D1716942

The Young Child and the Educative Process

The Young Child and the Educative Process

JOE L. FROST
The University of Texas at Austin

JOAN B. KISSINGER
The Colorado College

HOLT, RINEHART AND WINSTON   New York   Chicago   San Francisco   Atlanta
Dallas   Montreal   Toronto   London   Sydney

Library of Congress Cataloging in Publication Data

Frost, Joe L.
    The young child and the educative process.

  Includes indexes.
  1. Education, Preschool. 2. Child development.
I. Kissinger, Joan B., joint author. II. Title.
LB1140.2.F77   372.21   75-38537

ISBN: 0-03-085290-0

67890   032   987654321

Cover photo: A-Bar-Z Ponderosa School, Austin, Texas

To Lena Rexinger,
Arkansas Polytechnic College,
and Louise Berman,
University of Maryland,
teachers whose commitment
to young children
has been an enduring
source of inspiration

Preface

The Young Child and the Educative Process is designed primarily for early childhood teacher education programs. During the four years of its development, the material included here was used in a program in early childhood education in which several courses, including a practicum, were "blocked" together. The program was under the direction of a faculty-graduate student-undergraduate student team. The entire sequence was centered in field sites—private and public schools enrolling children from ages 3 through 8. The block experience was characterized by faculty-student team planning, controlled tutorials with children, small- and large-group seminars, videotape and live analysis of student teaching in classroom settings, integration of pre-service and in-service training, and retreats for group dynamics training.

The authors' experience with this program demonstrated that the present book may be effectively used alternatively (1) for a single undergraduate course, (2) for an undergraduate course and a practicum combination, and (3) for a graduate course for students entering early childhood education at the graduate level. In addition, the numerous practical ideas founded upon theory and research make *The Young Child and the Educative Process* a useful resource for persons presently working in preschools, kindergartens, day care centers, and Head Start programs.

Parts I and II present historical perspectives, recent psychological theory, and the intervention programs of the past decade. Practical program considerations built upon these foundations are given in Parts III, IV, and V. The development of language and thinking and ways to enhance them within the educative process are the focus of Chapters 6, 7, and 10. The influence of Jean Piaget is particularly strong in these chapters because his explorations of cognitive development have provided by far the richest resource on this subject yet available.

The student is assisted in planning and evaluating (Chapter 8), creating the classroom environment (Chapter 9), enhancing affective development (Chapter 11), and managing classroom behavior (Chapter 11). Play, the principal avenue for cognitive, social, and motor development during the early years, is given special attention in the final chapter. The practical examples and case studies throughout the book, although discussed within particular chapters, actually overlap in promoting the child's total development—cognitive, affective, physical, sociocultural. Developing positive parental involvement in early childhood programs is a theme that pervades the entire book.

For their contributions to the publication of this book, the authors express appreciation to colleagues who served as field editors, to Dick Owen and Fran Bartlett of Holt, Rinehart and Winston, to the many graduate and undergraduate students who offered positive criticisms, and to the young children who inspired the ideas within. The authors express special gratitude to Betty, to Marv, and to their children, who encouraged and who shared time with this project.

Austin, Texas   *J. L. F.*
Colorado Springs, Colorado   *J. B. K.*
January 1976

CONTENTS

Introduction

Almost exactly 10 years ago Project Head Start was born out of the federal government's "War on Poverty." For the first time, a comprehensive program of services for young children (3-, 4-, and 5-year-olds) and their families was launched nation-wide. The years since then have been marked by intense activity in early childhood education. While there were a few notable events in the field before 1965, the current emphasis upon early childhood is unmatched in history. Never before has there been such a proliferation of programs designed specifically for preschool children. Never before has there been such a concern for the rights and needs of the young child on the part of educators, parents, public agencies, organizations, and the federal government. A statement from the *Congressional Record* during the 1974 Week of the Young Child illustrates that concern:

Young children are our future—the future of parents, workers and decision makers of the world. Such an important resource for our future needs to be nurtured and preserved so that we can draw upon it when we need to. All adults share the responsibility for developing this resource. We far too frequently give priority to short-term goals and neglect the long-range educational and developmental needs of children. Think of what our future and theirs would be like if we put children first! (Quoted in *Young Children* 1974:196).

1

The rights and needs of the young child were also identified in the *Congressional Record* statement:

By birth, every child in this nation has a right to:
  Protection from physical and psychological danger.
  Security provided by adults who care for him.
  Support and nurturance from a stable home and other agencies of a concerned
    society.
What are the needs of the young child?
  To live and play in places which are safe, healthy and nurturing.
  To acquire knowledge and skills in order to become a competent person.
  To develop positive attitudes about himself and others. (Quoted in *Young
    Children* 1974:196)

THE INTERVENTION DECADE: 1965–1975

Several factors may be cited in accounting for the flurry of activity in early childhood education today. First, the success of intervention programs of the past decade stimulated increasing research and funding to establish experimental centers for young children. Second, several major theories arising out of recent psychological and educational research influenced thinking concerning the young child. Finally, changing social and cultural patterns in American and international life led to the introduction of new ideas and practices in child-rearing.

Earlier Programs

Beginning in 1962, a number of researchers, among them Martin Deutsch, David Weikart, Susan Gray, Walter Hodges, Merle Karnes, Carl Bereiter, and Siegfried Engelmann (Chapter 4), established small-scale experimental programs enrolling children from impoverished conditions, including many children normally classified as "educable mentally retarded." Even in the early years of experimentation, the groundwork was laid for future early childhood programs that would predominantly serve the specific needs of economically deprived children, who continue to comprise about one third of the total child population in the United States.

With the advent of the Head Start programs of the late 1960s came the first federal effort to support the education of young children. These programs were the first of any significant scope to deliberately solicit children from impoverished homes. They were also the first programs to marshall a broad array of community resources to work in early childhood education and to develop large-scale utilization of parents. The apparent early success of the programs sparked the release of unparalleled amounts of federal dollars to establish further experimental centers planned around the needs of the young child.

The Research

During the 1940s and 1950s, a number of studies of both animals and humans supported the conclusion that restricted patterns of living such as those found in severely impoverished areas could lead to deficiencies in human development. J. McVicker Hunt's (1961) influential book *Intelligence and Experience* also stimulated a turnabout in thinking by presenting a research base for the proposition that intelligence is not fixed at birth but may be altered by conditions of environment. Research pointed consistently to a close linkage between poverty and mental retardation. To a large extent, work in this area gave impetus to the establishment of Head Start and other publicly funded programs.

Perhaps the most quoted study which was influential in directing public attention to the young child during the mid-1960s was Benjamin Bloom's (1964) *Stability and Change in Human Characteristics.* Bloom analyzed eight major longitudinal studies that had been conducted in a number of the child research institutes established near the beginning of the scientific era in child development (Chapter 3). He concluded that the years between conception and age 4 are critical in terms of the development of intelligence. Moreover, Bloom proposed that the effects of environment upon intellectual development appear to be greatest in the early, most rapid, periods of development.

In the last 10 years, several major theories arising from psychological research have become the basis for a number of early childhood programs and practices. For the sake of discussion, these theories have been identified in this book as psychosexual-personality, normative-maturational, behavioral-environmental, cognitive-transactional, and humanistic (Chapter 5). For example, emerging psychosexual-personality theories provide insight in preparing young children in human relations (Chapter 11); behavioral-environmental theory (S-R psychology) underlies behavior modification techniques (Chapter 11); cognitive-developmental theory (Jean Piaget, Chapter 7) is a base for approaches to promoting logical thinking and language (Chapter 10) and to some extent play (Chapter 12); humanistic psychology gives useful clues for fostering affective development (Chapter 11). Yet no single theory is sufficiently comprehensive to deal with the complexities of child behavior. For example, behavior modification—a useful tool when properly applied—can hardly be inferred from cognitive-developmental or humanistic theory. On the other hand, the rich bases offered by Piaget for the promotion of thinking are not available from B. F. Skinner's stimulus-response theory. It is intriguing to note that it is not the philosophers who would restrict education to a single brand of theory:

Thus sects arrive: schools of opinion. Each selects that set of conditions that appeals to it; and then erects them into a complete and independent truth; instead of treating them as a factor in a problem, needing adjustment. (Dewey 1902:4)

I think the stimulus-response schema, while I won't say it is false, is in any case entirely incapable of explaining cognitive learning. . . . So you see it [Piaget's developmental theory] is indeed a stimulus-response theory, if you will, but first you add operations and then add equilibration. (Piaget 1964:15, 19)

It is very difficult, I have found, to communicate to others my simultaneous respect for and impatience with these two comprehensive psychologies [psychoanalysis and behaviorism]. So many people insist on being either pro-Freudian or anti-Freudian, pro-scientific or anti-scientific psychology, etc. In my opinion all such loyalty positions are silly. Our job is to integrate these various truths into the *whole* truth, which should be our only loyalty. (Maslow 1954:3)

Changing Patterns in American Life

Family living patterns in the United States have changed markedly in recent years, and these changes have had their impact on child-rearing. Out of economic necessity and as an outgrowth of the new consciousness generated by the women's movement, increasing numbers of mothers with young children hold full-time jobs. The number of working mothers with children under the age of 6 increased from 3 million in 1959 to 4 million in 1969 (White House Conference on Children 1970:61). Divorces and illegitimate births were also on the increase during that period, so that by 1970 the number of children under age 14 being raised in fatherless homes was 7 million (White House Conference on Children 1970:22). The intact, two-parent family has traditionally been regarded as the most appropriate setting for healthy child growth and development. But the realities of present family structure, or lack of it, have made it clear in recent years that alternative—but high-quality—child care arrangements must be provided.

THE SCOPE OF EARLY CHILDHOOD EDUCATION

The term "early childhood education" encompasses a broad array of programs, sponsorships, philosophies, and goals. Infant programs, nursery schools, and kindergartens are available for young children from infancy through age 5. In addition, day care centers provide child care for groups of preschool children. These centers frequently operate 10–12 hours per day. Some early childhood programs extend their services to include after-school and summer care for older, school-age children. Some group day care homes are available for before- and after-school care for up to 12 children in a private home. Family day care provides care for small groups of children within the family context in private homes. Such a setting is especially suitable for infants and children under the age of 3 or for some handicapped children. However, the growing trend is to place handicapped children in normal settings and provide additional services or training for them. In this way, young children profit from relating to each other.

Some early childhood programs are private facilities. The majority of all-day centers, for example, are privately operated (Lazar and Rosenberg 1971:74). Franchises of child care centers for profit also exist. Institutions sometimes sponsor early childhood programs. Churches, for example, operate preschools to further religious training or to satisfy a community need. Some labor unions, industries, and businesses offer day care facilities to their employees or members. Day care centers or nursery schools are established at some universities to accommodate the children of students or for research purposes. Groups of parents desiring quality early education at low cost sometimes work together to operate a parent cooperative program. The parents cooperate in all aspects of the program—financial, administrative, and instructional. The availability of public kindergartens and public preschools has also increased. In addition, a variety of early childhood programs are operated with federal funding, such as Head Start, parent-child centers, and programs for migrant and Indian families, non-English-speaking families, and families living in poverty.

The philosophies and goals of early childhood programs vary considerably. Some early childhood programs are concerned only with the physical safety of the child while he or she is away from home. Other programs emphasize a particular aspect of the child's development, such as cognitive development, social development, or language. Still other programs, Head Start, for example, are quite comprehensive. These programs extend beyond the child to the family and encompass health care, pychological and social services, and parent participation and policy-making. In spite of the diversity in early childhood education, *all good* programs strive to meet similar general goals:

To foster health and physical development.
To provide for intellectual stimulation.
To promote social awareness.
To promote a positive self-concept.
To promote curiosity and creativity.
To promote positive, fulfilling family life for all members of the family.

EARLY EDUCATION IN OTHER COUNTRIES

The USSR

Day care around the world has been examined by American investigators seeking broader perspectives upon which to base decisions about early education. It is only natural that the schools of our chief technological rival, the Soviet Union, would be a prime object of inquiry. Traditionally, in the United States, the major responsibility for early child care has been the family. In the Soviet Union, the children's collective, a communal body concerned with the education of children, assumes a major responsibility. Bronfenbrenner (1970) presented a detailed analysis of differences between the Soviet collectives and U.S. day care centers. The picture he painted of Soviet care is essentially a positive one. Beginning at birth, the Russian baby receives a great deal of physical stimulation, and breast feeding is almost universal. Freedom of movement is the rule, and contacts with adults are affectionate. Children and adults of all ages share in the caretaking role, thus providing more diffuse mothering than is usually found in the United States. At all levels of upbringing, self-discipline (internalized obedience) is stressed. The public collectives enroll 10 percent of all children under 2 years and about 20 percent of children between 3 and 6, representing the most extensive group program of early child care in history. Socialization training toward becoming the "new Soviet man or woman" (Bronfenbrenner 1970) stresses sharing and cooperating in group activity, with the adult gradually withdrawing from the leader role. However, Meers (1970:8) concluded from his observations of Soviet day care programs that "if there is an unstated, implicit political intent in these programs it has less to do with the creation of the ideal Communist than with the creation, in the younger generation, of a 'national' citizen who is free from regional and ethnocentric biases." But the *Program of Instruction* (Chauncey 1969a) and the *Teacher's Commentary*, which are used as the basic texts for the training of all Soviet preschool personnel, leave little doubt of the political intent and of the standardized curriculum:

The education of the future citizens of a Communist society requires from the teachers in preschool institutions the . . . study of Marxist-Leninist theory and the new program of the Communist party of the Soviet Union, participation in the political life of the country, and observance of the moral code of the builders of communism. . . . Every kindergarten should serve as a model of the Communist education of children. (Chauncey 1969a:5)

In his experience in both eastern Europe and the USSR, Meers (1970:12) found that children in group day care "were singularly lacking in verve and spontaneity; they consistently appeared depressed." Among the many photographs taken in the course of his tours, there is only one smiling child—the child's mother was the group's caretaker. It is interesting to note that among the 17 photographs of preschool children (apparently) in Bronfenbrenner's (1970) book, in only one stand-up (posed) photograph and one role-playing context are children smiling. Obviously, smiling for pictures is not a reliable base for judging the merits of a country's preschool program. Although many of the Soviet training techniques for young children described by Bronfenbrenner have possible positive implications for American preschools, the more pessimistic attitude of Meers also deserves attention. While early childhood education in the United States may learn from examinations of the

Soviet experience, it is doubtful that the U.S. system of institutionalized day care would adopt a single manual for all programs.

Denmark

In Denmark, emphasis is placed upon building day care centers near the children's residences. Many small centers are preferred to a few large ones. The kindergarten, serving children 3 to 6 years, supplements day care with educational services. Academic and preacademic work, music, art, physical activity, and napping are conducted from detailed instructions (Wagner and Wagner 1971). Only children of working parents are eligible for the kindergarten. Kindergarten teachers receive four years of training. As in the USSR, Danish children enter elementary school at age 7. After-school day care is provided for working parents.

Israel

Israeli day care centers are provided for infants, toddlers, and older children. For a minimal fee, children of lower-income working parents are provided food, rest, and play supervised by caretakers with limited training. Middle-class Israeli mothers who work typically prefer to employ babysitters for their children. The day care patterns are much like those in the United States. Day care centers are used not because they are superior but from sheer economic necessity (Gewirtz 1971).

The kibbutz, or communal settlement, is the form of Israeli child-rearing that has captured most attention in foreign countries. It is a predominantly agricultural settlement of about 100–400 members with communal ownership of property, communal responsibility for work, and communal responsibility for children. The children live in separate children's houses with their age groups and are under the supervision of trained caretakers. The children interact daily with their parents during "children's hour" (Bettelheim 1969). Contrary to popular opinion, the child-rearing practices are quite unlike those used in typical day care centers. Gewirtz's (1971) comparison of kibbutz rearing to institution rearing revealed some interesting differences. In the kibbutz, more time was spent in feeding, and there were twice as many shifts of location during the day. Caretaking activities by adults in the kibbutz were of longer duration, and more adults were in contact with children. There was also twice as much physical contact and much more time was spent with parents during the day. The kibbutz child is exposed to much more varied stimulation than the child reared in a conventional environment. The children's residences emulate to some degree the larger world of adults, containing, for example, a laundry, an animal farm, a kitchen, play yards, and areas for eating, sleeping, and studying. The major lesson to be learned from the Israeli experience appears to be that if child care services are to be successful, if they are to enhance the healthy development of children, if they are to help the parents improve their conditions of life—then such facilities must become integral parts of the communities they serve, where goals and responsibilities can be shared alike. (Gewirtz 1971:48)

Great Britain

The British primary schools are also influencing American early childhood education. Patterned from the work of Maria Montessori, Jean Piaget, and especially John Dewey, about one fourth of England's primary schools fit the pattern commonly called the open school (Rogers 1969). They are characterized by vertical age grouping, with 5-, 6-, and 7-year-olds commonly sharing a classroom. They emphasize learning over teaching, process over product, the development of independence, and aesthetic appreciation. Curriculum emerges from the natural explorations and interests of the children (Stephens 1974). Many U.S. preschools, kindergartens, and primary schools are today being modeled after the British experience. It should be noted that many open schools drawing from the work of Dewey and using similar educational practices were in existence in the United States during the 1940s and 1950s. While U.S. schools shifted to emphasize academics and structure during the post-Sputnik era, the British continued to develop their more flexible school programs. It is safe to say that another swing of the pedagogical pendulum will bring a new shift in viewpoint before many years pass—indeed, a "back to basic skills" movement is already picking up force.

THE FUTURE

The field of early childhood education has grown rapidly since 1965. It has benefited from the genuine concern and effort not only of educators but of government leaders, with more funding, increased enrollments, greater diversity in programs, parent involvement, and research support. It is an exciting time to be involved in early childhood education.

The tenth birthday of Project Head Start was celebrated on May 14, 1975. At that time, Caspar W. Weinberger, U.S. Secretary of Health, Education and Welfare, presented a citation that fittingly reiterates the giant strides made in the decade since 1965 and reflects the expectations for early childhood education of the future:

In recognition of ten years of outstanding service to more than 5.3 million children and their families; of the opportunities provided by dedicated staffs, volunteers, parents, public servants and other citizens to enable these children to reach their full potential; and as testimony to the steadfast and abiding belief in family strength, this Citation is hereby given to Project Head Start, 1965–1975, with the confidence that the program will continue to pioneer in the field of early childhood development for the benefit of all our children for generations to come. (Weinberger 1975:2)

REFERENCES AND FURTHER READING

Bettelheim, B. 1969. *The Children of the Dream*. New York: Macmillan.

Bloom, B. S. 1964. *Stability and Change in Human Characteristics.* New York: Wiley.

Bronfenbrenner, U. 1970. *Two Worlds of Childhood: U.S. and U.S.S.R.* New York: Russell Sage Foundation.

Chauncey, H. (ed.). 1969a. *Soviet Preschool Education.* Vol. I: *Program of Instruction.* New York: Holt, Rinehart and Winston.

Chauncey, H. (ed.). 1969b. *Soviet Preschool Education.* Vol. II: *Teacher's Commentary.* New York: Holt, Rinehart and Winston.

Dewey, J. 1902. *The Child and the Curriculum.* Chicago: University of Chicago Press.

Gewirtz, H. B. 1971. "Child Care Facilities and the 'Israeli Experience,'" in E. H. Grotberg (ed.), *Day Care: Resources for Decisions.* Washington, D.C.: Office of Economic Opportunity.

Hunt, J. McV. 1961. *Intelligence and Experience.* New York: Ronald.

Hurley, R. 1969. *Poverty and Mental Retardation. A Causal Relationship.* New York: Vintage Books.

Lazard, I., and M. E. Rosenberg. 1971. "Day Care in America," in E. H. Grotberg (ed.), *Day Care: Resources for Decisions.* Washington, D.C.: Office of Economic Opportunity.

Maslow, A. H. 1954. *Motivation and Personality.* New York: Harper & Row.

Meers, D. R. 1971. "International Day Care: A Selective Review and Psychoanalytical Critique," in E. H. Grotberg (ed.), *Day Care: Resources for Decisions.* Washington, D.C.: Office of Economic Opportunity.

Piaget, J. 1964. "Development and Learning," in R. E. Ripple and V. N. Rockcastle (eds.), *Piaget Rediscovered: A Report of the Conference on Cognitive Studies and Curriculum Development*, Cornell University, Ithaca, N.Y.

Rogers, V. R. 1969. "English and American Primary Schools," *Phi Delta Kappan*, October.

Stephens, L. S. 1974. *The Teacher's Guide to Open Education.* New York: Holt, Rinehart and Winston.

Wagner, M. G., and M. M. Wagner. 1971. "Day Care Programs in Denmark and Czechoslovakia," in E. H. Grotberg (ed.), *Day Care: Resources for Decisions.* Washington, D.C.: Office of Economic Opportunity.

Weinberger, C. W. 1975. "HEW Headquarters Celebrates 10th Birthday of Head Start," *Head Start Newsletter*, May–June 1975. Washington, D.C.: Office of Child Development.

White House Conference on Children. 1970. *Profiles of Children.* Washington, D.C.: Government Printing Office.

Young Children. 1974. 29 (4), May.

HISTORICAL BASES
for Early Childhood Education

Jean-Jacques Rousseau, 1712–1778
The Bettmann Archive

1

Antecedents of Early Childhood Education in America

The study of the history of early childhood education is a worthwhile endeavor for several reasons. History reveals how slowly early childhood education came into its own as an organized effort in the interest of the young child. In light of the slow advance of early childhood education over hundreds of years, one can appreciate the rapid developments that have occurred in the last 10 years alone. The history of early childhood education also provides an overview of the theoretical foundation from which early childhood program philosophy is drawn. The theories of child development and behavior that emerged through history serve as the criteria upon which to base decisions about methods, materials, and content. Finally, a study of early childhood history reveals the origins of contemporary curriculum practices and trends. Many contemporary ideas about the nature of the young child and ways to work with him were introduced by a few notable people throughout history. Ideas complemented each other and trends developed. Analysis of historical efforts helps the educator understand how and why contemporary practices emerged. Several conclusions can be drawn from the study of the history of early childhood education:

1. It has taken America a long time to recognize the young child.
2. Historic philosophies and principles of education have influenced contemporary practice.

3. The outlook for the young child was improved as a result of the child-oriented organizations and institutions and the scientific study of children that developed in the first half of the twentieth century.
4. The current emphasis upon early childhood education is unparalleled in history.

The field of early childhood education as it exists in the United States and most of the free world today rests on the accomplishments of a common core of visionary people. A few of these individuals were recognized in their own time as outstanding intellectual pioneers, while others, skillful and dedicated, worked in relative obscurity to contribute to expanding knowledge and practice. This chapter focuses upon the major contributors to early childhood education. The first section briefly traces the strands of contemporary educational philosophy and practice which emerged here and there over many hundreds of years, beginning in the age of Greece in about the third century B.C. The next section introduces a few individuals in educational history whom we have labeled men of vision. The discussion here focuses upon Jean Jacques Rousseau, Johann Pestalozzi, and Friedrich Froebel. The ideas of these eighteenth- and nineteenth-century scholars are strikingly modern in tone and represent a radical break with the educational thinking current in their time. These are milestone thinkers whose work led to landmark events. The professional in early childhood education today draws daily from these rich sources for philosophy and practice. The final section of the chapter focuses on the introduction of the kindergarten in America in the middle of the last century.

TRACES OF CONTEMPORARY PRACTICE IN EARLY EDUCATIONAL PHILOSOPHY

Greece and Rome

Concern with the education of young children can be traced at least as far back as Greek and Roman times. In Greece, the aims of education differed from one city-state to another, with educational practice largely a reflection of the social and political orientation of each area. Sparta, for example, with its emphasis on military preparedness and rigorous discipline, encouraged the development of such qualities as strength, courage, endurance, cunning, patriotism, and obedience. In the interest of defense against war and service to the city-state, the family in Sparta was virtually suppressed. More democratic in spirit, Athens stressed individual freedom and the teaching of moral and social values. In contrast to the subjectivity of the Greeks, the more objective Romans emphasized the practical: education was viewed as training for life. Early education was directed by the parents both in the home and beyond it. The notion of a formal school period, beginning at age 6, was borrowed from the Greeks, but the importance given to practical training so overshadowed philosophy and the arts that permanent contributions to future generations were relatively minor. Even in this early period educational philosophy was influenced by social conditions of the day, just as today social conditions have influenced the creation of Operation Head Start and the press for quality day care.

As long ago as the third century B.C., the Greek philosophers Plato and Aristotle recognized the importance óf educating children before they entered school, usually at 6 years. For Plato, the purpose of education was to prepare individuals to serve the state. He believed that the state should raise children from early infancy to ready them for this total commitment of self and to free their parents for similar service. Aristotle saw public education as a right to which the people who supported the state were entitled. Out of Aristotle's philosophy emerged the first thinking that linked home and school, for Aristotle envisioned children up to the age of 7 being educated at home by a mother or nurse. Aristotle, however, added a tutor to his educational scheme after the age of 7 to ensure a sound academic program. In his philosophy lie the roots of liberal education, for he advocated a broad course of study, one that introduced the student to numerous fields to stimulate the mind.

From the Middle Ages Onward

The period of the Middle Ages (400–1400) bequeathed little of value for future educators of young children. The Greek and Roman heritage was lost and formal education was through Church-established schools and apprenticeship. On the whole, the child was viewed as a miniature man or woman and was generally held in low esteem by adults. Such an attitude was engendered in part by an extremely high mortality rate, for one is not likely to become attached to something that will probably be lost. The world continued to be a difficult place for children well into the American colonial period. The early settlers regarded children as economic tools which could contribute to the hard work required to clear farms, raise crops, and, later, work in factories. Families were large and discipline was strict. Children were to be seen and not heard, and they were expected to obey immediately and unquestioningly.

As schools were established, corporal punishment became the standard method for enforcing order and instilling motivation to work. Unfortunately, the legacy of this view of discipline continues to be evident in many U.S. schools even today. In 1969, for example, a National Education Association survey found that 65 percent of the elementary school teachers and 55 percent of the secondary school teachers polled favored "judicious use" of bodily punishment. The use of punishment with young children sometimes takes on a more subtle form, but one that is equally cruel and humiliating, as the following incident, reported in *The Austin* (Texas) *Statesman* in 1973, reveals:

Once upon a time there was a little boy. He was full of fun. He wasn't mean, but he loved to run and jump and play and sing and be sure everyone was his friend.

He was in first grade. He was 6 years old. The other children in his classroom liked him. So did the children at recess. So did the children in the lunchroom.

But not the "lunch lady." (Do you know what a lunch lady is? She watches for spilled milk and left-over spinach and for "fooling around.")

The lunch lady did not like the little boy. She liked a quiet lunchroom. To make it quiet she would blow this big loud whistle. Really loud. And just in that noisy silence she would point a finger at someone.

Because the lunch lady didn't like the little boy, she would blow the whistle right behind him. Sometimes it made him spill the milk the lunch lady was supposed to make sure wasn't spilled. Sometimes it made him pinch the boy sitting next to him. Sometimes it made him want to cry.

After the lunch lady would blow the whistle, she would walk around the table. Real slow she would walk around. And then would come that finger. Then she would say the dreaded words: "Tomorrow, it's the bad table for you."

MARTIN LUTHER (1483–1546).   The Protestant Reformation of the sixteenth century stimulated massive changes, not only in religion but also in politics, economics, social life, and education. The outspoken Martin Luther, the leader of the Reformation in Germany, did much to help modify the educational views of his time. He proposed universal, compulsory education and suggested that the state assume responsibility for supporting primary schools for Christians. Luther stressed that the primary goal of education was to teach religion, an emphasis that has not endured in public schools today. Among his innovations which have influenced contemporary education, however, was Luther's insistence that music and physical education be included in the curriculum. "Music drives away all cares and melancholy from the heart and gymnastics produce elasticity of the body and preserve the health," he wrote. Luther also believed that the family in the home was the educational institution of primary importance. This is particularly interesting in light of contemporary educators' focus upon parent involvement in education in the form of parenting classes, parent-child centers, home start, and family life programs.

JOHN AMOS COMENIUS (1592–1670).   Luther's educational ideas were reinforced a century later by the Czech theologian John Amos Comenius, who broadened the scope of "universal education" by recommending that *all* children receive formal schooling. In *The Great Didactic* he proposed an educational ladder beginning with the mother school for children up to 6 years and progressing through the vernacular school for ages 6–12, the Latin school for ages 12–18, and the university for ages 18–24. With Comenius, the threads of contemporary practice in the education of the young child become clearer and stronger. Comenius, for example, wrote *Visible World*, the first text using pictures to teach children. He proposed a series of textbooks suited to the interests of the child at each level of his instruction. The well-being of the child was of central importance in his thinking, and he focused on play as a vehicle for promoting healthy development. Comenius saw humor as a means for lightening the grim realities that marked the lives of children of his day. This emphasis upon child self-esteem was further developed by his call for "humor and lightness" in every lesson. The skillful teacher, Comenius recognized, can make a child eager to learn, but the acquisition of knowledge cannot be forced. The idea that children learn by doing, a view later emphasized by John Dewey, may have had its roots in the philosophy of Comenius. "Let children learn to write by writing, to sing by singing and to reason by reasoning," Comenius preached. Similarly, his emphasis on things rather than words comes up again and again in various forms, as we will see, in the philosophies of Rousseau, Pestalozzi, Froebel, Montessori, and Piaget.

MEN OF VISION: A BREAK WITH TRADITION

We have called the French philosopher Rousseau, the Swiss educator Pestalozzi, and the German educator Froebel men of vision because each originated an approach to the teaching of young children that broke with the traditional education of his time and place. Moreover, the ideas of these thinkers have had a notable and lasting impact on the field of early childhood education as it has developed to the present day. All three of these men recognized the importance of the early years and the influence of the environment upon the child's development.

Jean-Jacques Rousseau (1712–1778)

Rousseau's *Émile*, published in 1762, made a strong case for beginning a child's education early. Not to be taken in a literal sense, it is a speculation on child-rearing principles that are in harmony with nature and not practical methods for educating children. "The whole duty of education," Rousseau wrote, "is to discover human nature, particularly as it exists in the child, and be guided by its dictates." We receive education from nature, from men, and from things. Since we cannot change nature, we must direct the other two toward it. Rousseau felt that "subjugation, torment, and constraints" were placed upon nature by such practices as leaving young children in the care of servants who bound them up in swaddling clothes so that they caused no trouble and required no care. Mothers themselves, he believed, should care for their children. The role of the father was equally important. For Rousseau, the heart of education was family life, a view that is shared by many people today. Again and again, modern thinking resounds in Rousseau's philosophy. In fact, Rousseau might be called the grandfather of modern child psychologists. He outlined four stages of child development, the first two of which are pertinent to early childhood education. The first stage of development spans the first five years of life. Rousseau, like Dewey, Piaget, and contemporary educators, emphasized physical activity as the curriculum for this stage. For the second stage of development, encompassing ages 5–12 years, children were to learn totally from their own direct experience and exploration of the environment. This point of view had been expressed earlier by Comenius and was to be reiterated later by Pestalozzi, Froebel, Dewey, and Piaget.

Rousseau's education began in the nature of the child. He broke with tradition in stressing that young children were not miniature adults: "Nature requires children to be children before they are men. By endeavoring to pervert this order, we produce forward fruits, that have neither maturity nor taste, and will not fail soon to wither or corrupt." Rousseau distinguished the manner and content of teaching young children from those used with older children and adults and emphasized individual differences in children. Education should grow out of native interests and curiosity, he felt, and memory work should be abandoned in favor of activities that foster judgment and the ability to reason. He emphasized the value of play and the vast difference between a child's interests and values and those of an adult. The child was to receive no kind of verbal instructions; his learning was to come only from experience. He was to receive no kind of punishment, was never required to ask pardon, and was incapable of immorality. Rousseau's reliance on the natural unfolding of the child stands in stark contrast to many contemporary infant-stimulation programs designed to counteract the effects of inadequate mothering. To Rousseau, the most important and most useful rule in education was "not to gain time, but to lose it."

Johann Pestalozzi (1746–1827)

Rousseau's beliefs in the natural growth of the child, unfettered by society, were put into practice a generation later by Johann Pestalozzi. Pestalozzi represents a landmark in early childhood education, for he actually taught young children and applied the ideas of earlier educational theorists to the classroom. His work marks the beginning of a new era of formal thought about schooling for young children.

Pestalozzi attacked several long-standing educational patterns of his day and to some extent was successful in changing them. In his work and in actual practice he deplored three practices in particular: that children of the poor were excluded from schooling; that schooling was characterized by rote learning, which he called "superficial verbosity"; and that cruel punishment was commonly used. Pestalozzi especially enjoyed teaching poor children, holding that every child's personality was sacred. Like Comenius before him and like Froebel, Lawrence Frank, and the humanists who were to follow him, Pestalozzi believed that schools should protect and nurture the child's self-esteem. Kindness ruled in Pestalozzi's school, and to the amazement of his contemporaries, he abolished flogging. Love, he ruled, was the basic foundation from which to work and was essential to the natural development of the child's physical and intellectual abilities. Pestalozzi saw every child as having potential and capability, regardless of his station in life. Like Rousseau, he believed there were individual differences in children's interests, needs, and rates of learning. He was an originator of the notion of readiness, that children must not be forced to learn through rote memorization but must be allowed time and experience to *understand.* Direct concrete experience (*Anschauung*), sometimes called "object lessons," preceded verbosity and meaningless words in Pestalozzi's curriculum. The idea that objects and events must be seen, felt, and observed in their concrete form was to be central later in the thinking of Dewey, Montessori, and Piaget. Pestalozzi also insisted upon repetition of newly learned actions —not blind repetition, but the kind related directly to the concrete experience. A number of the ideas Pestalozzi employed in his own teaching are found at work in some contemporary programs, especially in the British primary schools. For example, his students were of mixed ages, with the older ones tutoring the younger ones, and they engaged in real-life situations for learning such as counting the number of steps taken, actually setting up a business, and utilizing nature and its resources. In *Leonard and Gertrude,* Pestalozzi (1907) described the method of instruction of an ideal teacher, Gertrude. At the beginning of the schoolday the children helped wash the dishes and then prepared for the daily round of lessons. These included singing hymns, reading aloud from the Bible, performing assorted household tasks, and pronouncing syllables from an old ABC book for practice in correct and distinct articulation. Gertrude never adopted the tone of an instructor who would say, "Child, this is your head, your nose, your hand." Rather, she would say gently, "Come here, child, I will wash your little hands," "I will comb your hair," "I will cut your fingernails." All that Gertrude's children knew, they knew so thoroughly that they could in turn teach the younger children.

Friedrich Froebel (1782–1852)

Among the many scholars who studied in Pestalozzi's school was Friedrich Froebel. During his first brief visit to the school, Froebel noted that he experienced a variety of emotions—elevation, depression, arousal, bewilderment. Froebel was sympathetic toward the goals of the school, but he felt that Pestalozzi's method was both successful and lacking at the same time. Pestalozzi's method of teaching and his choice of subject matter, Froebel believed, did not call upon the nature of the child enough. Froebel spent years grappling with the question of what is the purpose and the method for teaching children. Still seeking the answer to his question, he returned to Pestalozzi's school some time later for a two-year stay in the stimulation and fervor of that environment. The result of his years of philosophical searching was the kindergarten, a form of preschool education designed to assist in the educational care of young children. The American kindergarten was to descend from the one begun by Froebel in Blankenburg, Germany, in 1837. The principles underlying this new educational venture stemmed from varied schools of educational and philosophical thought, most notably the reflections of Rousseau and Pestalozzi.

Froebel's philosophy of education was also influenced by idealism. Throughout his life, Froebel was a rather introspective person and a meditator. His mother died when he was only 9 months old and he never received the kindness and parental interaction he needed as a child. Growing up in the environs of a beautiful forest, he turned inward toward the solitude and beauty of nature. As a young man, the conditions were right in Germany near the end of the eighteenth century, and Froebel was swept up in the wave of idealism being spread by the poets and philosophers. This idealism was a spirit of faith in the powers of the mind, of thought, and of ideals. For Froebel, thought, and subsequently his philosophy of education, became a quest for unity and inner harmony with God. Indeed, God stands at the very core of his educational scheme, and this obsession with the idea of the unity of all things with God permeates his philosophy.

Among his notable contributions to early childhood education was a recognition of the importance of the early years of training and experience. His fervent support of childhood was the result of both his keen observations and the sadness of his own young life. Froebel, like Rousseau, also envisioned several stages in the development of the individual, which he described as childhood, boyhood, and manhood. They were to be duly respected in that order. As we will see, the notion of developmental stages or levels is of central importance with modern educational psychologists such as Jean Piaget and Robert Havighurst. To Froebel, education was to be based upon the child's inner unfolding. Man, Froebel felt, was not a sponge that soaked up knowledge from without; rather, he unfolded like a carefully tended plant. Froebel saw the same unfolding in all of creation. His emphasis on the inner unfolding of the child places Froebel's ideas within the predeterministic school of child development, which holds that all aspects of the child's development have been determined previously by heredity (see Chapter 3). Like any tender young plant, the child needs protection and nourishment from the adult rather than force and restraint.

Consistent with recognition of the early years and of developmental

Friedrich Froebel, 1782–1852.
The Bettmann Archive

hann Pestalozzi, 1746–1827. The Bettmann Archive

21

stages, Froebel's curriculum was built around the child's inner urges and native impulses. This principle persists to guide contemporary theorizing but continues to challenge the best minds in education. Like Rousseau and Pestalozzi, Froebel emphasized education that emanated from the child and, hence, from life itself. Education of this nature was divorced from the memorization routines so prevalent in his time. Instead, education should grow out of the natural interests and motivation of the child but be tempered with guidance from the educator. It is the educator who places the child in a stimulating learning environment where the logical outcome is self-direction and self-control.

Froebel's curriculum called for active involvement of the children and contained carefully sequenced activities. His vehicle of instruction was play, which he viewed as both instructive and enjoyable. So much of education of his day imposed dull, passive tasks upon children that Froebel designed his own materials. His "gifts," consisting of such objects as balls, cylinders, cubes, and blocks, were objects to be handled, examined, manipulated, counted, measured, divided, and so on. They were for arranging activities and were to be used alone until all possible meanings were explored. Then they were used in combination with other gifts for further development of ideas. They were designed to help the child understand his environment. In contrast, the "occupations" were designed to give children an enjoyable means of practicing skills while using their imagination. The occupations involved such things as paper cutting and folding, weaving, stringing, drawing, threading, and painting. The occupations invited controlling, modifying, transforming, and creating activities. The gifts were discovery oriented, while the occupations were to lead to inventiveness. Froebel's gifts and occupations were enumerated in *The Education of Man* (Froebel 1877) as follows:

GIFTS
Bodies
Gift one: Six colored worsted balls, about an inch and a half in diameter.
Gift two: Wooden ball, cylinder, and cube, one inch and a half in diameter.
Gift three: Eight one-inch cubes, forming a two-inch cube.
Gift four: Eight brick-shaped blocks, forming a two-inch cube.
Gift five: Twenty-seven one-inch cubes, three bisected and three quadrisected diagonally, forming a three-inch cube.
Gift six: Twenty-seven brick-shaped blocks, three bisected longitudinally and six bisected transversely, forming a three-inch cube.
Surfaces
Gift seven: Squares, entire and half. Equilateral triangles, entire, half, and thirds.
Lines
Gift eight: Straight (splints of various lengths) and circular (metal or paper rings of various sizes; whole circles, half circles, and quadrants are used.)
Points

Gift nine: Beans, lentils, or other seeds, leaves, pebbles, pieces of card-board or paper, etc.

Reconstruction

Gift ten: Softened peas or wax pellets and sharpened sticks or straws to enable the child to reconstruct the surface and solid synthetically from the point.

OCCUPATIONS

Solids

Plastic clay, card-board work, wood-carving, etc.

Surfaces

Paper-folding, paper-cutting, parquetry, painting, etc.

Lines

Interlacing, intertwining, weaving, thread games, embroidery, drawing, etc.

Points

Stringing beads, buttons, etc.; perforating, etc.

THE INTRODUCTION OF THE KINDERGARTEN IN AMERICA

With the description of the philosophy and school of Froebel, the stage is set for the introduction of the kindergarten in the United States. Mrs. Carl Schurz, a former student of Froebel's in Germany, opened a kindergarten in her home in Watertown, Wisconsin, in 1855. Originally intended for her own children, the kindergarten was later expanded to include other German-speaking pupils. Elizabeth Peabody became interested in the new venture through contact with Mrs. Schurz and established the first English-speaking kindergarten in Boston in 1860. In 1867, she traveled to Germany to further study the kindergarten with Froebel's disciples. Thereafter, she grew even more zealous in her support of its principles and began a lecture tour to spread the kindergarten cause. One who heard her lecture in Springfield, Massachusetts, was Milton Bradley, founder of the Milton Bradley Company. Bradley too was unhappy with American schools at that time, with their emphasis on passivity, rote memorization, and harsh discipline. He compared schools of this type which he himself had attended to the pleasurable ways his parents had helped him learn with understanding at home through the use of tangible objects. Bradley was deeply moved by Mrs. Peabody's description of the children's pleasure, understanding, and creativity while using Froebel's kindergarten materials. A few months later, the Milton Bradley Company published its first book and the first illustrated kindergarten guide published in the English language, *Paradise of Childhood, A Practical Guide to Kindergarteners.* Thereafter, the company continued to develop and produce kindergarten materials based upon Froebel's gifts and occupations (Shea 1960:101–115).

Froebel's gifts are also said to have had significant effect on the later work of the great American architect Frank Lloyd Wright, who wrote in his autobiography:

The strips of colored paper, glazed, and "matt," remarkably soft, brilliant colors! Now came the geometric by-play of these charming checkered color combinations! The structural figures to be made with peas and small straight sticks; slender constructions, the joinings accented by the little green pea-globes. The smooth shapely maple blocks with which to build, the sense of which never afterward leaves the fingers: so *form* became *feeling*. . . . And the exciting cardboard shapes with pure scarlet face—such scarlet! Smooth triangular shapes, with white-back, and edges, cut in rhomboids, with which to make designs on the flat table top. What shapes they made naturally if only you would let them! . . . That early kindergarten experience with the straight line; the flat plane; the square; the triangle; the circle! . . . These primary forms and figures were the secret of all effects . . . which were ever got into the architecture of the world. (Quoted from Saunders and Keister n.d.: 1)

The first publicly supported kindergarten in the United States was established in St. Louis in 1873 by William T. Harris and Susan Blow. Harris, later U.S. Commissioner of Education, was superintendent of the St. Louis schools and Blow was the first teacher of the public kindergarten. Blow wrote a number of books on kindergarten education, including *Symbolic Education* (1894) and *Educational Issues in the Kindergarten* (1908). In the editor's Preface to *Symbolic Education*, Harris cited statistics to show the growth of kindergartens during their relatively brief existence in the United States:

In 1892 an inquiry sent out from the Bureau of Education obtained information of the existence of 2,000 private kindergartens and 459 public kindergartens. Of the former, 1,148 failed to respond to the inquiry sent them. The 852 private kindergartens that reported had 1,602 teachers and 33,637 pupils. The 459 public kindergartens reported 933 teachers and 31,659 pupils enrolled during the year. The returns showed a total of nearly 2,500 kindergartens, with an enrollment of 65,296 pupils in the 1,311 that reported. . . . It may be safe to estimate the number of kindergartens at 3,000, the teachers at 5,000 and the pupils at 100,000. (Blow 1894: vii, viii)

Roughly coinciding with the early development of kindergartens in the United States was the rise of a man who is universally regarded as the outstanding educational theorist of modern times, John Dewey (1859–1952). Dewey integrated many of the ideas of Comenius, Rousseau, Pestalozzi, and Froebel. Although his philosophy is extremely broad in scope, it has particular relevance for early childhood education. Almost simultaneous with the development of Dewey's work in this country was the establishment in Italy of the *casa dei bambini*, or Children's House, by the great educational reformer Maria Montessori. Preschools of the first half of the twentieth century represent a fusion of the ideas of Froebel, Dewey, and Montessori. The philosophies and practice of Dewey and Montessori are examined and compared in Chapter 2.

SUMMARY AND CONCLUSIONS

The study of early childhood education reveals how contemporary philosophy and practice evolved over hundreds of years of history. For example, many contemporary educators focus upon the vital role of the family in the process of education. Parent involvement in education is encouraged in a variety of ways, including volunteers in the classroom, resource people, home start, parent-child centers, and parenting classes. The idea of a home-school partnership can be traced back through history to the ideas of Aristotle. Aristotle believed that education during the first seven years of a child's life should be conducted at home under the direction of a mother or nurse. A tutor was included in Aristotle's scheme to ensure that the child's education was adequate. Many years later, the French philosopher Jean-Jacques Rousseau supported Aristotle's notion of the importance of the family when he described in *Emile* the vital role of both the mother and the father in the education of the young child.

Other aspects of Rousseau's thinking are shared by many people today. Rousseau believed that education should grow out of the natural interests of the child and that the child should learn from direct experience. Earlier Rousseau had broken with tradition when he proposed that young children are unique beings and not miniature adults. He distinguished the manner and content of teaching young children from that of adults and older children. Rousseau recognized the existence of stages of child development, an idea that was later supported and expanded by others such as Froebel and Piaget. Pestalozzi and Froebel put Rousseau's ideas into actual practice in the classroom. The students taught by Pestalozzi and Froebel were actively involved in the learning process. This practice represented a radical shift from the traditional method of teaching students primarily through rote memorization. The idea that children learn best from active involvement with concrete materials was further supported in the twentieth century by Dewey, Montessori, and Piaget.

Contemporary early childhood programs which focus upon the child's self-esteem and emotional well-being also have roots in educational history. Comenius advocated more humor in the child's lessons to lighten the grimness of his life. Pestalozzi expanded the philosophy of Comenius. He abolished flogging and governed his school with kindness and love. Like Froebel, Frank, and the humanists who were to follow him, Pestalozzi believed that the child's personality was unique and sacred. Pestalozzi also believed that there were individual differences in children, in their interests, and in their educational needs.

Several other contemporary educational practices can be traced through history. Pestalozzi encouraged the older children in his school to tutor the younger ones. He also mixed the ages of the students within his classroom. The emphasis upon music and physical activity in the early childhood program was advocated much earlier by Martin Luther. Play as the young child's vehicle for learning was advocated in educational history by Comenius, Rousseau, and Froebel.

The first publicly supported kindergarten in the United States was opened in St. Louis in 1873 by William T. Harris and Susan Blow. The kindergarten movement spread rapidly, and by 1892 approximately 3000 public and private kindergartens were in operation servicing some 100,000 children.

SUGGESTED ACTIVITIES

1. Visit several early childhood programs in your community. Look for examples of some of the educational ideas listed below which were introduced throughout history. What are the historical foundations of those ideas and how have they contributed to the examples of contemporary practice you observed?
   a. Home-school partnership and parent involvement in education.
   b. Importance of family life in the process of education.
   c. Curriculum based upon real-life experiences.
   d. Integration of the natural interests and curiosity of the children within the curriculum.
   e. Use of concrete experiences in the classroom curriculum.
   f. Children's manipulation of materials and active participation in learning.
   g. Judgment and reason as opposed to rote memorization.
   h. Play as a vehicle for learning.
   i. Nurturance and protection of the child's self-esteem.
   j. Music and physical education within the curriculum.
   k. Mixed age groups within the classroom.
   l. Children as tutors.
   m. Existence of stages of child development.
2. Write down some of the historical ideas that you would incorporate into your own philosophy of education. Write down some of the curriculum practices that have emerged from history which you feel are important to use in a program for young children. Give the reasons for your choices.
3. Select one of the individuals discussed in this chapter who influenced early childhood education. Study the contributions of this person in greater depth. Read translations of his writings and critiques of his philosophy of education. Note the forces that stimulated the thinking of this individual and that inspired his philosophy. Analyze the ways in which he has influenced early childhood education today.

REFERENCES

Blow, S. 1908. *Educational Issues in the Kindergarten.* New York: D. Appleton.

Blow, S. 1894. *Symbolic Education.* New York: D. Appleton.

Bruner, J. S. 1966. *Toward a Theory of Instruction.* Cambridge, Mass.: Harvard University Press.

Comenius, J. A. Orig. 1632; reprinted 1896. *The Great Didactic*, M. W. Keatinge, trans. London: Adams and Charles Black.

De Guimps, R. 1890. *Pestalozzi: His Life and Work.* New York. D. Appleton.

Divoky, D. 1973. "Corporal Punishment in U.S. Schools," *Learning*, 1 (4) : 22–27.

Fletcher, S. S., and J. Welton (eds.). 1912. *Froebel's Chief Writings on Education.* London: Edward Arnold and Company.

Froebel, F. 1887. *The Education of Man*, W. N. Hailmann, trans. New York: D. Appleton.

Kilpatrick, W. H. 1916. *Froebel's Kindergarten Principles.* New York: Macmillan.

Pestalozzi, J. H. 1907. *Leonard and Gertrude*, E. Channing, trans. Boston: Heath.

Rousseau, J.-J. Orig. 1762; reprinted 1951. *Emile*, F. and P. Richard, eds. Paris: Garnier.

Saunders, M., and M. E. Keister. N.d. *Nurturing Creativity: The Role of Living Space in the First Years of Life.* Greensboro, N.C.: Institute for Child and Family Development, University of North Carolina.

Shea, J. J. 1960. *It's All in the Game.* New York: Putnam.

FURTHER READING

Anderson, L. F. *Pestalozzi.* New York: McGraw-Hill, 1931.

Braun, S. J., and E. P. Edwards. *History and Theory of Early Childhood Education.* Worthington, O.: Charles A. Jones, 1972.

Broome, J. H. *Rousseau: A Study of His Thought.* New York: Barnes & Noble, 1963.

Lawrence, E. (ed.). *Friedrich Froebel and English Education.* New York: Philosophical Library, 1953.

Michaelis, E., and H. K. Moore (eds.). *Froebel's Letters on the Kindergarten.* London: Swan Sonnenschein and Company, 1891.

Pestalozzi, H. *The Education of Man.* New York: Philosophical Library, 1951.

Weber, E. *The Kindergarten: Its Encounter with Educational Thought in America.* New York: Teachers College Press, Columbia University, 1969.

John Dewey, 1859–1952
The Bettmann Archive

Maria Montessori, 1870–1952
The Bettmann Archive

John Dewey and Maria Montessori

John Dewey and Maria Montessori are discussed together in this chapter for several reasons. First, Dewey and Montessori were contemporaries, working and influencing the shape of early childhood education during the same general period of time. Second, despite the many differences between their educational philosophies, their ideas reveal several underlying similarities. Finally, their contributions to education are still very much in evidence in schools for young children today.

JOHN DEWEY (1859–1952)

John Dewey became a household word during his lifetime. Praised by many and scorned by some, Dewey exerted an unparalleled influence upon educational thinking and stimulated a national, and to some extent, an international educational movement from the "traditional" to the "progressive." The noted philosopher Harold A. Larrabae pronounced him "the ablest philosopher America has yet produced," and Alfred North Whitehead classed him with Augustine, Aquinas, Bacon, Descartes, Locke, and Comte as one who made philosophic thought relevant to the needs of his own day. On the other hand, a renowned American naval officer, Vice-Admiral H. G. Rickover, expressed the view that Dewey exerted a "pernicious influence" on

American education. There is no doubt that Dewey's far-ranging influence on education has persisted to this day. American schools are still struggling with curriculum interpretations and misinterpretations arising from the influence of Dewey's pen and the teaching of his disciples. The British infant schools, recently brought to the attention of the world by the Plowden Report (Plowden 1967), are based upon a mixture of the findings of Piaget, Montessori, and Dewey. American participants in an international seminar (I.D.E.A. 1970) summed up the conceptual framework of the British infant school as "education the way John Dewey dreamed it should be but never saw in practice." Dewey himself was a great exemplifier of putting his own ideas into practice. His work reveals the scientific processes of a great thinker. A lifelong student, his work frequently reflected analytical efforts to bring order to the philosophizing of his predecessors and contemporaries. For instance, *Schools of Tomorrow* (1915) contains frequent citations from Rousseau and references to Pestalozzi, Froebel, and Montessori. Although Dewey stated in the Preface that he did not intend to offer an analysis of educational systems, this was, nevertheless, in part accomplished. Inescapably, Dewey, too, was a captive of his own exposited principle: "Intelligent activity is distinguished from aimless activity by the fact that it involves selection of means—analysis—out of the variety of conditions *that are present*, and their arrangement—synthesis—to reach an intended aim or purpose."

Progressivism versus Traditionalism

Dewey is generally heralded as the leader of the progressive movement as contrasted to the traditional education of his day. Traditional education, according to Dewey, was characterized by

imposition from above and from outside. It imposes adult standards, subject matter, and methods upon those who are only growing slowly toward maturity. . . . Learning here means acquisition of what is already incorporated in books and in the heads of the elders. Moreover, that which is taught is thought of as essentially static. (1915:18–19)

Dewey was opposed to the passive role of the student in traditional schools, to heavy reliance upon adult-imposed subject matter, and to the use of rote memorization. In *My Pedagogic Creed* (1929), he summarized his ideas about the progressive school. School, Dewey believed, was primarily a social institution representing life as vital to the child as that carried on in the home. Education, then, was a process of living each day and not a preparation for future living. As such, school functioned as a mini-society and called for democratic cooperation, sharing, humaneness, mutual decision-making, the fellowship of occupations, and the interest of the students. This view may be linked to the importance contemporary educators give to process skills in the curriculum; that is, to teaching for such lifetime skills as decision-making, creating, valuing, problem-solving, and awareness (see Chapter 11). Dewey defined the ultimate goals of schools when he raised concern about the relation of traditional school practices to democratic ideals.

Can we find any reason that does not ultimately come down to the belief that democratic social arrangements promote a better quality of human experience, one which is more widely accessible of human experience, one which is more widely accessible and enjoyed, than do non-democratic and anti-democratic forms of social life? Does not the principle of regard for individual freedom and for decency and kindliness of human relations come back in the end to the conviction that these things are tributary to a higher quality of experience on the part of a greater number than are methods of repression and coercion or force? Is it not the reason for our preference that we believe that mutual consultation and convictions reached through persuasion make possible a better quality of experience than can otherwise be provided on any wide scale? (1929:34)

Dewey hastened to clarify his notion of democracy in the classroom: It did not mean treating everyone alike or providing unlimited degrees of freedom. There was freedom and opportunity for all, but wisely based upon the needs of the individual.

With the rise of the progressive movement in education, Dewey was somewhat chagrined by the either-or extremist interpretation of progressive versus traditional schools of thought. In *Experience and Education* (1963), written after considerable experience with the progressive schools and in light of criticisms of his theory, Dewey attacked the extremist view. Educators "should think in terms of education itself rather than in terms of some 'ism' about education," Dewey argued, "even such an 'ism' as 'progressivism.'" He declared that "an educational philosophy which professes to be based on the idea of freedom may become as dogmatic as ever was the traditional education which is reacted against."[1]

Experience

The belief that experience, any experience, is the best teacher is perhaps the most common misinterpretation of Dewey's philosophy. The result in practice has been such extremes as providing nursery school and kindergarten experiences that are almost exclusively socially oriented and elementary school classes that allow children to engage almost exclusively in "what they are interested in doing." In reality, Dewey attacked the traditional schools on these very same grounds:

[1] All quotations from *Experience and Education* by John Dewey are used by permission of Kappa Delta Pi, an honor society in education (P.O. Box A, West Lafayette, Indiana 47905). Copyright © 1938 by Kappa Delta Pi.

It is a great mistake to suppose, even tacitly, that the traditional schoolroom was not a place in which pupils had experiences. . . . The proper line of attack is that the experiences which were had, by pupils and teachers alike, were largely of a wrong kind. (1963:26)

Everything depends upon the *quality* of the experience which is had. (1963:27)

Dewey (1963:74) viewed the environment of the child as steadily expanding, gaining momentum through experience: "The environment, the world of experience, constantly grows larger and, so to speak, thicker." He called for a stimulating environment which would enable children, first of all, to be able to experience. Moreover, since education was a process of living, the child's primary experiences should be with real-life situations rather than with secondary book learning. Experiences should be firsthand as a foundation for building true understanding. Knowledge discovered for oneself was knowledge that lasted, Dewey stressed. He also felt that educational experiences should stem from children's natural interests rather than be imposed by an artificially contrived curriculum. Dewey's school was not haphazardly planned: "It does not follow that progressive education is a matter of planless improvisation" (Dewey 1963:28). He called for the school to state its philosophy in words, and from this would emerge decisions about subject matter, methods of instruction and discipline, equipment, and school organization. Dewey's call for a thoughtful plan behind curriculum experiences was an early version of our contemporary focus on instructional goals and objectives (see Chapter 8).

Continuity and Sequence

In Dewey's scheme, every attempt to discriminate between worthwhile and nonworthwhile experiences involved the principle of *continuity*, or the experiential continuum. Its basic characteristic was that "every experience enacted and undergone modifies the one who acts and undergoes, while this modification affects, whether we wish it or not, the quality of subsequent experiences" (Dewey 1963:35). Growth is an exemplification of the principle of continuity. It may occur in any direction, good or bad, and it may result from experiences that are educative or miseducative. For growth to occur, experiences must be related to one another in an organized, sequential manner. The greater maturity of the adult places him or her in the role of selector and organizer of the experiences of children. This is a grave responsibility, for implicit in it is determining what attitudes and tendencies are being developed in children and to judge which are detrimental to and which are supportive of growth. Thus Dewey stressed the requirement of *skill* in teaching. He also recognized clearly the *sequential*, *cumulative* nature of development and learning: "It is also essential that the new objects and events be related intellectually to those of earlier experiences" (Dewey

1963:75). Although he did not use extensively the medical terminology which has gradually crept into education, he understood the principle and the promise of *diagnosis*. Dewey identified and explained a critical factor in diagnosing and teaching, namely, the increasing complexity of knowledge resulting from experience and maturation:

Those who deal with the pre-school child, with the kindergarten child, and with the boy and girl of the early primary years do not have much difficulty in determining the range of past experience or in finding activities that connect in vital ways with it. With older children, both factors of the problem offer increased difficulties to the educator. It is harder to find out the background of the experience of individuals and harder to find out just how the subject matters already contained in that experience shall be directed so as to lead out to larger and better organized fields. (1963:75)

Dewey recognized the importance of planned continuity and sequence within the curriculum, yet he recognized the educational value in making time for the unexpected:

The basic material of study cannot be picked up in a cursory manner. Occasions which are not and cannot be foreseen are bound to arise wherever there is intellectual freedom. They should be utilized. But there is a decided difference between using them in the development of a continuing line of activity and trusting to them to provide the chief material of learning. (1963:79)

Interaction

Any normal experience is an interplay of two conditions, internal and external. The fully integrated individual is built up as successive experiences interact and a world of related objects is constructed. The educator is concerned with the situations in which interaction takes place. The external conditions of an experience cover a wide range—what the teacher does, how he or she does it, equipment, materials, and games chosen, and the total social setup of the situation. One problem with traditional educators, according to Dewey, was that they failed to consider a second factor in creating an experience, namely, the abilities and interests of the learners. He noted that "the principle of interaction makes it clear that failure of adaptation of material to needs and capacities of individuals may cause an experience to be non-educative quite as much as failure of an individual to adapt himself to the material" (Dewey 1963:47).

The Learning Process

Dewey believed that the only freedom of enduring importance was *freedom of intelligence*, not just freedom of physical movement, though this too was important. For example, he rejected the typical fixed rows of seats and chain-gang procedures of the traditional school as being opposed to the natural flow of life. At the same time, he saw freedom of physical movement as a *means* toward intellectual freedom—freedom that represented power to set purposes, to judge wisely, to evaluate desires by their consequences, and to reconstruct and remake impulses and desires into coherent plans of activity. The participation of the learner should be central in the learning process, Dewey believed, since children learn by being actively involved. Young people learn by doing, and thus Dewey set out to narrow the gap between school and life itself. In his view, the purpose of the teacher was to ensure that situations were fully utilized. The plan and the action were cooperative enterprises occurring through reciprocal give and take.

I have heard of cases in which children are surrounded with objects and materials and then left entirely to themselves, the teacher being loath to suggest even what might be done with the materials lest freedom be infringed upon. Why, then, even supply materials since they are a source of some suggestion or other? (1963:71)

The teacher, then, was not a passive observer, and the curriculum was not an assorted grab bag. The teacher's role was to determine the most effective and appropriate way for each child to experience the discipline of life. The educator was knowledgable in both the learning potential within the activities and materials available and in the needs and skills of the students. Dewey envisioned the teacher as a guide, monitoring each experience to interject assistance, encouragement, and new direction throughout.

Methodology

Dewey was a scientific, not an intuitive, teacher.

The methods of science also point the way to the measures and policies by means of which a better social order can be brought into existence. . . . So far science has been applied more or less casually. . . . There is nothing in the inherent nature of habit that prevents intelligent method from becoming itself habitual; and there is nothing in the nature of emotion to prevent the development of intense emotional allegiance to the method. (1963:81)

The scheme of problem-solving—sensing a problem, analyzing it, proposing solutions, testing them, and drawing a final hypothesis—was basic to his curriculum and to his philosophy. Accordingly, educators had only two alternatives between which to choose if they were not to drift aimlessly. One was to return to the intellectual methods and ideals of those centuries before the scientific method was developed. The second was systematic utilization of the scientific method for intelligent exploration and exploitation of the potentials of experience.

MARIA MONTESSORI (1870–1952)[2]

Maria Montessori defied the sexual lines of distinction of her time to become the first woman in Italy to receive the degree of doctor of medicine. (She later repeated the feat by becoming the first woman in Italy to receive a Ph.D. degree in anthropology.) During her early work as assistant doctor at the psychiatric clinic of the University of Rome, she became interested in feeble-minded children then housed in lunatic asylums. In working with these children, Montessori adopted the methods of Itard and Seguin, the French physicians who had treated such cases 50 years before her time. Jean Itard had experimented with methods of teaching deaf-mutes in an institute in Paris while he was studying treatments for diseases of the ear. Later, while caring for a retarded child for eight years, Itard expanded his pioneer methods to educational treatment of all of the senses. Edouard Seguin was also a teacher and physician. He expanded Itard's educational method while working with children committed to insane asylums. Montessori studied the methods of Itard and Seguin and concluded that mental deficiency in children could more appropriately be treated by educational rather than medical techniques. This led to the development of her Orthophrenic School, designed for the treatment of feeble-minded children, in which she personally trained special teachers. Herein lies one historical bond between the field of early childhood education and that of special education.

The striking notion that emerged from her work during this period (1898–1900) was that methods for educating the feeble-minded could also be used successfully with normal children. While those around her were admiring the progress of her "idiots," Montessori herself was searching for the reasons why healthy children in regular schools were achieving at so low a level that they could be matched by her "unfortunate" children. It should be noted that Montessori distinguished between children who had organic retardation or impairment and children with no identifiable organic problem who had been labeled by the regular school system as feeble-minded because of their poor academic performance. The previous lack of progress of the latter group she attributed to the children's having been approached with inappropriate pedagogical philosophies and techniques.

In 1907 Montessori opened her first *casa dei bambini* (Home of Children) in Rome's San Lorenzo slum district. A housing association, desirous of protecting its property from vandalism by the many young children in the area, offered Montessori space for a school. The reports of her success (Fisher 1940; Stevens 1913) far exceeded the hopes of her sponsors. Not

[2] The authors express their appreciation to Steve Jackson, Linda Jackson, Gay Ross, and Mark Ross of the staff of the Escuela Montessori de Montopolis, Austin, Texas, for their assistance in the preparation of this section.

only was vandalism prevented, but these 3- to 7-year-old children were alert pupils. They learned "cleanliness," "manners," "grace in action," and "proper diet," and they became familiar with animals, plants, and manual arts. Their work with the didactic apparatus that Montessori was developing aided their sensory and motor training, and many learned the fundamentals of counting, reading, and writing before they were 5 years old.

News of her success spread rapidly throughout the world through accounts in the press and publication of her own first extensive description of her methods (Montessori 1964). She came to the United States as the guest of Thomas Alva Edison and addressed an overflow audience in Carnegie Hall. This led to the formation of La Montessori Society with Alexander Graham Bell as President. There was a mild explosion of interest in the method during the early 1900s. The number of articles about her work numbered 54 in 1912 and peaked at 76 in 1913. After that, interest and articles rapidly diminished, amounting to fewer than five publications a year by 1918. Reinterest in the Montessori method began in the United States in about 1958. At that time, Nancy Rambusch opened the Whitby School in Greenwich, Connecticut, after receiving training in Europe as a Montessori teacher. Here she succeeded in promoting widespread renewed interest in the Montessori method (Lillard 1972).

Criticisms of "overly intellectual" education for preschool children by a number of prominent American educators, especially William Heard Kilpatrick of Teachers College, Columbia University, led to a widespread reaction against Montessori schools which lasted from the 1920s until the 1950s or later. Kilpatrick was a follower of the philosophy of Dewey. He objected to Montessori's didactic materials, stating that they were limiting, unstimulating, and did not foster social development. He further stated that the didactic materials were artificial as compared to real-life experiences. Montessori's philosophy, according to Kilpatrick, was far behind the times because it was so strongly influenced by Seguin, whose work had appeared 50 years earlier (Orem 1969:9–15).

The Montessori Method

Montessori's writings are much too varied to fit a rigid classificatory scheme, yet certain elements characterize her methodology. The Montessori method is more accurately called an approach, based on an attempt to understand the child's own natural developmental process. This approach leads to the exploration of didactic materials (and related activities on the part of the child) which are in a sequence according to the child's increasing natural capacities, interests, and competencies. The adult guides the child to work with materials appropriate to his development in a particular area, maintains the order of physical environment (which Montessori felt aided the children in their development of a mental order and of self-confidence), and

helps the child develop a social order through allowing him the most free-dom possible, consistent with his ability to handle it.

EXPERIENCE.   Although the notion of experience was a fundamental part of her method, Montessori's conception of the nature of experiences was much more limited than was Dewey's. Like Dewey, she emphasized proc-esses rather than content, the *how* as opposed to the *what* of learning. Motor education occurs through experiencing real-life situations having to do with the child's care and management of his or her environment. Motor education involves such experiences as the everyday actions of walking, sitting, and handling objects; personal care such as washing one's hands; household management such as scrubbing, polishing, and sweeping; gardening; gym-nastic exercises; and rhythmic movements. Sensory experiences in the Mon-tessori method are fostered through the use of didactic materials with which the child can interact independently since they are self-teaching. Involvement with these materials sharpens the child's ability to discriminate and teaches concepts of shape, size, color, and texture. All of the senses are involved—visual, tactile, auditory, olfactory, and taste. Education of the senses, espe-cially auditory training and discriminatory ability, emerges into language education, writing, reading, and arithmetic activities.

CONTINUITY AND SEQUENCE.   Montessori envisioned a curriculum designed to match the needs of the child from preschool to postgraduate. She provided sequences of materials and methods tested in the laboratory classroom. The technique of the Montessori method follows natural physio-logical and psychological development. Each task has a carefully designed sequence of preparation, practice, and perfection, from simple to complex. Sensory motor tasks are perfected first, and from these develop reading, writing, and arithmetic. Each activity has a fixed method of presentation followed by a prescribed method of practice.

Each task in the prepared environment of a Montessori classroom has roots in earlier developments and serves as roots for future, more complex, developments. The teacher herself is prepared internally (spiritually) and externally (methodologically) to prepare an environment for children that aids each child in the mastery of skills and the full development of his per-sonality. Montessori saw these tasks as sequential in nature because a child's natural development is sequential (walking lays groundwork for running, and so on), with certain subtasks, sometimes numerous and diverse, essen-tial for the achievement of a particular higher-order task. She attempted to *match* the activities offered to a child to the child's current level of physical and mental development. The child's prolonged practice with a didactic material allows the child to develop, stabilize, and make permanent a par-ticular physical capability or intellectual skill. The child's movements, dis-criminations, and reasoning become increasingly refined and accurate with practice. This emphasis on the child's self-educative activity makes the correction of his mistakes by the teacher unnecessary.

INTERACTION.   Like Froebel, Montessori understood the importance of using materials appropriate for children. She designed a set of didactic teaching materials, which made auto-education possible. The materials have only one correct way in which to be manipulated, and in this way they provide immediate, self-correcting feedback to the child as he or she works. The environment is structured to support concentration and individualization of work. It is a controlled or prepared environment in which the materials and the way to handle them are presented in a prescribed way. The child then practices with the material at his or her own pace. In her scheme, Montessori was far ahead of her time in stressing the importance of sensory education for children. Her materials call upon using each of the senses, one at a time. Moreover, stressing that education begins with sensory motor activity links Montessori's ideas with those of Piaget, who believes that motor activity is the first form of intelligence (see Chapter 7).

THE LEARNING PROCESS.   The heart of the learning process is the child's interaction with the self-teaching materials. The teacher is viewed as a perceiver of child needs, a preparer of the environment, a programmer of materials and lessons, a protector of rights to learn, and the provider of a living model. The teacher's language and nonverbal behavior must reflect the best that is available culturally. This requires extensive preparation and practice. The Montessori teacher makes a radical break with traditional teaching by guiding the child to auto-education possibilities with didactic materials rather than imposing knowledge on the child through lecture and rote memorization. Montessori stressed that the teacher should serve as an observer and guide and not as an authoritarian source of learning. In fact, all of the assistants selected for her earliest *casa dei bambini* lacked formal training, a fact to which Montessori attributed much of her early success. Montessori urged her teachers to observe children carefully and collect anecdotes for gaining analytical information about them. She favored a longitudinal rather than a cross-sectional or statistical method of studying children, and she stressed the need for the development of a science of child care. In the classroom, there is little need of teacher talk as children are encouraged to make discoveries for themselves. During "presentations" of didactic materials especially, the adult shows silently how to do the task, in order to avoid dividing the child's attention. The child learns to care for his own environment, putting away things for himself and cleaning up after himself. Furniture is scaled to child sizes. The emotional environment is one of love, security, and consistency. Montessori believed that through providing a physical environment geared to the child's convenience rather than the adult's habit (child-size furniture, and so on), adults concretely manifest their love and respect for the child as an individual (and vice versa).

ORDER AND THE COLLECTIVE INTEREST.   Like Dewey, Montessori rejected much of traditional education. The principles of cooperation, kindness, and responsibility were the roots of the Montessori method in much the same way that democracy was the foundation of Dewey's philosophy. Montessori emphasized the welfare of the group, even to the point of personal self-sacrifice. Like Dewey, she believed in personal freedom, but hers was freedom within clearly specified limits, as the reader shall see throughout this discussion. Montessori believed in the goodness of children and in respect for their native abilities. In her teaching, she focused upon the child's natural interests, his particular stage of development, and his active participation in the learning process. Just as Dewey saw organization and purpose behind curriculum experiences, order was important to Montessori also. She believed that a prerequisite for all creation was organization and structure and that the child developed a more efficient and orderly mind as he developed such habits of order as putting things in their places, maintaining a consistent schedule, and respecting the work and rights of others as a correlate of receiving such respect himself.

In the case studies that follow, a "typical day" in a Montessori school for a 3-year-old, a 4-year-old, and 5-year-old will illustrate how the basic elements of Montessori practice and philosophy are put into operation in the classroom.

TYPICAL DAY IN A MONTESSORI CLASS FOR A 3-YEAR-OLD, BEN

Ben's mother leaves him at the gate at 8:30, where his teacher says good morning and they shake hands. Ben, having been shown early in the year where coats are hung and how to take his coat off, does this by himself as soon as he enters the room. First, he gets a small folded cloth from a basket, goes to his table, and carefully dusts it. After shaking the cloth out outside, he refolds it and puts it back. After some wandering around and watching other children working, Ben takes a pouring exercise to his table and pours popcorn back and forth between pitchers for about five minutes, stopping to pick up any spilled kernels when he hears them fall. After putting this away, he goes on choosing other activities such as building a tower of ten successively smaller pink wooden cubes, watering plants with a small pitcher, and sorting out small bars of beads of different lengths and colors.

After putting this material away, Ben begins to wander through the room. The guide notices and takes the opportunity to give him a presentation on how to work with one of the cylinder blocks. She asks Ben to come with her, goes to the shelf, and carries the block to his table slowly, so he can see how she carries it with both hands and how she walks around rugs on which other children are working. After bringing her stool to Ben's table, the guide waits until Ben is watching her quietly and then begins taking the cylinders one by one out of the block and placing them on the table. When they are all out, she takes the smallest cylinder by the knob on its top and very slowly puts it back into its hole. One by one she replaces the other cylinders. When she has finished, she invites Ben to do it. She waits for a minute or two while Ben begins, then quietly returns to her place while Ben continues. Later, when Ben has had enough of this activity and is ready to put it away, the guide watches him from a distance to be sure he remembers where this work came from on the shelf. If he has forgotten, the guide might give Ben a moment's help by inviting him to bring the cylinder block with him and follow her to the shelf (for now Ben has seen how to carry the material and is eager to do this himself).

Around mid-morning, the guide asks all the children to listen and then tells them it is time to put their work away and have juice and cookies. After Ben has put away his work, he waits at his table for his glass of juice and cookie, which other children pass to him on trays. Perhaps Ben is asked to pass the basket of napkins. After everyone has had juice and the tables are clean, Ben and the other children sit in a circle with the guide and sing songs, talk about what they did the night before at home, and so on. If Ben is relatively new, he may still be a little shy, but no one presses him to say anything until he wants to. The children might count to see how many are present that day, how many have on red shirts, how many have on black shoes. By the time they are finished with their group activity, it is time for Ben, who goes home at 11:30 because he is 3, to put his coat on again. He walks out to meet his mother after shaking hands with the teacher and saying goodbye.

TYPICAL DAY IN A MONTESSORI CLASS FOR A 4-YEAR-OLD, DORINA

After hanging up her coat, Dorina dusts her table, then decides to wash her table with soap and water. She brings all the materials to her table and arranges them on her chair. After washing her table as she was shown how, she might decide to wax and polish it, or she might decide to simply let it dry and do some other work. Having spent a long time scrubbing her table, Dorina only has time to do a couple of other things before juice, perhaps tracing one of the few letters she still doesn't know in the sandpaper cutouts glued on tablets. Today Dorina is asked by the guide to pour glasses of juice for the children and to take them around on a tray. Having done various types of pouring for over a year, Dorina is able to handle this. In the later part of the morning, Dorina spends the rest of the time sitting at the science table observing the aquarium and then goes to the art corner and draws a picture of the fish with crayons. Dorina is now just old enough to stay for lunch and the afternoon, so she gets her lunch and eats at her table as do the rest of the older children. Her mother forgot to cut her sandwich into quarters this morning, so the guide asks Dorina if she would like her to cut it for her. (In another year, after she has had practice with exercises such as peeling and slicing a banana and a carrot, Dorina will be able to do this for herself.) After lunch, Dorina and two other children play a game with the guide at a rug. Dorina builds the tower of pink cubes on the rug. Then, while all the children close their eyes, the guide removes one cube from the tower and holds it behind her back. After they open their eyes, one child tries to say where the cube is missing. Or perhaps they use the smallest and largest cubes from the tower alone to talk about "bigger" and "smaller." During the last part of the afternoon, Dorina goes to the bell table and practices matching one set of bells against the other set and putting them in the diatonic scale, or perhaps she makes a drawing using one of the "metal insets" with a pencil, paper, and an underlayer at her table.

TYPICAL DAY IN A MONTESSORI CLASS FOR A 5-YEAR-OLD, WILLIAM

As soon as he has hung up his coat, William goes to the table and takes up where he left off on his work the day before. He has a roll of adding machine tape on which he is writing the numbers from one to one thousand, and today he will finish it. When he finishes, just before juice time, he takes it to show several of his friends, and then to the guide, who tells him that he can put his name and the date on it and then put it in his drawer for work to be taken home on Friday. After juice, William takes a basket and goes to the garden to collect leaves. When he returns he matches the leaves to outline cards showing various leaf shapes at the science table. He makes written labels for the leaves in a "book" he is making which he will staple together when he has enough pages. While he is working on this one of his friends wanders by and, having nothing interesting to do at that moment, pulls William's hair. Perhaps William tells his friend he is busy, and as the friend drifts off, perhaps William pokes him. Let us say they are in the mood for a tussle. The guide might, if she thinks William is still interested in the work with the leaves, suggest that he return to it, and then lead William's friend off in search of some interesting work for him. Or she might suggest that William put the work away and go outside for a while if he doesn't feel like working. Alternatively, according to the situation, the guide might ask both boys to sit at their tables until they feel ready to work. At lunch, William and the other children have a lively discussion with the guide about how people in other cultures eat their food, what they eat, and so on. William mentions that Chinese people eat with chopsticks—he saw a picture of it in a book he was reading last week. Three older children decide to work after lunch on a long division problem using beads and cards with numerals on them. This occupies almost an hour, after which William spends the rest of the time comparing the various wooden rods in the set of graduated number rods to objects in the room such as the window sills to see how long each one is.

These "typical days" represent but a few of the pedagogical materials in a Montessori classroom and give only a brief indication of how a social order is developed. Since each guide is an individual with a different style, and since each child has the freedom to work individually with work he has been shown how to use, the day of any one child would not be the same tomorrow or the same as the day of any other child; but these suggestions in fictional form may give some indication of the flavor of daily activities in a Montessori classroom.

Critical Analysis of the Montessori Method

William Boyd (1914:135) aptly noted: "It is her [Montessori's] ideal to be a scientist pure and simple, an observer of the real facts of child development and nurture, unbiased by any preconceptions as to the nature and end of the process." But, he suggests, "Even to disclaim a philosophy, as Montessori does, implies a philosophy." He credits Montessori with offering appropriate criticism, though previously made by others, of traditional schools, but he oversimplifies her contributions to child teaching-learning when he states, "Criticism and teaching devices, however helpful in a casual way, are insufficient as a basis for such an educational reconstruction as she aspires to effect" (Boyd 1914:137). In not providing a definite philosophy of life, Boyd (1914:137–138) believes that Montessori fails: "Unlike Pestalozzi, whose genius and work are recalled at times by hers, she has not succeeded in evolving a coherent and unified scheme of thought out of her experimentation." Yet among the heterogeneous detail of the Montessori system, Boyd (1914:140) selects two ideas as more fundamental than the rest: "The first is the need for freedom and spontaneity on the part of the developing child. The second is the importance of the training of the muscles and the senses in the first stages of education. By these the system stands or falls." Boyd, however, wrote at a time when only the earliest of Montessori's writings were published; the didactic materials and her educational thinking continued to change for almost 40 years after his critique was published.

Contemporary Research on the Montessori Method

The potential of Montessori's contributions for contemporary research and the possible links between her contributions and contemporary theories of child development and teaching are largely unexplored. One notable exception to this state is the work of Travers (1968), who analyzed the characteristics of children implicit in the Montessori method. He identified characteristics of children stressed in Montessori's book, *The Montessori Method* (Montessori 1964), concluding that some of her principles appear to have their roots in psychology dating back to Aristotle, some have obscure origins or represent speculation, while others may represent novel contributions. Travers drew attention to Montessori's lack of depth in several instances. For example, he replied to Montessori's (1964:231) statement, "To one whose attitude is right, little children soon reveal profound individual differences" by pointing out:

This proposition reflects the interest shown by Montessori's contemporaries in individual differences, but there is little implied in her writing concerning the effects that individual differences should have on teaching. She also has nothing to say about the nature of the dimensions of individual differences. (Travers 1968:96)

Again, however, the book to which Travers refers is among Montessori's earliest, which leaves open, at least, the question of whether her later writings clear up this problem.

Hunt's (1964) analysis of the Montessori method, contrasted to that of

Travers, is quite positive (with certain reservations). In his Introduction to Montessori's book, Hunt (1964) specified a number of reasons for the period of relatively little interest in the method as well as for the recent attention given it. Certain conceptions, dissonant with those of Montessori, and with contemporary research, were prevalent in the United States during her professional lifetime. First among these earlier misconceptions was that school experience for very young children (3- and 4-year-olds) is unimportant. Second was the belief that intelligence is fixed at birth. Third was the belief in predetermined development. Fourth was the belief that all behavior is motivated by instincts, by painful stimuli, by homeostatic needs, by sex, or by acquired drives based on these. Fifth was the belief that the response side of the reflex is the one essential in education. Sixth was the desire of teachers for what they thought of as an orderly classroom and for control of the educational process.

Despite general adherence of Montessori method to contemporary thought about the above notions, Hunt warns that we must not be overconfident that our own present-day theorizing is completely correct, for we must continue to subject emerging views to analytical scrutiny. Furthermore, there may be the danger of developing a cult that will restrict innovation. Hunt concludes that although interesting and potentially valuable, Montessori's didactic apparatus is not sacrosanct.

Carefully planned experiments designed to reveal whether, and to what extent, Montessori programs have been successful are rare indeed. Educators still rely upon unsystematic observation rather than research in judging the worth of the Montessori approach. During recent years, however, some research evidence has accumulated.

One notable study by Karnes and her associates (1970) compared four preschool programs for disadvantaged children utilizing pre- and postbatteries of standardized tests. Intellectual functioning was measured by the Stanford-Binet; language development was measured by the Illinois Test of Psycholinguistic Abilities; vocabulary comprehension was measured by the Peabody Picture Vocabulary Test. The four classroom designs were planned to represent levels of structure along a continuum from the traditional nursery to the highly structured preschool, with teacher-child interaction as the critical dimension of structure. The traditional and community-integrated programs represented the less structured end of the continuum; the Montessori program embodied some elements identified with a child-centered or traditional approach and a methodology incorporating considerable structure; and the experimental program was heavily structured, emphasizing learning tasks from school-related curriculums especially designed to enhance cognitive and language development.

The performance of the four groups of subjects on all tests varied in a rather consistent fashion. The experimental and traditional groups made gains on all instruments; however, the gains of the experimental group were consistently larger. In contrast, the gains of the community-integrated and Montessori groups were smaller and less consistent. Consequently, one might assume that structure is unessential for maximum progress of the disadvantaged child. This did not seem to be the case, for careful examination revealed that the Montessori program, unlike the experimental program, provided structured emphasis upon motor-sensory development without apparently giving similar concern to verbal development. This resulted in somewhat regressive language behavior. Further, certain other arbitrary elements in the research design may have placed the Montessori group at a disadvantage— the age criterion did not coincide with the multiyear age span advocated by Montessori, the program was short-term, and later analysis may show delayed effects of Montessori training.

Despite such reservations, Karnes and her associates (1970:76) believe that the magnitude and consistency of the experimental group gains "clearly endorse the importance of providing a setting in which the child moves to physical mastery of a concept while he is required to make appropriate and increasingly complex verbalizations." The conclusions of this study seem to conflict with some of Montessori's statements. For example, the finding that direct involvement of the teacher promoted language development contrasted with Montessori's (1964:231) statement, "It is necessary, therefore, that the teaching shall be rigorously guided by the principle of limiting to the greatest possible point the active intervention of the educator."

Meizitis (1971) reviewed different comparative research studies of Montessori schools and several non-Montessori preschools such as traditional, structured cognitive, and no schooling at all. For middle-class populations, children in highly structured programs scored higher on a measure of achievement, but there were few or no significant differences between groups on other measures of ability or on sociomotivational and cognitive-style measures. The comparison with disadvantaged children, however, revealed strikingly different conclusions. Montessori-trained groups made greater gains than disadvantaged children without schooling, but made non-significant gains in comparison to traditionally trained groups. However, Montessori-trained children achieved lower gains in comparison to the children in the structured cognitive program.

It appears that a cognitive-oriented curriculum including intensive direct verbal stimulation with adult modeling in a highly structured classroom environment presents the ideal conditions for producing immediate impact on the cognitive achievement of the predominantly Negro Head Start groups included in the above studies. (Meizitis 1971:55–56)

Another interesting finding from the Meizitis review was that Montessori groups from both middle-class and disadvantaged populations scored significantly higher on measures of task persistence, reflection, and self-reliance, suggesting a challenging avenue for further research exploration in the future. In light of the fact that interest in the Montessori method is once again rising and applications of her program are increasing, more research is sorely needed to place this educational approach in proper perspective. It should be noted that the early approaches were modified during Montessori's later work and continue to be modified through the work of her followers.

Montessori Work Today

In 1926, Maria Montessori founded the Association Montessori Internationale (AMI) to carry on centers to train teachers in education based on her work. Her son, Dr. Mario Montessori, did considerable work within AMI, succeeding his mother as its head upon her death in 1952. A pedagogical committee, made up of AMI training center directors from all over the world, deals with the updating of materials, presentations, and teacher-training techniques. AMI has its world headquarters in Amsterdam. National organizations exist in many countries, and teacher-training centers are located in the United States, Great Britain, Ireland, Italy, France, Canada, Mexico, Argentina, the Netherlands, India, Ceylon, and other countries. In 1956, Nancy McCormick Rambusch founded a new organization called the American Montessori Society (AMS), which now has its headquarters in New York City and operates its own training programs in a number of cities in the United States.

SUMMARY AND CONCLUSIONS

John Dewey's ideas about the nature of education stimulated the movement from traditionalism to progressivism. Dewey's philosophy and ideas still serve as basic principles of education in many programs for young children today.

According to Dewey, traditional education was characterized by rote memorization, by adult-imposed subject matter, and by a passive role of students. In his progressive ideas, Dewey viewed education as the process of living and not a preparation for future living. As such, the school should function as a miniature society and call for cooperation, mutual decision-making, harmony among activities, humaneness, sharing, and active participation. This point of view may be linked to the contemporary view of the importance of the process in the curriculum as opposed to the product. Through the process, such lifetime skills as decision-making, creating, valuing, problem-solving, and awareness are developed. Education as Dewey saw it demands an active role on the part of the students. Learning emerges from real-life experiences as opposed to strictly book learning. The *quality* of the experience is important, for learning will not occur from just any experience. Knowledge and understanding require firsthand, concrete experiences that stem from the natural interests of the child. The scheme of problem-solving—sensing a problem, analyzing it, proposing solutions, testing them, and drawing a final hypothesis—was basic to Dewey's philosophy. To Dewey, knowledge that is discovered for oneself is knowledge that lasts.

Dewey's approach to education was not haphazard. He called for the school to state its philosophy in words. A thoughtfully planned curriculum provides sequence and continuity among experiences. The teacher, in Dewey's educational scheme, has the grave responsibility to select and to organize the most appropriate experiences for the young child.

Maria Montessori, a contemporary of Dewey, also left her mark upon early childhood education. Since the late 1950s, interest in the Montessori method has grown steadily in America. Montessori's method is more accurately called an educational approach which features the programming of tasks by a teacher in a prepared environment of didactic materials. The set of didactic teaching materials she designed are used to this day in some form in many early childhood programs. Montessori was also a forerunner in stressing the importance of sensory education for young children. Her teaching materials were designed to engage each of the senses in the learning process. This emphasis upon sensory-motor activity for the young child links Montessori's ideas with those of the contemporary psychologist Jean Piaget. Piaget's theory holds that motor activity is the child's first form of intelligence. Montessori's work also historically links early childhood education with the field of special education. More than 50 years earlier, the French physicians Itard and Seguin used sensory education as the treatment for mentally retarded children. Montessori's philosophy of education was heavily influenced by the methods of Itard and Seguin. Montessori went even further, however, and expanded the ideas of special, sensory education to normal children.

The few contemporary studies of the Montessori method that have been conducted have yielded mixed results. Travers (1968) pointed out several examples of lack of depth in the approach. For example, while Montessori demonstrated that she recognized the importance of individual differences in children, she did not indicate what the effects of this recognition should be on teaching. Hunt's (1964) analysis is more positive, but suggests that the method needs to continue to be subjected to analysis. A study by Karnes and her associates (1970) found that direct involvement of the teacher promotes children's language development, a finding that is in conflict with Montessori's principle of limiting the active role of the educator. Meizitis (1971) found that middle-class children in more structured programs scored higher than Montessori groups on a measure of achievement but not in the other areas measured. Montessori-trained groups, however, made greater gains than disadvantaged children without schooling, but nonsignificant gains compared to children in traditional groups.

The Association Montessori Internationale, with headquarters in Amsterdam, maintains teacher-training centers in the method throughout the world, and national Montessori organizations exist in many countries. The American Montessori Society, located in New York City, operates programs in several U.S. cities.

SUGGESTED ACTIVITIES

1. Visit several early childhood programs in your community. Be sure to include an open school. Identify the principles from Dewey's philosophy of education which have been put into practice there. Give examples from your observations.
2. Visit a Montessori classroom. Observe carefully the types of teaching materials used, the nature of the learning activities, and the teaching methods. Note the role of the student and the role of the teacher in the educational process in a Montessori classroom.
3. Visit a Montessori classroom and a traditional classroom of children of the same age. Compare the two programs in regard to the materials, curriculum activities, teaching methods, classroom organization and management, role of the students, and role of the teacher. Identify similarities and differences between the programs.
4. Compare a Montessori program with a special education program you have visited. What similarities in the two programs can you identify? What features of the special education program did you observe that can be traced to Montessori's philosophy and method of education?
5. Discuss the principles and practices in your own classroom which have been influenced by the philosophy and work of Dewey and Montessori. Consider the following categories in relating their work to application within your own classroom and program: classroom management and organization, materials used, role of the teacher, teaching methods and strategies employed, curriculum, and role of the child.

REFERENCES

Boyd, W. 1914. *From Locke to Montessori*. London: George G. Harrap.

Dewey, J. Orig. 1938; reprinted 1963. *Experience and Education*. New York: Macmillan Company.

Dewey, J. *My Pedagogic Creed*. Orig. 1897; reprinted 1929 in booklet of the Progressive Education Association.

Dewey, J., and E. Dewey. 1915. *Schools of Tomorrow*. New York: Dutton.

Fisher, D. C. 1912. *A Montessori Mother*. Reprinted in 1940 as *Montessori for Parents*. New York: Henry Holt.

Hunt, J. McV. 1964. "Revisiting Montessori," Introduction to M. Montessori, *The Montessori Method*. New York: Schocken Books.

Institute for Development of Educational Activities, Inc. (I.D.E.A.). 1969. *The British Infant School, Report of an International Seminar*. Dayton, O.: The Institute.

Karnes, M. B., J. A. Teska, and A. S. Hodgins. 1970. "The Effects of Four Programs of Classroom Intervention on the Intellectual and Language Development of Four-Year-Old Disadvantaged Children," *American Journal of Orthopsychiatry*, 40:58–76.

Lillard, P. P. 1972. *Montessori: A Modern Approach*. New York: Schocken Books.

Meizitis, S. 1971. "The Montessori Method: Some Recent Research," *Interchange*, 2(2).

Montessori, M. Orig. 1912; reprinted 1964. *The Montessori Method*, A. E. George, trans. New York: Schocken Books.

Orem, R. C. 1969. *Montessori and the Special Child*. New York: Putnam.

Orem, R. C. 1967. *Montessori for the Disadvantaged*. New York: Capricorn Books.

Plowden, Lady Bridget, et al. 1967. *A Report of the Central Advisory Council for Education (England), Department of Education and Science*, Vols. I and II. London: Her Majesty's Stationery Office.

Stevens, E. Y. 1913. *A Guide to the Montessori Method*. New York: Frederick A. Stokes.

Travers, R. 1968. "Analysis of the Characteristics of Children Implicit in the Montessori Method," in J. L. Frost (ed.), *Early Childhood Rediscovered*. New York: Holt, Rinehart and Winston.

FURTHER READING

Dewey, J. *The School and Society*, 2d ed. Chicago: University of Chicago Press, 1943.

Dewey, J. *How We Think*, 2d ed. Boston: Heath, 1933.

Dewey, J. *Democracy and Education*. New York: Macmillan, 1916.

Itard, J. M. G. *The Wild Boy of Aveyron* (orig. 1801), G. and M. Humphrey, trans. New York: Appleton-Century, 1932.

Montessori, M. *Dr. Montessori's Own Handbook*. Cambridge, Mass.: Robert Bentley, Inc., 1964.

Rambusch, N. M. *Learning How To Learn: An American Approach to Montessori*. Baltimore, Md.: Helicon, 1962.

Seguin, E. *Idiocy and Its Treatment by the Physiological Method* (orig. 1866). Albany, N. Y.: Educational Reprints, Teachers College, Columbia University, 1907.

Standing, E. M. *The Montessori Method: A Revolution in Education*. Fresno, Calif.: The Academy Library Guild, 1962.

Day-nursery playroom, 1875

The Bettmann Archive

Movements in Child Study and Child Development

Concurrent with the work of Dewey during the last quarter of the nineteenth century, Darwin's theory of biological evolution was influencing education. Dewey himself was influenced by Darwin, in that he believed that education should center around the individual's natural adaptation to life. Darwin's theory influenced popularly accepted notions that heredity influences growth and development, that man evolved through stages of development over time, and that intelligence is genetically determined. These new ideas strengthened earlier theories concerning man's innateness and the existence of developmental stages as proposed by the men of vision (Chapter 1). The result was the emergence of the normative-maturational theory of child development. Perhaps as an outgrowth of Darwin's theory concerning how human beings evolved, interest grew in studying how children develop. The time was right for the rise on the American scene of the child psychologist and the child study movement. From an approach that stressed studying children "scientifically" grew three new psychological theories— the psychosexual, the behavioristic, and the gestalt. All of them played a part in the growing controversy between the progressive and traditional schools of educational thought. At the same time, the kindergarten interests merged into legitimate organizations to promote the interest of the young child nationally. The kindergarten movement was given such impetus that it extended downward and gave birth to nursery schools. From this spreading interest in the young child and from child development theories also grew child research centers, parent cooperatives, and new ideas concerning curriculum development.

The present chapter briefly reviews the historical shaping of early childhood education from the time of Dewey through the 1950s. It examines the variety of programs for young children that developed historically out of the new theories of child development, the wave of interest in curriculum development, and the earlier strings of educational thought.

THE CHILD STUDY MOVEMENT

G. Stanley Hall (1846–1924)

G. Stanley Hall and Dewey were contemporaries. While Dewey was becoming increasingly involved in the progressive school of educational thought, Hall was looking at the young child along different lines. Hall was greatly influenced by Darwin's work and drew heavily from it in emphasizing heredity and the study of growth as it unfolds naturally. He believed that each child recapitulates earlier stages of civilization during the growth process. Hence, study of the child could reveal the essence of mankind's development. Hall, considered the father of the child study movement, introduced the new thinking in 1891 in his essay, "The Contents of Children's Minds on Entering School." Even though a few minor magazine articles concerned with the study of children had appeared before this, it was Hall's study that stimulated widespread interest and led to concentrated effort in the field. The scientific study of children was a major breakthrough, for up to this time no systematic attention was given to understanding individual differences in growth and capacities or to exploring the learning process. In fact, the world of 100 years ago regarded the study of children as an invasion of rights. The few scientists who kept records of children usually used their own offspring as subjects.

Hall's professional training and experience were extensive. After graduating from Williams College in 1867, he studied in Germany for two years and then returned to the United States to receive a second degree from United Theological Seminary in 1871. After holding three successive chairs at Antioch College between 1872 and 1876, he studied under William James at Harvard, and received his doctorate in 1878. He then pursued further studies at several German universities, working with such noted investigators as Wilhelm Wundt and Ferdinand von Helmholtz. In 1882, Hall established the first psychological laboratory in the United States at Johns Hopkins University in Baltimore. With his students, who included Arnold Gesell and Lewis Terman (discussed later in this chapter), he conducted research in child and adolescent psychology and in education. He founded the first American psychological journal, *The Pedagogical Seminary*, in 1891 and became the first president of the American Psychological Association. Hall's first objective report, "The Contents of Children's Minds on Entering School," relied upon a questionnaire to inventory children entering Boston schools. Teachers questioned groups of three students about their knowledge of subjects usually familiar to children upon beginning school, such as growing plants, parts of the body, animals, natural geography, geometric figures, colors, and occupations. The major conclusion was that one must assume that children know very little of pedagogic value upon entering school. Following the report of this study, Hall and his students designed questionnaires to examine a wide variety of topics, including sense of humor, sense of self, memory, anger, dreams, moral and religious experiences, and motor ability. These were circulated to teachers and parents throughout the United States.

Hall's methods of interpretation were quite naive in light of present standards. Statistical treatment was confined to a few percentages. His sampling methods were faulty, and many of his questions suggested the answer. Bradbury (1937:23–25) pointed up Hall's shortcomings in conducting "A Study of Fears" (1897): "The syllabus was filled out by 1,701 people, mostly under twenty-three years of age, gathered in different places and methods without great uniformity, and 386 supplementary reports and many returns or special points, all written on nearly 4,000 pages." Although Hall's study may be criticized in terms of the reliability and validity of the questionnaire used, the conclusions he derived from these data have a distinctly modern note. He concluded that there is no one without fears, that fears are necessary and healthy, and that many fears are the result of heredity because the experience of the individual and even that of the near forebears cannot explain all fears. (The influence of the recapitulation theory is evident here.) Yet it is clear that Hall was inclined to generalize beyond the limits of his data. To prove the hereditary nature of certain fears would require an elaborate and extensive series of investigations meeting scientific criteria little realized or appreciated until recent times.

Hall was to have considerable influence upon the kindergarten movement. In a seminar for kindergarten teachers on child development research in 1895, Hall's criticisms of Froebelian methodology so infuriated the group that all but two teachers walked out (Osborn, Logue, and Surbeck 1973:14). The two remaining teachers, Anna Bryan and Patty Smith Hill, were leaders in their own right in the emerging movement to modify the standard Froebel kindergarten. Bryan gave a dissenting speech to the kindergarten department of the National Education Association in 1890, attacking the slavish following of Froebel's principles in kindergartens. She later established kindergartens for poor children and trained young women in teaching methods. Hill attended the first class. Later, both Bryan and Hill turned to Dewey's ideas as a source for kindergarten practice and became leaders in the movement toward progressivism in the schools, as we shall see.

Hall continued to assail the traditional kindergarten in his speeches and his writing. He criticized the Froebelian kindergarten for its gross indifference to health problems of children as evidenced by lack of hygienic physical environments. Attention should be directed, he said, toward the child's body rather than his soul. Too much emphasis was being placed on the gifts and occupations. Hall's studies showed that the sequence of motor development was from fundamental, or gross motor, activities to accessory, or fine muscle, activities. Consequently, the child needed a great deal of opportunity to engage in bold, active movement. Believing that too much fine muscle activity resulted in tension and nervousness on the part of the child, Hall emphasized free play as the vehicle for needed development. He described four stages of human development—infancy, childhood, youth, and adolescence.

Hall's criticisms were the subject of discussion at the International Kindergarten Union in 1898 and, eventually, led to widespread revision of curriculums. Through the influence of his students, a number of child study societies and associations were formed in the United States and in Europe. The logical outcome of these efforts, an institute emphasizing the scientific rather than the educational values of studying children, was not to be founded until 1917 in Iowa. That date marks the end of the child study movement and the beginning of systematic, organized studies of child development in institutional settings.

Edward L. Thorndike (1874–1949)

While Hall was working in the field of child psychology, Thorndike was engaged in pioneering work in animal psychology. The work of this psychologist was also to have an effect on education. While studying under William James at Harvard in 1897, with whom Hall had earlier studied, Thorndike began experimenting with chicks. Later, he expanded his work to include cats, dogs, and monkeys. He found, for example, that hungry animals when placed in a closed box with visible food outside would engage in a hit-or-miss struggle until accidently striking a lever that when pressed gave them access to the food. In each successive trial fewer errors were made, until the animals were able to go directly to the lever. As animals engage in problem-solving activities, they learn to use responses that were previously successful in similar situations (Thorndike 1913). Thorndike called this associative shifting, a type of behavior similar to Pavlov's conditioned response. From his extensive experimentation with animals, Thorndike postulated three fundamental laws of learning—the laws of exercise, effect, and readiness. The law of exercise, or use, holds that an individual must have opportunities to repeat an act frequently if he is to learn that act.

Thus the emphasis upon habit formation emerged, influencing the curriculum of the kindergarten and other levels of schooling. Unfortunately, the law was widely abused in schools. For example, children were required to perform such tasks as writing spelling words and certain phrases hundreds of times to "fix" learning.

Thorndike's law of effect states that if learning is followed immediately by pleasure or satisfaction, the learning is strengthened and leads to increased effort on the part of the learner. Conversely, learning that is associated with displeasure is weakened and the learner's efforts will decrease. This law, highly oversimplified, was to influence the work of many other psychologists. For example, the principles of reinforcement associated with the work of B. F. Skinner and the contemporary behavior modification movement can be traced to Thorndike.

The third law, the law of readiness, simply means that the learner must be ready to learn. The laws of exercise and effect are of no use if the learner is not ready. Readiness results from the individual's interests, needs, and maturation and is determined by observing the learner's attitude toward a learning task. The concept of readiness was envisioned much earlier by Pestalozzi and by Dewey.

Thorndike's later works rejected the law of exercise and deemphasized the role of displeasure or punishment, a switch in position that, unfortunately, was not embraced by most schools of the period. Application of his principle of stimulus-response (S→R) learning to kindergartens was slow in gaining acceptance in the midst of the "naturalistic" views of Hall and Dewey. The conception of the human organism as a response mechanism subject to the control of conditioned stimuli was in extreme opposition to the prevailing Froebelian views. Moreover, educators, then and now, are quite emotional about the application of principles gleaned from studies of "frightened animals" to the nurture of children. Nonetheless, studies of behavior modification, using the principles developed by Thorndike and his predecessors, are coming into their own in the 1970s. Thorndike, along with other major psychologists and educators of his period, laid the groundwork for the child development movement emphasizing the scientific study of children for its own sake.

THE CHILD DEVELOPMENT MOVEMENT

The child study movement, stirred by psychologists like Hall and Thorndike, blossomed into the child development movement as a result of criticisms of the methodology used in child study. Growing numbers of psychologists and increased sophistication in experimental methods naturally resulted in better research. Nonetheless, the child study movement left an enduring effect on the field of early childhood. It contributed the framework upon which much of modern psychology is built. Hall himself described the contributions of the movement shortly after the shift of emphasis to scientific child psychology.

The wave of interest in child study which swept over this country some three decades ago, and even inundated Europe, was a cultural movement of great importance, no matter what value we attribute to its scientific results. It taught us that the child and its characteristic traits are ages older than adulthood, which is a comparatively recent superstructure, and that success in life is far more dependent than we had realized on a happy childhood. Another effect of the movement was to give psychology, which has been slower and more reluctant than even religion to recognize evolution, something of a genetic trend, which has been greatly reinforced of late, at least for a large and important group of scientific minds, by the new conceptions of childhood contributed by the psychoanalysts . . . . the value of not only the school but every institution is how much it contributes to bring individuality to the fullest and most mature development of which it is capable. (1921:v–vi)

The founding of the Iowa Child Welfare Research Station in 1917 under the direction of Bird T. Baldwin marks the beginning of an era in which childhood was a subject of major scientific interest. Children were to be studied "not by the parent, the teacher, the philosopher, or the educator, but by the scientist" (Bradbury 1937:35). In 1921, the Iowa station published the results of its studies on mental growth curves of normal and superior children. The establishment of the Iowa Child Welfare Research Station in 1917 was followed by the founding of the Merrill-Palmer School in Detroit in 1920; the Child Welfare Institute at Teachers College, Columbia University, in 1924; the Institutes of Child Welfare at the University of Minnesota and in Toronto in 1925; and the Yale Psycho-Clinic in 1926. In 1927, two other major institutions for child study were founded, the Institute of Child Welfare at the University of California and the Brush Foundation at Western Reserve University, Cleveland. During the same year, the Child Research Council in Denver began operations.

New Schools of Psychological Thought

In the early twenties, the scientific study of children began in earnest. The result was an interest in intelligence testing and the emergence of three new psychological theories of behavior. Lewis Terman, a former student of Hall, was conducting studies on gifted children. The result was his monumental volume, *Genetic Studies of Genius*. It was Terman also who revised Binet's intelligence test for American use, the new version appearing in 1916 as the Stanford revision. Arnold Gesell, another student of Hall, was studying maturation and stages of development in children. Gesell published his normative data in 1925. (Because of the originality and lasting impact of his work, an adaptation and further discussion of Gesell's developmental scales is presented in the next section.) During the same period in Vienna, Sigmund Freud was mapping the subconscious world of the human mind and developed the method of psychoanalysis. Freud emphasized the sexual basis of behavior. Thorndike and his students extended their work into studies of ability and achievement tests. In 1901, Ivan Pavlov's salivating dogs introduced the conditioned reflex into psychology. His work came to the attention of U.S. psychologists through a book, *Objective Psychology*, written by Vladimir Bekhterev and translated into English in 1913. An animal psychologist at The Johns Hopkins University, John Watson, was very much influenced by the work of both Pavlov and Thorndike. Watson started the school of behaviorism in 1914 and shifted psychological emphasis from introspection and consciousness to the study of mechanistic behavior. By 1920, the idea of conditioning (see Chapter 11) was a widely accepted psychological principle. Three German psychologists, Max Wertheimer, Wolfgang Köhler, and Kurt Koffka, took issue with Thorndike's and Watson's interpretations of learning behavior. They held that every experience is a gestalt, or whole, which cannot be understood by analyzing its parts. The school of gestalt psychology, or the study of the wholeness of behavior, emerged from their work. Thus, competing schools were developed and studies of both animals and humans became increasingly intense and sophisticated. In varying degrees, the results of five strands of psychology were influencing early childhood education during the twenties: Thorndike's stimulus-response theory, Freud's psychoanalysis, Watson's behaviorism, Wertheimer's gestalt theory, and Gesell's normative-maturational theory.

Arnold Gesell (1880–1961)

In his interest in developmental stages, Gesell is linked to Rousseau, Froebel, and Hall. Gesell's work, however, was much more detailed and extensive than any before him. His maturational-developmental theory was widely accepted by educators and psychologists alike during the 1920s and 1930s and preempted contemporary developmental testing. Gesell was among the first to recognize the importance of early childhood in human development. In an early publication, Gesell (1925:4) stated that

we must grant, at the outset, that the preschool period exceeds approximately the first seventy months of the scriptural allotment of seventy years—only one clock hour, reckoning the entire span of human life as a day. But during that hour the major portion of the total stream of development flows under the bridge.

Including the neonatal period, Gesell gave separate consideration to 10 successive stages of development which characterized the period of early childhood. Because of the extensive range of development during the early months of life, Gesell described four stages of maturity for the first year. These he designated as the neonatal period, 4 months, 6 months, and 9 months. Beyond this level, the chronological age descriptions include the 12-month level, the 18-month level, and the 2-, 3-, 4-, and 5-year-old levels (see Table 3-1).

Although his schedule of development is very relevant in contemporary times, Gesell's maturational-developmental theory is not widely accepted today because it explains development primarily on the basis of nature while disregarding nurture or the effects of the environment. To Gesell, the rate and course of development was predetermined by the process of maturation.

Infants are individuals, because the intrinsic forces of maturation operate to keep them from being the mere pawns of culture. The impacts of culture are incessant and often they tend to produce uniformity, but even the tender infant preserves an individuality, through the inherent mechanisms of maturation. We may be duly thankful for this degree of determinism. Did it not exist, the infant would be a victim of the malleability which behaviorists once ascribed to him. (Gesell and Ilg 1943:41)

According to Gesell, developmental trends and fluctuations are expressions of evolutionary processes and not the products of the environment. Thus, linkages are formed with Darwin's theories of evolution. In one of his own books, Gesell's (1948:43) chapter on "Charles Darwin and Child Development" stated, "We may well go back to Darwin for vitalization of outlook and even of method." Gesell also supported earlier views of recapitulation, for he emphasized that it took vast ages for man to bring walking, talking, manipulating, and thinking capacities to their present rich forms. In regard to these views of the role of heredity or predeterminism, Gesell stands in contrast to the prevailing beliefs of many contemporary psychologists and educators who work with young children.

THE KINDERGARTEN MOVEMENT

At the turn of the twentieth century, as Hall was conducting his child studies, kindergarten educators were torn between two camps: the idealistic, introspective school of Froebel and the progressive, scientific school of Dewey. Froebel's view had "maturational" overtones; education was to assist in the unfolding of symbolic premonitions and spiritual ideals. Dewey's child had the potential for growth to be shaped by environmental interaction. The Froebelian conservatives and the Deweyian progressives engaged in bitter debates at conferences of the International Kindergarten Union. Other kindergarten organizations were also the meeting grounds for professionals involved in the new kindergarten movement. An American Froebel Union was established in 1878 by Elizabeth Peabody, who earlier had established in Boston the first English-speaking kindergarten (see Chapter 1). In 1884, the new Froebel Union organized a kindergarten department in the National

TABLE 3-1 Normative Summary

Three Years	Four Years	Five Years
Motor Characteristics	*Motor Characteristics*	*Motor Characteristics*
Draws a circle from copy	Draws cross from copy	Draws triangle from copy
Draws a horizontal stroke imitatively	Traces diamond path	Draws prism from copy
Creases a piece of paper neatly	Hooks fish in 15 or 30 seconds with right or left hand	Hooks fish three times in 1 minute
Aligns a card to an edge		
Language	*Language*	*Language*
Uses pronouns, past and plural	Distinguishes four prepositions	Defines words by use
Names three objects in a picture	Uses descriptive word with picture	Knows three or more words in vocabulary list
Can tell simple stories	Repeats twelve syllables	Interprets humor
Distinguishes prepositions, *in, under, behind*		Speaks with noninfantile articulation
Adaptive Behavior	*Adaptive Behavior*	*Adaptive Behavior*
Builds bridge imitatively	Folds paper diagonally	Builds keystone gate
Builds block tower of four or more	Draws three completions in incomplete man	Completes four of eight forms
Discriminates between two short lines	Completes patience picture	Discriminates weights
Combines two parts of severed picture	Puts two blocks in cup	Performs three commissions
Personal-Social Behavior	*Personal-Social Behavior*	*Personal-Social Behavior*
Can open door	Uses building material constructively	Draws recognizable man and tree
Can carry breakable object	Buttons clothes	Laces shoes
Asks questions of elders	Goes on errands outside of house	Puts on coat and hat alone
Puts on shoes	Washes self	Uses play material with advanced constructiveness
		Replaces material in box neatly

SOURCE: Adapted from Arnold Gesell, *The Mental Growth of the Preschool Child*. New York: Macmillan, 1925.

Education Association and, one year later, merged with the new department (Haven 1908). In 1892, a new kindergarten section was established in the National Education Association with the aim of serving *all* kindergarten interests. The battles between the progressives and the traditionals were carried on among the membership. A typical round-table presentation on free play saw the conservative factor expressing alarm at abandoning the process of imitation and the progressives extolling the possibilities of growth in freedom of activity (Weber 1969:69). Continuing dissension led to the establishment of a Committee of Nineteen in 1903, charged with the task of formulating a clear statement of contemporary thought concerning kindergartens. It was chaired by Susan Blow, who had established, with William Harris, the first public kindergarten in St. Louis (see Chapter 1). The committee finally presented its report to the International Kindergarten Union in 1909. Three reports were presented. A conservative view was written by Blow and a liberal view by Patty Smith Hill, a well-known progressivist educator. (Hill was later associated with the laboratory school at Teachers College, Columbia University, and was instrumental in the formation of the National Association for the Education of Young Children.) A liberal-conservative, or middle-of-the-road, view was written by Elizabeth Harrison and was signed by Lucy Wheelock. The liberal report revealed the "new psychology" coming into play, and the theory of evolution was accepted as a viable hypothesis with implications for research in human development. A brief statement in this report exposed an important link with the work of Thorndike; "emphasis upon the child's physical development and upon the formation of correct habits of acting, feeling and thinking is the best method of furthering the development of the mental and moral powers" (International Kindergarten Union 1909:129).

REVISION AND EXPANSION IN EARLY CHILDHOOD EDUCATION

During the 1920s, early childhood education was legitimized. A flurry of activity led to the establishment of many child-oriented organizations and institutions. In 1925, Patty Smith Hill invited 25 selected representatives to Columbia University. This group, in 1926, formed the National Committee on Nursery Schools, which, in 1929, became the National Association for Nursery Education. It has since been renamed the National Association for the Education of Young Children (NAEYC), with headquarters in Washington, D.C. The association is being revitalized in the 1970s through the unprecedented interest in early childhood development. The NAEYC promotes its goals through local and state affiliates, national conferences, and publications, including the official publication, *Young Children*. The following goals and objectives are listed on the inside front cover of each issue of *Young Children*:

The expressed purpose of NAEYC is to serve and to act on behalf of the needs and rights of young children, with primary focus on the provision of educational services and resources. In implementing this goal, NAEYC

- endeavors to uplift the competence of all persons working with young children;
- develops "position statements" in issues or areas of critical concern through a series of NAEYC Commissions of Infants, Mass Media, Day Care, Professional Developments and Staff Patterns and Relationships;
- participates in the development of standards which will ensure high quality programs for young children;
- assists individuals and groups as they learn to become more effective in influencing and accomplishing legislation related to the total well-being of children;
- disseminates information about pending Federal legislation and interprets issues and alternatives involved;
- serves as a public information agency striving to accomplish a commitment by this nation to provide for every child that which is his birthright—the very best beginning in life that is within our knowledge and skills to give him.

In 1930, one year after the founding of NAEYC, a second major organization for children was organized. The Association for Childhood Education International (ACEI) was the result of a merger between the International Kindergarten Union and the National Council of Primary Education. These groups founded the *Journal of Childhood Education* in 1924. In later years, this publication became the official journal of ACEI, and the title was shortened to *Childhood Education*. The organization of ACEI is similar to that of NAEYC, with a series of local, state, regional, and national groups active in promoting common goals. The purposes of the Association are:

To work for the education and well-being of children, infancy through adolescence;

To promote desirable conditions, programs and practices in the schools—nursery through the elementary;

To raise the standard of preparation and to encourage continued professional growth of teachers and other educational leaders in this field;

To bring into active cooperation all groups concerned with children in the school, the home and the community;

To inform the public of the needs of children and how the school program must be adjusted to fit those needs.

The age range of children in early kindergartens was 3 to 7 years. However, as the programs became more closely associated with public schools, the age range was gradually narrowed. By the early 1920s, 4- and 5-year-olds were admitted to kindergartens, with preference given to those already 5 if space or resources were limited. Nursery schools accepted very young children, with some schools taking 18-month-olds. In this period, the average entering age was 2 years 5 months (Davis 1932). By the mid-twenties, the kindergarten was an established part of many educational systems. Half-day sessions were the rule. A survey of kindergartens (Davis 1925:62) showed that time was divided as follows: 36 percent to physical education, 33 percent to the general arts, 16 percent to general assemblies, 9 percent to language and literature, and 6 percent to music. There was also flexibility to allow for excursions, outdoor play, special days, and special needs of children. The following schedule outlines a typical day (Davis 1925:58):

8:10– 9:20	Self-adopted activity
9:20– 9:30	Period for replacing material
9:30– 9:50	Conversation—discussion or problems in connection with work, discussion of health habits, of nature study, the need for being careful in crossing streets, etc.
9:50–10:10	Luncheon
10:10–10:20	Rest
10:20–10:30	Games and rhythms
10:30–10:45	Songs and stories

"Undoubtedly the most important development of the twenties was the elaboration of a theory of normative stages of growth," Lazerson (1972:46) noted. Thorndike and Watson gave to teachers the research base for establishing proper conditions for learning and reinforcing correct responses. However, practitioners still needed assistance in determining the appropriate child behavior for a particular stage of development. A number of child research institutes took up this task, but the work of Gesell was the most thoroughgoing with respect to providing normative data about children.

THE NURSERY SCHOOL MOVEMENT

The nursery school movement developed separately from the kindergarten movement and was largely influenced by the work of Rachel and Margaret Macmillan in England. The Macmillans were contemporaries of Dewey. While working with children of the poor in health clinics, they conceived the idea of a nursery school and coined the term. The basic idea was to nurture the whole child, socially, physically, emotionally, and intellectually. The nursery school had a more social foundation than the religious foundation of Froebel's kindergarten. Many of the activities originated by the Macmillans are still included in early childhood programs today, such as personal hygiene, care of plants and animals, indoor and outdoor segments, and the use of sensory materials such as music, sand, and water. Here, the Macmillans were influenced by the French psychiatrist Seguin, who also influenced Montessori's ideas on sensory education.

During the twenties and simultaneous with the establishment of child research institutes discussed earlier in this chapter, early childhood education in America was extended downward through the spread of the nursery school movement. The reasons for the downward extension of early education at that time were similar to those cited during the 1970s for further extension of early childhood education to infancy. Research in child development stressed the importance of the early years in later growth, while studies of infant mortality, illegitimacy, and inadequate infant care reinforced this idea. In addition, large numbers of women were entering the labor force during the 1920s. Stimulated by World War I, the number of working women increased from five million in 1900 to eight million in 1920 (Lazerson 1972:48).

In 1920, the Women's Education Association of Boston organized the Ruggles Street Nursery School to serve children of the working class. The director was Abigail Eliot, a social worker who had studied at the Rachel Macmillan Nursery School and Training Center in England (Pearson 1925:19–21). The school program revealed the influence of Froebel and Dewey as well as the Macmillans. During the period of "quiet occupations," the child selected from a closet containing a variety of material—Froebel's gifts, certain Montessori apparatus, and Macmillan materials. Other nursery schools in the United States during the early twenties were the Harriet Johnson Nursery School started by Lucy Sprague Mitchell in New York City, the Merrill-Palmer Nursery School in Detroit, a nursery school at Teachers College, Columbia University, and a preschool unit at the University of Iowa. The only programs for parent education in 1920 were a few voluntary parent groups organized by the Federation for Child Study (Frank 1962:208). The idea of nursery schools spread slowly thereafter, and they were usually associated with a university or a child welfare agency. Only a few were privately owned and operated. The 1920s also saw the beginning of parent cooperative nursery schools, with the first established by a group of faculty wives at the University of Chicago in 1916. By 1929, there were some 300 in operation (Lazerson 1972:48). Parent coops emerged because of the growing interest in the early years of development, a desire for quality education at a low cost, with parents sharing the classroom work, and a desire for parenting education, including meetings or classes on child development and child-rearing. The biggest growth of parent cooperative nursery schools, however, came in the 1950s. In 1960, the American Council of Cooperative Preschools was formed and in 1964 changed its name to Parent Cooperative Preschools International (PCPI). The current membership is about 10,000 (Osborn, Logue, and Surbeck 1973:17).

THE SPREAD OF THE CHILD DEVELOPMENT POINT OF VIEW

The period of the twenties and thirties was one of intense activity in specialized child study. The work of three educators in particular, Lawrence Frank, Robert Havighurst, and Daniel Prescott, had a significant influence on the educational philosophy and practice of early childhood educators today. Each in his own way espoused the child development point of view and called for schools for young children that would meet the basic needs of life and living.

Lawrence Frank (1890–1969)

Much of the university-based research during the twenties and thirties was supported by the Laura Spelman Rockefeller Memorial, a fund administered by Lawrence Frank. Operational from 1923 to 1930, the memorial supported the fields of child study and parent education with five-year renewable grants to universities and aid to the National Research Council Committee on Child Development and the National Council on Parent Education (Frank 1962:214). Frank's influence exceeded the contributions he made as research executor of the fund. He studied the psychology of personality and pioneered in the use of projective techniques for diagnosing personality. Even more important, he spearheaded efforts to influence early childhood curriculum toward a child development point of view and to focus upon human basic needs. In an address to the National Association for Nursery Education, Frank (1938:379) made a strong case for the orientation of schools to the fundamental needs of the child, which, he said, are "in truth the fundamental needs of society." Frank reacted against the practice of dictating the nurture and education of children by religious, ethical, and moral ideas, by political and economic requirements, and by social class lines.

It is safe to say that most of these traditional patterns of child training and nurture derive from ideas and beliefs and strong convictions that have little or no relevance to the immediate needs of the child. Civilized man in many cases has survived *despite*, not because of, these methods of child care, as we are now beginning to realize in the light of recent investigation. Curious as are these practices of physical and physiological training, the variety of practices in psychological training are even more astonishing, since here we find methods and procedures for bringing up children in the most fantastic, distorted patterns of conduct and feeling. . . .

An effective program of early-childhood education based upon the needs of the child will inevitably change our society far more effectively than any legislation or other social action. (1938:354–355)

As the infant grows toward adulthood, Frank noted, he faces a series of life tasks that cannot be evaded or denied if he is to grow healthily. These include:

Warmth, nutrition, and bodily care.
Rest, sleep, and play.
Security, feelings of being protected, tactual contacts, and soothing, sympathetic reassurance.

Simplified enlightenment on problems such as sex and procreation.

Learning to recognize and observe the inviolabilities that every culture establishes with respect to objects, persons, places, and times.

An image of self and the kind of person he would like to be.

Frank disagreed with the prevailing view among psychologists that hostility and aggression are inborn characteristics of all individuals. He believed that human nature is essentially plastic and subject to educational direction toward friendliness and cooperation. He rejected the use of fear as an educational and psychological instrument in early child-rearing: "Fear, and the resentment or hostility it often generates, are indeed the major emotional drives in our social life and give rise to much unsocial and antisocial behavior" (Frank 1938:375). What the child needs, but seldom receives, he stressed, is adult help in determining a clear definition of the situation and the conduct appropriate to the situation so that he will *learn* what is permitted and what is not permitted. In building good preschools, Frank believed, the tendency of professionals to standardize and substitute academic training for sympathetic understanding and insight into children and their needs must be reexamined.

Robert Havighurst (1900–   )

Ideas about "life tasks" were elaborated and refined by Robert Havighurst, who sharpened his own observations by discussing with and observing the work of Frank and Daniel Prescott. Havighurst proposed that living in a complex modern society such as that of the United States involves a long, continuous series of learning tasks—the *developmental tasks* of life—if one is to be a happy person.

A developmental task is a task which arises at or about a certain period in the life of the individual, successful achievement of which leads to his happiness and to success with later tasks, while failure leads to unhappiness in the individual, disapproval by the society, and difficulty with later tasks. (Havighurst 1948:2)

The developmental tasks originate from *physical maturation*, such as learning to walk, from *cultural pressure*, such as learning to read, and from the *personal values* and aspirations of the individual. In most cases, developmental tasks arise from combinations of these factors acting together. Havighurst proposed developmental tasks for infancy through later maturity. He listed as the major tasks for infancy and early childhood:

Learning to walk.
Learning to take solid foods.
Learning to talk.
Learning to control the elimination of body wastes.
Learning sex differences and sexual modesty.
Achieving physiological stability.

Forming simple concepts of social and physical reality.
Learning to relate oneself emotionally to parents, siblings, and other people.
Learning to distinguish right and wrong and developing a conscience.

The major implications of developmental tasks for education have to do with determining and stating educational philosophy. The purpose of the school is to assist the child, through coordinated efforts of the school and society, to achieve the developmental tasks appropriate to him. In a more specific classroom orientation, Havighurst recommended that the teacher *study* the child to determine what developmental tasks he is working on and to establish conditions that are favorable for learning those tasks. "When the body is ripe, and society requires, and the self is ready to achieve a certain task, the *teachable moment* has come" (Havighurst 1948:5; italics added).

Daniel Prescott (1898–1970)

The movement to change education from a completely empirical art to a social process making full use of scientific knowledge gained force during the forties and fifties through the Institute for Child Study at the University of Maryland, under the direction of Daniel Prescott. With his staff, Prescott served between four and five thousand members of the educational profession each year toward the end of his tenure at Maryland. School systems were assisted in providing a three-year sequence of professional growth through child study (Prescott 1957:xii). Participants organized scientific knowledge about children into an integrated theory of human development. They learned to gather and objectively record, through anecdotal records, information about individual children in order to work out specific plans for the teaching-learning process for both individuals and groups. Techniques for identifying and referring children with special learning problems were developed. In addition, participants were helped to develop and abide by a strong code of professional ethics regarding the worth and dignity of individual human beings (Prescott 1957:447–448). Prescott's application of scientific knowledge to problems of education was based upon a number of religious, philosophical, and ethical assumptions which he classified under "sources of values." The assumptions were:

RELIGIOUS, PHILOSOPHICAL, AND ETHICAL ASSUMPTIONS
1. Every human being is valuable.
2. Every human being has the right to strive for those relationships and experiences which promote his optimum development.
3. Whatever promotes wholesome development is moral; whatever blocks or prevents optimum development is evil.
4. Every human being has the right to be treated at all times in ways that show respect for his dignity and permit him to retain respect for himself as a person.
5. The Golden Rule is the soundest ethical principle against which to evaluate the

behavior of individuals, the programs of social institutions, and the policies of nations.

SOCIAL ASSUMPTIONS
1. Every child must, inevitably and properly, internalize the culture of his family, social group, community and nation into which he is born.
2. Every individual has certain rights which cannot be abridged.
3. The democratic procedure is the best procedure yet worked out for carrying on the decision making that is a part of all social living.
4. Each individual must be reared in such a manner that he is capable and desirous of assuming responsibilities that go with freedom to make basic choices.
5. The scientific method is the best process yet devised for using the mind to distinguish fact from fallacy.

SCIENTIFIC ASSUMPTIONS
1. Behavior is caused and is meaningful.
2. The causes which underlie behavior are always multiple.
3. Each individual is an indivisible unit.
4. The human individual develops. No child or youth was born as he is or necessarily destined to become what he is.
5. Every human being is a dynamic energy system, not just a machine acted upon from without.
6. Dynamic self-actualization is made possible to an individual by the existence of an organizing core of meanings (values) at the center of the personality.
7. Each individual is different from every other.[1]

EVOLVING VIEWS OF LEARNING AND CURRICULUM

Early childhood curriculum during the thirties and forties distinguished between preschool and primary school needs. It was not until the 1950s that the different emphases were to evolve into new views of curriculum for young children. During the thirties and forties, the content of preschool curriculum maintained a strong Deweyian influence. It dealt with the immediate environment and focused on "learning by doing." The preschool projects of the 1920s had given way to units of work and centers of interest, allowing the child to "develop" in a lifelike setting under conditions of flexible planning. The units tended to center around such topics as seasons and holidays. The interest centers were separate areas organized around instructional materials such as blocks; housekeeping, woodworking, art, and science materials; and books and puzzles. The primary school, on the other hand, emphasized the development of skills and the acquisition of knowl-

[1] From *The Child and the Educative Process*, by Daniel Prescott, pp. 27–30. Copyright 1957 by McGraw-Hill Book Company. Used with the permission of McGraw-Hill Book Company.

edge. Pressures for modifying preschool curriculums were particularly great in regard to the teaching of reading. Reading specialists urged kindergarten teachers to "adopt as one of their aims the development of those attitudes and habits which make for reading readiness" (Gray 1927:213). This emphasis eventually led to widespread acceptance in public school kindergartens of "programs" of reading readiness. Unfortunately, these programs were most often sets of workbooks providing for a great deal of repetitious practice and busy work, but poorly correlated to the underlying bases for reading. Kindergartens of the 1970s are still plagued with this troublesome, ill-founded practice. During the fifties, preschool curricula based upon social-personal needs came under even more intense criticism. Was the environment rich in social interaction and exemplary in providing for emotional needs also providing for optimum *intellectual* development? Two major forces appear to have influenced criticism of preschool curriculums, namely, Russian technological competition and comparison of preschool and primary school emphases. As will become apparent in subsequent chapters, this initial criticism was strengthened during the 1960s by the accumulation of research data that supported increased emphasis in the curriculum upon intellectual development.

Expanding Program Bases: The Sixties and Seventies

The past decade has seen rapid expansion of program types. During the early 1970s, several therapy approaches bearing limited resemblance to Freudian psychoanalysis were being assimilated into classroom settings, such as Glasser's (1965) Reality Therapy and Harris' (1967) Transactional Analysis. The behavioristic approaches of Thorndike and Watson were employed by preschool educators up to about 1960 in a kind of back-door fashion. As part of the predominating child development school, they openly rejected such behavioristic doctrine as ignoring internal feelings and need states and reacting solely upon observable responses. Nor did they concern themselves with breaking down behaviors into "bite-sized" pieces for purposes of instruction, or with developing systematic schemes for behavior modifications through reinforcement principles. However, the careful study of observable behaviors for purposes of determining child needs *was* a central feature of curriculums during this period and remains alive in many teacher-preparation programs in child development in the seventies. A major influence in preschool program development was the normative-maturational view of Gesell and his followers. The failure of practitioners to develop programs of cognitive stimulation before the sixties seems to have been based in large part upon the established notions of predeterminism. These notions held sway until the research of the sixties (Chapter 4) established strong support for emphasizing the interaction of nature and nurture in child development. The influence of normative-maturational theory was also felt in the derivation and utilization of developmental "needs." These were often defined according to characteristics of mental, emotional, physical, and social development placed into normative age-stage schemes and translated into curriculum. This practice is experiencing a rebirth during the 1970s. In building "performance-" or "competency-based" programs, professionals are preparing sets of behavioral objectives that bear a striking resemblance to normative age-stage characteristics. The wise curriculum specialist will exercise caution lest catalogs of competencies become the contemporary entry in education's historical list of practices most likely to be abused.

Traditional practice in promoting the development of young children was to remain relatively fallow until the mid-sixties when a series of events led to frantic activity in the field. These events, as will be seen in Chapter 4, and the actions they generated were unparalleled in educational history and stimulated a "rediscovery" of early childhood education (Frost 1968). Ironically, a central figure in this rediscovery, Jean Piaget, had been actively studying children and publishing his work since 1921. However, his methods were criticized and his work was presented essentially as an isolated endeavor. The reemphasis on early childhood education in the United States during the 1960s paralleled a "discovery" of Piaget. Piaget is now the man of the hour among developmental psychologists and educators. His contributions, which serve as a primary source for early childhood curriculum, are presented in Chapter 7.

SUMMARY AND CONCLUSIONS

A number of trends were established in early childhood education during the first half of the twentieth century. Through the work of G. Stanley Hall, there emerged two unique phenomena on the American scene, the child psychologist and the child study movement. When Hall opened the first psychological laboratory in the United States dedicated to the study of children and founded the first American psychological journal, he further advanced the trend toward psychological and educational research. While Hall was studying children, Edward Thorndike was pioneering work in animal psychology. As a result of his study of animal behavior in problem-solving situations, Thorndike postulated three fundamental laws of learning. His laws were quickly accepted by educators and initiated the tendency to utilize the findings from animal research in the field of education. As the number of psychologists grew, the child study movement gave way to the child development movement and the serious study of children through more scientific methods. Out of the scientific research into child growth and development emerged rudimentary frameworks for schools of psychological theory—the normative-maturational, psychosexual, gestalt, and behavioristic. These schools of psychology were the foundations for the emergence of contemporary early childhood curriculum practice (Chapter 5).

During the twenties, early childhood education was legitimized, and the trend to promote the well-being of the young child through child-oriented organizations and publications was established. Nursery schools developed alongside kindergartens and established the trend of nurturing the whole child—socially, physically, emotionally, and intellectually. Many trends in the nature of early childhood program activities also emerged through the nursery school movement. Emphasis upon personal hygiene, the care of plants and animals, both indoor and outdoor activities, and the use of sensory materials such as music, water, and sand are still contemporary early childhood practices. In the attention to sensory materials, nursery schools were influenced by Seguin and again link early childhood education to the field of special education. Early childhood education was extended downward through the growth of the nursery school movement. The reasons for this downward extension were similar to those that accounted for the further downward extension of early childhood education to infancy in the seventies; that is, the research showing the importance of the early years in later growth and the growing number of working mothers.

Early childhood education was to remain relatively fallow in the application of the new psychological theories until the mid-sixties. Freudian psychoanalytical theory was never applied in classrooms. During the early seventies, however, several therapy approaches bearing some resemblance to psychoanalysis, such as Glasser's (1965) Reality Therapy and Harris' (1967) Transactional Analysis, are beginning to be used in classroom settings (Chapter 11). The behavioristic approaches of Thorndike and Watson were employed in a kind of back-door fashion by preschool educators at the time. Yet, the careful study of children's behaviors to determine the needs of the young child was a central feature of curriculum development during this period and remains so in many teacher-preparation programs in the seventies. From the twenties through the fifties, the major influence in preschool program development was the normative-maturational view of Gesell and his followers. Practitioners failed to develop programs of cognitive stimulation before the sixties largely because of the established notions of predeterminism. These notions held sway until the research of the sixties (Chapter 4) established strong support for early childhood programs that take into account the interaction of nature and nurture. The influence of normative-maturational theory was also felt in the trend to identify developmental "needs." These needs were generally characteristics of mental, emotional, physical, and social development. They were organized into normative age-stage schemes and translated into curriculum.

SUGGESTED ACTIVITIES

1. Visit a nursery school and a kindergarten in your community. Determine the goals of both programs. Observe the types of activities, materials, and methods used in each. Compare the similarities and the differences in the two types of programs.
2. Study one of the psychological theories of child development (normative-maturational, psychosexual, behavioristic, gestalt) in greater depth. Identify the major principles in the theory you investigate.
3. Familiarize yourself with the journals of the major early childhood organizations. How does the information in the journals promote the interests of the young child?
4. Identify the early childhood organizations, institutions, and agencies within your own community. Determine the goals, membership, and activities of each. Determine the ways in which each promotes the interests of the young child.

REFERENCES

Bradbury, D. E. 1937. "The Contribution of the Child Study Movement to Child Psychology," *Psychological Bulletin*, 34(1):2–38.

Davis, M. D. 1932. *Nursery Schools: Their Development and Current Practices in the United States.* Washington, D.C.: Government Printing Office.

Davis, M. D. 1925. *General Practice in Kindergarten Education in the United States.* Washington, D.C.: National Education Association, Research Committee of the Department of Kindergarten Education.

Frank, L. K. 1962. "The Beginnings of Child Development and Family Life Education in the Twentieth Century," *Merrill-Palmer Quarterly*, 8(4):207–227.

Frank, L. K. 1938. "The Fundamental Needs of the Child," *Mental Hygiene*, July.

Frost, J. L. (ed.). 1968. *Early Childhood Education Rediscovered.* New York: Holt, Rinehart and Winston.

Gesell, A. 1948. *Studies in Child Development.* New York: Harper & Brothers.

Gesell, A. 1945. *The Embryology of Behavior.* New York: Harper & Brothers.

Gesell, A. 1925. *The Mental Growth of the Preschool Child.* New York: Macmillan.

Gesell, A., and F. L. Ilg. 1946. *The Child from Five to Ten.* New York: Harper & Brothers.

Gesell, A., and F. L. Ilg. 1943. *Infant and Child in the Culture of Today.* New York: Harper & Brothers.

Glasser, W. 1965. *Reality Therapy: A New Approach to Psychiatry.* New York: Harper & Row.

Gray, W. S. 1927. "Training and Experiences That Prepare for Reading," *Childhood Education*, 3, January.

Hall, G. S. 1921. *Aspects of Child Life and Education.* New York: D. Appleton.

Hall, G. S. 1897. "A Study of Fears," *American Journal of Psychology*, 8:147–249.

Hall, G. S. 1891. "The Contents of Children's Minds on Entering School," *Pedagogical Seminary*, 1:139–173.

Hall, G. S. 1883. "The Contents of Children's Minds," *Princeton Review*, 2:249–272.

Harris, T. A. 1967. *I'm OK—You're OK: A Practical Guide to Transactional Analysis.* New York: Harper & Row.

Haven, C. T. 1908. "International Kindergarten Union: Its Origin—Why It Was Organized," *Proceedings of the Fifteenth Annual Meeting of the International Kindergarten Union.*

Havighurst, R. J. 1948. *Developmental Tasks and Education.* New York: McKay.

International Kindergarten Union. 1909. "Views of the Liberal Kindergarteners of the Committee of Nineteen," *Proceedings of the Sixteenth Annual Meeting.*

Lazerson, M. 1972. "The Historical Antecedents of Early Childhood Education," *Early Childhood Education: Seventy-first Yearbook of the National Society for the Study of Education.* Chicago: University of Chicago Press.

Osborn, D. K., C. Logue, and E. Surbeck. 1973. *Significant Events in Early Childhood Education.* Athens, Ga.: Early Childhood Education Learning Center, University of Georgia.

Pearson, E. W. 1925. "The Ruggles Street Nursery School," *Progressive Education*, 2, January–March.

Prescott, D. A. 1957. *The Child in the Educative Process.* New York: McGraw-Hill.

Thorndike, E. L. 1913. *The Psychology of Learning.* New York: Columbia University Press.

Weber, E. 1969. *The Kindergarten: Its Encounter with Educational Thought in America.* New York: Teachers College Press.

FURTHER READING

Anderson, J. E. "Child Development: An Historical Perspective," supplement to *Child Development*, 1956, 27 (2):181–227.

Auleta, M. S. (ed.). *Fountains of Early Childhood Education.* New York: Random House, 1969.

Braun, S. J., and E. P. Edwards. *History and Theory of Early Childhood Education.* Belmont, Calif. Wadsworth Publishing Company, 1972.

Bronfenbrenner, U. "Developmental Theory in Transistion," in *Child Psychology: Sixty-second Yearbook of the National Society for the Study of Education.* Chicago: University of Chicago Press, 1963.

De Mause, L. *The History of Childhood.* New York: Psycho-history Press, 1974.

Frank, L. K. "Human Development: An Emerging Discipline," in A. J. Solnit and S. A. Provence (eds.), *Modern Perspectives in Child Development.* New York: International Universities Press, 1963, pp. 10–36.

Frank, L. K. "Research in Child Psychology: History and Prospect," in R. G. Kounin, J. S. Kounin, and H. F. Wright (eds.), *Child Behavior and Development.* New York: McGraw-Hill, 1943, pp. 1–16.

Weber, E. *The Kindergarten: Its Encounter with Educational Thought in America.* New York: Teachers College Press, 1969.

Contemporary and Behavioral Science Bases for Early Childhood Education

Ford Foundation, William Simmons

Bridging the Seventies: A Decade of Development and Reappraisal

As an outgrowth of the child study and child development movements of the early part of the century, research into the way children grow and develop continued with vigorous intent during the 1940s and 1950s. From the great body of accumulated research data there emerged in the mid-sixties a new era in early childhood education. For several reasons this was a period of unparalleled growth in programs for young children that emphasized intellectual stimulation and cognitive growth. First, research with both animals and humans had demonstrated that environmental stimulation during infancy and early childhood significantly affected later development and achievement in school. Second, studies had demonstrated the link between environmental deprivation during the early years of life and mental retardation. Finally, longitudinal growth studies by Benjamin Bloom (1964) identified the early years as the period of most rapid growth in human characteristics and an optimum period for development.

THE RESEARCH

Deprivation Studies of Animals

Over the years, a large number of researchers tended to reach similar conclusions about the striking effects of sensory deprivation during infancy on later adult behavior. Melzack and Scott (1957) studied dogs reared in isolation from birth. Confined in small cages with no objects to explore and no chance to acquire pain expectancies, the dogs were unable to learn to avoid pain when released at maturity. The results of a similar study by Melzack and Thompson (1956) showed that dogs reared in isolation were unable to acquire normal social interactions when released at maturity. In another study, Riesen (1947) compared chimpanzees reared in darkness with a normal control group. The normal animals quickly learned to avoid objects associated with a painful electric shock, while the animals reared in darkness required many weeks of repetition of cues before becoming capable of utilizing the visual cue to avoid pain. Thompson and Heron (1954) investigated the effects of modifications of the environment on later problem-solving ability in dogs. Twenty-six Scotch terrier puppies were selected from several litters. Half were given an opportunity for enriched learning experiences by being placed in homes as pets. The remaining animals were subjected to varying degrees of isolation from the time of weaning to 18 months of age. Following this period, the performance of the home-reared animals was markedly superior on 15 of 18 problem-solving tasks.

Obviously, it is hazardous to attempt to draw parallels between animals and humans with respect to the effects of environmental conditions. Nonetheless, the relationships seem to have some degree of relevance when animal studies are placed in perspective with studies of environmental deprivation of humans.

Deprivation Studies of Humans

Bugelski (1965), Hebb (1947, 1949), and Hunt (1961, 1964) have reported many studies supporting the theory that perception is learned behavior. Children increase their awareness and their ability to organize information collected through the senses by exploration in an environment rich with objects to explore. This finding is in direct opposition to the traditional theory of perception as innate and structurally determined. (Hunt's (1961) widely quoted book presents the implications for early childhood education.)

For ethical reasons, it has not been possible to conduct rigorously controlled studies of sensory deprivation, but poverty and abuse have supplied numerous cases. Goldfarb (1953), for example, compared two groups of adolescents. One group had been institutionalized as infants, and another had been placed in institutions much later. The early-institutionalized group showed such evidences of emotional deprivation as being relatively apathetic and immature during the adolescent years. Dennis (1960) reported that in a Teheran orphanage, where there was little variation in stimulation, 60 percent of the 2-year-olds could not sit alone and 85 percent of the 4-year-olds could not walk alone. Such results are borne out by the senior author's personal observations of infants in the Corpus Christi, Texas, Child Development Center during 1972–1973. The center enrolls welfare-recipient children between the ages of 6 weeks and 4 years. One set of twins entering the center at 7 months of age were unable to turn over in their cribs without assistance, their muscles were weak and flaccid, stomachs were distended, visual-attending behavior was lacking, and hemorrhaging was in effect from diaper rash. Five months later, both children had made startling gains. One approached the normal range in physical development, and overall appearance improved dramatically. Efforts were underway to assist the mother in proper caretaking and stimulation so that the infants could continue a normal pattern of development.

Research into Mental Development

In addition to examining the more general long-range effects of abuse during infancy and early childhood, research in the mid-sixties focused on the effects of inadequate attention to mental development. Gutierrez (1972) presented evidence that the report of the President's Panel on Mental Retardation (1962) served as the blueprint for Project Head Start. The panel recognized four major influences on the performance of slum children:

1. A lack of achievement motivation.
2. The failure of the home to develop modes of thinking and perceiving common to middle- and upper-class children.
3. An emotionally crippling family organization.
4. Inadequate social facilities in health, education, and welfare.

Researchers point consistently to a close link between poverty and mental retardation. Much of this evidence was collected by Rodger Hurley (1969) in *Poverty and Mental Retardation: A Causal Relationship.* Senator Edward M. Kennedy summarized the consensus of investigators in the Preface to this work:

the supposed mental retardation of many of the poor is not mental retardation at all, but environmental deprivation, which includes being "served" by institutions that do not perform in the way the public believes they do. . . . There is no known or irreversible cause for over ninety per cent of the mental retardation in America —unless the cause be in fact a number of all too remediable social and economic forces that become translated, ultimately, into personal tragedies.

Perhaps the most quoted studies of the effects of environmental stimulation on "mentally retarded" children are those by Skeels (1965). In one case an experimental group consisted of 13 mentally retarded children. These children were transferred at an early age to an institution where they were provided with personal relationships with adult mentally retarded women. Later, 11 of the children were transferred to adoptive homes. A control group of 12 children, initially at a higher level of intelligence, remained in a relatively unstimulating environment for a prolonged period. In the initial study, the children in the experimental group showed a decided increase in rate of mental growth, while the control group showed progressive mental retardation. In a follow-up study conducted after the children had reached adulthood, all subjects in the experimental group were found to be self-supporting, and none was a ward of any institution. Eleven of the 13 were married, and 9 had children. The median grade in school completed was the twelfth, and one girl who had an initial IQ of 35 had graduated from high school and taken one semester of college work. Of the 12 children in the control group, one died in adolescence following continued residence in a state institution for the mentally retarded. Four others were still wards of institutions, one in a mental hospital and three in institutions for the mentally retarded. Only two of the group had married, and one of these was divorced. Two of the four females were sterilized in late adolescence. Extrapolated to post-1963 prices, the cost to the state for one of these cases would have been over $100,000. The logical conclusion is that prevention of mental retardation through improved child-care measures is most desirable from both financial and humane points of view.

The Work of Benjamin Bloom

Another influential study that directed attention to infancy and early childhood and that stimulated the rapid development of programs during the mid-sixties was *Stability and Change in Human Characteristics* by Benjamin Bloom (1964). This widely acclaimed study was initiated while Bloom was a fellow at the University of Chicago Center for the Advanced Study of the Behavioral Sciences. The three-year project was based primarily on eight major longitudinal studies: the Iowa Studies (Baldwin 1921), the Harvard Growth Study (Dearborn and Rothney 1941), the Chicago Study (Freeman and Flory 1937), the Berkeley Growth Study (Jones and Bayley 1941), the Brush Foundation Study (Ebert and Simmons 1943), the Fels Institute Study (Sontag, Baker, and Nelson 1958), the California Growth Study (Macfarlane 1938), and the Michigan Study (Olson 1955). Although the major concern was to describe the development of particular human characteristics, certain secondary areas were also explored. These included the effect of environmental forces upon human characteristics and the relationship of the description of the characteristic's development to the literature on the influence of early experiences. The data on physical development revealed the very rapid early development of height followed by a period of steady but slow growth, and then the adolescent spurt. The influence of environment on increase in height is clearly demonstrated by studying extreme environments. The effects of environment are most marked during the period of most rapid normal development; that is, during infancy and early childhood.

Bloom investigated the stability of IQ by comparing a number of longitudinal studies and making allowances for instrument reliability and sample variability. He found that "intelligence is a developing function and that the stability of measured intelligence increases with age" (Bloom 1964:88). His data suggested that in terms of intelligence at age 17, about 50 percent takes place between conception and age 4, about 30 percent between ages 4 and 8, and about 20 percent between 8 and 17. Bloom stressed the effects of environment on intelligence. "Abundant" or "deprived" environments, he believes, can make about a 20-point difference in IQ. The effects of environments appear to be greatest in the early, most rapid periods of development. It should be stressed that all of Bloom's findings are based on present tests, present child-rearing practices, present educational methods, and Western culture. Evidence is available to support the contention that development of intelligence does or could continue into the adult years.

The absolute scale of vocabulary development and the longitudinal studies of achievement (teachers' marks, achievement test batteries, and reading comprehension) employed by Bloom indicated that about 50 percent of general achievement at age 18 had been reached by age 9. This finding has led directly to the development of more stimulating educational environments during the early years.

Bloom's analysis of interests, attitudes, and personality was based primarily on ratings and observations of individuals by others. He concluded that major development of personality takes place during the early years. "By an average age of about two, it seems evident that at least one-third of the variance at adolescence on intellectual interest, dependency, and aggression is predictable. By about age five, as much as one-half of the variance at adolescence is predictable for these characteristics" (Bloom 1964:175). Bloom proposed that environmental stability and change are linked to developmental stability and change. When the environment is relatively stable over long periods, a particular human characteristic will tend to be more stable than when the environment is changing. Environment tends to have its greatest effects in the periods of most rapid normal development and its least effects during periods of little or no change in normal development. At the later stages of development, only the most powerful environments produce marked changes. Thus, optimal environments are necessary for the individual to achieve his full hereditary potential.

ENVIRONMENTAL INFLUENCES: REVERSIBLE OR IRREVERSIBLE?

The research of the 1960s projected an image of irreversible damage to children as a result of environmental deprivation in infancy. That image is a bit more bleak than most recent evidence would allow. Kagan, for example, recently presented evidence that "the first two years of life are not a good predictor of future functioning in all environmental contexts" (Kagan, Hall, and Klein 1972:2). In an isolated Guatemalan village, he observed "listless, silent, apathetic infants; passive, quiet, timid three-year-olds; but active, gay, intellectually competent eleven-year-olds" (Kagan, Hall, and Klein 1972:2). Kagan reported the mothers in this village nursed the children on demand, without talking or interacting with them, and left the infants isolated in dark huts during the day. On tests of maturational and intellectual development, they were four to five months behind American infants. Paradoxically, the 11-year-olds scored higher than Americans on a set of culture-fair tests (ostensibly, tests for which results are not affected or are affected only slightly by the culture of the subject). Since the culture has been fairly constant for a very long period of time, Kagan assumed that these 11-year-olds were also "retarded" as infants but had somehow recovered. Therefore, he concluded, "the first two years of life do not inexorably doom you to retardation." Kagan's experience led to a reorganization of biological-environmental influences. Experience can slow down or speed up the emergence of basic functions by several months or a few years, but nature will win in the end. "The capacity for perceptual analysis, imitation, inference, language, symbolism, and memory will eventually appear in sturdy form, for each is an inherent competence in the human program" (Kagan, Hall, and Klein 1972:5).

If Kagan's conclusions are correct, they have important implications for American educational practice. The tendency to judge poor test performance upon school entry or at age 6 as an indication of *permanent* defect in intellectual ability rather than merely a difference in maturational rate could be disastrous for a child. Apparent permanent retardation of poor children appears to be, in reality, relative retardation due to rank ordering of children on academic achievement. Kagan believes that Americans are confusing "relative retardation" with "absolute retardation." If a 10-year-old child can't play hockey, we never say he is retarded. But if he can't multiply, he's retarded. Children do not learn to play hockey or multiply unless they are taught. In sum, "There are few dumb children in the world if one classifies them from the perspective of the community of adaptation, but millions of dumb children if one classifies them from the perspective of another society" (Kagan, Hall, and Klein, 1972:29). Despite the appeal of Kagan's work, the results cannot yet be considered definitive. There is some criticism of the testing. For example, one may demonstrate that environmental influences are reversible by using a sensitive test for young children, ages 5–6, and a test with a low ceiling for older children, ages 9–11. Also, longitudinal study of the infants in Kagan's study may show unexpected environmental and/or developmental patterns not detected in his cross-sectional analysis.

CONTEMPORARY PROGRAMS FOR YOUNG CHILDREN

The response to the accumulated body of research just examined was a proliferation of new, experimental programs for young children. Several different programs are described here to illustrate the wide range of methodology, materials, and purposes that characterized the programs of the sixties.

Project Head Start[1]

With evidence accumulating to promote the need for early childhood development, political maneuvers in Washington began to set the stage for a comprehensive, nation-wide program of assistance for young children. During the summer of 1965, over 550,000 children participated in a preschool program called Project Head Start. Head Start is a program for helping children of limited opportunity who are to enter kindergarten or first grade following participation in the program. It was one of several community action programs operated under the Office of Economic Opportunity. Conceived in November 1964 and implemented in June 1965, Head Start has continued to gain favor among people of all walks of life. Moreover, the research support for expansion of programs for young children has strengthened with time. On February 19, 1969, former President Nixon called for a national commitment to provide for children an opportunity for healthful and stimulating development during the first five years of life. On April 9, he took a major step toward fulfilling this commitment by announcing the delegation of Project Head Start to a new Office of Child Development within the Department of Health, Education and Welfare. Robert H. Finch, then Secretary of HEW, commented upon the delegation, saying, "Today, our nation's schools and child care programs are in the process of changing toward a more comprehensive approach to the physical, social, and intellectual development of children and their families." He proposed to strengthen Head Start through a series of measures: (1) providing greater program length and continuity by converting summer programs into experimental or regular full-year programs; (2) doubling the size of the Parent and Child Center program to $12 million; (3) substantially expanding the Follow-Through program; (4) increasing technical assistance and evaluation efforts; and (5) experiment-

---

[1] This section is adapted with the permission of the publishers from Joe L. Frost and G. Thomas Rowland, *Compensatory Programming: The Acid Test of American Education* (Dubuque, Iowa: William C. Brown, 1971), pp. 52–56.

ing with new program models; larger Head Start grantees were to devote 5 per cent of their approved slots for experimental curriculums and programs.

RATIONALE FOR THE PROGRAM.   The Head Start program was cast in the context of a child development center, providing a broad array of services to children. For the first time in American education, a comprehensive attack upon the developmental problems of poor children became operational, a program utilizing the services of civic associations, parents, schools, churches, and other social institutions. Volunteers played an active role. In 1969, over 120,000 were active in the program. Since its inception, over 600,000 volunteers, including doctors, nurses, parents, low-income people, and high school and college students, have participated. Recognizing that children from low-income homes often arrive at school under distinct handicaps, the originators of Head Start designed the program so as to evaluate and meet the special needs of disadvantaged children.

The Instructional Program. Head Start programs are tailored to the needs of local children and their families. Although certain broad goals were established by the Office of Economic Opportunity, local programs varied widely in interpretation and implementation. The goals were as follows:

Improving the child's health.

Helping the child's emotional and social development by encouraging self-confidence, self-expression, self-discipline, and curiosity.

Improving and expanding the child's mental processes, aiming at expanding the ability to think, reason, and speak clearly.

Helping children to get wider and more varied experiences which will broaden their horizons, increase their ease of conversation, and improve their understanding of the world in which they live.

Giving the child frequent chances to succeed. Such chances may thus erase patterns of frustration and failure, and especially, the fear of failure.

Developing for the child a climate of confidence which will make him want to learn.

Increasing the child's ability to get along with others in his family and, at the same time, helping the family to understand him and his problems—thus strengthening family ties.

Developing in the child and his family a responsible attitude toward society, and fostering feelings of belonging to a community.

Planning activities which allow groups from every social, ethnic, and economic level in a community to join together with the poor in solving problems.

Offering a chance for the child to meet and see teachers, policemen, health and welfare officers—all figures of authority—in situations which will bring respect and not fear.

Giving the child a chance to meet with older children, teenagers, and adults who will serve as "models" in manners, behavior, speech, etc.

Helping both the child and his family to a greater confidence, self-respect, and dignity. (Office of Economic Opportunity 1965: 17–18)

Classes in Head Start are limited to twenty children, with fifteen recognized as ideal. Each class has a teacher and an aide. Special Head Start training institutes are conducted for both teachers and aides. A full-day program might follow this plan:

7:00– 9:00	Breakfast, quiet play, listening to records, helping to get school ready.
9:00–12:00	Core of 3-hour work-play schedule.
12:00– 1:00	Lunch.
1:00– 3:00	Nap, rest or quiet time.
3:00– 5:00	Outdoor play. In case of bad weather, dancing, singing games, gymnastics; enriched with care of pets, trips, cooking projects, helping to close shcool for day. (Office of Economic Opportunity 1967:21)

Evaluation of Programs. The "Six Months Later" study (Wolff and Stein 1967), made in the fall of 1965, compared kindergarten children with Head Start experience and children with no such experience. All these children attended the kindergarten of four public elementary schools in New York City. The Head Start children in these schools attended centers selected for the study on the basis of the following criteria: (1) the centers were rated "very good" to "excellent" by the supervisory staff of the summer Head Start programs; (2) one was all black, another predominantly Puerto Rican, and the third was mixed in racial and ethnic composition.

Four measures of social educational "readiness" for the first grade work were selected for comparisons: (1) the child's initial adjustment to classroom routines, and the length of time it took him to become fully adjusted to school routines; (2) the child's behavior toward his teacher and his peers; (3) the child's speech, work habits, and listening habits; (4) the child's educational attainments.

Although the reported results are rather difficult to interpret, the Head Start children, contrasted to a control group of their classmates, appeared to rank higher on the Caldwell Preschool Inventory after six months in kindergarten. Enthusiasm of the parents for the Head Start program was unanimous. The kindergarten teachers had mixed opinions about the advantages of Head Start. But those with kindergarten classes containing 50 percent or more Head Start children were more positive than were the teachers with fewer than 50 percent in attendance. For all schools combined, Head Start children were rated higher in initial school adjustment by their teachers. Of the twelve teachers responding, none felt that Head Start had helped the child relate to the teacher. However, teachers agreed that Head Start had assisted children in adjusting to the regular school routine.

The most comprehensive study of Head Start effects presently available was conducted for the Office of Economic Opportunity from June, 1968, through May, 1969, by Westinghouse Learning Corporation and Ohio University (1969). The basic question posed by the study was: *To what extent are the children now in the first, second, and third grades who attended Head Start programs different in their intellectual and social-personal development from comparable children who did not attend?* A sample of children from 104 Head Start centers who had gone on to elementary school was matched with control children from the same schools. These controls had not attended Head Start. Formal tests were administered. Parents of both groups, directors of the 104 centers, and primary grade teachers were interviewed. Separate data analyses were conducted for those children who had attended summer and full-year programs.

The findings led to the following major conclusions:

1. Summer programs appear to be ineffective in producing any gains in cognitive and affective development that persist into the elementary grades.
2. Full-year programs appear to be ineffective in regard to measures of affective development used in the study, but appear to be somewhat effective in producing gains in cognitive development that could be detected in grades one, two, and three. Programs appeared to be of greater effectiveness for certain subgroups of centers, most notably in all-black centers in southeastern United States and in scattered programs in the central cities.
3. Head Start children, whether from summer or full-year programs, still appear to be in a disadvantaged position with respect to national norms for the standardized tests of language development and scholastic achievement.
4. Parents of Head Start enrollees voiced a strong approval of the program and its influence on their child. They reported substantial participation in the activities of the center. (Westinghouse Report 1969:0–5)

Possible explanations for the limited effectiveness in terms of the measures employed are the delays in measurement until the children had been exposed to primary school curricula; the positive effects of Head Start may have been offset by the impoverished environment to which the child returns after he leaves school; first grade may produce an intellectual spurt in the non-Head Start child similar to the spurt observed for the Head Start child during his initial Head Start experience; Head Start may suffer from poor implementation; the program may be more effective for certain types of children than for others. Finally, no distinct type of program was evaluated, because Head Start programs are locally planned and the broad program goals are subject to great variation in interpretation. Despite the generally negative tone of this study, recommendations were made that appear to reflect faith in Head Start.

1. Summer programs should be phased out as early as feasible and converted into full-year or extended-year programs.
2. Full-year programs should be continued, but every effort should be made to make them more effective. Some specific suggestions are:
   a. Offering intervention programs of longer duration, perhaps extending downward toward infancy and upward into the primary grades.
   b. Varying teaching strategies with the characteristics of the children.
   c. Concentrating on the remediation of specific deficiencies as suggested by the study, for example, language deficiencies or deficiencies in spelling or arithmetic.
   d. Training parents to become more effective teachers of their children.
3. In view of the limited state of knowledge about what would constitute a more

effective program, some of the full-year programs should be set up as experimental programs (strategically placed on a regional basis) to permit the implementation of new procedures and techniques and provide for an adequate assessment of results. Innovations which prove to be successful could then be instituted on a large scale within the structure of present full-year programs. Within the experimental context, innovations such as longer period of intervention or total family intervention might be tried.

4. Regardless of where and how it is articulated into the structure of the federal government, the agency attempting the dual research and matching missions presently assigned Head Start should be granted the focal identity and organizational unity necessary to such complex and critical experimental programs. Their basis of funding should take cognizance of both the social significance of these missions and the present state of the art of programs attempting to carry them out. (Westinghouse Report 1969:0–7)

The negative tone of portions of the Westinghouse Report are offset by a study prepared by the Kirschner Associates (1970). The study was designed to determine Head Start's effect on community institutions. Head Start had a positive effect in 44 out of 47 changes investigated in depth. These changes included increased involvement of the poor with institutions, increased institutional employment of local people, greater educational emphasis upon the needs of the poor and of minorities, and modification of health institutions and services to better serve the poor.

Project Follow-Through

The typical finding that emerged from the many evaluative efforts of Head Start was that enrollees in the program made statistically significant IQ gains during their attendance. Control groups of children not attending a preschool program made no gains (Wolff and Stein 1967; Cunningham 1968; Temp and Anderson 1967). Typically, however, Head Start children tended to lose most of their IQ gain advantage over their non-Head Start peers during the first year of public schooling. This "wash-out" stimulated the development of Project Follow-Through, which was authorized under Title II of the Elementary and Secondary Education Act of 1965. Its purpose was to maintain and supplement in the early grades the gains that had already been made by low-income children coming from a full-year Head Start experience or a comparable preschool program. In keeping with the trend toward broad-scale intervention, Follow-Through offers several types of services: instruction, nutrition, health, social work, psychological services, and staff development. The major elements in a child's environment—the school, the family, the neighborhood, and the community—ostensibly work together to minimize adverse influences and to maximize beneficial effects on learning and development. Out of the proliferation of early childhood programs of the 1960s, a number of different models were selected for implementation in Follow-Through classrooms around the nation.

Despite problems of funding, control, and inadequate evaluation procedures, it now appears that Follow-Through has met its major goals. Attitudes of teachers are more positive, children are responding to school in a more favorable manner, there are fewer attendance problems, and children are exhibiting greater curiosity, self-direction, and creativity than before. In addition, achievement in academic skills has increased in many classrooms.

EXPERIMENTAL PROGRAMS IN EARLY CHILDHOOD EDUCATION

Even before the development of Head Start, there were a few major experimental programs in early childhood education developed by imaginative researchers. For example, the long-term program directed by Susan Gray at George Peabody College in Nashville, Tennessee, was begun in 1959, and the well-known program of David Weikart in Ypsilanti, Michigan, was started in 1962. These projects continue to channel useful information into the literature for early childhood educators as long-term research findings become available.

The Early Training Project and the Perry Preschool Project

Gray's Early Training Project for Disadvantaged Children (Klaus and Gray 1968) set the pattern for most of the early childhood programs that followed by focusing upon low-income children and their families. Thereafter, in the 1960s, a large number of experimental programs were established, all seeking effective ways to overcome the limitations of poverty on young children. In Gray's project, it was presumed that low-income homes lacked a range and variety of stimuli and passed on a restricted language style. The program was designed to "make up" for these restrictions through providing a high ratio of adults to children, devoting more time to certain materials, and using systematic reinforcement according to the achievement of desired behaviors. For example, in the beginning the child who could say "milk" got a second glass. Later, however, he had to make a complete request for milk. The curriculum stressed achievement motivation, persistence, delayed gratification, interest in school-like activities, and identification with achieving role models. This program also paved the way for increased attention to home involvement. It provided home visitors who made arrangements for the children's health checkups, obtained school-related information about children, helped parents reinforce the goals of the school, and suggested home-based activities that would expand the child experiential environment.

Weikart's (1967) program, the Perry Preschool Project and later a part of the High-Scope Foundation, was designed after the developmental theories of Jean Piaget. Thinking tasks such as temporary relations, seriation, and classification were the content of the curriculum. However, socialization experiences were also included to assist the child in developing autonomy and responsibility.

The Bereiter-Engelmann Program

Both the Gray and the Weikart programs represent a striking contrast to the Academic Preschool developed by Carl Bereiter and Siegfried Engelmann (Bereiter and Engelmann 1966) in 1964. Their curriculum focused directly on objectives designed to teach language, reading, and arithmetic at a rapid pace. During each of three daily 20-minute periods, as many as 500 responses could be required of each child and five or six tasks could be presented. The approach was a no-nonsense one, with the teacher quickly correcting mistakes and making heavy work demands of children. Like other experimental programs for young children, the initial intelligence gains were impressive, with an average increase of 17 IQ points in a year. Later experimenters, however, criticized the program for its "insensitivity" to affective development and for its "narrowness" of content.

Other Approaches to Preschool Programs

Before the end of the 1960s, other educators tested a variety of approaches to stimulating young disadvantaged children. Marion Blank and Frances Solomon (Blank and Solomon 1968) developed an intriguing tutorial approach characterized by short, individualized tutorial sessions. The method of Socratic dialogue was used to stimulate the child to think and to reflect. The Regional Educational Laboratories also sponsored a variety of early childhood programs. Southwest Educational Development Laboratory in Austin, Texas, for example, sponsored the development and implementation of an early childhood program for English-speaking children and a bilingual program for Mexican-American children (Nedler 1969). Children in the bilingual program were exposed to a daily three-hour activity using carefully sequenced instructional activities in visual training, auditory training, motor training, language, mathematics, science, art, and music.

The results of programs for 4- to 6-year-olds gradually led investigators to reflect on the possibilities for even earlier intervention. Perhaps the impressive gains in intelligence would not fade out in later years if intervention started during infancy and was continued into the school years. With such thoughts in mind, a number of programs were established. By this time professionals were convinced that programs for young children should be broadened to include the family and associated problems. It was clear that the school, working alone, could not compensate for disruptive, unhealthy home conditions. Two of the best-known contemporary programs are described in some detail to illustrate the scope of activity deemed to be desirable in the mid-seventies.

A Home Learning Center Approach to Early Stimulation

A project called the home learning center approach is centered at the Institute for Development of Human Resources at the University of Florida. Directed by Ira J. Gordon, the principal goal is to "simultaneously raise the chances that a young child will reach a higher level of intellectual and personal development and that the significant adults in his life will gain in competence and feelings of self-worth" (Gordon 1973).

RATIONALE FOR THE PROGRAM.   Gordon and his colleagues accept the view that the earliest years of life are critically important in intellectual and personal development. They acknowledge the insufficiency of information about acceptable instructional materials and tasks for stimulating this development as well as practical procedures to reach rural and urban families whose children need stimulation techniques. The early project, an approach to early intervention into the lives of babies (Gordon 1970), provided beginning answers to these concerns with children from 3 months to 2 years. A continuation of the investigation (Gordon 1973) sought to provide information about early stimulation procedures for 2- to 3-year-olds before they moved into more organized and institutionalized early childhood centers.

DESIGN OF THE STUDY.   The approach during the early infant studies was to use low-income women to teach mothers how to stimulate infants in their own homes. The major questions investigated were concerned with (1) the actual teaching process, (2) the efficacy of the paraprofessional parent-educator, (3) the effects on the mother, and (4) the problem of sex differences in infant performance. The stimulation procedure developed in the early project for infants remained the procedure through the later project for 2- and 3-year-olds. Piagetian principles and measurement tasks were converted into instructional activities. The basic process of using low-income women as parent-educators in the home was continued, and a major change was instituted. "Backyard centers" were established for the 2- and 3-year-olds. In these centers additional instruction beyond the home visit was provided.

One phase of Gordon's work (Gordon 1973), begun in 1968, sought answers to the following questions:

A. Can a combined home visit and home learning center approach, using non-professionals as the key educators of parent and child, be sustained for children ages two to three and their mothers?
B. Can intellectual and personality stimulation materials be developed which can be easily taught to the mother and child by nonprofessionals?
C. Does early child stimulation, provided through a program such as this, have continuing effects as youngsters reach kindergarten and the beginning of school years?

In addition, Gordon tested a number of specific hypotheses regarding intellectual performance and self-concept of the children as well as the self-concept and social activity of mothers. The sample consisted of 158 families in either experimental or control status in the early (infant) project plus an additional 100 new families. Criteria for original selection were, "indigent," single birth, no breach or Caesarian delivery, no complications for the mother or infant, no evidence of mental retardation, no evidence of mother's mental illness, and residence in Alachua and 11 other surrounding counties. The 100 new families were added to the longitudinal population in 1968 to investigate the effects of training on mothers and children not previously exposed to the project. Experimental and control groups were established for various groups, infancy through 3 years of age.

Treatment variables were length and timing of instruction and presence of instruction. Dependent variables were changes in mother and child. There were three steps in treatment: (1) development of materials, (2) training of the parent and child development trainers, and (3) implementation in parent education and home learning centers.

Tasks and materials for both the home and the learning center were developed from several major resources, including the work of Piaget and Montessori. These resources were used to suggest goals which were sequenced and organized in terms of age. Through a continuous process of field testing and revision, the materials were refined for usage. One set of materials, *Home-Centered Learning Activities for Twos and Threes* (New York, St. Martins Press, 1971), is available in book form.

Each child spent four hours a week in two separate sessions at a backyard center located in neighborhoods close to the population distribution. This center was simply a home especially equipped for at least five children. The home learning center director was a low-income woman from the target population who had been a parent-educator home visitor in the earlier phases of the project. Program activities focused upon (1) strengthening interpersonal relationships between mother and child; (2) cognitive development; (3) developing feelings of competence in the child; and (4) building the mother's sense of accomplishment. In addition, the parent-educator worked with the mother once a week, explaining and demonstrating activities and exercises to be used by the mother at home. This activity was integrated with that of the backyard center. In the work with infants, materials already in the home were used. However, some materials, such as clay, blocks, and books, were introduced for the older children.

Gordon (1973) reported the following results for the activity phase begun in 1968: (1) Within the first three years of life, children who received experience earlier were not superior to children entering the program later and receiving experience. (2) The longer the children were in the program, however, the better their performance. (3) There were no significant sex differences within each group. (4) There was a low positive correlation between self-concept and intelligence measures. (5) Although there were no differences in academic or career expectations, experimental mothers were significantly more involved in their children's learning than the controls, and 78 percent reported that they saw their child in a more positive light.

The longitudinal assessment of the effects of the program over time indicate that

a home visit program using paraprofessionals as home visitors on a once-a-week basis in the first two years of life, combined with a small group setting for four hours a week for children two-to-three years old, lead to (1) improved cognitive performance of the children as a function of time in the program, and (2) positive attitudes and behaviors of mothers toward their children. Further, the relationships between maternal attitude and behavior to child performance found at ages two and three not only increase our scientific knowledge but also provide support for the development of parent-oriented service programs. (Gordon 1973: 114)

IMPLICATIONS.   A number of implications seem to be justified from the evidence. First, the program seems to be viable. Positive results have accrued and participation has been over 70 percent. The curriculum materials developed from the project offer a basic framework from which others can develop and extend on their own. Gordon stresses, however, that it is the *process* that he would wish emulated rather than the product. The inadequacy of available tools for assessing intellectual and affective domains remains a source of frustration for researchers and a sphere of critically needed research activity. For example, what 2-year-old behaviors might be inferred to relate to high self-concept? It appears that longitudinal studies provide clearer insights for working with young children than short-term intervention projects. It takes continuous involvement to produce lasting effects.

Finally, Gordon urges that we go beyond simple education and health to require a range of social supports in housing, jobs, adult education, and social services. This suggests a synergistic (working together) rather than a reductionistic or specific, narrow skills development approach to meeting the needs of young children and their families (Gordon 1975).

Verbal Interaction Project: Mother-Child Home Program

The Mother-Child Home Program, directed by Phyllis Levenstein, was initiated in 1967. There were four major components: (1) a focus on mother-child pairs; (2) the use of trained "toy demonstrators" who worked with the mother and child in their home; (3) Verbal Interaction Stimulus Materials (VISM), consisting of toys and books which formed the basis of the mother-child-demonstrator relationship; and (4) supervision, which included selection of VISM according to specific criteria, development of methods to insure proper presentation of VISM, and the monitoring of the work of the toy demonstrators (U.S. Department of Health, Education and Welfare 1972). Levenstein and her associates chose to focus on the family as a preventive force. The incidental curriculum of the home was seen as the focus for providing concept-rich verbal interaction built around common toys and books (Levenstein 1970, 1971, 1975; Levenstein and Levenstein 1971). The mother was seen as the ultimate agent of intervention and motivation (Levenstein and Sunley 1968). The original hypothesis was that the treatment would foster cognitive growth as measured by IQ tests.

The program operated originally in three low-income housing projects in the Long Island, New York, communities of Freeport, Glen Cove, and Manhasset. Parents were of low socioeconomic status and had an educational level of high school or less. Forty percent of the mothers were receiving welfare, and 90 percent were black. In 1967–1968, the treatment group consisted of 34 mother-child pairs, and the comparison groups contained 9 and 19 pairs. During this period, professional social workers were employed as the toy demonstrators who visited the homes to stimulate verbal interaction between mother and child with the VISM. In 1968–1969, nonprofessionals trained and supervised by social workers acted as the toy demonstrators for all 2-year-old children entering the program. Presently there are two groups of children, one group entering at age 2 and another group of 3-year-olds who are in their second year of the program. Toy demonstrators visit the mother-child pairs twice each week for a half-hour home session. A toy or book is introduced to the child while encouraging him to talk and to respond to questions. The mother is drawn into the session and is encouraged to use verbal-stimulation techniques modeled by the demonstrator. The mother is also encouraged to read to the child and to play with him between visits. The mother and demonstrator prepare a toy chest for storing the 11 toys and 12 books which are used in the lessons. These are presented to the child as gifts after their introduction each week. The VISM are selected according to such *stimulating* qualities as strong primary and secondary colors, durability and safety, usefulness in encouraging large muscle activity and dexterity, usefulness in developing spatial organization, presence of geometric shapes, tactile qualities, provision of sound stimuli, and possibilities for problem-solving activity, imaginative play, and self-rewarding activity. Interaction techniques are designed in a simple-to-complex sequence according to eight categories of verbally stimulating behavior: giving information. eliciting responses from the child, describing toy manipulation aloud, giving positive motivation, verbalizing social interaction by inviting or cooperating, encouraging reflection, encouraging divergence, and engaging the child's interest in the book or toy.

Evaluation instruments include the Peabody Picture Vocabulary Test and either the Stanford-Binet used for the older children or the Cattell Infant Intelligence Scale used for the younger children. The average IQ gain for the 1970–1971 school year was 16 points, with an initial IQ mean of 88.3 and an end mean of 103.8. Tables of longitudinal data completed in February 1973 show some interesting trends. Five experimental groups, 64 months after pretesting, had maintained an average IQ gain of 14 points. The range across groups was 7–19 points. The general growth pattern shows a sharp leveling off after the first year, but gains were generally retained into the first grade. The three control groups showed average gains of −4.77, 19.3, and 6 points, respectively. With the exception of the second control group, the experimental groups showed a decided advantage in IQ growth and status. Examination of the learning environments of the second control group may show that some unexpected treatment was present during the periods of rapid gain.

ANALYSIS OF EXPERIMENTAL PROGRAMS

Analysis of the major experimental preschool programs of the sixties reveals a number of common features. All of them selected children on the basis of low socioeconomic status of the family; objectives ranged from being moderately well defined to well defined; class size was less than 25 children; the adult-pupil ratio was 1 to 7.5 or less; paraprofessionals were employed; medical and nutritional services were provided; parental involvement was the rule; the research designs tended to include standardized testing (predominantly, the Stanford-Binet and the Peabody Picture Vocabulary Test) and control groups; the mean IQ gains of the experimental groups ranged between 10 and 20 points the initial year from pre- to post-testing. Despite the heartening results from these programs, researchers still do not know the *precise* factors that cumulatively contribute to the gains made by participants in the programs, nor do they know the extent of the contribution of specific elements of program methodology and organization. Some of the relevant aspects of methodology include diagnosis, lesson presentation, goal setting, modeling, questioning, and evaluating. Organizational dimensions include equipment and supplies, classroom environment, class size, pupil-adult ratio, health services, and the like. It appears that the effects of *none* of these factors have been measured except in extremely global terms. Further, it seems particularly questionable to base the bulk of our judgments upon the results of IQ tests, for it is now clear that significant IQ gains can be achieved for young children through a wide variety of program types.

THE SHIFT TO FAMILY AND ECOLOGICAL INTERVENTION

Early childhood education is undergoing a redirection in emphasis toward family intervention and toward a more encompassing or ecological form of intervention. The recurring factors that have pointed to the need for such redirection include: the slow-down and fade-out effect on IQ of children enrolled in early intervention programs; the heavy expense associated with institutionalized intervention; a series of studies relating school performance with family background (see Bronfenbrenner 1973); and the success and economy of such parent approaches as the Gordon and the Levenstein programs. Bronfenbrenner (1973) has proposed ecological intervention as the direction of the future. He refers to the major transformation of the child's environment and that of the persons principally responsible for his or her care and development as ecological intervention. Such major transformation must include provisions for health care, nutrition, employment, housing, and associated status and motivation for parenting. The home cannot fulfill its function as a child-rearing unit unless basic ecological requirements are present. Frost and Hawkes (1966) pointed out that it is foolish and utopian to expect impoverished people living in degradation to pull themselves up by their bootstraps. Some individuals are indeed able to do this, but many others are crushed under the weight of their condition. It appears that children of middle-class families who are able to provide for good health care, nutrition, and other physiological needs do not typically need intervention programs. Their children tend to perform well in school and to realize a reasonable degree of academic fulfillment. But for the disadvantaged, needy family, ecological intervention "may well be the most powerful strategy for achieving substantial and enduring growth in IQ and in other more significant spheres of development" (Bronfenbrenner 1973:102). Thus, successful intervention seems to be closely tied to the willingness of society at large to support political movements that are aimed at promoting self-sufficiency among families to the degree that all have the assurance of physiological need fulfillment. Parents should be involved as partners in the educational enterprise in ways that will reinforce the effects of existing programs and sustain them after the program is concluded.

The future of early childhood education, it would seem, must also take into account the wide range of heterogeneity found among all family groups, suggesting that no one setting or method of care giving will be appropriate to the needs of everyone. A variety of resources must therefore be available. Some families will need access to high-quality, out-of-home centers because all the adults in the family desire or are required to work. Such a situation is not bound to a particular income level. Many families will need in-home assistance to learn better child stimulation and care activities so that their children will develop in a normal fashion. Some parents will need encouragement to spend more time with their children in order that the goals of the school can be carried over into the home. Some schools or day care centers will need to consult with parents so that their goals and activities are congruent with the desires of the parents for their children. Since most families need access to a broad range of care-giving resources during the time their children are growing to maturity, the relevant issues are quality, availability, and mutual respect and cooperation.

SUMMARY AND CONCLUSIONS

During the forties and fifties, research into child growth and development continued vigorously. The cumulative research findings ushered in a new era in early childhood education in the mid-sixties, a period of unparalleled growth in programs for young children. The primary emphasis of most of these programs was some form of intellectual stimulation and cognitive development. A few conclusions can be presented based upon the relatively firm experimental findings of the programs:

1. Infancy and early childhood are "optimum periods" for development. The nature and quality of experiences and care during these periods are essential elements in producing optimum growth.
2. Dramatic cognitive gains (IQ) are possible from a wide range of program types, drawing from every major psychological base and employing widely divergent instructional modes.
3. Early gains in IQ tend to "wash out" by the time the child is in the second or third year of primary school. The few exceptions involve programs with carefully planned follow-through activities.
4. The family is the most economical and effective setting for child care yet devised.
5. The good nursery school, day care center, kindergarten, early childhood center, and so on, is of value in promoting health, intellect, and social growth. A constructive school, however, cannot compensate for a destructive family environment. The destructive family environment will continue to take its toll —evenings, weekends, holidays, and summers—despite the best efforts of the constructive school. In the worst homes, children are often doomed to inferiority if they survive at all. The optimum time to begin family intervention is prior to conception.
6. The optimum combination of care-giving sources *appears* to be a close, supporting family during the infant and toddler stages with access to a high-quality child care center for portions of the day beginning at age 3 or 4. Individual conditions such as a working mother or inadequate resources would modify this general pattern, calling for intervention in the family context and provision of out-of-home care.

Early childhood education is undergoing a redirection of emphasis in caring for young children. This redirection is toward family intervention and toward a more encompassing form of intervention. These two elements appear to go hand in hand. The family cannot fulfill its functions as the child-rearing unit unless other basic requirements for living are met. Intervention must include health care, nutrition, employment, housing, and status and motivation associated with parenting. The heterogeneity among family groups must also be taken into account in early childhood education of the future. The heterogeneity of life-styles and needs suggests that no *one* setting or method of child care giving is appropriate for everyone.

SUGGESTED ACTIVITIES

1. Visit a Head Start center in your community. Determine the goals of the program. Determine how the goals are accomplished. Determine the extent of community involvement in the program and the nature of that involvement.
2. Investigate animal research further. Read about some of the research studies conducted with animals and the findings of those studies. Determine the implications of the findings from these studies for the field of early childhood education.
3. Select two or three of the experimental early childhood programs discussed in this chapter. Do additional reading to find out more about each of these programs. Compare and contrast these programs with respect to such elements as clientele, program goals, class size, adult-pupil ratio, paraprofessionals employed, community services provided, parental involvement, and experimental base.

REFERENCES

Baldwin, B. T. 1921. "The Physical Growth of Children from Birth to Maturity," *University of Iowa Studies in Child Welfare*, 1 (1).

Bereiter, C., and S. Engelmann. 1966. *Teaching Disadvantaged Children in the Preschool*. Englewood Cliffs, N.J.: Prentice-Hall.

Blank, M., and F. Solomon. 1968. "A Tutorial Language Program To Develop Abstract Thinking in Socially Disadvantaged Preschool Children," *Child Development*, 39 (2) : 379–389.

Bloom, B. S. 1964. *Stability and Change in Human Characteristics*. New York: Wiley.

Bronfenbrenner, U. 1973. "Is Early Intervention Effective?" unpublished paper.

Bugelski, B. R. 1965. *The Psychology of Learning*. New York: Holt, Rinehart and Winston.

Cunningham, G. 1968. *A Head Start Control Group*. Austin, Tex.: Child Development Evaluation and Research Center.

Dearborn, W. F., and J. W. M. Rothney. 1941. *Predicting the Child's Development*. Cambridge, Mass.: Sci-Art Publishers.

Dennis, W. 1960. "Causes of Retardation among Institutional Children," *Journal of Genetic Psychology*, 96: 47–59.

Ebert, E., and K. Simmons. 1943. "The Brush Foundation Study of Child Growth and Development," *Monographs of Society for Research in Child Development*, 8 (2).

Freeman, F. N., and C. D. Flory. 1937. "Growth in Intellectual Ability as Measured by Repeated Tests," *Monographs of Society for Research in Child Development*, 2 (2).

Frost, J. L. 1970. "Application of a Structure Process Approach to Inservice Teacher Education and Compensatory Programming," in J. L. Frost and G. R. Hawkes (eds.), *The Disadvantaged Child, Issues and Innovations*, 2d ed. Boston: Houghton Mifflin.

Frost, J. L., and G. R. Hawkes (eds.). 1966. *The Disadvantaged Child: Issues and Innovations.* Boston: Houghton Mifflin.

Frost, J. L., and G. T. Rowland. 1971. *Compensatory Programming: The Acid Test of American Education.* Dubuque, Iowa: William C. Brown.

Goldfarb, W. 1953. "The Effects of Early Institutional Care on Adolescent Personality," *Journal of Experimental Education*, 12:106–129.

Gordon, I. J. 1975. "Intervention in Infant Education," unpublished paper prepared for the Texas Conference on Infancy, Austin, June.

Gordon, I. J. 1973. "A Home Learning Center Approach to Early Stimulation: A Summary of Progress Reports of the Institute for Development of Human Resources," in J. L. Frost, (ed.), *Revisiting Early Childhood Education.* New York: Holt, Rinehart and Winston.

Gordon, I. J. 1970. *Baby Learning Through Baby Play.* New York: St. Martins Press

Gutierrez, A. 1972. "Analysis and Comparison of the Lyndon Baines Johnson Education Papers and Head Start Research," doctoral dissertation, University of Texas at Austin.

Hebb, D. O. 1949. *The Organization of Behavior.* New York: Wiley.

Hebb, D. O. 1947. "The Effects of Early Experience on Problem-Solving at Maturity," *American Psychologist*, 2:306–307.

Hunt, J. McV. 1964. "The Psychological Basis for Using Preschool Enrichment as an Antidote for Cultural Deprivation," report of the Arden House Conference on Preschool Enrichment of Socially Disadvantaged Children, December 16, 1962, *Merrill-Palmer Quarterly*, July.

Hunt, J. McV. 1961. *Intelligence and Experience.* New York: Ronald.

Hurley, R. 1969. *Poverty and Mental Retardation: A Causal Relationship.* New York: Vintage Books.

Jones, H. E., and N. Bayley. 1941. "The Berkeley Growth Study," *Child Development*, 12:167–173.

Kagan, J., W. J. Hall, and R. E. Klein. 1972. "Cross-Cultural Perspectives on Early Development," paper presented to the Annual Meeting of the American Association for the Advancement of Science, Washington, D.C.

Kirschner Associates, Inc. 1970. *A National Survey of the Impacts of Head Start Centers on Community Institutions.* Washington, D.C.: Office of Child Development, U. S. Department of Health, Education and Welfare, May.

Klaus, R. A., and S. W. Gray. 1968. "The Early Training Project for Disadvantaged Children: A Report after Five Years," *Monographs of the Society for Research in Child Development*, 33(4)1–66.

Levenstein, P. 1975. "The Verbal Interaction Project," symposium at American Orthopsychiatric Association Conference, Washington, D.C., March.

Levenstein, P. 1971. "Learning Through (and From) Mothers," *Childhood Education*, December, pp. 130–134.

Levenstein, P. 1970. "Cognitive Growth in Preschoolers through Verbal Interaction wth Mothers," *American Journal of Orthopsychiatry*, 40:426–432.

Levenstein, P., A. Kochman, and H. A. Roth. 1973. "From Laboratory to Real World: Service Delivery of the Mother-Child Home Program," *American Journal of Orthopsychiatry*, 53:72–78.

Levenstein, P., and S. Levenstein. 1971. "Fostering Learning Potential in Pre-schoolers," *Social Casework*, February, pp. 74–78.

Levenstein, P., and R. Sunley. 1968. "Stimulation of Verbal Interaction Between Disadvantaged Mothers and Children," *American Journal of Orthopsychiatry*, 38:116–121.

Macfarlane, J. W. 1938. "Studies in Guidance," *Monographs of the Society for Research in Child Development*, 3(6).

Melzack, R., and T. H. Scott. 1957. "The Effects of Early Experience on the Response to Pain," *Journal of Comparative and Physiological Psychology*, 50:155–161.

Melzack, R., and W. R. Thompson. 1956. "Effects of Early Experience on Social Behavior," *Canadian Journal of Psychology*, 10:82–90.

Nedler, S. 1969. "Early Education for Spanish-speaking Mexican Children—A Comparison of Three Intervention Strategies," paper presented at the National Conference of the American Educational Research Association, Minneapolis, Minn., March.

Office of Economic Opportunity. 1967. *Project Head Start: Daily Program I.* Washington, D.C.: Government Printing Office.

Office of Economic Opportunity. 1965. *Project Head Start.* Washington, D.C.: Government Printing Office.

Olson, W. C. 1955. *Child Development.* Boston: Heath.

President's Panel on Mental Retardation. 1962. *A Proposed Program for National Action To Combat Mental Retardation.* Washington, D.C.: Government Printing Office.

Riesen, A. H. 1947. "The Development of Visual Perception in Man and Chimpanzee," *Science*, 106:107–108.

Skeels, H. M. 1965. "Effects of Adoption on Children from Institutions," *Children*, 12:33–34.

Sontag, L. W., C. T. Baker, and V. L. Nelson. 1958. "Mental Growth and Personality Development: A Longitudinal Study," *Monographs of the Society for Research in Child Development*, 23:1–143.

Temp, G., and S. B. Anderson. 1967. *Project Head Start—Summer, 1966—Section Three: Pupils and Programs.* Princeton, N.J.: Educational Testing Service.

Thompson, W. R., and W. Heron. 1954. "The Effects of Restricting Early Experience on the Problem-Solving Capacity of Dogs," *Canadian Journal of Psychology*, 8:17–31.

U.S. Department of Health, Education and Welfare. 1972. "Mother-Child Home Program, Freeport, New York," in *Model Programs: Compensatory Education.* Washington, D.C.: Government Printing Office.

Weikart, D. P. 1967. *Preschool Intervention: A Preliminary Report of the Perry Preschool Project.* Ann Arbor, Mich.: Campus Publishers.

Westinghouse Learning Corporation and Ohio University (Westinghouse Report). 1969. *The Impact of Head Start. Preliminary Draft; An Evaluation of the Effects of Head Start Experience on Children's Cognitive and Affective Development.* Washington, D.C.: Government Printing Office.

Wolff, M., and A. Stein. 1967. "Head Start Six Months Later," *Phi Delta Kappan*, March.

FURTHER READING

Association for Childhood Education International. *Parenting.* Washington, D.C.: The Association, 1973.

Dittman, L. L. (ed.). *The Infants We Care For.* Washington, D.C.: National Association for the Education of Young Children, 1973.

Evans, E. B., and G. F. Sain. *Day Care for Infants.* Boston: Beacon Press, 1972.

Evans, E. D. *Contemporary Influences in Early Childhood Education,* 2d ed. New York: Holt, Rinehart and Winston, 1975, Chapter 1.

Fallon, B. J. (ed.). *40 Innovative Programs in Early Childhood Education.* Belmont, Calif.: Lear Siegler, Inc./Fearon Publishers, 1973.

Far West Laboratory for Educational Research and Development. *Early Childhood Education.* Report #42, "How To Select and Evaluate Materials." New York: Educational Products Information Exchange Institute, 1972. (Package contains resource manual, program selection manual, and descriptive filmstrips of experimental early childhood programs.)

Frost, J. L. "At Risk," *Childhood Education.* 1975, 51: 298–304.

Frost, J. L. *Revisiting Early Childhood Education.* New York: Holt, Rinehart and Winston, 1973, Part 8.

Goodlad, J. I., M. F. Klein, J. M. Novotney, and associates. *Early Schooling in the United States.* New York: McGraw-Hill, 1973.

Honig, A. S. *Parent Involvement in Early Childhood Education.* Washington, D.C.: National Association for the Education of Young Children, 1975.

LeShan, E. J. *The Conspiracy Against Childhood.* New York: Atheneum, 1971.

Parker, R. K., (ed.). *The Preschool in Action: Exploring Early Childhood Programs.* Boston: Allyn and Bacon, 1972.

Pines, M. *Revolution in Learning.* New York: Harper & Row, 1966.

Stanley, J. C. (ed.). *Compensatory Education for Children, Ages 2 to 8.* Baltimore, Md.: The Johns Hopkins Press, 1973.

Stanley, J. C. (ed.). *Preschool Programs for the Disadvantaged: Five Experimental Approaches to Early Childhood Education.* Baltimore, Md.: The Johns Hopkins Press, 1972.

Weber, L. *The English Infant School and Informal Education.* Englewood Cliffs, N.J.: Prentice-Hall, 1971.

Weikart, D. P., L. Rogers, C. Adcock, and D. McClelland. *The Cognitively Oriented Curriculum.* Washington, D.C.: National Association for the Education of Young Children, 1971.

A-Bar-Z Ponderosa School, Austin, Texas

5

Behavioral Science Foundations
for Early Childhood Education

The previous chapters reviewed the historical antecedents of early childhood education from the time of Plato and Aristotle to the 1970s. Significant throughout is the way people and events in history have built upon each other over time. Chapters 1 and 2 reviewed the earliest strings of educational thought in terms of traces of contemporary practice in early education, the men of vision, the progressive school of John Dewey, and the Montessori method. Chapter 3 discussed the emergence of the child development movement in education. The normative-maturational theory of Gesell was influenced by his association with Hall and their mutual regard for Darwin. Psychosexual-personality views stemmed from the pioneering work of Freud and were elaborated by Erikson and other followers. Strings of thought are difficult to trace directly to the very early philosophers (Plato and Aristotle), but later figures such as Luther, Comenius, Rousseau, Pestalozzi, Froebel, Dewey, and Montessori undoubtedly influenced (directly and indirectly) most of the great thinkers to follow. Cognitive-transactional theory and humanistic theory are linked to the cognitively oriented school (Weikart) and the open school. Out of the laboratory studies of animals by Thorndike and Pavlov and the work of Watson and Skinner grew behavioral-environmental theory and behavior analysis methods. Chapter 4 discussed how the interest in child study and in psychology resulted in the accumulation of a large body of research data. The outgrowth of this research was a proliferation of experimental programs for young children which included Project Head Start. Subsequent research revealed a "wash-out" of the successful IQ gains made by the children in these programs as they moved into the public school primary grades. The result was Project Follow-Through, which encompassed a number of different program models designed to maintain the earlier gains. These different types of programs represent varying points of view about the learning process. Of interest in this discussion of historical influences on early childhood education is that certain elements of each of these contemporary programs can be traced to particular schools of psychological theory (Chapter 3), to the beginnings of educational thought (Chapter 1), and to the philosophy of Dewey (Chapter 2).

The present chapter discusses these historical points of interest, as illustrated in Figure 5–1. The body of psychological-developmental theories from which contemporary early childhood programs draw their scientific support are categorized in this chapter as psychosexual-personality, normative-maturational, behavioral-environmental, cognitive-transactional, and humanistic. In order to illustrate how these theories have contributed to contemporary early childhood programs, fundamental assumptions of the theories are presented, points of view are compared, and representative programs and program elements corresponding to particular theories are identified. The practice of extracting views about curriculum and instruction from psychology is somewhat tenuous, for there is no *direct* linkage between knowledge about how children learn and develop and how one should go about instructing them or how one should prepare the learning environment. A leap of faith is taken and some degree of overgeneralization is present because of limited knowledge about these relationships. Nonetheless, the authors have risked overgeneralization in postulating relationships between theory and instructional practice because they believe that logic and practice based upon a preliminary science is better than vague hunches, superstition, or no science at all.

PSYCHOSEXUAL-PERSONALITY THEORY

Psychosexual-personality theory has roots in the psychoanalytical work of Sigmund Freud. Early psychoanalytic theory saw the individual as governed by irrational impulses as he passed through a series of psychosexual stages (Cowles 1971:794). These stages included the oral period, the anal period, the phallic, or oedipal, period, and the latency period. The manner in which the child passed through these stages determined in large degree whether he would become a healthy or unhealthy adult. Although Freud had only limited contact with children, he believed that the child developed his feelings about acceptance during the oral period, his traits of orderliness and punc-

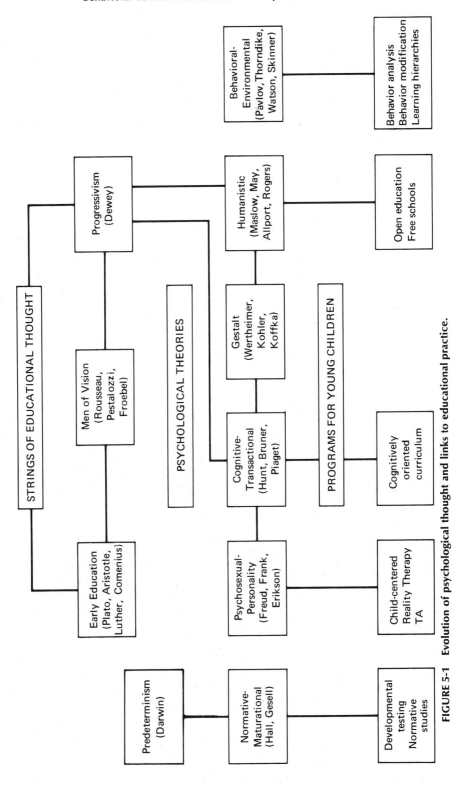

FIGURE 5-1   Evolution of psychological thought and links to educational practice.

tuality during the anal stage, his awareness of love directed toward parents during the phallic period, and his projection of love outside the family circle during the latency period. According to the psychoanalytic point of view, if the child's basic drives are not satisfied, he may experience permanent personality distortions. The symptoms of personality distortion are regression, fixation, denial, sublimation, and repression. Recognition and analysis of these symptoms provide information about the meaning of the child's behavior. The corrective method of the psychoanalyst is therapy. Freud's monumental contributions to personality theory were felt most heavily in one-to-one therapy sessions between psychiatrist and patient. Only recently have useful implications along this line been developed for children in group and school contexts.

Freud's work was carried on by many disciples, including his daughter Anna and Erik Erikson. Erikson received a portion of his training with Anna Freud in Europe and taught and practiced in the United States at such institutions as Harvard, Yale, and the University of California at Berkeley. His work is significant because it expands the theory of psychoanalysis to include the study of human strengths as well as human problems and the relationship of social and cultural experiences to the developing ego. Erikson conceptualized stages of growth in the development of a healthy mature ego, or personality. Each stage holds a central task or problem that must be solved if the child is to attain the next stage. A reasonably satisfactory level of solution provides the foundation for future progress and secures a degree of personality strength (Erikson 1963). The major implication of Erikson's theory seems to be that teachers or care givers must provide an emotional environment in which children engage in both anxiety-producing and pleasure-producing experiences. The child who never faces anxiety-producing situations, either real or imaginary, cannot be expected to learn to cope with life. On the other hand, the child must have many successful, pleasurable experiences if interest and healthy growth are to be maintained.

The contributions of classical Freudian theory can be seen only tangentially in contemporary early childhood programs. However, the proponents of three types of child development programs, the traditional nursery schools, Head Start, and the Bank Street program, draw in varying degrees from Erikson's theory in the construction of learning climates conducive to healthy emotional development. Furthermore, growing attention is being directed to new therapeutic approaches. For example, Glasser (1965) feels that Freudian psychoanalytic procedures are frequently ineffective and proposes reality therapy as a very different therapeutic approach. This approach rejects the concept of mental illness and does not allow the patient (student) to evade responsibility by delving into his history for possible causes for his behavior. Rather, he is assisted in learning to fulfill two essential needs: to love and be loved, and to feel worthwhile to himself and to others. A second therapeutic approach, transactional analysis (TA), is currently being applied to problems of intra- and interpersonal relationships on a rapidly broadening scale. TA is a concept developed by Eric Berne (1961, 1964, 1972) and popularized through a best-selling book by Thomas Harris (1967). Like reality therapy, TA (see Chapter 11) confronts the individual with the fact that he is responsible for what happens in the future, regardless of what happened in the past. However, Harris disagrees with Glasser's denial of the importance of the past in understanding present behavior. We cannot change the past, but the past projects itself into present lives and must be dealt with. Both approaches resulted from dissatisfactions with therapeutic approaches that disregard morality in the treatment process. These new therapeutic approaches are applicable to problems of individuals in classrooms at every level. Harris makes broad claims for TA, applying the system to problems in marriage, child-rearing, mental retardation, racial prejudice, creativity, violence, student revolt, religion, and international affairs. Thus, it appears that the influence of Freud and psychosexual-personality theory, greatly modified over time, is in a position to have further impact upon contemporary thought and practice in early childhood and other levels of education.

NORMATIVE-MATURATIONAL THEORY

The normative-maturational view draws its power from two major sources, normative studies such as those of Gesell and the predeterministic views of such figures as Darwin, Hall, and Gesell. In the extreme, the predeterministic views applied to practice gives a distorted picture of the child as a creature of his genes in consort with a teacher who must bide her time until the teachable moment arrives through the methodological process of maturation. The normative view, in the extreme, paints an equally dismal classroom picture of grade-level standards, rigid ability grouping based on standardized tests, letter grades, grade-age expectations, and predetermined curriculum. Unfortunately, extreme, ill-founded misinterpretations of normative-maturational theory set the pattern for most contemporary American schools. Gesell, however, promoted a point of view quite foreign to the classroom picture just painted. Throughout his work, normative stages were offered as approximate norms of developmental sequence that are always relative and not absolute. He also viewed each child as an individual, though "tailor-made" by the maturational process. Gesell's point of view stands in sharp contrast to the contemporary interactionist view which stresses that both nature and nurture combine to influence development. The degree of relative influence of each is presently unclear and is being widely debated.

Normative-maturational theory appears to have left its mark upon programs for young children which employ standardized testing and normative studies. Standardized tests are useful in research activity, group analysis, and, through attention to individual items, diagnostic activity. Normative studies provide sets of child characteristics that are useful in determining sample developmental sequences (see Chapter 8). These assist in deciding possible curriculum sequences. In contemporary practice, the specific developmental tasks that comprise stages of development are hierarchically organized and used as checkpoints for child growth. The "tasks" are often rewritten as behavioral objectives. The crucial concern in contemporary practice lies in what manner the resulting sequence of objectives is used. Employing a developmental task as a learning objective must be preceded by a careful diagnosis of the child's needs. The child must *not* be expected to fit a particular task or sequence. The task, objective, or sequence must be designed to match the needs of the child. There is no expectation in the healthy environment, implicit or explicit, that the child should measure up to a chronological or grade norm.

BEHAVIORAL-ENVIRONMENTAL THEORY

Behavioral-environmental theory draws from the stimulus-response-reinforcement theories of B. F. Skinner (1938, 1953, 1968), his contemporary disciples, and his predecessors Hall, Thorndike, and Watson. Behavioral theory views the child as a passive, receptive organism, essentially a creature of his environment. He is primarily responsive to cues, or stimuli, that initiate behavior and to reinforcement which ensures the repetition of that behavior. Reinforced behavior is repeated; unreinforced behavior is extinguished.

Skinner (1972) proposes that we can no longer afford freedom, and so it must be replaced with control over man, his conduct, and his culture. This is to be accomplished by environmental manipulation. "Behavior is shaped and maintained by its consequences," Skinner maintains. His radical propositions associated with his belief that autonomy, the inner man, and God are myths drew the wrath of psychoanalysts, humanists, and theologians. Despite strong attacks, neither theory nor practice is washing its hands of behaviorism.

The behavioral-environmental view has been put into practice as behavior modification, currently exemplified by the well-known early childhood behavior analysis and follow-through model of Bushell and associates at the University of Kansas. Although Bereiter and Engelmann (1966) do not give credit to any particular figure or school of thought, their academic preschool and the Distar materials later developed are also tied closely to behavioral theory. Insofar as early childhood curriculum and instruction employ systems approaches, behavioral objectives, hierarchical sequencing, and behavior modification, they are also tied in greater or lesser extent to behavioral-environmental theory. Taken in isolation, such procedures could well result in rigid, uninspired, dehumanized schools. If, on the other hand, both theory and practice are realistically interpreted in the broader sphere of human insight, useful tools for curriculum development become available. Abraham

Maslow, one of the chief spokesmen for humanistic psychology, clarified his position in regard to both psychoanalysis and behaviorism:

It is very difficult, I have found, to communicate to others my simultaneous respect for and impatience with these two comprehensive psychologies. So many people insist on being *either* pro-Freudian *or* anti-Freudian, pro-scientific *or* anti-scientific psychology, etc. In my opinion all such loyalty-positions are silly. Our job is to integrate these various truths into the *whole* truth, which should be our only loyalty. (1954:3)

COGNITIVE-TRANSACTIONAL THEORY

Cognitive-transactional theory includes the information-processing models of J. McVicker Hunt (1961) and Jerome Bruner (1966), Piaget's theory of cognitive development, and gestalt psychology. In contrast to the behaviorist view, cognitive-transactional theory views the child as being shaped through transactions with his environment. The child is an active, seeking being. In this respect, cognitive-transactional theory is linked to the ideas of Dewey. The child is not viewed as totally dependent upon *external* forces for his motivation. Piaget looks at this idea as *internal reinforcement* added to stimulus-response theory. Of internal reinforcements, he says:

They are what I call equilibration or self-regulation. The internal reinforcements are what enable the subject to eliminate contradictions, incompatibilities, and conflicts. All development is composed of momentary conflicts and incompatibilities which must be overcome to reach a higher level of equilibrium. Berlyne calls this elimination of incompatibilities internal reinforcement. . . . So you see that it is indeed a stimulus-response theory, if you will, but first you add operations and then you add equilibration. That's all we want! (Piaget 1964:19)

In his theory of cognitive development, Piaget espouses the idea that the sequence of human development is invariant. However, the rate and timing of development is highly variant or different for every individual. Further, Piaget proposes that development cannot be forced, although it can be retarded by teaching. Cognitive-transactional theory is linked to contemporary programs where the pedagogical emphasis is upon the broadening of mental structures rather than upon their vertical acceleration. The principal curriculum method stemming from this theory is operations upon objects by the child. Piaget holds that all children develop through a series of developmental stages characterized by identifiable classes of learning tasks. These learning tasks, such as reversibility, classification, and seriation, are the *content of curriculums* extracted from cognitive-developmental theory. The cognitively oriented curriculum of David Weikart in Ypsilanti, Michigan, is the best-known experimental early childhood model employing the theory. In addition, Celia Stendler Lavatelli of the University of Illinois has developed a kit of teaching materials oriented to Piaget-inspired learning operations;

and Constance Kamii, formerly of the Ypsilanti public schools, has studied with Piaget and proposed designs for curriculum development (Sonquist and Kamii 1968; Kamii 1973). Certain proponents of the British infant school credit Piaget as a source for curriculum. In reality, however, the infant schools appear to draw most of their ideas from the philosophy of Dewey. The "open" style of these schools also ties them in some degree to humanistic psychology.

HUMANISTIC THEORY

Humanistic psychology has deep roots in the philosophy of humanism, which focuses upon man and his potential. It represents a sharpening and rediscovering of historical trends—of the philosophies of the men of vision who emphasized the child as unique and different from the adult, of the various self psychologies, organismic psychologies, Freudian psychology, gestalt psychology, and existential psychology. Humanistic psychology is exemplified in the ideas of Maslow, who conceived it as a counter to behaviorism and psychoanalysis, and in the ideas of Allport, Rogers, and May.

Gordon Allport

Allport made major, initial contributions to the body of theory which was later to be called humanistic psychology. In his Yale lectures sponsored by the Terry Lecture Foundation, he described with clarity and vision his psychology of becoming (Allport 1955). He viewed with concern the widespread disagreement among psychologists regarding the nature of the growth and development of personality. He recognized no single brand of modern psychology as completely adequate in accounting for the organization and growth of the individual person, and he believed that the psychologist must consider the organismic system as a whole and show how parts of that system are related to one another. Allport struck out at dogmatism and proposed that psychology enlarge its horizons without sacrificing its gains; that attention be focused upon the study of healthy human beings rather than sick and anxious people or captive and desperate rats who are primarily concerned with preservation of life. Allport ventured the opinion that, unlike plants and lower animals, man is not merely a creature of cell structure, tropisms, and instinct; that all of the animals in the world are psychologically less distinct from one another than one human is from other humans. The individuality of man extends infinitely beyond the puny individuality of plants and animals. Therefore, we should refuse to carry over the indifferences of other sciences to the problem of individuality. Allport made no pretense of having final and complete solutions to issues that confront a psychology of becoming. He offered provisional solutions based on preliminary evidence, trusting that future research would strengthen or amend them.

Rollo May

The existential approach was prominent in European psychology and psychiatry for two decades before it was introduced in the United States during the mid-fifties. In 1959 a symposium on existential psychology was held at the annual convention of the American Psychological Association in Cincinnati. The papers presented were meant to show how and why an impressive group of American psychologists and psychiatrists were profoundly interested in the existential approach to human beings. They were later published (May 1961). In the symposium, May stated that existentialism means centering upon the *existing* person; it is the emphasis on the human being as he is *emerging, becoming.* The word "existence" comes from the Latin *exsistere*, meaning literally "to stand out, emerge." This view, in Western culture, has been set over against *essence*, which emphasizes immutable principles, truth, and logical laws. American psychologists are becoming increasingly emphatic in saying one cannot adequately describe or understand a living human being, or any living organism, on an "existentialist" basis. May took very seriously the dehumanizing dangers in our tendency in modern science to make man over into the image of the machine, into the image of the techniques by which we study him. He expressed fear that man was actually in the process of losing self-consciousness. As a practicing therapist, he favored phenomenology[1] as the first stage in the existential psychotherapeutic movement. Techniques will change, not in a hit-or-miss fashion but dependent upon the needs of the patient at given times. The existential psychological movement, in May's judgment, was not at all "unscientific." It simply did not fit the particular methods then in vogue. Methodology always suffers from a cultural lag. He strongly affirmed the existential view that questions regarding the image of man should be answered on the *human* level, pointing toward a psychology of mankind.

Carl Rogers

The symposium paper by Carl Rogers (1961) identified two divergent trends existing in the field of psychotherapy. These were the "objective" and the "existential."

THE "OBJECTIVE" TREND. This trend represented the rigorous hard-headed devotion to reductionist theories, to operational definitions, and to experimental procedures that lead us to understand psychotherapy in purely objective rather than subjective terms.

THE "EXISTENTIAL" TREND. This trend gained rapid popularity in the United States during the 1950s. Maslow, May, Allport, and Rogers place

---

[1] Phenomenology is the endeavor to take the phenomena as given. It is the disciplined effort to clear one's mind of the presuppositions that so often cause us to see in the patient only our own theories or the dogmas of our own systems.

themselves in this group. These psychologists insist, in a variety of ways, that they are concerned with the whole spectrum of human behavior and that human behavior is, in some significant ways, something more than the behavior of laboratory animals. The concern in therapy is with an existing, becoming, emerging, experiencing being.

In the judgment of Rogers, the warm, subjective, human encounter of two persons is more effective in facilitating change than is the most precise set of techniques growing out of learning theory or operant conditioning.

Abraham Maslow

Maslow (1961:53) defined existentialism, in a symposium presentation, in a personal way, in terms of "what's in it for me": "To me it means essentially a radical stress on the concept of identity and the experience of identity as a sine qua non [essential] of human nature and of any philosophy or science of human nature." If the study of the uniqueness of the individual does not fit into what we know of science, then so much the worse for the conception of science. It, too, will have to endure re-creation. To Maslow, no theory of psychology will ever be complete that does not incorporate centrally the concept that man has his future within him, dynamically active at this present moment. We must realize that only the future is in principle unknown and unknowable. This means that all habits, defenses, and coping mechanisms are doubtful and ambiguous because they are based on past experience. Only the flexible, creative person can really manage the future, only the one who can face novelty with confidence and without fear. Much of what we now call psychology is the study of the tricks we use to avoid the anxiety of absolute novelty by pretending the future will be like the past. Existentialism may be an additional push toward the establishment of another branch of psychology—the psychology of the fully evolved and authentic self and its ways of being. This possibility of a new branch of psychology was later to be fulfilled when Maslow (1962b) conceived of humanistic psychology as a "third force," countering behaviorism and psychoanalysis. According to humanistic psychology, the goal of education is the ultimate self-actualization of a person. The method upon which the theory is based is a normative one—studying superior human beings (self-actualizers) and using their choices as models for education. In other words, one attempts to help people to achieve the highest human possibilities by studying those who appear to be living those experiences.

Humanistic psychology suffers from the lack of a substantial theoretical foundation, due in large part to the difficulty involved in researching affective and psychic processes. The central themes are the whole child, inner drives, and the affective dimensions of man. The open school and the free school typify humanistic theory in practice, implicitly and explicitly. In the open school, such as the British infant schools, children are assisted in the development toward self-fulfillment through flexible guidance in an informal learning environment built around centers of interest, multiple-age grouping, and attention to real-life problems through subject integration.

The free schools represent a second major group of schools drawing force (implicitly) from humanistic psychology. The goal is the creation of an environment conducive to creativity and interest in learning. Such schools are seen as alternatives to both public and private schools. The free school prototypes, over 1000 in number, reveal an intriguing view of the learning process. The *New Schools Exchange*[2] illustrates excitement of discovery and discontent with traditional schools through its "People Seeking Places" advertisements:

Wants very much to teach in a place that accepts kids as pretty wonderful human beings.

Want a pleasant opportunity to expand our minds in an atmosphere of joyful learning. Experience: five years attempting to teach English in high school; suspended and later dismissed for attempting to relate to students on a human level.

I'm willing to travel, to work for room and board, in fact to try anything that sounds interesting. (No. 141)

In the same issue, program developers described their efforts under the caption, "We Have Created a School Where . . ."

the student's natural curiosity, freed from the burdens of competition and threats, and guided by an affirming environment, will lead him to a quest for knowledge of himself and the world.

students can study whatever they choose, there are no required classes, grades, textbooks, or tests. Although the student understands that the responsibility for his education rests squarely upon his own shoulders.

Free schools are presently failing at a rapid rate. Jonathan Kozol, a dominant force behind their existence, offers a perspective on the problem. He believes it is time to "come right out and make some straightforward statements on the misleading and deceptive character of certain slogans that are now unthinkingly received as gospel." The best teacher is *not* the one "who most successfully pretends that he knows nothing" (Kozol 1973:471–472). The teacher is not a "wandering mystic" afraid or unable to express his convictions, but one who lives fully his own life values and does not shrink from providing adult direction. Thus the progress in making schools "open" or "free" places is in a preliminary, pioneering state. It is recognized that neither of these schools has or is overtly and deliberately drawing its ideas from the postulates of humanistic psychology. Yet their practice appears to represent the closest approximations to that theory applied to childhood education.

[2] 2840 Hidden Valley Lane, Santa Barbara, California 93103.

SUMMARY AND CONCLUSIONS

Contemporary early childhood programs draw their scientific bases from the body of available psychological-developmental theories that emerged through history. Although there is no *direct* connection between how children learn and develop and how one should prepare the learning environment or instruct them, some theory-instruction relationships can be postulated.

The theory of Erik Erikson has been applied in contemporary education more than has classical psychoanalytic theory per se. Erikson is a disciple of Freud and expanded Freud's ideas to include the relationship between social and cultural experiences and the developing personality. Proponents of three types of child development programs, the traditional nursery school, Head Start, and the Bank Street program, draw in varying degrees from Erikson's theory in the construction of learning climates conducive to healthy emotional development. A further outgrowth of psychosexual-personality theory has been the new therapeutic approaches such as Reality Therapy and Transactional Analysis, which are being increasingly implemented. It appears that the influence of Freud and psychosexual-personality theory is in a position to have further impact upon contemporary thought and practice.

Normative-maturational theory has influenced contemporary programs that employ standardized tests and normative studies for the purposes of curriculum development and evaluation. Behavioral-environmental theory has been put into practice in contemporary programs as systems approaches, behavioral objectives, hierarchical learning sequences, and behavior modification. Application of cognitive-transactional theory can be seen in programs that emphasize the broadening of mental structures and where the instructional method is the direct operation upon objects by the children. Humanistic theory in contemporary practice is typified by open schools and free schools where the primary concern is inner drives and the affective dimension of the child.

SUGGESTED ACTIVITIES

1. Study one of the psychological-developmental theories discussed in this chapter in greater depth. Identify the key principles of the theory you investigate. What are the implications of these key principles for early childhood education?
2. Determine the theoretical base for some of the early childhood programs in your community. How does the particular theory influence the program goals? In what ways does the curriculum and the instructional methods and materials reflect the program's theoretical base?
3. Visit an open school. Observe the instructional methods, the materials, curriculum, teacher-pupil roles, and program goals. What evidence of the application of humanistic theory can you find?

REFERENCES

Allport, G. W. 1955. *Becoming: Basic Considerations for a Psychology of Personality.* New Haven, Conn.: Yale University Press.

Bereiter, C., and S. Engelmann. 1966. *Teaching Disadvantaged Children in the Preschool.* Englewood Cliffs, N.J.: Prentice-Hall.

Berne, E. 1972. *What Do You Say After You Say Hello?* New York: Bantam Books.

Berne, E. 1964. *Games People Play.* New York: Grove Press.

Berne, E. 1961. *Transactional Analysis in Psychotherapy.* New York: Grove Press.

Bruner, J. 1966. *Toward a Theory of Instruction.* Cambridge, Mass.: Harvard University Press.

Buhler, C. 1971. "Basic Theoretical Concepts of Humanistic Psychology," *American Psychologist,* 26(4). Reprinted in J. L. Frost (ed.), *Revisiting Early Childhood Education.* New York: Holt, Rinehart and Winston, 1973.

Cowles, M. 1971. "Four Views of Learning and Development," *Educational Leadership,* 28(8):790–795.

Dewey, J. 1902. *The Child and the Curriculum.* Chicago: University of Chicago Press.

Erikson, E. 1963. *Childhood and Society.* New York: Norton.

Freud, A. 1960. *Psychoanalysis for Teachers and Parents.* Boston: Beacon Press.

Freud, S. 1949. *An Outline of Psychoanalysis.* New York: Norton.

Gagné, R. M. 1968. "Learning Hierarchies," presidential address, Division 15, American Psychological Association, August 31.

Glasser, W. 1965. *Reality Therapy: A New Approach to Psychiatry.* New York: Harper & Row.

Harris, T. A. 1967. *I'm OK—You're OK: A Practical Guide to Transactional Analysis.* New York: Harper & Row.

Herrnstein, R. 1971. "I.Q," *Atlantic,* 228(3):43–64.

Hunt, J. McV. 1961. *Intelligence and Experience.* New York: Ronald.

Illich, I. 1970. *Deschooling Society.* New York: Harper & Row.

Jensen, A. R. 1969. "How Much Can We Boost I.Q. and Scholastic Achievement?" *Harvard Educational Review,* 39(1):1–123.

Kamii, C. 1973. "A Sketch of the Piaget-Derived Preschool Curriculum Developed by the Ypsilanti Early Childhood Program," in J. L. Frost (ed.), *Revisiting Early Childhood Education.* New York: Holt, Rinehart and Winston.

Kelley, E. C. 1962. "The Fully Functioning Self," in Yearbook of the Association for Supervision and Curriculum Development, *Perceiving, Behaving, Becoming.* Washington, D.C.: The Association, pp. 9–20.

Kozol, J. 1973. "Free Schools: A Time for Candor," in J. L. Frost (ed.), *Revisiting Early Childhood Education.* New York: Holt, Rinehart and Winston, 1973.

Maslow, A. H. 1971. *The Farther Reaches of Human Nature.* New York: Viking Press.

Maslow, A. H. 1962a. "Some Basic Propositions of a Growth and Self-Actualization Psychology," in Yearbook of the Association for Supervision and Curriculum Development. Washington, D.C.: The Association, pp. 34–49.

Maslow, A. H. 1962b. *Toward a Psychology of Being.* Princeton, N.J.: Van Nostrand.

Maslow, A. H. 1961. "Existential Psychology—What's in It for Us?" in R. May (ed.), *Existential Psychology*. New York: Random House, pp. 52–60.

Maslow, A. H. 1954. *Motivation and Personality*. New York: Harper & Row.

May, R. (ed.) 1961. *Existential Psychology*. New York: Random House.

Piaget, J. 1964. "Development and Learning," in R. E. Ripple and V. N. Rockcastle (eds.), *Piaget Rediscovered*, a report of the Conference on Cognitive Studies and Curriculum Development, Cornell University, Ithaca, N.Y., March.

Rogers, C. R. 1961. "Two Divergent Trends," in R. May (ed.), *Existential Psychology*. New York: Random House, pp. 85–93.

Skinner, B. F. 1972. *Beyond Freedom and Dignity*. New York: Knopf.

Skinner, B. F. 1968. *The Technology of Teaching*. New York: Meredith Corporation.

Skinner, B. F. 1953. *Science and Human Behavior*. New York: Macmillan.

Skinner, B. F. 1938. *The Behavior of Organisms*. New York: Appleton-Century-Crofts.

"Skinner's Utopia: Panacea, or Path to Hell?" 1971. *Time*, September 20, pp. 47–53.

Sonquist, H. D., and C. Kamii. 1968. "Applying Some Piagetian Concepts in the Classroom for the Disadvantaged," in J. L. Frost (ed.), *Early Childhood Education Rediscovered*. New York: Holt, Rinehart and Winston, pp. 169–180.

U.S. Department of Health, Education and Welfare. 1970. *Model Programs in Childhood Education*. Washington, D.C.: Government Printing Office.

U.S. Department of Health, Education and Welfare. 1969. *Selected Exemplary Programs for the Education of Disadvantaged Children*. Washington, D.C.: Government Printing Office.

FURTHER READING

Bigge, T. *Learning Theories for Teachers,* 2d ed. New York: Harper & Row, 1971.

Carpenter, F. *The Skinner Primer*. New York: Free Press, 1974.

Child, I. L. *Humanistic Psychology and the Research Tradition: Their Several Virtues*. New York: Wiley, 1973.

Erikson, E. *Childhood and Society*, 2d ed. New York: Norton, 1963.

Frost, J. L. (ed.), *Revisiting Early Childhood Education*. New York: Holt, Rinehart and Winston, 1973, Part 7.

Illich, I. *Deschooling Society*. New York: Harper & Row, 1970.

Kohlberg, L. "Early Education: A Cognitive-Developmental View," *Child Development*, 1968, 39:1013–1962.

Kohl, H. *The Open Classroom*. New York: Vintage Books, 1969.

Kozol, J. *Free Schools*. Boston: Houghton Mifflin, 1972.

Matson, F. W. (ed.). *Without/Within: Behaviorism and Humanism*. Monterey, Calif.: Brooks/Cole Publishing Company, 1973.

Maslow, A. H. *Toward a Psychology of Being*. New York: Van Nostrand, 1968.

Richards, F., and I. D. Welch (eds.). *Sightings: Essays in Humanistic Psychology*. Boulder, Colo.: Shields Publishing Company, 1973.

Smedslund, J. *Becoming a Psychologist: Theoretical Foundations for a Humanistic Psychology*. New York: Halsted Press, 1972.

Language and
Cognitive Development
in Young Children

A-Bar-Z Ponderosa School, Austin, Texas

6

Language Development in Young Children

A major responsibility of early childhood programs is to assist children in extending and enriching their verbal abilities. This responsibility is made complex by a variety of factors. The sounds and symbols of language differ not only from country to country, but within a country language patterns vary widely across regions, communities, neighborhoods, and ethnic groups. Dialect differences are everywhere obvious, with each shaped by the needs of the particular societal group it serves. This chapter considers both innate and environmental factors in the development of language in the young child. It reviews the sequence of language learning (see Table 6-1) as well as some of the major assumptions about how language is learned. The intimate relationship between language and thinking is also explored. Chapter 7 focuses on the development of thought in the young child. Later, in Chapter 10 of Part V, the teacher's role in enhancing both language and thinking within the educative process is examined in detail.

TABLE 6-1 Sequence of Language Development

Approximate Age	Vocalization and Language
12 weeks	Cooing stage (squealing, gurgling sounds); 7-phoneme repertoire; vowel-consonant ratio 5:1.
20 weeks	Vowel sounds interspersed with consonant sounds.
6 months	Cooing changing to babbling; one-syllable utterances (*ma, da, mu, di*); produces most of the vowel elements and half of the consonants; 12-phoneme repertoire.
12 months	Distinctive intonation patterns; utterances signal emotion; pseudo-imitation of sounds; words are emerging (*mama, dada*); definite signs of understanding words and simple commands; 18-phoneme repertoire.
18 months	Repertoire of words between 3 and 50; intricate babbling; rapid progress in understanding; forms simple 2- and 3-word sentences ("telegraphic" speech) which linguistically code basic cognitive relationships such as actor-objects.
2 years	2- to 5-word utterances, predominance of nouns; absence of articles, auxiliaries, verbs, prepositions, and conjunctions; one third of sounds clearly articulated; vocabulary 50–300 words, although not necessarily adult in meanings; babbling outgrown; characteristic child grammar rather than imitation of adult; understands language directed at him.
3 years	Average sentence length 4 words; rapid increase in articulation proficiency; learns 50 new words each month to age 5; vocabulary 100–1000 words; grammar approaching that of adult; intelligible utterances.
4 years	Average sentence length 5.3 words; complete sentence stage; good mastery of inflections; use of relational words; mastery of fundamental grammatical rules; utterances consistent with adult grammar.
6 years	Vocabulary of 2562 words (M. E. Smith 1926); vocabulary of 49,500 basic and derived words (M. K. Smith 1941).
8 years	Mature articulation; vocabulary increases into adulthood.

THE EMERGENCE OF LANGUAGE

The First Year

From the moment of birth, the child learns from his surrounding world. At first he is a relatively passive recipient of attention directed to him by adults. Carroll (1970) points out, however, that the infant early develops the capacity to recognize and react differentially to adult voices. Very soon, the young child learns that his actions have an effect on his comfort, and he sets about to exercise this skill. His primary means for effecting change is vocalization, which initially has no pattern or meaning but later is connected to need fulfillment. By the age of 3 or 4 months the child is associating patterns of vocalization with satisfaction of need. Crying may bring relief from discomfort. If the infant feels contented and comfortable, he expresses his feelings of pleasure and satisfaction by cooing, emitting vowel-like sounds. Or he may even laugh out loud. His vocalizations, in turn, solicit pleasurable pats, comforting touches, smiles, and soothing voices. Through such inter-action, the child receives reinforcement, exercises his maturing speech appa-ratus, and develops a simple but effective means of communication.

Even during the first few weeks, language growth is related to the child's sensorimotor activities. The child imitates himself. He repeats actions and tries new actions that are similar to ones previously learned. Intertwined with his actions and in parallel fashion, he develops the foundation for lan-guage by making utterances and then repeating and imitating them. The cooing stage of the first few months is rapidly replaced by the babbling stage, characterized by repetition of syllables (*da-da, ga-ga*) for the sheer delight of uttering them. Babbling may begin as early as the third month for some infants and not until the sixth or seventh for others. Between the sixth and the twelfth month, the child's language system becomes quite flexible and differentiated. He recognizes some words and phrases and responds accordingly. For example, he may raise his arms when his mother asks, "Want to come?" or he may look at the dog or the clock in response to "Puppy—where's puppy?" and "Tick tock, Tick tock." He incorporates intonation and inflection to lend meaning and emphasis to his cooing and babbling. He may shout or squeal when angry, frustrated, or very excited. Rising inflection and tempo become linked with the emotions of pleasure and surprise, while lower inflection and tempo become associated with dis-comfort and displeasure. In addition, such expressive behaviors as smiling, frowning, physical contact, and speed of movement also become associated with emotions and language and are a part of the child's communicating, thinking, and acting repertoires. He may, for example, race across the room in his walker or on his hands and knees to grab his father's legs and screech with glee. He may stare into space, knit his brows, and emit a quiet grunt as he listens to some loud noise in the background.

12–24 Months

By the end of the first year, a normal child free from hearing or speech impediments begins to use whole words. Over the next six months, his understanding of words and phrases increases, so that he grows from *com-plying* with a simple request when accompanied by a gesture—"Throw daddy a kiss"—to *pointing* to a named object such as eyes or ball to *follow-ing* a simple direction—"Bring the book here to me." The young child between 1 year and 18 months of age enjoys the sound of words and delights in listening to songs and rhymes and playing with picture books. He increas-ingly coordinates his wants with finger pointing, utterances, and correct labels. By 1½ to 2 years, he begins to form two- and three-word sentences. He expresses what he experiences, for example, "Allgone milk" and "Mommy bye-bye." He parrots adults and talks to people, pets, and toys. The emergence of teeth help him to produce new sounds.

2–4 Years

By age 2, the child is talking. Between ages 2 and 4, language develops at a remarkable rate, and "the child whose language development is seriously delayed for any reason labors under an almost unsurmountable handicap in his social and academic relationships" (McCarthy 1954:494). From age 2 on, language is commonly used as an indication of mental development: "It is pretty well agreed that linguistic development is a good index, though, of course, not a complete one, of the general powers of children in their earlier years" (Watts 1948:34). The importance of this period is dramatized further by the fact that by approximately age 4 the child has miraculously acquired almost full knowledge of the grammatical system of his native language. Most children, having already mastered the grammar, or rules, of their native language, *do not learn* them from their teachers (Cazden, Baratz, Labov, and Palmer 1972:153).

SEQUENCE IN LANGUAGE ACQUISITION

Some children are talking a great deal at 1½ years, while others a year older are not talking at all. Children of the same age differ markedly in both understanding and talking. Although *rate* of language acquisition varies from child to child, all children acquire language in the same basic sequence. During the first few months of life, the child develops a simple, basic grammar. The first words are unitary labels for objects, events, or persons, such as "doll," "dog," or "Mommy." They are closely associated with the child's actions at the moment and may have broad meaning. For example, "dog" may mean that the child wants the dog or that he wants the listener to look at the dog. Or he may see a bone or toy belonging to the dog and merely be commenting that it is the dog's. As the child begins to put two words together at 18 or 20 months, the linguist can begin to analyze the structure or grammar and the semantic (meaning) relationships of his language (Mussen, Conger, and Kagan 1969). Children's mastery of certain fundamental grammatical and semantic rules by the age of 3 or 4 represents an extraordinary intellectual accomplishment. These basic rules are used by the child to generate new and more complex language.

Suppose a child comes in from the yard and says, "I digged a hole," or comes back from a drive in the country and says, "We saw some sheeps and oxes." In saying digged, sheeps, and oxes, he produced words that are not actual utterances in English. We can be fairly sure, therefore, that he has not heard these from anyone and so is not simply imitating. As long as a child speaks correctly he may only be producing utterances he has heard. We cannot, after all, keep track of every morpheme, word, and sentence a child has had a chance to learn to imitate. When he speaks incorrectly or unlawfully he is not likely to be imitating.

In the case of such unlawful utterances as digged and sheeps, we are, in addition, able to guess the source of the creations. They seem to be overgeneralizations of the regular forms of the past and the plural. As it happens, English verbs and nouns do not all follow the regular inflectional paradigms. By treating irregulars as if they were regulars, the child exposes the inductive operations of his mind and reveals to us his possession of a productive formula. (Brown 1965:297)

Brown (1973) supports the claim of invariant sequence in the child's acquisition of language. What determines the order of language acquisition is cumulative complexity, both semantic (meaning) and grammatical (structure), in the system. Variation in the ways families interact *and* variation in general intelligence influence only the *rate* of language progression, not the sequence. For example, some parents restrict their child's language development by oversimplification or engaging in baby talk long after the child has outgrown a need for it. Watts (1948:34) described such an incident. When a small child was told in a public place to look at the "bow-wow," the child replied, "Don't say 'bow-wow,' Mother; people will think you can't say dog."

Piaget (1926) also has long held that intelligent behavior develops through *invariant* stages (see Chapter 7). He sees logic and language as related processes in which language is the expressive vehicle for logic. He has theorized the existence of three stages between the ages of 4 and 7. In the first stage, genuine interchanges are absent because the child is primarily egocentric; he is lacking an intent to communicate with others. Language activity during this stage is related to parallel play. The child talks and plays by himself without any primary intent to communicate with those nearby. If a peer of like stage happens to overhear, he may appear to hear, but his response is unrelated to the original child's comments. In stage two, children interact on common activities but not on conversational topics. They operate on the same concrete materials and engage in primitive arguments. In stage three, there is genuine interchange of information. Arguments are supported with logic and explanation.

INNATE CAPACITY FOR LANGUAGE LEARNING

For a decade linguists and psychologists have debated the issue of whether or not children are born with an ability to learn language. Scholars are taking hard-line positions in favor of the existence of general innate capacities for acquiring learning principles which may be brought to bear in mastering language.

The child must bring to the language-learning situation some amount of intrinsic structure. This structure may take the form of general learning principles or it may take the form of relatively detailed and language-specific information about the kind of grammatical system that underlies natural languages. But what cannot be denied is that any organism that extrapolates from its experience does so on the basis of principles that are not themselves supplied by its experience. (Fodor 1966:106).

The emphasis currently being directed toward intrinsic structure of language and innate abilities of children does not rule out the existence of experiential factors in language learning. No one is born talking. Language is learned through many rich associations with speakers of the language. The child must be exposed to fluent speakers. The language and dialect he learns will be the language and dialect of the significant adults in his life, usually his parents. Either-or arguments can be dismissed with confidence.

On the one hand, it is inconceivable that the child's data (experiences) contribute no linguistic information, for this would mean that all such information is intrinsic. On the other hand, it seems that the data cannot contribute all the relevant information, for this would be logically incompatible with the fact that the child eventually learns to deal with utterances of sentences he has not previously encountered. It appears that the theory we want must lie somewhere between the two. (Fodor 1966:107)

The course of language development is similar for all children. One of the most remarkable findings from research on language development is that children in all cultures representing many language groups pass through similar stages in learning their native language. All children, whatever their unique group, appear to have their own built-in sets of subconscious but similar strategies for mastering language, thus suggesting the existence of *language* universals. Language universals refer to certain underlying properties that are common to all languages and that make it possible for all children to learn language in a similar manner. Of course, languages differ from each other in a multitude of obvious surface ways. However, underlying these differences are such universal elements as the organization of each particular language according to basic rules of sound and the existence of grammatical elements that make it possible to form words, phrases, and sentences.

As a result of his studies of children, Lenneberg (1964) concurs with the idea of man's biological·propensity to acquire language and offers four specific arguments in support of this position: (1) the existence of relationships between verbal behavior and sensory and cognitive counterparts; (2) the existence of an extremely regular sequence of events in the acquisition of speech, such as principles of semantics and syntax, which is unaffected by cultural or linguistic variations; (3) the existence of remarkable human abilities to learn language in the face of dramatic handicaps such as congenital blindness, deafness, and criminal neglect; and (4) the presumption that language cannot be taught to subhuman forms.

ENVIRONMENTAL FACTORS IN LANGUAGE DEVELOPMENT

Although powerful innate potential is present and necessary in language development, this potential is made functional by conditions of nurture. The child must live in an environment that is relatively rich in objects to explore and in the presence of adults who talk to him and support his language efforts. All languages appear to be essentially equivalent in complexity of structure and in potential for generating logical thought. It does not necessarily follow that conditions of nurture are equal in all cultures or subcultures characterized by a particular language or dialect. Thus, the realization of equivalent levels of thought across language and dialect groups or geographical regions is partly bound to opportunity and income.

Imitation

Until recently, writers were almost unanimous in stressing the role of imitation and the power of experience in language learning. McCarthy (1954) concluded that linguistic development during the second year of life is dependent largely upon imitation, citing as evidence that the congenitally deaf child does not learn to speak at all because he is deprived of opportunity for imitation. However compelling and logical the argument, imitation is not the total answer to language learning. Cazden et al. (1972) point out that "children use the language they hear as examples to learn from, not as samples of language to learn." Lenneberg puts it this way:

Children . . . can repeat correctly only that which is formed by rules they have already mastered. This is the best indication that language does not come about by simple imitation, but that the child abstracts regularities or relations from the language he hears, which he then applies to building up language for himself as an apparatus of principles. (1969:638)

The stages of language that children pass through are remarkably similar from child to child, but the grammar that emerges in each is strikingly different from adult grammar.

For example, while children are learning to form noun and verb endings, at a certain period in their development they will say *foots* instead of *feet, goed* instead of *went*. Children do not hear *foots* or *goed*. These words are overgeneralizations of rules which each child is somehow extracting from the language he hears. (Cazden et al. 1972:154)

All this does not mean that children never imitate language in the learning process. The importance of imitation in language development cannot be denied, for the child learns to speak precisely the language and dialect of those closest to him. The speech patterns of children from disadvantaged economic or cultural environments are those of their parents, despite constant exposure to standard English on television and at school. The child's choice of *speech sounds* to express meaning as well as his *vocabulary* is the result of imitation. But essentially, the child discovers for himself the meaningful patterns or rules underlying language. In the main, these rules are unconscious and unstated. The child builds from his language models to generate rules that are not furnished by those models. The lawful rules or basic structure of a language are not possible utterances in the language. Imitation, then, is not a complete answer to language learning, for the behavior to be learned is not modeled. Similarly, language rules or base forms of language are not uttered by children and, consequently, are not available for selective reinforcement by the parents. Therefore, the traditional approaches of psychologists, providing opportunities for imitation and then using reinforcement, are of no *direct* value in the development of base structures for language learning. Yet these factors do indeed play an important role in promoting the *production* of verbal utterances for which children somehow generate inherent rules and extrapolate more complex language.

Reinforcement

Another mistaken view concerning how children acquire language is that adults mold the child's speech by correcting wrong responses and reinforcing right responses. A number of experiments in natural settings have shown that neither correcting nor reinforcing takes place with sufficient frequency or consistency to be a potent force in language learning. Brown and Hanlon (1970) studied two kinds of adult responses to child language: approval and disapproval. Parents generally paid no attention to nonstandard syntax or to the grammaticalness of the utterance and did not seem to be aware of it. What parents did approve or disapprove about the utterance was the truth of the statement the parents thought the child was intending to make. Brown (1973) deduced from inquiry and observation that parents generally correct not faulty syntax but "naughty" words and the tendency on the part of the child to regularize irregular allomorphs, such as *digged* and *goed*. "But syntax—the child saying, for instance, 'Why the dog won't eat?' instead of 'Why won't the dog eat?'—seems to be automatically set right in the parent's mind with the mistake never registering as such" (Brown 1973:412). Since approval and disapproval are not applied directly and systematically to the consequence in question, improved syntax, one can state only that there are no selective pressures operating on children to bring their speech in line with adult models. It is important to note that this says nothing about deliberate teacher influences or the possible consequences of using systematic behavior modification procedures.

Parent and Sibling Influences on Language Development

The language interaction between mothers and children plays an important role in language learning. In addition to correcting socially inappropriate words and erroneous statements, the mother clarifies word meanings and provides information for the child about his activities and concerns. Gordon (1973) found a significant relation between maternal language behavior and the development of abstract concepts. Both the number of different words and the number of interrogatory sentences mothers used with their 2-year-olds during regular five-minute free play times was significantly related to the children's performance on the Stanford-Binet at age 3 and at age 4. Gordon (1973) also demonstrated that mothers can be taught to increase their amount of verbal and instructional interaction with their infants and young children. The emphasis, however, must be on *inter*action: talking *at* the child, without attending to his responses, was found to be negatively related to his development as measured by the Bayley scores.

The matter of sequence and complexity of language is also involved in promoting language development.

Mothers do use simpler language with young children than with other adults, and as the child's utterances become longer and more complex, so do the mother's. Other than this simplification, there is no sequencing of what the child has to learn. He is offered a cafeteria, not a carefully prescribed diet. And seemingly impelled from within, he participates in the give-and-take of conversation with adults and other children as best he can from the very beginning, and in the process takes what he needs to construct his own language system. (Cazden et al. 1972:155)

Children also teach each other. Older siblings sometimes spend several minutes correcting the pronunciation of a younger sibling until he gets it "right." An intriguing study by Shatz and Gelman (1973) showed that 4-year-olds adjust their speech to the age of their listeners. These adjustments occurred in both task-oriented and spontaneous situations and were independent of whether the speaker had a sibling or was talking to a sibling. Peer-directed speech resembled adult-directed speech. However, speech directed to 2-year-olds contained shorter utterances and fewer coordinate constructions, subordinate conjunctions, and certain forms of predicate complements. They also used more words to attract or sustain attention.

Language development can be enhanced by training and practice. In Russian studies (Mallitskaya 1960), babies of 9–10 months were oriented to objects and had the objects named. The procedure was then repeated. For example, the infant was given a ball and was told to perform different activities with it such as throw it, kick it, and so on. In this way, the babies learned to comprehend new words. Weir (1962) studied crib language and found that children practice to improve their linguistic ability. They correct their own pronunciation, drill themselves on sounds, and practice using words in sentences. A wide range of experimental studies of early childhood programs enrolling children from low socioeconomic groups (American Institutes for Research 1968; Bissell 1970) have shown that specific and systematic language training measures can make a positive difference in language development.

DIFFERENCES IN LANGUAGE SYSTEMS

Throughout U.S. history, immigrants have brought foreign languages to this country. Most immigrant parents promote English from the beginning, so that by the age of school entry their children are speaking English. The decline of their native languages is particularly rapid for families from European and other countries separated from the United States by vast distances and geographical barriers. This is not the case for Mexican-Americans of the Southwest who retain ties to Spanish-speaking Mexico or for Puerto Ricans on the East coast with ties to the island, nor is it true for certain isolated Indian groups living on reservations. For many of these children English is a second language and is taught as such in the schools. Educators are currently grappling with this situation with varied degrees of success. Teaching is further complicated by the existence of nonstandard dialects. The process of "educating" teachers usually rules out their speaking these dialects, even though they themselves may have used a dialect during childhood. Basically, according to Cazden et al. (1972:158), dialects differ from standard English only in a few rules: "the marking of the objective case in pronouns, agreement between third singular subject and verb, irregular forms of the perfect, the comparative and adverbial -ly, a few conjunctions, and such well-known markers as ain't." However, certain regional dialects, such as those of rural New England, Appalachia, and areas of the South, differ markedly from standard English. For example,

Southern dialects freely employ negative inversion for emphasis: *Didn't anybody see it* may be a question in the north. There are also deeper social differences in the south than elsewhere: *Ain't nobody see it* is the most nonstandard equivalent of the form just given. Most teachers in these areas come from the same region, and have an intuitive grasp of these grammatical forms, though not necessarily a full enough understanding to teach the contrasting sets of rules to children. (Cazden et al. 1972:158)

The nonstandard form of black English is relatively uniform wherever blacks are concentrated in northern cities or the rural South. When blacks and others who speak nonstandard English move out of their native areas, they find that their speech is regarded as substandard and deficient, a condition that results in social rejection as well. According to Labov, the dialect is a well-formed, sophisticated, complete system for communication.

The concept of verbal deprivation has no basis in social reality: in fact, Negro children in the urban ghettos receive a great deal of verbal stimulation, hear more well-formed sentences than middle-class children, and participate fully in a highly verbal culture; they have the same basic vocabulary, possess the same capacity for conceptual learning, and use the same logic as anyone else who learns to speak and understand English. (1969:1)

The work of Labov and other prominent linguists such as Stewart, Shuy, Baratz, and Cazden is intriguing and invaluable because of its potential effects on modifying attitudes and social and educational practices directed toward speakers of nonstandard dialects. It should be pointed out, however, that some prominent psychologists do not accept completely the conclusion of Labov. For example, Bruner and Greenfield (1969; Bruner 1971) agree that no human language can be shown to be more sophisticated than any other. But they do not accept the view that every language is equally powerful for organizing thought. Also, the relatively close association of nonstandard dialect with poverty adds a critical variable of environment to influence the use of language and thinking that will serve the child in the larger society.

The culture of poverty and the conditions of life that it creates as well as the expectations it generates in parents and children, has the effect of leading some to use the instrument of language analytically and reflectively, while others are not so affected. The result of a failure to so use language is that it makes it difficult for the child to take advantage of the usual forms of thought and discourse employed in school settings. In effect, where the child, by background, has been kept from developing a typical middle-class analytical style, he is slowly but surely excluded from schooling and thereby excluded from access to the powerful tools of the technology and of the mainstream culture. (Bruner 1971:104)

Teaching Speakers of Nonstandard Dialect

The arguments concerning proper teaching for speakers of nonstandard dialect are volatile and limited to incomplete evidence. One extreme says that teachers should ignore substandard dialect or treat it as inferior and useless for learning. The other extreme says that teaching should be exclusively in the dialect of the child. Some regard substandard dialect as evidence of mental inferiority, while others contend that all dialects are equally powerful for logical thought. In the strictest sense, there is no "standard" dialect. Even standard English is governed by arbitrary rules, developed over generations and drawn from many languages and cultures over decades of development. From a linguistic point of view, standard English is no better than any other variety of English. Language is a tool for communicating thoughts, feelings, and emotions. In some contexts, one variety of English is more effective than others. For example, an individual with a well-formed Boston dialect would likely be less effective than a native dialect speaker in rural Appalachia. In respect to communicating in a highly technical context, or in communicating in a variety of geographical regions, standard English is more likely to have wider utility. It is for this reason that schools promote the expansion of the nonstandard dialect speaker's language to include standard English. In contemporary programs, there must be no explicit actions on the part of teachers that suggest inferiority of the native dialect or language. In actual practice, many well-meaning but misinformed teachers do indeed reject children in implicit (correcting their speech) and explicit ways ("fining" children for "improper" language). In the main, however, the theoretical if not always practical view has been to *take children where they are* and *build on what they bring to school*. Teachers and parents alike tend to reject artificiality in either extreme. Existing language should be accepted and used. Children are not to be taught a second dialect in the highly structured methods used to teach a second language to adults. Neither are teachers to employ nonstandard dialect as a primary teaching method. In response to a Ford Foundation grant for the above purpose, the NAACP described the project as a "cruel hoax" which could harm generations of blacks. Whether or not children should be taught standard English in order to participate fully in the technologically oriented mainstream society is indeed a value judgment. Moreover, it is becoming increasingly clear in this early phase of the energy shortage that not all values of the mainstream society—material overabundance, for example—are worth pursuing. Nonetheless, a decision not to participate in the mode of the mainstream would have its effect as well.

Less technical societies do not produce so much symbolic embedding or so many ways of looking and thinking. Whether one wishes to judge these differences on some universal human scale as favoring industrial man is a matter of one's values. But, however one judges, let it be clear that a decision *not to* intervene in the intellectual development of those who live in less technically developed societies cannot be based on the careless claim that it makes little difference. (Bruner and Greenfield 1969)

INTERRELATIONSHIPS BETWEEN LANGUAGES AND THINKING

Through living richly in the presence of people and objects, the developing child accumulates the raw materials, or schemata, of thinking: percepts, images, memories, and concepts. The *manipulation* of these raw materials is called thinking. The child's *ability* to think is called intelligence. Intellectual activities, or thinking processes, include perceptual thinking, associative thinking, inductive thinking, problem-solving, critical thinking, and creative thinking. Language is used in all the activities normally associated with intelligent behavior and the vehicle for expressing it. The close relationship between language and thinking suggests that conditions which facilitate the growth of either are essential for the growth of both. However, Piaget (Piaget and Inhelder 1969:90) raises controversy as to whether all types of thought are essentially linguistic or nonlinguistic in nature. He cites evidence that "language does not constitute the source of logic but is, on the contrary, structured by it. The roots of logic are to be sought in the general coordination of actions (including verbal behavior) beginning with the sensori-motor level (infancy)." The child's mental structures in infancy, his sensorimotor schemes, are elaborated through his operations on his environment. This developing schematism continues to develop and structure thought throughout early childhood. As children grow beyond the sensorimotor period, language liberates thought from immediate space and time and allows it to range over vast stretches. Language is not an invention of the child. It is, rather, an instrument of thought based on the child's sensory schemes and actions. With the emergence of representative thought, thought aided by language, language plays an ever-increasing role in the formation of mental schema. It becomes completely an instrument or tool of thought. Yet "neither imitation nor play nor drawing nor image nor language nor even memory . . . can develop or be organized without the constant help of the structuration characteristics of intellect" (Piaget and Inhelder 1969:91).

We turn next to the development of intelligent, thoughtful behavior in young children by sampling the comprehensive work of Piaget.

SUMMARY AND CONCLUSIONS

Language is an instrument of thought based on the child's sensory schemes and actions. Children have an innate capacity for language learning. Although the *rate* of language acquisition varies from child to child, all children acquire language in the same basic sequence of development. Experiential factors play some part in language development; that is, the child must live in an environment that is relatively rich in objects to explore and in the presence of adults who talk to him and who support his language efforts. Imitation and reinforcement are of value in promoting the production of utterances but are of no direct value in the development of base structures for language learning.

Specific language training measures can have a positive effect on language development, but whatever the approach used, differences in language systems must be taken into account. Children learning English as a second language and children speaking nonstandard dialects should be approached in positive ways that support the strengths of the system they bring to school. As language programs are developed, the teacher selects activities that promote thinking behavior, thus capitalizing on the close relationship between language and thinking.

SUGGESTED ACTIVITIES

1. Observe several children between the ages of 3 and 6. Tape record each of them as they play or as they engage in a conversation with someone. By playing back the recordings, identify as many specific points as possible to describe

each child's stage of language development. Consider such things as number of utterances, length of utterances, nature of the vocalizations, intonation, inflection, presence of full sentences, types of sentences, egocentric or socialized speech, signs of comprehension, types of grammar, different parts of speech, and so on.

2. Repeat the procedure described above at a later date using the same children. Look for changes and growth in their language.

3. Explain the current position of linguists on standard versus nonstandard English. Discuss the implications of this position for classroom teaching of children who speak nonstandard English. Translate those implications into examples of actual language teaching.

4. Visit several different programs for young children in your community. Observe the variety of ways that language development is enhanced in each of these programs.

REFERENCES

American Institutes for Research. 1968. *A Study of Selected Exemplary Programs for the Education of Disadvantaged Children.* Palo Alto, Calif.: The Institutes.

Bissell, J. S. 1970. "The Cognitive Effects of Preschool Programs for Disadvantaged Children," unpublished doctoral dissertation, Harvard University. Summary reprinted in J. L. Frost (ed.), *Revisiting Early Childhood Education.* New York: Holt, Rinehart and Winston, 1973.

Brown, R. 1973. *A First Language.* Cambridge, Mass.: Harvard University Press.

Brown, R. 1965. *Social Psychology.* New York: Free Press.

Brown, R., and C. Fraser. 1964. "The Acquisition of Syntax," in U. Bellugi and R. Brown (eds.), "The Acquisition of Language," *Monographs of the Society for Research in Child Development,* 29(1): 43–79.

Brown, R., and C. Hanlon. 1970. "Derivational Complexity and Order of Acquisition in Child Speech," in J. R. Hayes (ed.), *Cognition and the Development of Language.* New York: Wiley, pp. 155–207.

Bruner, J. S. 1971. "Overview on Development and Day Care," in E. H. Grotberg (ed.), *Day Care: Resources for Decisions.* Washington, D.C.: Office of Economic Opportunity, Government Printing Office.

Bruner, J. S., and P. M. Greenfield. 1969. "Language and Learning: Work with the Wolof," in D. A. Goslin (ed.), *Handbook of Socialization Theory and Research.* Skokie, Ill.: Rand McNally.

Carroll. J. B. 1970. "Language Acquisition, Bilingualism, and Language Change," *Encyclopedia of Educational Research.* New York: Macmillan.

Cazden, C. B., J. C. Baratz, W. Labov, and F. H. Palmer. 1972. "Language Development in Day Care Programs," in *Day Care: Resources for Decisions.* Washington, D.C.: Office of Economic Opportunity, Government Printing Office.

Chomsky, N. 1968. *Language and Mind.* New York: Harcourt Brace Jovanovich.

Chomsky, N. 1957. *Syntactic Structures.* The Hague: Mouton.

Fodor, J. A. 1966. "How To Learn To Talk: Some Simple Ways," in F. Smith and G. A. Miller (eds.), *The Genesis of Language*. Cambridge, Mass.: M.I.T. Press.

Gordon, I. 1973. *An Early Intervention Project: A Longitudinal Look*. Gainesville, Fla.: Institute for Development of Human Resources, University of Florida.

Hildreth, G. H. 1954. "Interrelationships Between Written Expression and the Other Language Arts," in *Interrelationships Among the Language Arts*. Research Bulletin of the National Conference on Research in English, pp. 4–12.

Hughes, V. E. 1953. "A Study of the Relationships Among Selected Language Abilities," *Journal of Educational Research*, 47:97–105.

Labov, W. 1969. "The Logic of Nonstandard English," paper presented at the Twentieth Annual Round Table Meeting on Linguistics and Language Studies, Washington, D.C.

Lefevre, C. A. 1965. "The Contributions of Linguistics," *The Instructor*, 64:103–104.

Lenneberg, E. H. 1969. "On Explaining Language," *Science* (May), 164:635–643.

Lenneberg, E. H. 1964. "A Biological Perspective of Language," in E. H. Lenneberg (ed.), *New Directions in the Study of Language*. Cambridge, Mass.: M.I.T. Press, pp. 65–88.

Loban, W. D. 1963. *The Language of Elementary School Children*. Champaign: Ill.: National Council of Teachers of English.

Mallitskaya, M. K. 1960. "A Method for Using Pictures To Develop Speech Comprehension in Children at the End of the First and Second Year of Life," *Voprosy Psikhol*, 3:122–126.

McCarthy, D. 1954. "Language Development in Children," in L. Carmichael (ed.), *Manual of Child Psychology*, 2d ed. New York: Wiley.

McNeill, D. 1966. "The Creation of Language," *Discovery*, 27(7):34–38.

Mussen, P. H., J. J. Conger, and J. Kagan. 1969. *Child Development and Personality*. New York: Harper & Row.

Piaget, J. 1926. *The Language and Thought of the Child*. New York: Harcourt, Brace.

Piaget, J., and B. Inhelder. 1969. *The Psychology of the Child*. New York: Basic Books.

Shatz, M., and R. Gelman. 1973. "The Development of Communication Skills in the Speech of Young Children as a Function of Listening," *Monographs of the Society for Research in Child Development*, 38(5).

Skinner, B. F. 1953. *Science and Human Behavior*. New York: Macmillan.

Smith, F., and G. A. Miller (eds.). 1966. *The Genesis of Language*. Cambridge, Mass.: M.I.T. Press.

Smith, M. E. 1926. "An Investigation of the Development of the Sentence and the Extent of Vocabulary in Young Children," *Student Child Welfare*, University of Iowa, 3(5).

Smith, M. K. 1941. "Measurement of the Size of General English Vocabulary through the Elementary Grades and High School," *Genetic Psychology Monographs*, 24:311–345.

Watts, A. F. 1948. *The Language and Mental Development of Children*. Boston: Heath.

Weir, R. H. 1962. *Language in the Crib*. The Hague: Mouton.

FURTHER READING

Bates, E. "Pragmatics and Sociolinguistics in Child Language," in D. Morehead and A. Morehead (eds.), *Language Deficiency in Children*. Boulder, Colo.: University Park Press, in press.

Blank, M. "Cognitive Function of Language in the Preschool Years," *Developmental Psychology*, 1974, 10:279–362.

Bloom, L. "Language Development Review," *Review of Child Development Series*. Chicago: University of Chicago Press (Society for Research in Child Development), 1975.

Cazden, C. B. (ed.). *Language in Early Childhood Education*. Washington, D.C.: National Association for the Education of Young Children, 1972.

Cazden, C. B., V. P. John, and D. Hymes (eds.). *Functions of Language in the Classroom*. New York: Teachers College Press, 1972.

Chukovsky, K. *From Two to Five*. Berkeley: University of California Press, 1963.

Dale, P. *Language Development: Structure and Function*. Hinsdale, Ill.: Dryden Press, 1972.

Frost, J. L. (ed.). *Early Childhood Education Rediscovered*. New York: Holt, Rinehart and Winston, 1973, Part 7.

Frost, J. L., and J. Thrift. "Language Development in Children," in P. Lamb (ed.), *Guiding Children's Language Learning*, 3d ed. Dubuque, Iowa: William C. Brown, in press.

Keenan, E. O. "Conversational Competence in Children," *Journal of Child Language*, 1974, 1:163–183.

Lapp, D., and R. D. Fram. "The Neglected I," *Elementary English*, 1975, 52:45–48.

Rosen, C., and H. Rosen. *The Language of Primary School Children*. Baltimore, Md.: Penguin Books, 1973.

Slobin, D. I. *Psycholinguistics*. Glenview, Ill.: Scott, Foresman, 1971.

Tough, J. *Talking Thinking Growing*. New York: Schocken Books, 1974.

Jean Piaget, 1896–
The Bettmann Archive

Cognitive Development in Young Children: Jean Piaget

In the last few years, the work of Jean Piaget has had a powerful impact on early childhood education around the world, particularly in the United States. His brilliant observations of thinking strategies provide the most comprehensive framework available for understanding the cognitive, or intellectual, development of the young child.

Piaget was born in Neuchâtel, Switzerland, on August 9, 1896. He was a precocious child, showing an unusually high degree of intellectual interest at an early age. His first paper, which concerned an albino sparrow he had seen in the park, was published when he was 10 years old. Piaget's early interests and studies were in the biological sciences. After receiving his doctorate at the University of Neuchâtel in 1918, he directed his study toward psychology, philosophy, and logic. This led to his association with Theophile Simon, who had earlier developed the intelligence test with the French psychologist Alfred Binet. Piaget accepted a position at the Binet Laboratory in Paris, standardizing some reasoning tests from the Binet scale in French. While working in this capacity, Piaget became intrigued with the incorrect responses of the children he worked with. He began to study the nature of the child's responses and the thought processes the child used in responding. This interest resulted in a series of publications and, ultimately, led to his life's work. In 1921, Piaget accepted the position of Director of Research at the Institute of Jean-Jacques Rousseau in Geneva and, later, became its Co-director. Students from all over the world have studied with him. He has been a prolific writer in the field of child psychology in his lifetime. Now in his seventies, Piaget continues to conduct research and add to his theory of intellectual development. Unquestionably, he is the foremost contributor to the study of cognitive development.

THE CLINICAL METHOD

Piaget devised an unstructured procedure for the study of intelligence. His procedure is directed by the child's responses and pursues the child's thinking. This method is quite different from standardized test procedure where the wording and the order of questions are predetermined and are exact. Piaget's "clinical method" of investigation was soon criticized for its "unscientific" nature. However, increasingly sophisticated research methods have led to many replication studies that confirm Piaget's major hypotheses. After implementing his clinical method, Piaget found that relying solely on verbalization from the child was inadequate because of varying verbal abilities in children. Consequently, he later expanded his clinical method to include free manipulation of materials along with free flow of verbalization. The following "experiment," for example, is designed to reveal the child's conception of number correspondence.

Lid (age four years, four months) put four pennies opposite four flowers. Is there the same number of pennies and flowers? *Yes, they're the same.* All right, now you're going to buy some flowers. Here are your pennies (six). You must give one penny for each flower. (We exchanged six flowers for six pennies, the pennies being arranged in a row while the flowers were in his hand.) Is there the same number of flowers and pennies? *Yes, they're the same. . . . No, they're not. Here there are more* (pointing to the flowers). Could we put one flower opposite each penny? *No, there are too many flowers* (he tried it and found that they corresponded exactly). *Yes, they're the same.* Let's begin again, shall we? (The exchange was made again, with the pennies spaced out and the flowers bunched together.) Will that be all right? *There'll be too many flowers. You'll see.* (He made the correspondence and was very much surprised at the result.) (Piaget 1965:58)

Piaget's three children were the subjects for his initial studies of the development of intellectual behavior. With the help of his wife, one of his former students, he observed his children closely during their early stages of development. He kept detailed notes on their behavior and devised experiments to test their intellectual capacities and to determine the patterns of development.

BASIC CONCEPTS IN PIAGETIAN THEORY

Piaget's work is *descriptive* in that it describes the children's intellectual development as it unfolds. In Piaget's framework, intellectual development is viewed in a wholistic, structural sense. For example, the organism inherits physical structures such as an eye and simple behavioral structures such as the reflex of sucking. Soon, these biological factors (having an eye, sucking) interact with environmental experiences (various objects to look at or to suck). The result is psychological structures on which intellectual activity is based. Each stage of the child's intellectual development from infancy to adulthood is characterized by different psychological structures. The infant, for example, uses particular organized behaviors, or actions, while the older child uses mental operations. To illustrate, the young child puts objects in his mouth. After awhile, as a result of his functioning within his environment, he learns that some objects he puts in his mouth are to suck, some are to eat, and some are not to be put in the mouth at all. The older child, in later stages of development, is able to organize his interactions with the environment by discriminating (tastes, smells, appearances), classifying (foods, non-foods), and so forth. The initial action of putting objects in the mouth emerges into increasingly more complex psychological structures. Piaget explains the nature of intelligence in this way:

Every structure is to be thought of as a particular form of equilibrium, more or less stable within its restricted field and losing its stability on reaching the limits of the field. But these structures, forming different levels, are to be regarded as succeeding one another according to a law of development, such that each one brings about a more inclusive and stable equilibrium for the processes that emerge from the preceding level. Intelligence is thus only a generic term to indicate the superior forms of organization or equilibrium of cognitive structurings. (1966:7)

The systematic changing of structures is called development. As the individual develops intelligence, his actions become progressively internalized and covert. The ultimate goal of this development is the ability to perform at the level of logical mental operations.

Piaget has termed organized behaviors *schemata.* The term "scheme" is used broadly, and it encompasses organized behaviors that are inherited (sucking scheme), organized behaviors that are learned (thumb-sucking scheme), and organized mental behaviors (categories such as food scheme). Moreover, the infant's behavioral schemata are very different from the older child's operational schemata (internalized intellectual behaviors).

Piaget believes that the idea of an *operation* is central to the understanding of the development of knowledge. Knowledge is more than a mental copy, or image, of an object or event.

To know an object is to act on it. To know is to modify, to transform the object, and to understand the way the object is constructed. An operation is thus the essence of knowledge; it is an interiorised action which modifies the object of knowledge. . . . An operation . . . is a reversible action; that is, it can take place in both directions, for instance, adding or subtracting, joining or separating. . . . Above all, an operation is never isolated. It is always linked to other operations, and as a result, it is always a part of a total structure. (Piaget 1964:8)

In Piaget's theory, structures change systematically (development), but *functions* remain invariant. Functions are methods of interacting with the environment, and they are biologically inherent. According to Piaget, the organism inherits two invariant functions: he is inclined to *organize* his structures into coherent systems that enable him to function more effectively, and he *seeks to adapt* to his environment. According to Piaget, the individual does not inherit specific intellectual responses; rather, he inherits an inclination to *organize* his structures into higher-level structures. For example, he can look at a toy, reach for it, grasp it, and shake it—separate structures organized into an effective system. The individual also inherits an inclination to *adapt* to his environment. Adaptation is accomplished through the two related processes of *assimilation* and *accommodation* (Ginsburg and Opper 1969:18–25).

Assimilation and Accommodation

The developing child does not submit passively to the objects in his world. Rather, he reacts to his environment in terms of the structures he already possesses. He deals with objects or events by incorporating them into his existing schemata or patterns of behavior. *Assimilation* is "the action of the organism on surrounding objects, insofar as this action depends on previous behavior involving the same or similar objects" (Piaget 1966:7). On the other hand, the environment acts *upon* the organism. It calls upon him to change his existing psychological structures in some way. This converse action is called *accommodation*. Surrounding stimuli do not *directly* affect the organism; rather, they operate on the organism by modifying the assimilatory cycle. Adaptation is an equilibrium between organismic actions upon the environment and vice versa, or an equilibrium between assimilation and accommodation.

Suppose Peter, a preschool child, goes to the park to play. He sees a fence with horizontal boards and decides to climb it. He tries to put his foot between the boards, as he would in climbing a ladder, but the space is not large enough. He tries to reach to the top of the fence to pull himself up, but he is neither tall enough nor strong enough. He looks around for help and sees a log nearby. After thinking a moment, he pulls the log over to the fence, climbs up on it, reaches for the top of the fence, and swings himself over to the other side.

Seen from Piaget's point of view, what has really happened in Peter's mind? The searching for alternatives and the solution to Peter's problem can be labeled *operations.* The actual (mental) subject matter, the problem of climbing the fence, is called a *schema.* Peter's unsuccessful ideas about climbing the fence can also be called a schema. He had been successful in past situations with these climbing ideas. Consequently, he *assimilated* the present problem into his previous experiences. However, his past experiences did not give him enough help. Therefore, he has had to *accommodate* himself to the new situation by finding a new solution: the use of the log as a footstool. Peter has thus *adapted* himself to the situation. He has reached a slightly higher stage of *equilibrium.* He has completed only one of a countless number of equilibration processes on the stairway to mature, logical thought. (Honstead 1968:136)

Assimilation and accommodation are called *functional invariants* because they are characteristic of all biological systems. They are complementary processes and operate simultaneously. Assimilation requires a degree of unity between the existing schemata and the new stimuli; accommodation takes place when this unity or continuity is disrupted by the interjection of unfamiliar stimuli. When this happens, the assimilatory cycle may remain disrupted or the organism may accommodate to the discontinuity, reestablishing the unity, or equilibrium. Such activity takes place whenever a teacher introduces new content into the classroom environment. She may introduce totally new content that is unfamiliar and too complex for adaptation by the existing schemata of the children, in which case they do not change. Or she may introduce content that is only slightly more difficult than previously assimilated content, and the student's cognitive structure will adapt and change. Consequently, *"education is defined as the controlled introduction of discontinuity into the educational environment of the learner"* (Frost and Rowland 1969:139).

Stage-Independent Theory

Mental development is usually explained in terms of the two principal factors of environment and heredity, and arguments regarding the relative contributions of the two are common in psychological literature. Piaget, however, assigns four general factors to mental development: *maturation, experience, social transmission,* and *equilibration.* He postulates that one of the fundamental aspects of intellectual growth is organism-environment interaction: that man plays an extremely active role in the formation of his cognitive world. In Piaget's view, development from one level of structure to another, from simply looking at a rattle, for example, to both looking at it and reaching for it, or to looking at it, reaching for it, and shaking it, is dependent upon all four general factors. Those four factors form that part of Piaget's theory termed "stage independent" (Flavell 1963:262) because they are relevant throughout all of development rather than only at certain stages of development (stage-dependent component). The stage-dependent component of Piaget's theory involves the separate stages of intellectual growth from birth to maturity. The two components are interrelated but separated for purposes of discussion.

MATURATION.   The maturation of physical structures with which the child is born, such as the brain, the central nervous system, and muscles for walking and coordination, is one factor that influences intellectual development. Certainly physical structures take time to develop fully and become organized into increasingly complex patterns of behavior. But maturation in itself is insufficient as an explanation of mental development, for the age of appearance of the different stages varies greatly. Moreover, the average age at which developmental stages appear also varies greatly from one society to another. Such great differences in rate of development cannot be totally due to maturation and must be influenced by other factors as well. "Maturation consists essentially of opening up new possibilities. The possibilities thus opened up also need to be fulfilled, and for this to occur, the maturation must be reinforced by functional exercise and a *minimum* of experience" (Piaget and Inhelder 1969:154).

EXPERIENCE.   The second fundamental factor influencing development is experience. Piaget recognizes physical, or concrete, experience as a basic factor in cognitive development. It is through direct, overt action on objects —when he has seen, tasted, heard, smelled, and handled the objects in his environment, for example—that the individual comes to know them. However, experience is also an insufficient explanation of intellectual development in itself. This explanation omits social and maturational factors. Moreover, certain concepts appearing at the beginning of the stage of concrete operations, for example, do not appear to be drawn from experience.

Let us take the conservation of the substance in the case of changing the shape of a ball of plasticene. We give this ball of plasticene to a child who changes its shape into a sausage form, and we ask him if there is the same amount of matter, that is, the same amount of substance as there was before. We also ask him if it now has the same weight and thirdly, if it now has the same volume. The volume is measured by the displacement of water when we put the ball or the sausage into a glass of water. The findings, which have been the same every time this experiment has been done, show us that first of all, there is conservation of the amount of substance. At about eight years, a child will say, "There is the same amount of plasticene." Only later does the child assert that the weight is conserved and still later that the volume is conserved. So, I would ask you where the idea of the conservation of substance can come from. (Piaget 1964:11)

Piaget rejects the notion that either experiment or experience shows the child that there is the same amount of substance. Weighing the ball could lead to the conservation of weight. Immersing it in water could lead to the conservation of volume. But conservation of substance is attained before either the conservation of weight or the conservation of volume. Piaget explains this phenomenon as a *logical necessity* "for something to be conserved even though no experience can have led to this notion."

Piaget has identified two types of mental experience that result from direct involvement with objects, *physical* and *logico-mathematical experience*. Physical experience consists of actions upon objects that draw out their physical properties such as size, color, and weight from the objects themselves. The child discovers that this block is heavier than that toy from his direct play and handling of the toy and block. Logico-mathematical experience consists of internally combining the results of the individual's actions upon objects rather than simply recognizing physical characteristics from the objects themselves. For example, the child places a group of marbles in a circle, counts them, and finds that there is a total of 10. Next, he rearranges the marbles into a row, recounts them, and again finds that there are 10 marbles. The child discovers that the sum of a group of objects is independent of their spatial order. He did not discover a property of marbles such as roundness or color, but discovered a property of the action of ordering.

SOCIAL TRANSMISSION.   The third major factor in mental development is social transmission, linguistic or educational. This factor alone is also insufficient to explain development because the child must be in a state for understanding information before it is useful. He must have the appropriate mental structure in order to assimilate information. For this reason, we do not teach highly advanced concepts to young children. Only when the child has firm control of logical structures that he has constructed for himself through his own actions and experience can he succeed in understanding more advanced linguistic expressions.

EQUILIBRATION.   The fourth factor in mental development is equilibration. Piaget calls this "the fundamental one," since this factor balances or regulates the other three. In the process of coming to know, the individual is *active* and thus is exposed to external disturbances in his environment. He makes compensatory reactions toward these disturbances because he tends toward equilibrium, toward a balance between his present structures and what he experiences in his environment. The process through which structures change from one level to another, then, is called equilibration. But equilibrium itself is only a goal of equilibration, or the process of structure changing, since only a state of relative equilibrium is ever reached. The result of this state is greater mental clarity, but this increased clarity only leads to even further disturbance. Consequently, in the equilibration process, the organism constantly progresses toward higher levels of equilibrium. In the movement from level to level, it is not possible to reach a second level unless equilibrium has been reached at the first, or lower, level.

Dynamic equilibrium appears to have biological significance in that the organism has an innate need to explore, to adapt, to achieve ever-increasing complexity of equilibrium. The more an individual learns, the more he wants to learn. It would follow that dynamic equilibrium is best understood as a state of being in which the organism is more comfortable and operating at peak efficiency. In such a state there would be few pressures introduced, as in teaching, that the individual could not handle by drawing upon the behaviors already mastered. In other words, the introduction of discontinuity would be controlled and matched to the learner's present state.

Stage-Dependent Theory

The stage-dependent portion of Piagetian theory is concerned with the developmental progression of intelligent behavior from birth through adolescence. Piaget has specified four broad stages of development: (1) a sensorimotor stage; (2) a preoperational stage; (3) a stage of concrete operations; and ultimately (4) a stage of formal operations. These four stages are in turn divided into substages or phases. The *sensorimotor* period begins at birth and lasts until the child is about 18 months to 2 years of age. Table 7-1 illustrates the multidimensional nature of development during this period. There are six substages within the sensorimotor period. From about 2 years to about 7 years, a *preoperational* period holds sway, a period of preparation for concrete operations. There are two phases within this period: the *preconceptual phase* (2–4 or 5 years) and the *intuitive phase* (4–7 years). The attainment of *concrete operations* occurs between 7 and 11 years. The final stage is that of *formal operations*, which occurs at about age 11 or 12 and extends into adulthood. Division of the child's development into stages and substages is possible because of the integration of structures into increasingly more complex ones.

The first property of a stage is reality, which means that certain patterns of behavior tend to cluster and that there are qualitative differences between behavioral clusters. The reality of stages makes them susceptible to analysis. The second property is that of invariance, meaning that there exists a constant, ontogenetic sequence in development that is only tangentially related to the chronological age of the subject. The unfolding of stages may be characterized by accelerations or retardations, but their sequence is constant. One does not enter the formal operations stage, for example, until he has achieved the mental structures characteristic of the concrete operations stage. Moreover, the transition from one stage to the next is gradual. It occurs over a long period of time, and the child exhibits different patterns of behavior along the way. A third property is an overall integrative structure through which the stages tend to be integrative and noninterchangeable. Each stage results from the preceding one, and each is incorporated into later stages. Finally, there appears to be a period of preparation for each new stage, characterized by the forming and organization of the structures of that particular period. This period may be considered a phase of achievement during which the structures appear to be organized, behavior tends to be relatively stable (dynamic equilibrium), and, consequently, behavior is open to assessment and prediction.

SENSORIMOTOR INTELLIGENCE

Substage 1

Immediately after birth, only hereditary structures such as reflexes are apparent. The infant grasps objects placed in his hand, the grasping reflex. He sucks when objects touch his lips, the sucking reflex. He makes responses to light and to sound. This is not an unimportant period, for the brain is growing rapidly. The bases for later, elaborate mental schemata are being formed through the consolidation of "reflex exercises." The infant needs to use the structures he has. This need is termed *functional assimilation*. As he uses his structures—the mouth, for example, in developing a scheme such as sucking behavior—he uses the scheme on many objects, not just one. This is referred to as *generalizing assimilation*. Soon he is able to distinguish one object from another to use in his schemata, and this is called *recognitory assimilation*. "The reproductive or functional assimilation that accounts for this exercise also gives rise to a generalizing assimilation (sucking on nothing between meals or sucking new objects) and a recognitive assimilation (distinguishing the nipple from other objects)" (Piaget and Inhelder 1969:7).

Substage 2

The exercise of reflex patterns during the first substage emerges into the development of first habits in the second substage. Beginning about the second month, the cumulative effects of practice result in the formation of first habits. J. M. Baldwin (in Piaget 1966:101) defines these as "the active reproduction of a result at first obtained by chance." Since the chance action —such as getting a finger in his mouth—interested the infant, he attempts to repeat it. When the behavior is repeated again and again for its interesting results, it has become habit. Since movements in this substage are centered on the infant's body rather than on external objects, they are referred to as primary circular reactions.

Substage 3

Between 4 and 8 months, a transition between simple habit and intelligence is reached. By this time, primary circular reactions have been acquired. The child becomes more mobile and, as a result, his interaction extends from his own body into the environment. His circular reactions are termed secondary,

TABLE 7-1   Multidimensional View of Development During the Sensorimotor Period

Developmental Unit	Intention and Means-Ends Relations	Meaning	Object Performance	Space	Time	Causality	Imitation	Play
Exercising the Ready-made Sensorimotor Schemata (0–1 mo.)								
Primary Circular Reactions (1–4 mo.)		Different responses to different objects					Pseudo-imitation begins	Apparent functional autonomy of some responses
Secondary Circular Reactions (4–8 mo.)	Acts upon objects	"Motor meaning"	Brief single-modality search for absent object	All modalities focus on single object	Brief search for absent object	Acts; then waits for effects to occur	Pseudo-imitation quicker, more precise	More responses done for their own sake
Coordination of Secondary Schemata (8–12 mo.)	Attacks barrier to reach goal	Symbolic meaning	Prolonged, multi-modality search	Turns bottle to reach nipple	Prolonged search for absent object	Attacks barrier to reach goal; waits for adults to serve him	True imitation—i.e., of novel response	Means often become ends; ritualization begins

Developmental Unit	Intention and Means-Ends Relations	Meaning	Object Performance	Space	Time	Causality	Imitation	Play
Tertiary Circular Reactions (12–18 mo.)	"Experiments in order to see"; discovery of new means through "groping accommodation"	Elaboration through action and feedback	Follows sequential displacements if object in sight	Follows sequential displacements if object in sight	Follows sequential displacements if object in sight	Discovers new means; solicits help from adults	True imitation quicker, more precise	Quicker conversion of means to end; elaboration of ritualization
Invention of New Means Through Mental Combinations (18–24 mo.)	Invention of new means through reciprocal assimilation of schemata	Further elaboration; symbols increasingly covert	Follows sequential displacement with object hidden; symbolic representation of object, mostly internal	Solves detour problem; symbolic representation of spatial relationships, mostly internal	Both anticipation and memory	Infers causes from observing effects; predicts effects from observing causes	Imitates: 1. complex, 2. non-human, 3. absent models	Treats inadequate stimuli as if adequate to imitate an enactment—i.e., symbolic ritualization, or "pretending"

From *The Origins of Intellect: Piaget's Theory*, 2d ed., by John L. Phillips, Jr. W. H. Freeman and Company, San Francisco, Calif. Copyright © 1975. Reproduced by permission.

since he now repeats actions on *objects* for the interesting results they evoke. The child is beginning to distinguish between ends and means. The ends are generally discovered accidentally, but he applies the same means to similar situations. For example, having perceived that grasping a cord attached to a rattle produces a certain effect, the child reproduces that motion "when you swing an object from a pole two yards from the crib" (Piaget and Inhelder 1969:10).

Substage 4

The period between about 8 and 12 months is characterized by more advanced acts of intelligence. Refinements in each of the previous substages lead to further development of the separation of means and ends. The child has the end result in mind right from the beginning, and true intention appears for the first time. During this substage also, the child will now pursue and obtain an object that has disappeared after being placed out of reach or hidden under a pillow. Thus, he has acquired the concepts of object permanence and the construction of space. Symbolic meaning comes into play, since the child now begins to distinguish objects on the basis of their sound alone. New objects are incorporated into the existing schemata. Determination, or intention to act upon objects, is increasingly evident.

Substage 5

At about 11 or 12 months, an important new behavior is formed—causality. Now the child can perceive objects other than himself as causes. After attempting vainly to secure an object placed on a rug just out of reach, he will pull the rug toward himself. Similarly, he learns to secure objects by pulling strings to which they are attached. In substage 5, between 12 and 18 months, the child now engages in experimentation and is no longer bound to stereotyped behavior patterns. This stage of seeking the new or the unusual for its own sake is termed tertiary circular reactions. For example, the child continues to reach for the handles on a low kitchen cabinet to grasp and shake as he has in the substage of secondary circular reactions. However, an interesting and unusual event now happens. The spring-loaded door flies open as he grasps the handle and then springs shut again. The child is surprised at first and then attempts to repeat the action as he has done in the previous stage. Now, however, the tertiary reaction becomes evident, for the child seeks the unusual. He does not merely repeat his original action but makes many changes in it as though testing the effects. He pulls the cabinet door open to different positions and watches the result as he lets it swing shut. He tries the effects of pulling on other handles in the room, drawer handles, handles on other cabinets, and appliance handles. Interestingly, the child now manipulates the environment just to find out what will happen.

Substage 6

Between 18 and 24 months, the sensorimotor period phases into the following period. The child develops new intellectual means through overt activity combined with *internalized thought*. The result is *insight*. Typically, the child initiates problem-solving or exploratory behavior by physical, trial and error activity as he has in earlier substages. Now, however, failing to reach a solution, he contemplates the problem to devise a workable strategy.

A child confronted by a slightly open matchbox containing a thimble first tries to open the box by physical groping (reaction of the fifth stage), but upon failing, he presents an altogether new reaction: he stops the action and attentively examines the situation, after which he suddenly slips his finger into the crack and thus succeeds in opening the box. (Piaget and Inhelder 1969:12)

The achievement of this last substage results from a succession of assimilations on varying levels, and it cannot be separated from the previous substages. It represents the development of complex combinations and internalizations that collectively make "insight" possible.

THE PREOPERATIONAL PERIOD

During the sensorimotor period, approximately the first 2 years of life, the child develops a considerable number of behavioral schemes for interacting with his environment. In all of these schemes, however, the child is only able to act upon objects that are present. A significant change in intellectual development occurs at about 1½ or 2 years of age, however. It is at this age that the child enters the preoperational period, and he remains in it until he is nearly 7. The period is sometimes divided into two parts: the preconceptual phase from 2 to 4 years of age and the intuitive phase from 4 to 7 years. Between 2 and 4 years, the *symbolic function* appears; that is, the ability to symbolize and represent objects or events that are *not* present.

Symbolic Function

During the preoperational period, the child begins to understand that all meaning implies a relationship between a *signifier*, or symbol, that represents something to the individual and the *signified*, or reality, that is represented. With the appearance of the symbolic function, the child is able to represent an object, event, or scheme (signified) by means of mental image, symbolic gesture, or language (signifier).

Mental images may take the form of holding some mental picture of an object or event to imitate later. Or the child may represent things through their sound (making a clucking noise with his tongue to represent the sound of a galloping horse) or through some motion (*very slight* movement of his body to represent a ride on a horse). Piaget believes that the precursor of mental images occurs during the sensorimotor period with the child's overt use of his body to imitate a model (*vigorously* rocking his body back and forth to represent a ride on a horse or stretching one arm in the air and turning it from side to side after observing an airplane fly overhead). When this ability to imitate is refined, the preoperational child is able to imitate internally. Gradually, the child learns to use signifiers for anticipating, predicting, and planning events. The meaning he attaches to a signifier is the child's understanding of the signified and not necessarily the real object or event as others understand it. The existence of mental image is demonstrated in *deferred imitation*, which is imitation of the signified, or model, after the signified has disappeared. Deferred imitation is illustrated by the following example. Julie's mother was babysitting for 18-month-old Ann while Ann's mother went to the hospital to have another baby. Sixteen-month-old Julie watched Ann climb up on a low coffee table, stamp around, and laugh, a behavior pattern she had never seen before. The next day, Julie climbed up on the coffee table and began to laugh and stamp around on top of it.

The symbolic function is revealed in *symbolic gesture* as well as in the use of mental images. Symbolic gesture, or play, is pretending in which the child represents through imitative gestures. For example, Robby was sitting on the grass with a box of assorted playthings. He pulled out a round plastic food container and turned it around in his hands several times. He looked at the container and laughed. Then he held it up to his mouth, put his head back, and made a sipping noise as if he were drinking.

Symbolic function is also evident in the language of the preoperational child. In the sensorimotor period, the child uses language with concrete objects with which he is presently interacting or desires. At about 2 years of age, the child begins to use words to represent things that are not present. To illustrate, when Michael's father came home from work, Michael told him about a visit he had had that morning from his grandmother: "Grandma come. Ice cream for Mike."

Characteristics of Preoperational Thought

The child's language during the preoperational period, however, is still quite simple. His concepts are not firmly established and are, in fact, only *preconcepts*. The distinguishing feature of these notions is that the concept level stays midway between the generality of the concept and its individual components without arriving at either; hence the term "preconcept." Kim, for example, did not recognize her grandmother when she saw her with a wig that was quite different in color and style from her natural hair. To Kim, Grandmother was no longer Grandmother when she looked different. The child in this case classifies the same thing as different things when its outer appearance changes. The opposite may also be true—that the preconcept child sees different things as the same. Richie, for example, enjoyed watching his neighbor's cat whose name was Emily. For a long time, Richie called every cat he saw "Em'ly."

The reasoning of the preoperational child is neither inductive (reasoning from the particular to the general) nor deductive (reasoning from the general to the particular). In Piaget's view, the young child's reasoning is *transductive* in that it relates the particular to the particular. For example, when mother was emptying a closet to clean and took out the umbrella, Lisa said, "Mommy gots the umbrella so it's raining out." Lisa related the umbrella (one particular) to the rain (another particular) and reasoned that the rain depended on the umbrella.

Another characteristic of preoperational thought and language is its *egocentricism*, the focusing of the child's attention on only one thing at a time. Children in this stage are extremely self-centered in behavior and in language, not in a selfish way, but because they are so absorbed in themselves. Sometimes the young child uses language to repeat what those around him say. He repeats words *not* to communicate with others but simply because he enjoys playing with their sound (an example of functional assimilation or exercising an acquired scheme.) Another part of the young child's speech is directed to talking aloud when no one else is present. Piaget believes that such egocentric language occurs because the young child has not separated the word from the action or the object. The young child tends to say the words aloud that are associated with whatever it is that he is doing. A third form of egocentric language occurs when the child talks aloud when he is in a group. His language is not directed to anyone in particular, nor does he expect a reply. Yet, he may actually believe that the others are listening and that he is communicating with them. His egocentricism, however, prevents him from engaging in give-and-take positions with the others and, thus, from communicating with them.

Centering, the tendency to focus only upon one dimension of an object or event, is also characteristic of preoperational thought.

For example, in a conservation experiment, the child is presented with a container of liquid, which is then poured into another container. The first container may be tall and thin, while the second is shorter but wider. The child, focusing on the height of the container, will not understand that the amount of liquid has been conserved; the same holds for the child focusing on the width of the container. Only when the child is able to relate the two dimensions, which are functionally compensatory, will he be able to demonstrate conserving behavior. (Frost and Rowland 1969: 151)

Preoperational thought is further limited by the child's "tendency to focus on the successive *states* of a display rather than on the *transformations* by which one state is changed into another" (Phillips 1969:64). In the above example, the child fails to focus on the actual transformation of the liquid from the state of tall and thin to the state of shorter but wider.

Perhaps the most limiting characteristic of preconceptual thought is its *irreversibility*. The learner can go from point A to B, but he cannot go back from B to A. For example, the preconceptual-reasoning child is asked, "Do you have a sister?" She replies, "Yes." "What's her name?" "Mary." "Does Mary have a sister?" "No."

THE DEVELOPMENT OF CONCRETE OPERATIONS

The transition period from preoperational thought to concrete operations is particularly relevant for early childhood educators. Children within the early childhood age range are developing concepts of classification, space, number, and seriation. Many children appear to profit from instructional activities designed to facilitate their transition. The inclusion of these concepts in programs for young children should follow carefully seriated steps designed to build sequentially upon preliminary steps. Chapter 10 provides a detailed discussion and examples of early childhood instructional activities that enhance the development of intellectual abilities in this period.

From 7 or 8 to 11 or 12 years of age, the stage of concrete operations occurs. In other words, concrete operations (mental actions) are limited in that children in this stage are capable of operational groupings only when they can see or work with concrete objects. They cannot perform the same operational groupings with imaginary objects or purely on a verbal level. The emergence of the stage of concrete operations is always rapid and sometimes sudden. These operations are made possible by a "thawing out" of intuitive structures. At this point in development, grouping occurs as the key to operational thought. Grouping is a complex structure. It refers to the mental processes attained by the child at about 7 or 8 years of age which explain what he can do. Grouping I, for example, refers to the mental processes explaining what the child can do in classification. Piaget has described nine groupings that appear in the stage of concrete operations. The properties of Grouping I described below, however, basically illustrate the properties of all the groupings.

Properties of Grouping I

The concrete operational child classifies objects on the basis of particular elements or properties. These properties of logical thought are four in number.

ADDITIVE COMPOSITION. The child begins to think of a whole as being constituted by its parts, and he learns that he can put parts together to form a class. He can identify vegetables and fruits; he can form these into a class including all foods. He can form hierarchies—classes and superclasses. In mathematical terminology, *composition* means that the result of an operation is a part of the system. For example, if $A + B = C$, then C as well as A and B are parts of the system.

ASSOCIATIVITY.   The child can put information together in various ways to solve problems. "Shown a long stick and a series of segments that add up to the same length, he is sure that the segments together will equal the long stick regardless of whether they are arranged in zigzag fashion" (Ragan and Stendeler 1966:55). In other language, $A \times (B \times C) = (A \times B) \times C$, or $A + (B + C) = (A + B) + C$.

IDENTITY.   In every system there is one and only one element that, when added to any other element, leaves the system unchanged. Suppose the child explores the question, "Is lettuce a vegetable?" The child distinguishes the characteristics of "lettuce" and of "vegetable" to make a one-to-one correspondence, whereupon he concludes that lettuce is a vegetable. The identity property is used in mathematics. In addition, the sum of zero and any number is that number $(X + 0 = X)$. In multiplication, the product of any number and 1 is that number $(X \times 1 = X)$.

REVERSIBILITY.   Every cognitive action is reversible. The child can combine subclasses to form classes and he can reverse the process. He can combine red beads with blue beads to form a class of all beads. He can also take away the blue beads to have only the red beads again.

Fundamental Aspects of Concrete Operational Development

Piaget and Inhelder (1969: Chapter 4) identify some aspects of concrete operational development which are briefly explained below. Some short experiments are included in the discussion to illustrate how the emergence of these aspects of development are built upon earlier stages of development. These sample experiments illustrate how the child's thinking and reasoning can be easily and informally assessed. The experiments in this section are drawn from Piaget's own experiments and from his explanations of the results. They are merely suggestions of the kinds of Piagetian tasks it is possible to administer to young children. The reader will undoubtedly wish to administer these experiments to young children as well as to devise additional informal tasks based upon individual needs and his or her reading of Piagetian theory. There are several points that the reader should bear in mind when administering Piagetian tasks or experiments. It is advantageous to tape record each of the experiments as they are administered for future reference and analysis. The experiments should be administered informally to each child, in a quiet place, and not all in one session. A small table with a chair for the child and one for the experimenter can be used to do the experiments. The experimenter should be thoroughly familiar with each experiment before presentation and should be sure that all directions are clear and are understood by the child. Sample questions for each experiment in this section are given. Questions may be repeated. Alternative questions are given in parentheses following each initial question in case rewording is necessary. The experimenter must be sure that any questions used in the experiments do not suggest a response for the child. Also, in administering the experiments, there are neither "correct" answers nor "incorrect" answers. Nor is there any particular score, or mark, involved. The purpose of these informal experiments is to reveal the child's thinking and reasoning for the subsequent planning of experiences that are appropriate to the child's mental processes. The reader should remember that the age at which the intellectual abilities appear is approximate and varies with individual children. However, the sequence of appearance is invariant. The reader should also note that Chapter 10 contains a further discussion and examples of ways to enhance thought processes in the early childhood program.

CLASSIFICATION.   The roots of classification can be traced to the sensorimotor period when the infant gives the first motor reaction to objects as classes, such as things to shake or things to grasp. Later, when children are instructed to "put the things that are alike together," they perform on several levels. Children of 3 or 4 years engage in simple sorting. They begin to arrange the objects according to such similarities and differences as color, shape, or size, but then may add objects randomly because they lack an overall defining property for the collection. They may also arrange the objects spatially, in rows or circles or in the form of a figure. Piaget and Inhelder (1969) call this first state *figural collections*. In the second state, at age 5 or 6, nonfigural collections, the child appears to form classes in that he divides objects into groups irrespective of any spatial form. He also differentiates these groups into subgroups—all the round objects, for example, from a larger set of objects. However, genuine classification does not emerge until the child enters the period of concrete operations (7–9 years). During this third state, the child engages in *double classifications*—"for example, classifying red or white squares and circles in four compartments according to two dimensions" (Piaget and Inhelder 1969:103). The child can now respond correctly to the question, "Are there more round objects or more red objects?" He can classify by more than one property at a time. He recognizes that one object may belong to more than one group, and he recognizes that *all* members of a class may be red but that only *some* are round, and so on.

SIMPLE CLASSIFICATION EXPERIMENT

Materials: a collection of small plastic toys which includes 8 dogs, 3 cats, 9 cars, 4 airplanes.

Procedure: Place the collection of toys on the table and ask the child, "What do you see?" (Tell me what each object is.) When the experimenter is sure that the child can identify each category, say, "Put the things that are alike in some way together." (Put the things that are the same together.) As the child works, say, "Tell me about what you are doing." When he is finished, say, "Tell me about what you did." "How did you know the things went together like that?" "What else?"

Part B: For the child who arranges classes hierarchically (a class and sub-classes), also ask, "Are there more cats or more animals?" "Are there more cars or more things to ride in?"

Discussion: Children between 2 and 5 years (first preoperational phase) engage in simple sorting. They may begin to form a class but then add objects randomly (dog, dog, cat, cat, car, airplane). This child sometimes notes similarities among objects but loses track of the standard with which he began for the class.

A child between 5 and 7 years (second preoperational phase) *appears* to classify. He uses all of the objects in the collection. He seems to have an overall plan that guides the classes he forms (all the animals in one pile and all the vehicles in another pile). He also arranges classes hierarchically—he forms a class of all the animals and then subclasses of all the dogs and all the cats; a class of all the vehicles and then subclasses of all the cars and all the airplanes. However, this child is unable to understand the relations among the different subclasses and the entire class. When asked, "Are there more dogs (cats) or more animals?" he is likely to center on what he *sees* there, which is the sub-classes, and answer incorrectly.

Genuine classification emerges between 7 and 9 years of age. This child, in the concrete operational period, is able to form classes hierarchically and to comprehend the relations among subclasses and the whole class (Ginsburg and Opper 1969: 121–127).

NUMBER AND SPACE. Number, in Piagetian theory, refers to understanding basic concepts such as one-to-one correspondence and conservation, rather than to rote counting or skill in computation. In the sensorimotor period, the infant shows a precursory discrimination of number through his motor behavior. Mother and baby play a bang-bang, tapping game. Mother says "bang-bang" at the same time that she taps her hand on the high chair tray. Baby laughs and taps the tray two times with the toy he is holding. Mother repeats her actions, but longer this time, "bang, bang, bang, bang, bang." Baby responds by going tap, tap, tap, tap, tap, tap, tap with the toy. As number develops later on, it proceeds from a one-to-one or term-to-term correspondence between two sets which results from the ignoring of differential qualities about the sets. In other words, one car is equivalent to one tree. One-to-one correspondence also requires serialization in space or time to avoid counting the same object twice. In this process, the concrete operational child is free from the visual, physical nearness or perceptual matching of the two sets. Now, his one-to-one correspondence is guided by the relationship between the members of the two sets; that is, he can begin matching anywhere in the rows, since he now considers the idea "one car, one tree, a second car, a second tree, etc."

Spatial measurement develops in close isomorphism to but independently of number and, like number, develops from the child's precursory notions of object relations. Spatial measurement begins with the dividing of space into segments. One segment must be taken as a unit and applied successively without overlapping to the whole, a form of seriation. The extension of measurement leads to the *conservation of area*—the recognition that area remains the same even though its appearance may change. The *transformation of perspective* is also characteristic of this period. The child visualizes mentally how objects would look if viewed from a different perspective.

ONE-TO-ONE CORRESPONDENCE EXPERIMENT: PART A

Materials: a box containing 15 plastic spoons; 7 paper cups.

Procedure: Say to the child, "Some friends of mine are going to have ice cream later. They're going to put the ice cream in these cups (as you bring out the paper cups). I have 1 cup for each of my friends (as you place each cup in a row about 2 inches apart). Now, each of my friends needs a spoon to eat his ice cream with (as you set the box of spoons on the side of the table). Put out here as many spoons as there are cups." (Put the same number of spoons on the table as there are cups.)

CONSERVATION OF THE EQUIVALENCE OF NUMBER EXPERIMENT: PART B

Ask the child to put each spoon in a cup. There will then be 7 spoons in 7 cups, or two sets of objects that are equivalent in number. Now test whether or not the child is able to conserve that equivalence when the sets are in a different physical arrangement. In full view of the child, take out the 7 spoons and place them in a *bunch* in front of the row of cups. The spoons will then be in a shorter row than the cups. Ask the child, "Are there the same number of spoons and cups?" If the child responds, "No," then ask, "Where are there more?" (Which has more, the spoons or the cups?) "If we put the spoons back in the cups, will there be a spoon in each cup?" "Why?" Ask the child to count first one row and then the other. Then ask, "Are there the same number of spoons as there are cups?" Have the child put each spoon back in each cup. Then repeat the experiment and the questions, but bunch the cups now instead of the spoons.

Discussion: In making a one-to-one correspondence, the child in the first preoperational phase is likely to make a tight row of spoons in front of the cups with each spoon very close to the one beside it. This child centers on the aspect of length of the rows, so that the row of spoons he makes will be just as long as the row of cups, but there will be many more spoons than cups. Since he is unable to focus on the aspects of length and density of the row at the same time, he does not make equivalent sets except accidentally or if working with only a few objects. In Part B of the experiment, even after making a one-to-one correspondence (being told by the experimenter to put one spoon in each cup), this child does not conserve the equivalence of number of the two sets. When the spoons are bunched and the row of cups are longer, he believes that there are more cups, and vice versa, even if he is able to count. This child is fooled by *the way things look*.

The child in the second preoperational phase is able to make a one-to-one correspondence and establish the numerical equivalence of two sets of objects. However, he does not really understand the one-to-one correspondence. He is subsequently unable to conserve the numerical equivalence, since he is fooled by the appearance of things when either the spoons or the cups are bunched into a shorter row. Also unlike the child in the first preoperational phase who centered on one dimension, the child in the second stage wavers, sometimes centering on length of the row and sometimes on density.

The concrete operational child (7–9 years) is able to both make two sets equivalent in number and to conserve that equivalence. Furthermore, he does so in a more intellectually advanced manner. The concrete operational child does not place the members of one set directly and visually next to the members of the other set to establish one-to-one correspondence. Rather, he is guided by the relationship between set members. He can begin matching anywhere in the rows, since he now works from the idea of "one spoon, one cup, a second spoon, a second cup, and so on" (Ginsburg and Opper 1969:145–152).

SERIATION.   The process of seriation consists of *arranging elements* according to increasing or decreasing size or some other characteristic such as shortest to tallest or thinnest to fattest. The property of "reversibility" can be applied, and the order of sequencing is reversed. The preoperational child in the preconceptual phase is unable to seriate, or he may partially seriate a collection of objects. In the later, intuitive phase, he generally can seriate but with difficulty in a trial and error fashion. Operatory seriation, which occurs at about 7 years, includes one-to-one correspondence and two-dimensional seriation, or varying objects by size and shape. Seriation has its origin in substage 3 of the sensorimotor period when the infant acquires a precursory notion of object relations. For example, he intentionally taps the container with which he is playing very lightly on the floor and then very loudly to obtain differences in sound.

SERIATION EXPERIMENT

Materials: a collection of 10 cardboard tubes differing in size only by 1 inch. The shortest tubes (from paper products) are made by smoothly cutting the larger tubes into different lengths so that tube width and color are the same.

The wise adult helps to create a learning environment rich in opportunities for listening, speaking, and problem-solving, for these are the foundations of later literacy in the language arts and related areas.

Tia Kummerfeld

Esquela Montessori de Montopolis, Austin, Texas

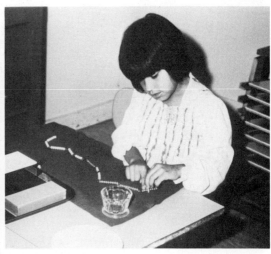

Esquela Montessori de Montopolis, Austin, Texas

In the Montessori classroom, the children are assisted in developing a social order that allows each child the most freedom consistent with his or her ability to handle it, taking into account the parallel rights of others. The emphasis upon self-responsibility in social learning also carries over into intellectual activity. The teacher gradually relinquishes a didactic role to the child's self-educative activity.

A-Bar-Z Ponderosa School, Austin, Texas

Societal roles (sex roles, family roles, job roles, and so on) are not inborn. They are learned through practice and observation. The adult does not insist that the child assume a particular role; rather he or she provides the setting and materials and guides the child toward taking advantage of the opportunities available for engaging in dramatic play.

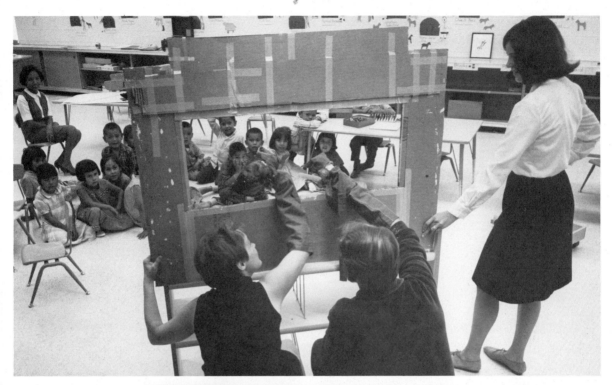

OEO

El Paso Community College Child Development Center

National Education Association Publishing, Joseph Di Dio

National Education Association Publishing, Joseph Di Dio

A-Bar-Z Ponderosa School, Austin, Texas

Sawing, sewing, and planting are examples of real-life activities that promote a wide range of social, intellectual, and psychomotor skills. Further, they are usually high-interest activities, for the child can now supplement the pleasure of doing with the reward of a tangible product.

160

A-Bar-Z Ponderosa School, Austin, Texas   A-Bar-Z Ponderosa School, Austin, Texas

Play Schools Association

Children need *time* to do the things that are necessary, like tying shoes, and they need time for simple, uncluttered fun like blowing bubbles or listening to seashells. Grimness is not essential to growth.

A-Bar-Z Ponderosa School, Austin, Texas

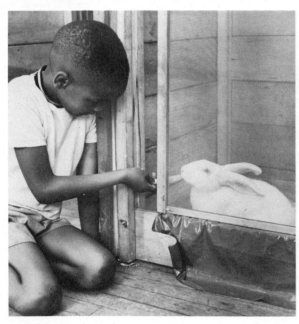

Play Schools Association

Merrick, N.Y., Public Schools

Activity periods allow for solitary roles that are related to various content areas such as reading and science, as well as time for small- and large-group activities.

Suzanne Szasz

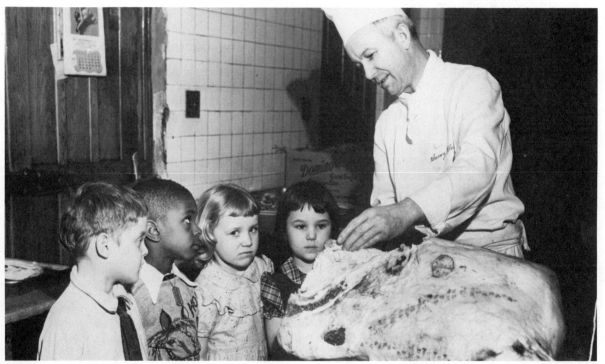

Manny Greenhaus

Trips outside the classroom provide real-life experiences that are not available in the school context. Such activities provide the tools of language and thought, allowing children to attach new meanings to concrete objects as they engage in symbolic play and as they interact in novel situations.

163

Procedure: Place the collection of tubes on the table in front of the child. Ask the child to select the smallest tube of all and then the biggest tube. When the child has done so, say, "Now put that smallest tube down first. Then put down one a little bit bigger, and then one a little bit bigger than that, and a little bit bigger until you have all the tubes in a row from smallest to the very biggest."

Discussion: The child between 2 and 5 years (first preoperational phase) generally cannot seriate or order the tubes. Some children in this phase may be able to seriate a few of the tubes but not all of them.

The child between 5 and 6 years is able to order the tubes. However, this child does so through trial and error and with considerable difficulty. He does not have an overall, systematic plan of finding the next bigger, and the next bigger, and so on. Instead, beginning with the smallest tube, he randomly selects another small one which may actually be third or fourth in the final ordering. It is only through trial and error, arranging and rearranging, that he finally succeeds in ordering the tubes.

The child of about 6 or 7 years of age seriates the tubes easily and properly. Generally, he begins with the smallest, then places the next smallest, and so on, as opposed to trial and error positioning and repositioning.

ONE-TO-ONE CORRESPONDENCE BETWEEN TWO ORDERINGS EXPERIMENT

Materials: 10 simple construction paper cowboys differing in size by ½ inch each; 10 construction paper horses differing in size by ½ inch each.

Procedure: Place the construction paper cowboys on the table in random order. Tell the child that you have some cowboys and that each cowboy has a horse to ride. (Place the horses in random order on the table.) "Each cowboy must have his own horse. Place one horse below each cowboy but not touching him. Be sure that the smallest horse goes with the smallest cowboy and the biggest horse goes with the biggest cowboy." When the child has finished ask, "Why did you put the horses and the cowboys that way?" (Tell me how you put the horses and the cowboys.)

Discussion: The child in the later preoperational stage (5–6 years) is able to produce a one-to-one correspondence between two orderings, but through trial and error. First he orders one set and then he orders the second set. Finally, he makes a one-to-one correspondence between the two previously ordered sets.

At about 6 or 7 years of age, the child is able to establish a one-to-one correspondence between two orderings in a more efficient manner than the younger child. He begins with either the smallest or the biggest cowboy and immediately places the corresponding smallest or biggest horse next to it, and so on (Ginsburg and Opper 1969:136–142).

CONSERVATION.   Perhaps the clearest indication that a child is operating at the *preconceptual* level is the absence of ability to conserve substance which normally takes place at about age 7 or 8. Conservation, then, gives a clear indication that the child has entered the concrete operations stage.

Piaget speaks of three major types of conservation, which occur in order. The first is the *conservation of substance* (7–8 years)—for example, the ability to specify that changing the shape of a lump of clay does not change the amount. The second is the *conservation of weight* (8–9 years). A scale balance is used to assess this ability. The child is asked if variable and standard objects weigh the same. *Conservation of volume* (11–12 years) is assessed by showing that each ball of clay, when placed in a container, causes the water to rise to the same height. One of the balls is then altered, and the child is asked if it will still make the water rise to the same height. Conserving behavior occurs initially during the substage of secondary circular reactions. In attempting to repeat an interesting event, the child conserves the behavior necessary to repeat it. For example, moving his arms has caused a rattle overhead in the carriage to shake. The child then limits his attempts to reproduce the behavior to arm movement, and he does not attempt other movements such as kicking his feet.

CONSERVATION OF SUBSTANCE EXPERIMENT

Materials: 2 balls of playdough or clay.

Procedure: Place two balls of playdough (clay) of identical size on the table. Ask, "Are the balls of playdough the same?" If the child does not think they are the same, let him add or subtract as much playdough as he thinks it takes to make them exactly the same. When he has finished, ask again if the two balls are the same. Next, roll one of the balls into a hot dog shape. Ask, "Is there as much playdough in this one (pointing to ball) as in this one (pointing to hot dog)?" "How can you tell?" Then ask, "Is there the same amount in each one or does one have more than the other?" "How do you know?"

Roll the hot dog back into the original ball shape. Again ask the child if the two balls of playdough are exactly the same, and let him take away or add to make the two balls exactly the same. Roll one of the balls into the shape of a hamburger pattie. Repeat the experiment and the questioning exactly as in the section above.

Roll the hamburger pattie back into the original ball shape. Repeat the experiment exactly as in the section above, changing one ball of playdough into a large, thin pancake shape.

Discussion: A child of about 4 or 5 years of age correctly states that the two original balls of playdough are exactly the same. When the shape of one ball is changed, however, the child believes that the two amounts are no longer the same and usually explains that one piece has more than the other. This child fails to conserve because he concentrates on only one dimension (hot dog is longer, so it's more, for example).

The child in the later preoperational period conserves, but he also changes his response through the experiment. Sometimes he concentrates on length and sometimes on width (sometimes the hot dog is more because it's longer, and sometimes the ball is more because it's wider).

At about 6 or 7 years, the child is able to conserve substance.

THE PERIOD OF FORMAL OPERATIONS

The period of formal operations begins at 11 or 12 years. It is characterized by the final development of the operational groupings and reaches the level of reflective intelligence. The child now formulates verbal hypotheses and is no longer bound to the concrete reality of objects. The concrete operational child dealt with what is; the formal operator explores what might be. The formal level problem-solver uses logical analysis and combinatorial experimentation. He sees reality as a limited subset of an almost unlimited world of possibilities. In this fashion, the child develops cumulatively toward ever-increasing complexity of thought. The formal operations would have no meaning without prior concrete operations and, similarly, concrete operations have no meaning without sensorimotor operations. Integration of structures is a fundamental concept in Piagetian theory.

IMPLICATIONS OF PIAGETIAN THEORY FOR EARLY CHILDHOOD EDUCATION

Piaget's work is primarily concerned with how intellectual development occurs rather than with the practical application of his theory in the classroom. Nonetheless, some general implications for early childhood education can be identified. First, a major emphasis in Piagetian theory is that intellectual, or cognitive, development is an active process, especially in the early years. The child learns from his active involvement with his environment. Shortly after birth, the child begins to manipulate and explore—with his eyes, his hands, and his mouth. Such manipulation enables him to develop behavioral schemes. New objects to explore and further manipulation result in expanded schemes and in new ones. Gradually, behavioral schemes become internalized thought. It is from the child's direct actions on objects that he comes to understand those objects and to develop behavioral and operational schemes with respect to them. The implication here is that schools for young children must allow and encourage *activity*. Young children should be given time and opportunity to freely explore and to manipulate the objects in their environment. Young children need concrete, realistic objects and firsthand experiences with which to interact.

According to Piaget, the child has an inherent inclination to adapt to his environment. The child adapts by dealing with his environment in terms of his present structures (assimilation). He also modifies his present structures according to the demands of the environment (accommodation). According to Piaget, the child tends toward equilibrium, or harmony, between his psychological structures and his environment. However, only a state of relative equilibrium is ever reached, since the sharpened structures that result from the equilibration process only lead to new disturbances. In other words, the more a child learns, the more he wants to learn. It follows, then, that early childhood programs must provide the young child with an *enrich-*

ing environment in which to learn. Enriching means that the learning environment is essential, not just nice or overflowing with entertaining materials. An enriched environment implies that education be extended beyond the four walls of a classroom to include the outdoors, nature, the neighborhood, community, the past, and the future. There is a further implication for early childhood education implicit in the principle of adaptation. The teacher must introduce *new stimuli* into the learning environment *that are only slightly more difficult* than previously assimilated content so that the child will be able to adapt and, hence, develop.

Several other implications emerge from Piaget's theory of intellectual development. Piaget states that *play* is important as an intellectually enriching experience. The child between 2 and 4 years manifests a significant development in his play, that of the symbolic function. With the development of the symbolic function, the child is no longer forced to act upon only those objects in his immediate environment, for he can now mentally recall absent objects or past events. In play, the young child can try out the real world without fear of mistakes or punishment. Play, therefore, it also important for the child's emotional development.

Informal talk is also important in the early childhood program for intellectual development. In the classroom filled with rich informal talk—questioning, hypothesizing, explaining, communicating, wondering—new interests as well as conflicting opinions and ideas result. It is from such conflicts that new thought processes emerge.

The stages of intellectual development that Piaget has identified are invariant. Children pass through the stages at different ages and rates, but all children pass through the same sequence of stages of intellectual development. This suggests that ongoing diagnosis is vital in order to determine the child's level of thinking for subsequent program planning. If, as Piaget says, the child's thinking process is different in quality from that of the adult, then it is urgent that the teacher strive to understand the child's thinking in order to plan appropriate enriching experiences. This further suggests that the adults who work with young children must be flexible in their interactions with them. The adult must tailor the program to the child's developing abilities rather than preplanning one program for all the students. The adult is perceptive in that she continuously observes and listens for clues to the child's thinking. The perceptive adult guides the child as he develops increasingly complex and internalized thought, offering challenging stimuli and appropriate experiences.

SUMMARY AND CONCLUSIONS

Jean Piaget is, undoubtedly, the foremost contributor to the study of cognitive, or intellectual, development in the young child. His theory describes the child's intellectual development as it unfolds. In his initial studies, Piaget observed his own three children during their infant and toddler years and kept detailed notes on their intellectual development. He devised the "clinical method" as the procedure for studying intelligence. It is an unstructured procedure that follows the child's responses and, hence, his thinking processes as he manipulates objects in experimental situations.

In Piaget's framework, the organism inherits physical structures such as an eye and simple behavioral structures such as the reflex of sucking. As the individual functions within his environment, his physical and behavioral structures result in *psychological structures.* Psychological structures are the foundation for cognitive activity, and there are different psychological structures at each stage of the child's development. The infant, for example, uses particular organized behaviors, or actions, while the older child uses mental operations. Piaget has termed organized behaviors *schemata.* The term "scheme" is used broadly and refers to both physical and mental organized behaviors. The infant's behavioral schemata are very different from the older child's operational schemata. *Operations* are internalized intellectual behaviors.

While structures change systematically (development) in Piaget's theory, *functions* remain invariant. Functions are methods of interacting with the environment. The organism inherits two functions; that is, he is inclined to *organize* his structures into coherent systems that enable him to function more effectively and he *seeks to adapt* to his environment. Adaptation is accomplished through the two related processes of assimilation and accommodation. The child deals with objects or events in his environment by incorporating them into his existing schemata (*assimilation*). Conversely, the child also modifies his existing psychological structures (*accommodation*). Assimilation and accommodation are complementary processes and operate simultaneously.

Mental development is explained by Piaget in terms of four general factors, *maturation, experience, social transmission*, and *equilibration*. He postulates that man plays an extremely active role in the formation of his cognitive world and that these four factors are relevant throughout all of his development. This part of Piaget's theory has been sometimes referred to as the stage-independent component. Piaget has also identified separate stages of intellectual growth from birth to maturity (stage-dependent component). A *sensorimotor stage*, which begins at birth and lasts until the child is 18 months to 2 years of age, is further separated into six substages of development. The second stage of development is the *preoperational period,* from 2 years to about 7 years. This period is sometimes divided into a preconceptual phase (2–4 or 5 years) and an intuitive phase (4–7 years). The third stage of intellectual development is the attainment of *concrete operations* between 7 and 11 years. *Formal operations*, the final stage of intellectual development, begins at about age 11 or 12 and extends into adulthood. According to Piaget, the age related to each of the stages is approximate and varies with individual children. The stages of development are integrative, and each stage results from the preceding one and each is incorporated into later stages.

The preoperational period, between the years 2 and 7, is of particular concern to early childhood educators. Entry into the preoperational period is marked by the appearance of the *symbolic function* between 2 and 4 years of age. Symbolic function enables the child to represent an object, event, or scheme (signified) by means of a mental image, symbolic gesture, or language (signifier). The child's thought during the preoperational period is quite simple. His concepts are not firmly established and are, in fact, only *preconcepts*. The child's thought and language in this period is *egocentric*. He uses *transductive reasoning* and tends to *center*, or focus, on only one dimension of an object or event at a time. The preoperational child's thought is further limited by its *irreversibility*.

Piaget's work is primarily concerned with describing intellectual development rather than with the practical application of his theory in the classroom. Nonetheless, some general implications for early childhood education can be identified. Programs for young children must allow and encourage *activity*, since cognitive development is an active process. The environment of the young child should be an *enriching* one for his psychological structures to change through the process of equilibration. Also, the teacher should introduce new stimuli into the environment which are only slightly more difficult than previously assimilated content for adaptation and change to occur. Piaget also states that *play* is important as an intellectually enriching experience. Rich, *informal talk*—questioning, hypothesizing, experimenting, communicating, wondering—should accompany the child's play because informal talk and play lead to new thought processes. Piaget postulates that the young child's thought processes are qualitatively different from the adult's. Consequently, ongoing *diagnosis* in the early childhood classroom is vital in order to determine the child's level of thinking for subsequent program planning of appropriate experiences.

SUGGESTED ACTIVITIES

1. Become thoroughly familiar with the experiments described in this chapter.
   a. Administer the tasks informally to several children of different ages. Tape record what they say and keep a written record of what they do for later analysis.
   b. Devise some additional simple experiments based upon your reading of Piagetian theory to assess different aspects of development discussed in this chapter. These might be experiments concerning the child's language; drawings; conservation of space, area, and length; time; perception; moral judgment and rules; or the content of the child's thought about such things

as dreams; beliefs about God, the sun, or moon, and so on. Administer these experiments informally to the same children you worked with in (a).

c. Analyze the tape recordings and your written observational records. Diagnose as many facets of intellectual behavior as possible according to the principles of Piagetian theory discussed in this chapter. Support your conclusions with specific examples taken from your taped and written records.

2. Interpret your conclusions about each child's stages of development from (1) above in terms of appropriate activities and materials in the classroom. Discuss and explain your interpretation.

3. Administer the exact procedure used in (1) to the same children at a later time in the year. Compare the results of both sessions for changes in each child's stages of intellectual development.

REFERENCES

Almy, M. 1964. *Young Children's Thinking and the Teaching of Reading.* U.S. Department of Health, Education and Welfare, Education Office Bulletin No. 19, pp. 97–102.

Braine, M. D. S. 1959. "The Ontogeny of Certain Logical Operations: Piaget's Formulation, Examined by Nonverbal Methods," *Psychological Monographs: General and Applied,* 73(5):1–43.

Braine, M. D. S., and B. L. Shanks. 1965. "The Conservation of a Shape Property and a Proposal About the Origin of the Conservations," *Canadian Journal of Psychology,* 19:197–207.

Bruner, J. S., R. R. Olver, and P. Greenfield. 1966. *Studies in Cognitive Growth.* New York: Wiley.

Dodwell, P. C. 1962. "Relations Between the Understanding of the Logic of Classes and of Cardinal Number in Children," *Canadian Journal of Psychology,* 16:152–160.

Dodwell, P. C. 1961. "Children's Understanding of Number and Related Concepts," *Canadian Journal of Psychology,* 15:29–36.

Elkind, D. 1961a. "The Development of Quantitative Thinking: A Systematic Replication of Piaget's Studies," *Journal of Genetic Psychology,* 98:37–46.

Elkind, D. 1961b. "Children's Discovery of the Conservation of Mass, Weight, and Volume: Piaget Replication Study II," *Journal of Genetic Psychology,* 98:219–227.

Erikson, E. H. 1950. "Eight Stages of Man," *Childhood and Society.* New York: Norton, pp. 247–274.

Flavell, J. H. 1963. *The Developmental Psychology of Jean Piaget.* Princeton, N.J.: Van Nostrand.

Frost, J. L., and G. T. Rowland. 1969. *Curricula for the Seventies.* Boston: Houghton Mifflin.

Ginsburg, H., and S. Opper. 1969. *Piaget's Theory of Intellectual Development: An Introduction.* Englewood Cliffs, N.J.: Prentice-Hall.

Gruen, G. E. 1965. "Experiences Affecting the Development of Number Conservation in Children," *Child Development,* 36:963–979.

Honstead, C. 1968. "The Developmental Theory of Jean Piaget," in J. L. Frost (ed.), *Early Childhood Education Rediscovered*. New York: Holt, Rinehart and Winston.

Hunt, J. McV. 1961. *Intelligence and Experience*. New York: Ronald.

Lovell, K., D. Healey, and A. D. Rowland. 1962. "Growth of Some Geometrical Concepts," *Child Development*, 33:751–767.

Phillips, J. L. 1975. *The Origins of Intellect: Piaget's Theory*. San Francisco: W. H. Freeman.

Piaget, J. 1966; French ed., 1947. *Psychology of Intelligence*. Totowa, N.J.: Littlefield, Adams.

Piaget, J. 1965; French ed., 1941. *The Child's Conception of Number*. New York: Norton.

Piaget, J. 1964. "Development and Learning," in R. E. Ripple and V. N. Rockcastle (eds.), *Piaget Rediscovered*. Ithaca, N.Y.: School of Education, Cornell University.

Piaget, J. 1951. *Play, Dreams, and Imitation in Childhood*. New York: Norton.

Piaget, J., and B. Inhelder. 1969; French ed., 1966. *The Psychology of the Child*. New York: Basic Books.

Ragan, W. B., and C. B. Stendler. 1966. *Modern Elementary Curriculum*. New York: Holt, Rinehart and Winston.

Sigel, I. E. 1971. "The Development of Classificatory Skills in Young Children: A Training Program," *Young Children*, pp. 170–194.

Sigel, I. E., and F. H. Hooper. 1968. *Logical Thinking in Children: Research Based on Piaget's Theory*. New York: Holt, Rinehart and Winston.

Sigel, I. E., A. Roeper, and F. H. Hooper. 1966. "A Training Procedure for Acquisition of Piaget's Conservation of Quantity: A Pilot Study and Its Replication," *British Journal of Educational Psychology*, 36:301–311.

Smedslund, J. 1961a. "The Acquisition of Conservation of Substance and Weight in Children, I: Introduction," *Scandinavian Journal of Psychology*, 2:11–20.

Smedslund, J. 1961b. "The Acquisition of Conservation of Substance and Weight in Children, II: External Reinforcement of Conservation of Weight and of the Operations of Addition and Subtraction," *Scandinavian Journal of Psychology*, 2:71–84.

Smedslund, J. 1961c. "The Acquisition of Conservation of Substance and Weight in Children, III: Extinction of Conservation of Weight Acquired 'Normally' and by Means of Empirical Controls on a Balance," *Scandinavian Journal of Psychology*, 2:85–87.

Smedslund, J. 1961d. "The Acquisition of Conservation of Substance and Weight in Children, IV: Attempt at Extinction of the Visual Components of the Weight Concept," *Scandinavian Journal of Psychology*, 2:153–155.

Smedslund, J. 1961e. "The Acquisition of Conservation of Substance and Weight in Children, V: Practice in Conflict Situations Without External Reinforcement," *Scandinavian Journal of Psychology*, 2:56–160.

Smedslund, J. 1961f. "The Acquisition of Conservation of Substance and Weight in Children, VI: Practice on Continuous vs. Discontinuous Material in Problem Situations Without External Reinforcement," *Scandinavian Journal of Psychology*, 2:203–210.

Smedslund, J. 1962. "The Acquisition of Conservation of Substance and Weight in Children, VII: Conservation of Discontinuous Quantity and the Operations of Adding and Taking Away," *Scandinavian Journal of Psychology,* 3:69–77.

Uzgiris, I. C. 1964. "Situational Generality of Conservation," *Child Development,* 35:831–841.

Vernon, P. E. 1965. "Environmental Handicaps and Intellectual Development," *British Journal of Educational Psychology,* 35:1–22.

Wallach, L., and R. L. Sprott. 1964. "Inducing Number Conservation in Children," *Child Development,* 35:1057–1071.

Wohlwill, J. F., and R. C. Lowe. 1962. "Experimental Analysis of the Development of the Conservation of Number," *Child Development,* 33:153–167 .

FURTHER READING

Battro, A. M. *Piaget: Dictionary of Terms,* E. Rutschi-Herrmann and S. F. Campbell, eds. and trans. New York: Pergamon Press, 1973.

Isaacs, N. *Children's Ways of Knowing.* New York: Teachers College Press, 1974.

Isaacs, N. *A Brief Introduction to Piaget.* New York: Agathon Press, 1972.

Kamii, C. "One Intelligence Indivisible," *Young Children,* 1975, 30:228–238.

Modgil, S. *Piagetian Research: A Handbook of Recent Studies.* New York: Humanities Press, 1974.

Osborn, J., and D. K. Osborn. *Cognitive Tasks: An Approach for Early Childhood Education.* Athens, Ga.: Education Associates, Early Childhood Education Learning Center, University of Georgia, 1974.

Piaget, J. *To Understand Is To Invent: The Future of Education.* New York: Agathon Press, 1972.

Schwebel, M., and J. Raph (eds.). *Piaget in the Classroom.* New York: Basic Books, 1973.

IV

Creating a Challenging and Healthy Learning Environment

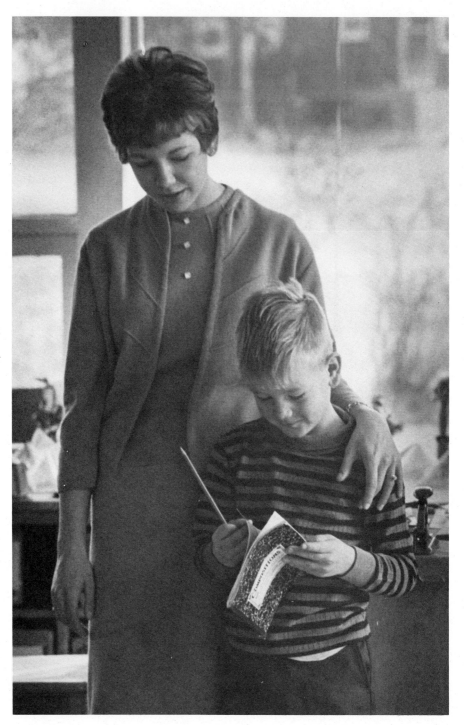

Suzanne Szasz

Planning and Evaluation

We have seen that various forces and events throughout educational history called attention to different aspects of the young child. As a result, early childhood education stressed different educational objectives over corresponding periods of time. The aims of the earliest kindergartens, for example, focused upon self-esteem, kindness, play, and firsthand experience, while the earliest nursery schools emphasized cleanliness, personal hygiene, and good health habits. The work of Freud, Prescott, Frank, and other psychologists and educators led to subsequent concern for the child's emotional and social well-being. This concern grew even stronger in the 1940s and 1950s. It was not until the sixties, however, with the cumulation of research and the emergence of the civil rights movement that the emphasis in early childhood education shifted to the child's cognitive growth and development. As illustrated in Chapter 4, numerous preschool programs emerged during that period, exemplifying a wide variety of program approaches and instructional techniques. Despite their unique features, basic aims of contemporary early childhood programs can be identified. This chapter discusses those basic objectives and their importance as the foundation for program planning and evaluation. A distinction is made among three types of evaluation—diagnostic, formative, and summative—and methods for implementing each type are discussed.

SOURCES OF EDUCATIONAL OBJECTIVES

Educational objectives arise from three major sources—society, psychology, and philosophy. Social trends influence the direction of education even more in contemporary times than in the past. As changes occur in life-styles, the economy, social and moral issues, and methods of communication, new priorities are reflected in the educational program. The advent of activities and programs designed to increase awareness of inflation, energy conservation, ecology, career education, child-rearing, sex education, and drug abuse all typify the way educational objectives are shaped by social forces.

Psychology also exerts a strong influence on the formulation of educational objectives. The flurry of experimental early childhood activity during the late 1960s relied in large part upon psychological assumptions about optimum conditions for child learning. Project Head Start, for example, stressed such objectives as improving health, expanding mental processes, developing feelings and attitudes of self-worth, self-confidence, respect, and belonging, and providing opportunities for success. Such goals appear to be linked to maturational and humanistic views of learning (Chapter 5). The behavior analysis approach of Bushell and his associates at the University of Kansas has its roots in stimulus-response or behavioral learning theory. The Weikart project draws heavily from Piagetian theory and is linked to the cognitive-transactional view of learning.

Educational objectives are also a reflection of philosophy. The nature and direction of the program is determined by what a teacher or staff believes to be the best type of classroom environment, the most effective instructional techniques and methods, and the overall intent or purpose behind the program's existence.

It is interesting to note that the historical emphasis on God as a source of educational purposes has all but disappeared from all except church schools.

EDUCATIONAL OBJECTIVES AS THE BASIS
FOR PLANNING AND EVALUATION

Educational objectives are statements of purpose or intent. On one level, when stated in such broad, general terms as "developing competence in problem-solving, attending, language, socialization, and coordination," they identify the long-range emphasis, or the goals, of the early childhood program. On another level, educational objectives are stated more specifically in terms of observable outcomes of instruction. In this case, they describe the specific kinds of student behavior toward which the instructional process is directed. Examples of objectives on this level include "points to the basic shapes of a circle, square, and triangle correctly each time when shown a set of 10 objects" and "identifies those things that are real and those that are make believe from a picture containing 12 objects." Educational objectives on both levels are the basis for planning and evaluation. On the broad level, educational objectives are the teacher's long-term plan assuring that a balanced program will be maintained, that all aspects of development—physical, intellectual, social, and emotional—have been taken into account in the program. Broadly stated objectives also guide the teacher in deciding how far the child has already progressed along the developmental continuum and what should happen next in his development. They further serve as the criteria for determining whether and to what extent the program accomplished what it set out to do. When educational objectives are stated on the more specific level, in terms of observable behaviors, they become the teacher's short-term plan to assure that individual needs are met. They take into account the child's specific areas of strength and weakness. They set the direction and the content of daily activities, and they are the focal point for continuous program evaluation throughout the instructional process.

In using educational objectives as the basis for evaluation, a distinction can be made among three types of evaluation or three distinct purposes for assessment. The three types of evaluation are diagnostic, formative, and summative. The purpose of diagnostic evaluation is to obtain information about the child's present status—what he can now do, how he presently behaves, in which stage of development he is currently functioning. Diagnosis is conducted *prior* to instruction. It helps the teacher determine *causes* of deficiencies, and it helps her in making decisions about instructional placement of the child. What areas of a child's development the teacher will diagnostically evaluate are determined by the educational objectives of the program. Formative evaluation is conducted *during* the instructional process. Its purpose is to assess the student's progress throughout a particular unit of study. Therefore, formative evaluation is continual, with periodic checking to determine which objectives have and have not been achieved. The results of this continual assessment are immediately fed back into the program to shape and give direction to planning as instruction proceeds. Summative evaluation is an overall assessment that occurs at the *end* of a year, a semester, or an area of study. It evaluates whether and to what extent the objectives have been met.

The teacher implements evaluative data in the instructional process through lesson planning, as illustrated in Figure 8-1. Although lesson plans are the teacher's source of guidance and direction, it is a rare day indeed when plans are followed to the letter. As teachers become increasingly skillful, they are likely to vary planned activities to seize emerging opportunities for enhancing interest and learning. When a child brings a new litter of kittens to school, for example, the planned language lesson gets a real boost. The alert teacher uses the opportunity to introduce new words, stimulate language of shy children, and tie abstract learnings to a real-life incident. Grasping opportunities to expand learning does not mean that the teacher dismisses the plan. Rather, she remains aware of the planned objectives but varies the activities in ways that seem most likely to result in learning and increased interest.

Name of Child(ren) _____   Teacher _____

_____   Date _____

_____

Diagnosis: Briefly describe the diagnosis and/or evaluation techniques used. Describe the results of evaluation which will be used to select or formulate objectives for this lesson or activity.

Observable Behaviors: Specify the desired behavioral change which you expect to result from this lesson.

Procedure: Describe how you will teach the lesson, step by step. Procedures should relate directly to the objectives. Apply criteria for selection of child activity. Describe special teaching methods (inductive, discovery, and so on) and techniques (questioning, reinforcing, and so on).

Materials: List the materials to be used in teaching this lesson.

Evaluation: Specify exactly how you will determine whether the objective(s) was (were) achieved. The proposed method of evaluation, for example, specific formal or informal test, checklist, or observation, should be described in *advance* of teaching the lesson or conducting the activity.

Result: Briefly describe the effect of this lesson on the child's behavior. The results serve as diagnosis for the next lesson. The results are determined by application of the evaluation scheme and are written *after* the children are dismissed.

FIGURE 8-1   Lesson plan format.

EDUCATIONAL OBJECTIVES FOR EARLY CHILDHOOD PROGRAMS

Educational objectives in early childhood programs encompass all aspects of development—psychomotor, cognitive, affective, and social. These aspects of development are inextricably mixed in the educative process so that development in one area is intertwined with development in the other areas. This intimate relationship is illustrated in Figure 8-2 and in the following description of objectives for early childhood programs for 3-, 4-, and 5-year-olds. These examples relate to the comprehensive developmental checklist in Appendix A.

Attending

Attending refers to the child's ability and willingness to direct his attention toward or to participate physically and responsively in particular events. It also includes increasing attention to detail, awareness of the environment,

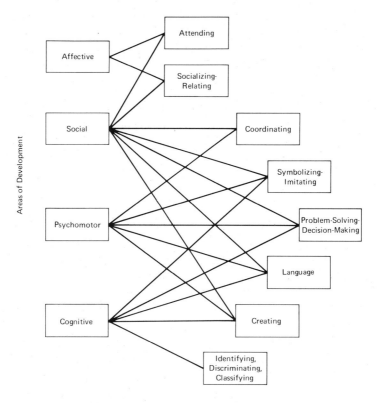

FIGURE 8-2   Objectives for early childhood programs.

and awareness of personal beliefs and values. Increasing ability to attend is desirable for socialization. Also, being able to attend in general is a prerequisite ability for selective attending, or forming preferences for and commitments to selected phenomena.

Examples   To sit with the group for a few minutes at story time.

To indicate having listened to the teacher's directions for leaving the story time group by following through.

For Janey to select her favorite record during the music activity.

Socializing-Relating

The educational objective of socializing-relating is concerned with developing inter- and intrapersonal relationships. It includes the child's willingness to interact with others as well as his skill in relating to them. It involves such skills as respecting the rights and property of others, being concerned about others, accepting responsibility, cooperating, growing in independence, and using self-control. This objective is related to attending in its importance for functioning acceptably in society. Skill in this area is also important for the individual's emotional well-being.

> *Examples*   For Peter to leave his mother readily at the door without crying or clinging to her.
>
> To join in the cleanup today by replacing all of the blocks to their proper shelves.
>
> To offer the tricycle to someone else during the outdoor playtime.

Coordinating

Coordinating refers to gross and fine motor skills which involve the whole body or body parts, such as using the feet for a specific purpose, speech production, and eye-hand coordination. Self-help skills such as dressing, toileting, and buttoning are also included here. Being able to coordinate the body and body actions is necessary for all other dimensions of functioning.

> *Examples*   To climb all the way up the slide and come down once during the morning outdoor period.
>
> To hold a cup with one hand.
>
> To catch a small ball on the first bounce.

Identifying, Discriminating, and Classifying

Increasing facility to use all of the senses to recognize and differentiate properties, events, and relationships is reflected in ability to identify, discriminate, and classify. This objective further includes skill in grouping, sorting, and ordering phenomena. All of these skills are prerequisites for more advanced cognitive activity.

> *Examples*   To correctly point to different food objects as they are named by the teacher.
>
> To sort objects into groups of heavy and light objects.
>
> For Danny to locate his name in all the places that it occurs on the experience chart.

Symbolizing and Imitating

Symbolizing and imitating include role-playing, dramatization, mimicry, and representation through art, verbalization, or print. This broad objective is important for the young child to gain understanding of social roles and social rules and to be able to function according to the expectations of society. Through symbolizing and imitating, the child has a chance to use and develop many other skills. He has the opportunity to classify, to discriminate, to use language, to understand concepts, to solve problems, to be creative, and to improve coordination.

Examples   To draw a circle correctly from a model.

To play an adult role in the housekeeping area.

To relate for an experience story the experience of going to the dentist.

Language

The broad objective of language refers to developing vocabulary, concepts, comprehension, grammar, and the ability to communicate verbally and nonverbally. As illustrated in Figure 8-2, language development is related to all other aspects of development.

Examples   For John to state his first and last names intelligibly.

To describe what is happening in a given picture in complete sentences.

To retell a story in correct sequence immediately after hearing it read.

Problem-Solving and Decision-Making

Problem-solving refers to increasing skill in analyzing a problem or situation, seeking and formulating solutions, and then testing the proposed solution. This objective involves thinking and reasoning skills, analyzing cause and effect relationships, and weighing alternatives as the prerequisites for making decisions more wisely. It includes creating, experimenting, questioning, explaining, testing, and evaluating.

Examples   To solve successfully a puzzle involving five pieces.

To propose a solution to the problem of too many children in the block area at one time.

To suggest why the straw floated and the nail sank in the water table activity.

Creating

Creating refers to expressing the usual and ordinary in new and original ways through the media of art, music, play, language, and print.

Examples   To construct with the large blocks.

To act out the story of the "Three Bears."

To draw a picture of what the boy's invention in the story might have looked like.

STATING OBJECTIVES IN TERMS OF OBSERVABLE BEHAVIORS FOR INSTRUCTIONAL PURPOSES

For objectives to be useful in the instructional process, they must be stated precisely. The teacher writes the objectives so that both the observable behavior desired in the student and the criteria of acceptable performance are given. To illustrate, consider the following objectives stated quite generally:

For Jimmy to be able to play ball.
For Danny to know his name.

Obviously, such sweeping generalities provide no clear basis for a specific lesson. No two people would be likely to agree on their exact meaning or their implications for instruction. On the other hand, compare the above objectives with the following objectives stated specifically:

After participating in this series of five activities, Jimmy will be able to catch a small ball on the first bounce.

Upon completion of this language activity, Danny will be able to locate his name in all five places that it occurs on the experience chart.

Failure to communicate clearly the intent of an objective is often due to the use of words that refer to behaviors which are not observable and therefore subject to various interpretations. The following examples illustrate observable as opposed to nonobservable behaviors:

Observable Behaviors	*Nonobservable Behaviors*
To identify	To know
To state	To understand
To volunteer	To appreciate
To join	To learn
To select	To feel

TASK ANALYSIS

Once the objectives have been determined and clearly stated, the next step is to sequence them to accommodate the movement of the child through the curriculum. A sequence of educational objectives is a powerful curriculum tool for the teacher in that it allows for the control of step size. It allows the teacher to match desired objectives with previously acquired abilities, or skills, of the learner. Each new cognitive, affective, social, or psychomotor ability is made up of other abilities that developed earlier. Understanding and/or ability is not possible without a structural base, and that base is developed over time from the materials and experiences available to the learner. In this sense, one way to view the educational process is as a process of building upon simpler acquired behaviors or as the introduction of *controlled* discontinuity or change. If instructional input is precisely congruent with existing structure or ability, then the structure will not change. The task of the teacher is to introduce tasks of complexity levels slightly in excess of established structure. Given such optimal conditions in a positive environment, the structure will change; that is, learning will occur.

Sequencing educational objectives requires the use of task analysis. The curriculum developer begins with any desired objective and asks, "In order to perform this behavior, what prerequisite behaviors must the child be able to perform?" This question is asked again for each identified behavior, and a hierarchy, or sequence, based upon behavioral prerequisites is developed. In Table 8-1, for example, the principle of task analysis is applied to the classification of objects, where the continuum of prerequisite behaviors ranges from complex to simple. The sequencing, task-analysis process is continued until the behaviors identified fit the range of presumed abilities of the children to be involved in the instructional process. That is, the lower-order objectives are sufficiently simple to accommodate the learning needs of the least sophisticated member of the learning group, and the higher-order objectives are sufficiently complex to challenge the most sophisticated learner in the group. The task-analysis and sequencing process is initially based upon professional decision and should be modified through trial. Applied in instructional practice, all this must be made relevant to individuals, not groups. Moreover, the cognitive emphasis must be viewed as inextricably intertwined with the affective, psychomotor, and social domains to build hierarchies of behavioral objectives there as well. In planning the instructional program, the teacher then links the planned *cognitive objectives* with *affective objectives* [to listen to each other describe the common property he identified with which to group his collection of objects; to actively participate in the classification activity (attending)]. These objectives are then tied in with *psychomotor objectives* [to arrange the objects into groups by moving them (fine movement); to match the teacher's model of objects by arranging a one-to-one correspondence (eye-hand coordination)] and, finally, with *social objectives* [to take turns describing the group of objects each made; to replace the objects used in the classification activity in their proper containers after the lesson (socializing-relating)]. The utilization of task analysis and sequencing in planning does not fix or prescribe the *method* of instruction.

TABLE 8-1 Example of Sequencing Objectives

Prerequisite Abilities	Sequence of Objectives
Combining subclasses to form a class	*Desired behavior:* To combine a subclass of brown dogs and a subclass of black dogs in the first collection to make a class of all dogs; to combine a subclass of big boats and a subclass of little boats in the second collection to make a class of all boats.
	Question: In order to perform the above behavior, what prerequisite behavior must the child be able to perform? ↓
Identifying many common properties to form many classes	To identify as many common properties among a collection of 15 objects as possible and to group them accordingly (possible properties include things that are big, little, brown, black, dogs, boats, etc.). ↓
Forming a class and a complementary class	To discriminate between things in a collection that are alike and things that are not alike by identifying and combining all the objects that are dogs and all the objects that are not dogs. ↓
Multiple classification	To keep in mind two properties of color and size at the same time in order to correctly find the missing object in a row containing a big brown dog, a little black dog, a big brown cat, _____. ↓
One-to-one correspondence	To match the objects in a row according to the two properties of color and size by making another row through one-to-one correspondence. ↓
Size as a property	To discriminate which objects in a collection of 15 are big and which are little. ↓
Color as a property	To discriminate which objects in a collection of 15 are brown and which are black.

RESEARCH ON LEARNING HIERARCHIES

The sequential structure of educational objectives may be likened to the "cumulative learning" theory of Gagné (1962, 1968). Gagné, perhaps the leading protagonist for the existence of learning hierarchies, postulated an ordered hierarchy of types of learning in which subordinate skills contribute to the acquisition of superordinate skills. In the original studies of learning, using programmed instruction, Gagné and Brown (1961) came to believe that differences in learning performance were more likely attributable to certain identifiable skills required for meeting the demands of the program rather than to differences in "intelligence." A number of questions were raised by their studies. First, asking what the individual would have to be able to do prior to a given behavior implies a search for subordinate tasks that will have positive transfer for the learning of the given task. Second, how does one judge the correctness of the order of skills in the hierarchy? Gagné (1968:5) provides general guidance: "Simple responses are subordinate to chains or multiple discriminations, which in turn are subordinate to classifying, which in turn is subordinate to using principles or rules." Often, one is unsure about the proper location of a particular capability, and empirical tryout of a hierarchy is appropriate. This process is essentially viewed as hypothesis testing, a legitimate activity for teachers. In fact, whenever one teaches for the achievement of a particular objective, the procedure, strategy, materials, or sequence involved become the hypothesis to be tested —given such and such, the abilities of the learner will change. Consequently, the teacher determines the validity of her hypothesis by the observable change noted in the students and modifies her strategies (hypotheses) on this basis. Given the complexity of hierarchies, however, it does not seem reasonable to project errors of a particular hierarchy to all hierarchies.

A third question proposed by Gagné (1968) seems particularly appropriate for the consideration of those who assume an either-or view regarding the validity of learning hierarchies in educational programming. Do hierarchies represent the only learning route or the most efficient route? Is each learner required to acquire *each* subordinate skill in order to learn the final task? The answer to both questions is no. The method of *analysis* of *tasks* tells us nothing about the learner. A given learner may be able to skip subordinate tasks. Another individual may approach the hierarchy with a set of skills from a different domain of knowledge which is not directly represented in the hierarchy. Yet another may engage in atypical combination of subordinate skills (see Figure 8-3). Given the present state of knowledge, a

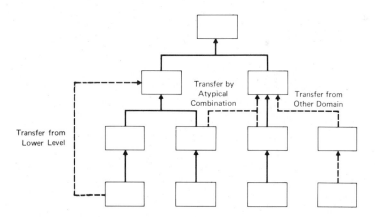

FIGURE 8–3   Latent consequences of cumulative learning. (From R. M. Gagné, "Learning Hierarchies," presidential address, Division 15, American Psychological Association, August 31, 1968.) Reprinted with the permission of the author.

learning hierarchy does not represent the most efficient route for any given learner. The hierarchy represents the "most probable expectation of greatest transfer for an entire sample of learners concerning whom we know nothing more than what specifically relevant skills they start with" (Gagné 1968:6).

Some Cautionary Notes

A learning hierarchy does not represent everything that can be learned or everything that is learned within a given domain. The reader must be alert lest he assume an overly simple view of the educational implications of hierarchies and sequences in learning. Gagné (1968:8) makes it clear that learning hierarchies *are not* "entities of verbalizable knowledge." He calls them "intellectual skills." What the learning hierarchies describe are "capabilities for action," or in computer language, "subroutines of a program; what they do not describe is the facts or propositions retrievable from memory as verbalizable statements."

Nor does the hierarchy represent that most important factor in learning, the potential for transfer that is generated through learning. Each new capability may generalize to a host of situations that are not represented in the sequences being taught. There are latent consequences of cumulative learning that are not represented on a given learning chart within a given curriculum.

Learners can acquire verbalizable knowledge, and even intellectual skills, from sequences of presentation that are altered in various ways from what may be considered "highly organized." The hypothesis I should like to reaffirm, however, is that regardless of presentation sequence, if one is able to identify the intellectual skills that are learned, he will find them to generate positive transfer in an ordered fashion. (Gagné 1968:11)

Gagné hypothesizes that intellectual skills and verbalizable knowledge are learned in different ways. The skills have an ordered relation to each other such that subordinate ones have a positive transfer to superordinate ones; but the verbalizable entities do not necessarily have this relationship. One need not, for example, learn the letters before learning their position in the alphabet. Verbalizable knowledge must surely have a rationale of its own. Nonetheless, the individual who can solve skills tasks also brings verbalizable knowledge to bear on the problem; that is, the skill cannot be learned in a vacuum. Both are essential for problem-solving. The relevant question at this point becomes which emphasis will predominate in the curriculum, intellectual skills or verbalizable knowledge—or put into common instructional terms, process or content. The predominating trend of professional thought suggests that process should be heavily emphasized. Knowledge, or content, can be "looked up" in a book, but skills, or processes, must be "built-in." Assuming the validity of this argument, it would seem that the construction and use of learning hierarchies, the sequencing of intellectual skills to be learned, are legitimate curriculum concerns.

METHODS OF EVALUATION

Changing behavior is the very essence of the educative process. The term "behavior" is used here in a broad sense to include all aspects of development—cognitive, psychomotor, social, and affective. To change behavior, the teacher at first performs diagnostic evaluation. She collects evidence to determine the nature of the child's behavior at a particular point in time. Instructional activities and experiences are then planned on the basis of the diagnostic data. During the ongoing instruction, the teacher conducts formative evaluation. She collects evidence to determine if and in what ways the child's behavior is changing. Such evidence is immediately fed back into the instructional plans to maintain and/or improve them. At the end of the activity unit, or some designated period of time, summative evaluation occurs. Summative evaluation determines if in fact that child's behavior did change as was planned. To ensure that the evidence for diagnostic, formative, and summative evaluation is objective and reliable, it must (1) be based on *observable* behaviors, not conjecture or feelings; (2) be systematically obtained in that it is conducted regularly and with the aid of some methodical tool or plan; and (3) be obtained from a variety of situations over a period of time. Several different ways to obtain objective and reliable evidence for evaluation and planning are discussed in the following sections.

The Case Study

One of the simplest ways to obtain information about a child is to observe him closely. The teacher observes the child in a variety of activities, both indoors and outdoors, to evaluate every aspect of his development. Although observation is a time-consuming task, it is possible for teachers to obtain such valuable data even with their already busy schedules. Observing two or three children a day in some predetermined order for just a few minutes provides an informative record of behavior over the semester or year. One form of observation is the case study, or anecdotal record, an objective study of one child over a period of time. (See also Chapter 11, which examines the use of the case study as a tool in managing child behavior.) The insights gained from studying one child are expected to have generalizing effects to other children. The common practice of studying a "typical child" to identify observable behavior and relate it to what is known about child development may be extended to the deliberate study of a child with obvious behavioral problems. Systematic observation of children with special problems can yield valuable information about possible causes of such behavior and may suggest ways to change that behavior. The case study is a useful tool when applied for these purposes. It enables teachers to shift their interactions with children from impulsive generalization to objective analysis.

In studying an individual child the teacher uses *scientific* methods. The validity of all information is checked carefully. Each anecdote relates exactly what the child did or said. Each situation is described in concrete terms, and the reactions of adults and peers to the particular child's behavior are described accurately. Subjective words and phrases such as "seems," "apparently," "I feel" are avoided in the anecdotes. As the study progresses, the teacher begins to make teaching and guidance decisions, including setting up motivational procedures. All of these decisions are made on the basis of documented evidence rather than intuition or guesswork.

The record may be divided into several sections—title page, background information, anecdotal record, summary, and implications for teaching. The sample record on Patty (p. 189) illustrates the type of information that is included in the middle three sections.

The *title page* includes the child's name, age, sex, grade, address, phone number, parents' names, and beginning date of record.

The section on *background information* is completed from school records, direct observation of the child in various school settings, talks with the child's religious leader, walks through the neighborhood, and talks with the child himself. It may include descriptions of the child's home environment and neighborhood, health and early developmental information, intelligence and achievement test data, and notes on social and emotional development.

A variety of techniques may be used to complete the *anecdotal record*. The sample case of Patty, as we shall see, follows a column organization. The first column on the left is reserved for the tabulation of categories—physical, affectional, peer, and so on—resulting from analysis of the anecdotes. The first column is filled in only *after* entries have been made in the other three columns—when the teacher has had a chance to analyze the information in each observation. The second column is for noting the date and time, and sometimes the place, of each observation. Time periods are important in assessing the occurrence and reoccurrence of behavior patterns. For example, a specific problem near the end of the day may reflect fatigue. The anecdote number is listed in the third column to facilitate communication about any particular observation. The fourth column contains the anecdotes.

The *summary* of the information in the record may be broken down into such categories as (1) physical, (2) affectional, (3) peer, (4) social and cultural, (5) self-development, and (6) self-adjustment, or other categories may be selected. The teacher analyzes each anecdote to decide which category best describes the behavior observed and then enters the appropriate category number(s) in the first column of the anecdotal record. When the summary is prepared, the teacher may refer to the category column to see how many occurrences there were of peer-related behavior, of self-adjustment behavior, and so on. On the basis of the summary information the teacher makes decisions about teaching procedures for the child and continues to observe the behavior of other children to determine how the new knowledge can be brought to bear in unique situations.

EXAMPLE OF AN ANECDOTAL RECORD—THE CASE OF PATTY.[1]
The following record was prepared by a graduate student in a summer Head Start program. It should be borne in mind that the record resulted from only 11 days in the center. The meaningful information gained in this short time illustrates the significance of brief, concentrated attention to the behavior of a child and suggests considerable promise for longer-term studies. Anecdotes 10–61 are not included in the sample case study. The summary of the record, however, takes into account the complete set of anecdotes.

BACKGROUND INFORMATION

Patty was born October 29, 1962. Her mother said she was a six-months' baby and that she had difficulties at Patty's birth. Her mother is pleasant but illiterate, having only finished the second grade. She could give no other details about Patty's weight and height when she was born, but did say Patty was mature enough to accompany her home from the hospital four days after her birth.

Patty is the youngest of eleven (Negro) children. Eight of them are still living at home. Their ages are 4, 6, 7, 9, 10, 12, 14, and 23.

The house they live in is in a very deprived area. It is a two-room house. A toilet and lavatory have recently been installed so that it would pass the housing code as rental property. Most of the window panes have been broken out and have been replaced by corrugated paper and boards nailed across the windows.

The neighborhood is typical of most slum areas. Tin cans, paper, and other trash are found on the unpaved street and in the yards.

Patty is the youngest child and sleeps in the same bed with four brothers and sisters. The mother stated that she "pretty nigh well" played in her own yard or in the house.

Patty's father died when she was less than one year old. He fell from the top of a building under construction.

Patty's mother takes in ironing. Her oldest son is unmarried and helps to support the family. The mother says all the children work when she can find "yardwork or something of the sort" for them. They give her the money "'cause it takes all I can git to keep the family together."

Patty's oldest sister was stabbed to death about two months ago. She had given Patty most of her maternal care. Patty did not witness the killing, but did see her dead sister and was present at all the other incidents following the death. After this time Patty became withdrawn and very seldom talked to anyone but

[1] From Joe L. Frost and G. Thomas Rowland, *The Elementary School: Principles and Problems.* Copyright © 1969 by Houghton Mifflin Company, Boston, Mass. Reprinted by permission of the publisher.

her ten-year-old sister. Patty has become attached to this sister, who stays with her practically all the time.

A doctor's examination (and conference with the mother) disclosed the following:

1. No childhood diseases (mother).
2. No serious diseases (mother).
3. Vision—20/20 both eyes (doctor).
4. Hearing—normal (doctor).
5. Teeth—gross cavities (doctor).
6. Slow response to simple tests (doctor).
7. Blank eye focus (doctor).
8. Reflex test—abnormal (doctor).

ANECDOTAL RECORD

Category	Date and Time	Anecdote Number	
1,2,3,4	June 26 8:30	1	Patty was brought to school by her older sister, Sue, who is ten years of age. Patty was eating a piece of sausage. Sue said that Patty did not want to come so she had to come spend the day with her. Patty is small and thin. She held on to her sister's skirt and followed her to a chair where they both sat down. Patty was tidy and clean in appearance.
1,3	Lunchroom 8:30	2	Entire class went to lunchroom for breakfast. Patty ate most of food given to her and carried her tray. She didn't talk to anyone and looked away when teacher tried to talk with her.
1,3,5,6	Classroom 9:30	3	Class was given color booklets and colors. She colored within the lines and in a neat manner. She was the only child to color the faces brown. She still hasn't talked to anyone.
6	10:00	4	The teacher told the children a story. She held Patty in her lap. She tried to get Patty to talk and finally did get her to say, "Yes, ma'am."
2,3,6	Playground 10:30	5	The class went to the playground. Patty's sister put her in a swing and pushed her. Patty smiled. She did not play with the other children. She let me carry her back to the classroom.
1,5,6	Classroom 11:00	6	Patty picked out a jigsaw puzzle and brought it over to me. She put the pieces back in place with little difficulty.

			I talked to her and she understood but made no attempt to talk to me.
2,3,5	Classroom 11:30	7	Patty and her sister played in the doll house, but from observation I did not see her talking to anyone. The children in the class do not respond to Patty. If they take something from her, she just looks at them.
3	Classroom 12:00	8	Patty and another girl began playing together in the sand pile. This is the first time I have seen her playing or making contact with anyone other than her sister.
1,3	Lunchroom 12:20	9	Patty sat by her sister and ate lunch. She ate everything on her plate. As soon as they finished eating, they walked to their home one block away.
3,5	10:00	62	Patty played with other children on the playground. She tried to push other children in the swings (swing them).
4,5	11:00	63	The doctors examined in one room and nurses checked eyes in the other. Two classes were involved at a time. Many children became restless. Patty sat and said nothing. She was very receptive to taking the eye test.
2,6	11:15	64	The doctor examined Patty. She sat quietly and wouldn't answer him. She was slow to do what he told her but didn't cry.
	11:30	65	The doctor said he would like to talk to Patty's mother. I walked to her home and she was ironing. She readily agreed to talk to the doctor and walked back to school with me. She said, "I cain't help my yunguns with school work 'cause I don't know nuffin myself. I had to quit school in the secunt grade." She said she was going to try sending Patty to kindergarten if she could "scrape up" the fees.
2,5,6	11:45	66	After Mrs. Dickson talked with the doctor, Patty asked her to go to the room and see her pictures. She was talking about the "life-size" form which had been cut from the mural paper. I went to the room with them. Patty ran to her form on the wall and said in the most pronounced voice I have heard from her, "See!"

Summary

Tabulations of selected behaviors:

  2 Cried when her sister left her.
 15 Eats well (most or all of her lunch).
  5 Held on to sister's skirt.
  6 Would not talk to other people when they tried talking to her.
 14 Talked to other people.
  6 Played with other children.
  3 Late to school.

Note: It was amazing to me that after observing Patty almost constantly, she was observed talking only fourteen times during the eleven days I observed her. I tried to watch for this in particular and suppose I got used to it, because I thought she talked more than this.

SUMMARY OF INFORMATION ABOUT PATTY—BY CATEGORIES

1. Physical

Premature birth (six month)
Small and thin
Gross cavities of teeth
Eats well
Abnormal reflex to reflex test
Needs more sleep
Normal hearing
20/20 vision
Blank eye focus

Summary

Patty is small and fragile looking. Except for abnormal reflexes and cavities of teeth, she is in good physical condition. She eats well and the doctor states that she has no obvious nutritional problems.

2. Affectional

Lives with mother
Cared for mostly by older sister
Cries when sister can't be with her at school
Holds older sister's skirt or hand most of the time
Smiles at people sometimes when they do things for her

Summary

Patty receives love and affection from her family, but constant attention from her ten-year-old sister. She has a great fear since her oldest sister's death.

3. Peer

Seldom talks to peers
Seldom plays with peers
Peers act as though Patty isn't there when she refuses to take part in activities

Summary

Patty has little to do with her peer group. She has progressed in her relationship with them as she continues coming to Head Start.

4. Social and Cultural

Lives in two-room house with nine others
House in middle of slum area, run down, boards and cardboard cover most windows, dark and dreary

Summary

Patty is a disadvantaged child coming from a poor socioeconomic area. She took her first bus trip this summer and never gets "uptown." She has never been to a movie, but watches inside; seldom leaves immediate neighborhood

Does not attend Sunday School

Has TV in home; toilet and lavatory

5. *Self-Development*

Colors faces brown

Smiles when she has a pretty dress

Neat in appearance

Clean

6. *Self-Adjustment*

Stopped talking after oldest sister's death

Decided attachment to ten-year-old sister

Cries when sister leaves her

Little relationship with those about her

Slow response when given simple tasks and often shows no response

TV. The family does not take a paper, and her only access to books is what her brothers and sisters bring home.

Summary

Patty apparently realizes she is a Negro because of coloring skin brown. She is kept clean and seems to take pride in the fact that she has on a clean dress.

Summary

Normal self-adjustment seemed to slow when Patty's oldest sister, who cared for her, died. She has formed a decided attachment for her ten-year-old sister, who stays with her constantly. She shows withdrawal tendencies, which I believe are caused by fear. As she has made some progress in her relationships with others in the short time she has been attending Head Start, continued contacts in kindergarten should help tremendously. Psychological testing has already been ordered for her in September, and immediate dental care is planned.

Developmental Checklists

Another approach to observation is through a developmental checklist. The teacher either uses the checklist as a guide in observing children or as a basis for designing informal, teacher-made tests. A developmental checklist serves many important functions. (1) It serves as a general outline for program activities. (2) It is a source for assisting teachers in determining next steps in the developmental-instructional sequence. (3) Through systematic checking, the progress of each child may be charted and used for instruction and assessment. The checklist found in Appendix A is sequenced, representing *rough averages* for children from about 3 to about 6 years of age, as follows:

Level III: 36 months to 48 months
Level IV: 48 months to 60 months
Level V: 60 months to 72 months

There are certain limitations to the developmental checklist presented here that should be observed. (1) The sequence presented is drawn from experience and research and is subject to variation from child to child. (2) The tasks presented are only *samples* of behaviors that are frequently demonstrated, but they are not necessarily the most important behaviors for individual children. (3) The major categories are arbitrary and are related to the educational objectives for early childhood education discussed earlier in this chapter. They are not necessarily consistent with the program categories used by everyone. (4) The chronological age ranges attached are rough averages; any individual child may be several months beyond or behind the average capabilities reached by other children of the same age. (5) The checklist behaviors were not selected to conform to a particular developmental theory or body of work (for example, Piaget, Gesell), but were chosen because they are simple, frequently observed, and commonly used in assessment and curriculum development.

Learning Centers

The wise teacher plans interest centers that serve both instructional and evaluation purposes. For example, a pan scale balance arranged alongside an assortment of objects (buttons, pine cones, seashells, blocks, pebbles) invites learning and concept formation about weight, size, proportion, and number. Moreover, immediate feedback to the child from the activity fosters self-discovery and independence. The teacher may simply observe the child at work in such an interest center, encourage him to verbalize about what he is thinking and doing, and make notes about her observations to use in later planning. The activity may be accompanied by a set of task cards (see Chapter 9) which propose problems in picture-word form and which are color coded according to levels of difficulty. Further evaluative information about the child is provided on the basis of his work with the task cards. The teacher may advance along the continuum of difficulty level of the task cards on a one-to-one basis with the child or in a small group. When the task cards are laminated or protected with clear contact paper, the child is able to record his discoveries directly on the cards. Thus the teacher may assess them later, at her own convenience.

Outdoor activities can be similarly arranged for evaluative as well as instructional purposes. For example, a simple beanbag toss game is used as an instructional tool for learning colors, for counting, for eye-hand coordination, and for gross motor activity. One can easily be made by painting the face of a clown on a large piece of sturdy cardboard which has also been fitted with a cardboard stand on the back for support. The object is to stand at a predetermined distance from the clown's face and toss beanbags through the openings. The openings are the clown's facial features, his eyes, nose, mouth, and ears. The rim of each of the facial features is painted a different color to match a similarly colored beanbag. The child names the color of the beanbag he chooses and attempts to toss it through the corresponding colored opening on the clown's face. The child, and one or more partners if he so chooses, keeps a count of successful tosses. Motor skill is further challenged by gradually increasing the distance between the child and the clown board. A game of this nature is not only instructional, but the teacher, through observation, is able to diagnose strengths and weaknesses in the participating children as well as evaluate growth at a later time.

Table 8-2 illustrates the many possible areas for instruction and for evaluation in learning centers. Additional examples of integrated and extended learnings that emerge from learning or interest centers are given in Chapter 9.

Inventories and Surveys

Using inventories and surveys with just two or three children for a brief period each day provides considerable information for evaluating and planning over the semester or year. These are especially useful techniques for evaluating the child's interests and attitudes. Identified topics of personal interest to a child such as dinosaurs or astronauts may be the take-off point for activities involving language arts, mathematics, science, art, music, fine muscle movement, planning, decision-making, problem-solving, creating, and so on (see Chapter 11). Examples of types of inventories and surveys the teacher may choose to conduct include:

1. Tallying which learning centers and activities the child selects and the amount of time he spends at each over a period of time to identify what kinds of activities interest him.
2. Recording the objects he brings to school from home to assess personal interests.
3. Recording the topics or the kinds of things he talks about over a period of time, at snack time or planning time or dismissal, to evaluate interests and attitudes.
4. Noting the peers and/or adults with whom he interacts, the amount of time he spends with each, and the nature of the interaction.
5. Tape recording or making a written record of what the child says to his peers and the manner in which he says it to determine if his attitude is bullying, domineering, aggressive, thoughtful, cooperative, dependent, and so on.
6. Tallying every instance in which a particular behavior of interest is demonstrated over a period of time, such as biting, hitting, temper tantrums, a gesture to help someone, participating in cleanup, sharing and so on.
7. Making a case study of the child and the way he functions on his own to assess his self-responsibilities, self-reliance, and independence.
8. Making a case study of the way the child reacts to people and situations to evaluate his awareness and control of his emotions.
9. Using a specific opportunity, such as group planning time, to tally the number of times the child does or does not listen to others, offers alternatives, shares ideas, and so on.

TABLE 8-2 Areas for Instruction and Evaluation in Learning Centers

	Awareness, Attitudes, Interests	*Language, Symbolizing, Imitating, Communicating*	*Problem-solving, Decision-making*	*Coordinating, Identifying, Discriminating, Classifying, Knowing*	*Creating*	*Attending, Relating, Valuing*
Housekeeping—dramatic play center, doll corner	Awareness of oneself of physical attributes of emotions and feelings Awareness of other people of one's family of community and social roles of one's environment	Through speech role playing hearing drama body movement gesture action	*Who* to be *What* to be *How* to be it *Where* to be it *When* to be it	Social roles and skills Social expectations One's environment	Risk-taking Originality Open-ended activity	Oneself Others Needs Values
Quantitative, manipulative, and scientific centers	Awareness of time space quantity number weight form natural phenomena technological advances	Through graphics pictures print spoken word	Sensing a problem Weighing alternatives Experimenting Analyzing Evaluating	Self-discovery through manipulation use of senses experimentation repeated encounters in new ways	Charts Records Graphs Displays Experiments Projects Ideas	Nature and beauty Mathematics as a language
Block center and blocks added to outdoor play	Awareness of space area shape	Three-dimensional display Language arts	Making decisions and solving problems in building and	Physical development large and small	Unlimited for all ages	Social role Sharing Cooperation Responsibility

	Role-playing	in working with others	muscle development / Concepts	Messing about / Fantasy	Natural materials
dramatic play sand play measuring and weighing activity			muscle development (lifting, carrying) eye-hand coordination balance, symmetry		
			Emotional-social development independence patience sense of accomplishment	Messing about and free exploration stage	Natural materials Achievement
Sand (dry, wet)	Tension release (splashing, squeezing, pounding)	Making decisions and solving problems in usage, working with others and planning	Concepts number, size, shape, quantity weight	Controlling the medium stage Fantasy Realism	
Mud (changed for variety and stimulation with beans, leaves, sawdust)	Soothing, pleasant, sensory satisfaction (soft, cool, smooth)		simple machines motion		
	Tongue-loosening qualities Expression through the medium itself		math and science concepts depth what floats what melts takes shape of container has weight exerts		
Water centers (changed by adding soap bubbles, food coloring, cornstarch, styrofoam squiggles)		Vocabulary development names of various tools, shape words, size words, words for relationships such as over, under, and			
Woodworking-construction center (add "beautiful junk": clothes-					

A multisensory experience

TABLE 8-2 Areas for Instruction and Evaluation in Learning Centers (continued)

	Awareness, Attitudes, Interests	Language, Symbolizing-Imitating, Communicating	Problem-solving, Decision-making	Coordinating, Identifying, Discriminating, Classifying, Knowing	Creating	Attending, Relating, Valuing
pins, flat sticks, etc.)			top, number-descriptive words such as jagged, wide, end, and pound	force reflects changes in texture Relationships cold-warm wet-dry solid-liquid Muscle development poking pulling pouring filling sifting holding Ego development sense of mastery		
Cooking activities	Smells Sounds Tastes See changes Feel textures	Through words the senses	How much ___? How to ___? Why did ___? What is ___?	Vocabulary development (mix, pour, sift, coarse, chop) Math concepts (number, measurement, shape, size)	Unlimited, using both cook and noncook recipes	Foods Other customs Different tastes Nutritious foods Sensible eating habits Health standards Personal hygiene
Art center	Awareness of color texture	Through fingerpaint tempera	Unlimited			

form medias	clay collage junk and scrap material crayons magic marker. chalk paper	Science concepts (property change, temperature) Language arts reading recipes packages talking questioning explaining following directions health safety nutrition Muscle development Vocabulary growth Number Size, shape, color Aesthetic appreciation	Unlimited	Beauty Symmetry Nature Responsibility Others' work
Creative movement, music, dance, rhythms, physical education	Body awareness Sound awareness Space awareness	Auditorially With the body With feeling Self-expression	Unlimited	Listening skills listening to sounds, words, notes, beats, rhythm, matching sounds Motor development Spatial and body awareness Directionality Sound Unlimited Sound Rhythm Mobility Other people's space

10. Making a case study of the way the child makes decisions, solves problems, or works in small groups.
11. Making an anecdotal record of the types of emotions the child expresses, what situations evoke particular emotions such as anger, happiness, anxiety, or fear, the way the child expresses his emotions, and the way he reacts when things don't go his way.
12. Creating questionaires about the child's feelings, interests, and attitudes. These are not paper and pencil questionaires. Rather, the teacher implements them casually as she chats with the child: "What things do you like to do in school?" "What is easy for you to do?" "Who is your best friend?" "Why?" Sometimes the teacher uses the questionaire topics as the basis for small-group discussion: "What makes you happy?" "If you could change something about our classroom, what would you change?" "Why?" "Who is your favorite person?" Or she may ask the children to draw a picture and then take down dictation about it: "Draw a picture of the things that are hard for you to do"; "Draw a picture of the things you did this vacation at home." Such simple questionaires are also useful tools to determine if the child is aware of his personal values and if he knows how to evaluate them for himself: "How do you feel about _____?" "What would you do if _____?" "What would you have done if you were in that situation?" "Is that the best thing to do?" "Should everyone do it that way?" "Should everyone feel like that?" (See also Chapter 11 for value identification.)

Samples of the Child's Work

Another way to evaluate is to maintain a file of the child's work. At various times determined by the teacher, such as weekly, biweekly, monthly, and so on, samples of the child's work in various areas are dated and added to the file. The method is to collect work samples on a regular basis so that the collected file is truly a representative sample and not merely the child's best effort or his poorest effort. A work file provides a long-range picture of the child's growth for use in evaluation. When the data are related to what is known about the child's development in the various areas, the method provides useful information to use in planning further instruction. Work that cannot be easily kept in a file, such as three-dimensional art work or examples of oral language or of behavior, is preserved by being written down in descriptive detail by the teacher.

The Initial Teacher-Parent-Child Conference

Whenever possible, the teacher arranges to meet the children before the first day of school so that the school setting and personnel will be familiar to them. She contacts each parent by telephone or by letter to arrange a mutually convenient time for a three-way meeting between parent(s), child, and teacher during the week before school begins. During each scheduled meeting, lasting at least 15–30 minutes per child, the teacher becomes acquainted with the child and also obtains some preliminary diagnostic information about him. If individual conferences are not possible, the teacher may gather preliminary evaluation data during the first few weeks of school. It is also useful to have a systematic plan formulated for gathering preliminary information about new entrants to the program or for use during special teacher-parent conferences called by either party early in the year. The preliminary form illustrated in Figure 8-4 exemplifies the type of evaluative data it is possible to obtain during initial interaction with children and/or parents.

The teacher obtains her diagnostic information informally, rather than create a possibly threatening test situation. As she chats with the parents, as she interacts with the child, and as he moves about the room, she focuses upon the specific aspects of behavior previously selected and isolated on the form. In the affective domain, she may focus upon the child's attitude about himself. Is he shy or apprehensive about the new experience? Does he cling to his mother throughout the conference or is he bold and forward? What are his feelings about coming to school? What are the parents' attitude toward the child? Are they warm and concerned or cold, insensitive, or punitive? What are the parents' expectations of the program? Do they see value in play as a vehicle for learning? The teacher focuses upon the child's interests, as evidenced by the toys and equipment he plays with during the conference, and by the things his parents state he is looking forward to in school or the things he likes to do at home. She may obtain some insight into the child's personal values and those of his family from the way he handles the equipment and materials in the room, what his parents say to him and to the teacher about their expectations for his behavior, and the way he responds to his parents.

In the cognitive domain, the teacher may focus upon the child's recognition of his name: "There's a special place in the room where you can keep all of your very own things while you're at school. Can you find the coat hook and the box that has your name on it?" If he can find it, she asks, "How did you know that was your very own place?" If the opportunity arises, she may carry the diagnosis further. For the child who chooses to draw, paint, or make something during the conference, she invites him to print his name himself on the item. Or the teacher prepares cheerful, inviting name tags for each of the children to wear on the first day. The room number, bus number, and teacher's name is already printed on one side. She casually invites the child to print his name on the tag himself. The teacher may choose to assess informally the child's knowledge of color by asking him the color of the label on the coat hook, the color of his name tag, or the color of some toy he plays with. She may assess some of the child's concepts as he explores the toys and equipment in the room: "Which is the biggest of those blocks?" "Which side of the scale weighs more?" "Which is the tallest letter in your name?" "Would you wear those dress-up clothes in the

Child's name ———————————————————— Date ——————————

Parent-Child Attitudes
1. The child acts: shy   aggressive   apprehensive   at ease   eager.
2. The child handles the classroom materials:
   not at all   cautiously   with curiosity   aggressively   dangerously.
3. The parents speak to the child with:
   warmth   concern   indifference   warnings   threats.
4. The child responds to his parents:
   with indifference   with fear   timidly   easily and warmly   not at all.
5. Do the parents express their expectations of the program? Yes   No   .
6. Their expectations are: subject-matter oriented   socially oriented
   developmentally oriented   other ————————————————
7. The parents view play: as a vehicle for learning   as useless
   no view given   other ——————————————————
8. Particular concerns expressed by the parents: ————————————
   ————————————————————————————————————

Interests

9. The toys, materials, or equipment that the child approached during the conference: ——————————————————————
   ————————————————————————————————————

10. The parents stated that the child is looking forward to the following in school: ——————————————————————
    ————————————————————————————————————

11. The things the child is interested in at home: ————————————
    ————————————————————————————————————

Concepts and Skills

12. The child is able to locate his name above his coat hook. Yes   No   .
13. The child can print his name: not at all   partially   well   .
14. The child appears to walk and move normally. Yes   No   .
15. The child has difficulty grasping materials and equipment. Yes   No   .
16. The child holds a pencil (crayon, paintbrush, magic marker, etc.) appropriately. Yes   No.
17. The child appears to have difficulty with coordination as he paints, draws, or prints: ——————————————————————
    ————————————————————————————————————

18. The child speaks clearly. Yes   No.
19. Any special handicaps: ——————————————————
    ————————————————————————————————————

20. Any indication of level of understanding of size concepts: ————————
    ————————————————————————————————————

21. Any indication of level of understanding of number concepts: ————————
    ————————————————————————————————————

22. Recognition of colors: ——————————————————————
23. Recognition of shapes: ——————————————————————

Additional Remarks

FIGURE 8-4   Preliminary evaluation information.

summer or in the winter?" "Why did that magnet pick up the paper clip and not the napkin?"

In the psychomotor domain, the teacher may focus upon the way the child walks and moves, the way he holds a pencil, crayon, paintbrush, or toy, or his coordination in handling equipment and materials and in writing or painting. She focuses upon the clarity of his speech. If he is handicapped in some way, she looks for immediate concerns in the way he deals with his handicap and any special adjustments to be made in the physical setting and in the curriculum.

After the get-acquainted conference, the teacher begins her record of information about the child and his behavior by completing the preliminary diagnostic form. She continues to add evaluative data for each child in all the domains of his development throughout the school year. Although the teacher has undoubtedly already basically arranged the classroom environment based upon her knowledge of young children and her program goals, she may make some program adjustments as a result of this initial diagnosis. She may adjust the developmental levels of some learning centers, add new ones, and/or tentatively cluster the children for small-group and individual work in particular areas of need.

Standardized Tests

Standardized tests, when used in conjunction with other forms of evaluation, add to the teacher's knowledge and understanding of the child. The use of standardized tests must be accompanied by the teacher's judgment in assessing the meaning of a measurement for a particular child and must be based upon her thorough knowledge and understanding of him. She must answer such questions as: Does this measure, or score, actually represent Sue's best effort? Was she feeling well today? Was the test designed for specific instructional purposes? Are the results useful in planning curriculum for Sue? This final question should be asked of every assessment procedure ordinarily planned for children. Tests are to be used to improve classroom instruction, not to satisfy someone's curiosity or to "make the school look good." The exceptions are for carefully planned research for gaining new knowledge and pre-post testing to weigh effects of curriculum in producing growth within groups of children.

Standardized tests must be used cautiously for there are a number of problems associated with them. Many standardized tests have been built from middle-class Anglo samples that do not accurately reflect the wide diversity of cultural and socioeconomic groups in the United States. The common standardized tests discriminate against some minority and low socioeconomic groups. In many cases, the test items are foreign to the environmental setting (subways for rural children) or the language is inconsistent with common usage of the children being tested (dialect differences and English tests for children whose first language is Spanish). Other problems involved in the use of standardized tests include the fact that some children simply are not motivated to common testing procedures and do not work at their best under such conditions. The performance of a child may be affected by the nature of the test, the friendliness and competence of the examiner, the rapport established, and the feelings of the child toward the test. Even more dangerous is the practice of using standardized test results for comparative rather than instructional purposes. Evaluation specialists, psychologists, and other professionals are only beginning to understand the varieties of mental, social, and emotional characteristics that form the complex human being. Evaluation in respect to these individual factors is in an infant stage. It is quite conceivable that hundreds of abilities are yet to be identified, much less subjected to precise, objective measurement. Standardized tests have the potential of being a useful tool for diagnostic, formative, and summative evaluation when (1) the limitations of the particular test are taken into consideration; (2) the results of the test are used together with the results of other evaluation procedures; (3) test results are used for instructional and not for comparative purposes; and (4) the interpretation of test results is accompanied by the teacher's judgment and personal knowledge of the child. The types of standardized tests which are commonly used in early education include intelligence tests, readiness tests, and achievement tests. Sources of some commonly used tests are found in Appendix B.

INTELLIGENCE TESTS.   Intelligence tests measure such abilities as cognitive functioning, creativity, and memory. Subtasks of cognitive functioning include spatial reasoning, classificatory reasoning, relational-implicational reasoning, systematic reasoning, and attention span. Subtasks for creativity are fluency and flexibility. For memory they include span and serial memory, meaningful memory, visual memory, and auditory memory (Holpfner et al. 1971). In theory, the differences between intelligence quotient (IQ) scores of children are differences in inherent ability. Consequently, IQ is presumed to remain constant for any given individual across chronological age. In reality, however, there are a number of reasons why the IQ is not constant from one age to the other. All children do not have the same experiences or the same opportunities to learn the skills that intelligence tests measure. White, middle-class children appear to be in a more favored position than children from low socioeconomic groups and from certain minority groups in regard to *opportunity* to learn IQ test skills. Also, the original purpose of IQ tests, which was to predict academic achievement, has little utility in practice. The early childhood experimentation of the late 1960s demonstrated that IQ scores change dramatically as children are moved from one educational environment to another.

READINESS AND ACHIEVEMENT TESTS.   Achievement testing is the most common type of testing in the public schools. As early as kindergarten, the child is introduced to a common form of achievement assessment, the readiness test. Since readiness tests assess whether the child has the prerequisite skills necessary to benefit from formal instruction, they can be a helpful tool for the teacher. A major weakness which must be kept in mind, however, is that in many schools testing for "readiness" has become synonymous with "reading readiness." The term "readiness" is actually much broader in scope. Brenner describes readiness from a developmentalist's point of view.

Each individual is different from every other one. Each individual is an entity of body and mind which develops interdependently through constant interaction between the organism and his various environments. Each behavior has multiple causes. The multiplicity and different characteristics of individual genes transacted through the multiplicity of nurture factors and life experiences makes each individual unique, with a different pattern and rate of maturation and readiness. Readiness for certain school demands occurs in each individual in a different way and at a different time. (1967:73)

Downing and Thackray (1971) compiled an extensive review of readiness literature which illustrates the broad scope of readiness. Their discussion of readiness is divided into four chapters, covering physiological factors; environmental factors; emotional, motivational, and personality factors; and intellectual factors. Contrasted to this broad view, common readiness tests are quite limited in scope, reflecting a major weakness in them. The widely used Metropolitan Reading Readiness Test, for example, measures only understanding of word meaning, listening and matching skills, knowledge of number and letter names, and pattern-copying ability; it includes also a draw-a-man test. The Harrison-Stroud Reading Readiness Profiles measure symbol usage, visual discrimination, context usage, auditory discrimination, combined use of auditory and context cues, and letter naming.

Some achievement tests have recently become available for use with preschool children. The Preschool Inventory is made up of 85 questions that yield scores on personal-social responsiveness, associative vocabulary, and numerical and sensory concept activation. A second preschool achievement test, the Basic Concept Inventory, consists of 90 items forming three major groupings—basic concepts, statement repetition and comprehension, and pattern awareness. This test is designed to measure achievement on the Bereiter-Engelmann program (see Chapter 4). The Preschool Attainment Record measures achievement on counting and operations with integers and oral semantic skills. In addition, it measures certain skills in other domains such as physical coordination, small motor coordination, health responsibility, and social skills.

TESTS OF PSYCHOMOTOR ABILITY. Psychomotor development is a gradual process of bringing the voluntary muscles under control. Skills in this area are learned rapidly during infancy and early childhood and, under normal conditions, appear to require little direct attention from adults. Consequently, this important aspect of development may be taken for granted or overlooked. Level of psychomotor development is not always either diagnosed or evaluated for the average child, the child who lacks any overt, obvious handicap. Moreover, planning for growth in this domain is often taken for granted as attainable through play with such typical preschool-kindergarten items as outdoor playground apparatus and indoor puzzles. Children do, however, need a more systematic program for psychomotor development based upon deliberate, continuous evaluation of developmental level and growth. There are some tests which have been used in early childhood education in this area such as the Valett Developmental Survey of Basic Learning Abilities, the Developmental Test of Visual-Motor Integration, the Metropolitan Readiness Test (eye-hand coordination), and the Southern California Perceptual-Motor Tests.

TESTS OF AFFECTIVE AND SOCIAL BEHAVIOR.   Affective development is more difficult to measure than intellectual and psychomotor development because it deals with subjective feelings and values which are not directly observable. For this reason, most early childhood programs do not treat this important area in a systematic way. Instructional objectives for the affective domain rarely are used and, until recently, research into affect was quite limited. Yet, despite this lack of attention, educators generally concede that affective development is at least as important as intellectual and psychomotor development.

A number of difficulties need to be overcome so that affective development will receive the attention it deserves. Some educators believe that teaching values and attitudes may "brainwash," or indoctrinate, children (Bloom, Hastings, and Madaus 1971). Another reason for hesitancy to teach for values and attitudes is that affective competencies are considered private matters. An individual's right to political and religious beliefs and his attitudes on social issues are protected by law and teachers are reluctant to infringe on these delicate areas. On the other hand, such personal matters do have direct effects on performance of cognitive competencies and must be treated if the individual is to develop fully. The child's privacy is protected by avoiding the assignment of grades or marks to affective objectives and by teaching him how to evaluate for himself. (See Chapter 11 for examples of ways to enhance affective development.) Evaluation is used for direct feedback to the student and for instructional improvement. Tests that are used in assessing affective development include the California Test of Personality, Coopersmith Behavior Rating Form, Measures of Self-Concept, and the Cincinnati Autonomy Test Battery. As in the evaluation of the other domains, the teacher uses standardized tests only when she feels that they will be useful in improving instruction and when they can be used in combination with other evaluation techniques.

Teacher-Made Informal Tests

Daily classroom activity affords numerous opportunities for the teacher to evaluate children through informal testing. The teacher simply devises a set of tasks to assess the attainment of whatever objectives she is interested in measuring. The hierarchy of program objectives is useful here in designing a range of behaviors for evaluation. Informal tests need not be written tests. The teacher may take each child aside and ask him a series of questions or ask him to manipulate some objects or materials. The items on the developmental checklists and many of the tasks designed by Piaget in his study of children lend themselves to informal evaluative tests (see Chapters 7 and 10). In designing informal tests, the teacher must be sure that the few tasks or questions she selects are representative of the observable behavior she is evaluating and that she does not change the questions or tasks from child to child if she is evaluating the entire class.

Self-Evaluation

It is enlightening when children are given the opportunity to evaluate themselves, a source of assessment whose value should not be dismissed lightly. The teacher may ask, "What do you think about your work today?" "Why did you work the problem this way?" "How do you feel about this paper?" "How could you show me you understand this story?" Awareness and acceptance of children's standards, which are often quite different from those of the teacher, can at least provide an understanding of those differences if not reconcile them entirely. When such evaluation is encouraged and treated with fairness and respect, children offer honest insight into the circumstances of their own accomplishments. Moreover, in the process-oriented curriculum, children are guided in learning how to set high standards for themselves and how to critically evaluate for themselves (see Chapter 10).

REPORTING EVALUATION TO PARENTS

There are a variety of methods to use in reporting evaluation to parents. Report forms that consist of a series of skills and behaviors may be the method of reporting. (Letter or numerical grades are of little or no value.) Other report cards employ a narrative format. Only a few general headings are indicated, for example, language, social adjustment, and mathematics. The teacher then writes a brief description of the child's progress and his strengths and weaknesses under each heading. Some schools choose to report evaluation at parent conferences and have samples of the child's work, test scores, and observation reports on hand as the basis from which to discuss the child's growth. Sometimes sending home a report card is combined with an immediate follow-up parent conference. Whatever method a program selects to report evaluation to parents, there are several important things for the teacher to remember. The purpose of reporting to parents is not to inform them solely of pupil achievements and weaknesses. Teachers should maintain continuous communication with parents so that reporting is viewed as just one more part of the line of communication between them. Parents feel welcome to share in the educative process when they are kept in constant touch with the program. Frequent newsletters inform them of such things as activities in the classroom, changes in the routine, the goals and purposes of the program, and the changing interests of the children. (see Chapter 10). Reporting to parents must also include the occasional phone call and brief note to share a child's discovery, a humorous anecdote, or some personal concern. Such a continuous approach to reporting utilizes its primary purpose, to maintain two-way communication in the best interest of the children involved.

EVALUATING THE PROGRAM

In addition to evaluating children, it is necessary to evaluate the program. Program evaluation is not an easy task. The teacher works individually and/or may be part of a staff team. All aspects of the program must be included in the evaluation. The evaluation team asks questions similar to those that follow and many more. The results of formative and summative evaluation are utilized to answer some of the program evaluation questions. Others are answered by the statement of philosophy, the activities and materials, or actual practice. Also, comparing other preschool programs as well as their evaluation techniques may be useful in formulating evaluative questions for one's own program.

Program Objectives
    Are both the long- and short-term objectives of the program identified?
    Are they operationally stated as observable behaviors?
    Are the long- and short-term objectives related to each other?

Curriculum
    What are the major characteristics of the curriculum?
    Does it represent implementation of the objectives?
    Is it sequenced?
    Is it based upon the needs of the children?
    Does it account for their interests?

Relationship to Community
    Does the program and the curriculum extend into the community?
    Does the program and the curriculum reflect community needs, concerns, and background?

Role of the Teacher and of the Child

What is the teacher's role in making decisions about the program?
What is the teacher's role in implementing the curriculum?
What is the child's role in curriculum planning and implementation?
How is the child viewed in the program?

Theoretical Basis

What theories of child development and learning is the program based upon?

Physical Setting, Materials, Teaching Methods

What is the nature of the physical setting in the classroom?
Does it allow the curriculum objectives to be implemented?
Does the daily schedule allow the curriculum objectives to be implemented?
Do children work primarily alone, in small groups, or in large groups?
What materials and equipment are used in the program?
What space is available, indoors and outdoors?
What expenses are involved in the program?

Resources

What size staff is used in the program implementation?
What size staff is needed to implement the program effectively?
How are parents, the community, and community resources utilized in the
 program?
To what extent are outside resources utilized in the program?

Evaluation

How is diagnostic information obtained?
How is the diagnostic information applied to the instructional process?
On what basis are children evaluated?
What tools and techniques are used for diagnosis, formative evaluation, and
 summative evaluation?
How is evaluation data utilized in program and instructional improvement?
How is evaluative information reported to parents?

CRITERIA FOR INSTRUCTIONAL EXPERIENCES

Once the educational objectives of the program are determined, the next step
is to select the appropriate experiences that will facilitate their attainment.
The criteria for instructional experiences serve as the teacher's guidelines in
choosing experiences for young children that are conducive to the achievement of the program objectives. The following criteria were influenced in
part by the philosophies of the significant individuals in educational history
discussed earlier in this book. They are also based upon psychological theory
and research. The criteria for experiences are the foundation from which the
activities and experiences suggested in subsequent chapters emerged. When

choosing between alternate activities, the criteria for instructional experiences suggest the most fruitful avenue for reaching a given end.

1. *The child has an active role in planning the activity.* The child is most likely to work with commitment if he is working toward purposes that he understands and had a part in developing. Given choices, the child will most often choose activities that are conducive to healthy growth. If the child is to learn *how* to plan for his own living, he must have opportunities for practice.

2. *The experiences selected call for activity rather than passivity.* Children are normally active, curious, and inquisitive, engaging in exploration during much of the day. Exploration and self-discovery are essential because children learn for themselves from direct experience with objects and events. Through active involvement with his environment, the child comes to know and to understand.

3. *The activities foster the development of cooperation through sharing of materials and ideas.* In our society, we see a highly developed spirit of cooperation which is essential to societal functions such as production and distribution of goods, provision of services, healthy social relationships, and advancing scientific knowledge. The child learns, through sharing, to give as well as to receive—a pattern that will become increasingly essential as natural resources are depleted.

4. *The child is an individual.* Each child is viewed as a unique human being with individual needs, interests, and learning styles. The educational experiences, therefore, provide for a range of methods, materials, and activities. Individuality is everywhere evident in the classroom through the variety of the children's work displayed and the diversity of ongoing activities.

5. *The experiences enhance self-esteem.* The experiences foster such positive feelings in the child as a feeling of importance, of being worthwhile, and of being successful. He is personally greeted each day and treated with warmth and respect. Important things in his life are remembered and talked about. His ideas are sought, shared, and used in the program. His work is handled with care and his interests are encouraged and extended.

6. *The activities provide for exploration of real-life, practical problems.* Theoretical problems and many problems identified by teachers or other adults for children are states of mind. Real-life, practical problems arise from situations and concerns related to the child. They are *his* problems. They capture *his* interest. *His* problems are subject to change with circumstances. The imposed problems are often viewed as immutable, unyielding to changing circumstances. All this is not meant to imply that the teacher is a passive partner in the educative process. Why even have a teacher if she is unable to offer suggestions or directives of one sort or another? It is a matter of degree and timing.

7. *Concrete materials and real situations are the chief media for explora-*

tion. Other factors being equal, concrete materials and real situations are superior to improvised models or abstract representations. A trip to the airport is better than hearing stories about the airport. In-class exploration of plants, animals, and so on, is better than group discussion or teacher lecture about them. Children need tangible, interesting objects to handle, manipulate, take apart, put together, explore, invite curiosity, and stimulate thinking.

8. *The curriculum grows out of the personal interests of the child.* The curriculum is an integrated one. It stems from the personal interests of the child. The child's interests are then extended as far as possible to include integration with reading, mathematics, language arts, social studies, science, music, art, books, poetry, field trips, community resources, and parent resources.

9. *Experiences are planned.* Experiences are not haphazard presentations. There is a thoughtful plan behind their nature and their occurrence which is based upon the needs and interests of the particular children involved and the educational objectives of the program.

10. *Experiences have sequence and continuity.* The experiences are sequenced along a continuum of simple to complex to accommodate the movement of the child. Experiences are also built upon each other to facilitate growth and allow for the introduction of controlled discontinuity.

11. *The emphasis is on the process rather than the product.* Through learning problem-solving processes, children are better able to cope with new, or novel, concerns. Problem-solving processes are more intellectually durable and economical than isolated information. Masses of facts or information are more conveniently stored in books and computers. Activities and experiences are thought-provoking, inviting creativity, imagination, and many alternatives to explore.

12. *The teacher assumes a mediating, guiding role rather than a didactic role.* The teacher is a student of children, making judgments about what the child can now do as a basis for determining what types of experiences would logically come next. She anticipates and prepares an ever-changing environment to match emerging developmental needs. Interaction with children in ongoing activities is the chief context for mediation and guidance. The chief means of mediation and guidance are informal comment, questioning, modeling, reinforcing rather than telling and directing.

13. *Child talk is valued.* Children are encouraged to talk and to question, and ample time is provided for them to do so. Wherever possible, the teacher provides opportunity for the children to use language in giving directions, planning activities, and explaining rules.

14. *Play is an important vehicle for learning.* The educative process occurs through the child's natural inclination to play. Play, as the child's work, is the avenue for diagnosis, concept-building, problem-solving, language development, decision-making, cooperation, creating, coordination, extending interests, building attitudes, and growing in awareness of values.

15. *Time is valuable.* There is time for "messing about," time for in-

volvement, and time for evaluation. Children are allowed plenty of time initially to freely manipulate and explore. Then they are allowed sufficient time for deep involvement. At the end of the experience, there is time to evaluate the experience and to make value judgments.

16. *Various levels of success are possible.* The child is not expected to achieve complete success or absolute accuracy in every activity. Stages of success are possible. He is credited for partial solutions, for *progress* from a previous base-line level.

17. *More than one solution is possible and there are alternate routes to a solution.* Knowledge is not seen as fixed and immutable. Varying styles of working are valued, and children learn of the relativity of events and outcomes. Divergent outcomes are expected and valued.

18. *The child engages in decision-making and understands the consequences of his actions.* As the child works in a cooperative group context, he is constantly interacting with other people. These interactions affect his own behavior as well as the behavior of those around him. The child is assisted in examining choices and the actions of himself and others so that he may discover cause-effect relationships and learn to act in ways that support positive peer relations. Through this process, he becomes more skillful in making choices. In examining relationships among choices, actions, and consequences, the child engages in the construction, selection, and identification of rules and standards that are essential for group living and scientific endeavor.

19. *The activities preserve and enhance understanding of cultural group mores.* Children of different cultural groups have the opportunity to interact in an atmosphere of adult respect for differences. Activities are designed to enhance mores by drawing from rich community sources of materials—physical and human.

20. *The activities are enjoyable.* Other factors being equal, activities are chosen simply because the children enjoy them. Grimness is not essential to growth.

SUMMARY AND CONCLUSIONS

Educational objectives encompass all aspects of development, psychomotor, cognitive, affective, and social, and are the basis for planning and for evaluation. Objectives for early childhood programs include attending; socializing-relating; coordinating; identifying, discriminating, and classifying; symbolizing and imitating; language; problem-solving and decision-making; and creating.

There are three types of evaluation or three distinct purposes for assessment. The three types of evaluation are diagnostic, formative, and summative. The purpose of diagnostic evaluation is to obtain information on the child's present status. Instructional activities and experiences are then planned on the basis of the diagnostic data. Formative evaluation is conducted during the ongoing instruction. The purpose of formative evaluation is to assess the child's progress through a particular unit of study. Summative evaluation is an overall assessment at the end of a particular period of time. It assesses whether and to what extent the objectives were achieved.

There are a variety of methods which the teacher may employ to obtain objective and reliable data for evaluation and planning. These methods include the case study, developmental checklists, inventories, surveys, samples of work, conferences, learning centers, teacher-made tests, standardizd tests, and self-evaluation by the children.

Evaluation that is reported to parents should be more than a report of the child's grades, or marks. Reporting to parents should be considered just one more part of the continuous line of communication between teacher and parents. Reporting to parents should also include information about classroom interests and activities, changes in routine, goals and purposes of the program, personal concerns, and anecdotes.

Evaluation in early childhood education should include evaluation of the program as well as evaluation of the children. Aspects of the program which are evaluated include program objectives, theoretical basis, community relationship, role of the teacher and child, curriculum, physical setting, materials, teaching methods, resources, and progress of the children.

In selecting appropriate experiences to facilitate the attainment of the educational objectives, the following criteria for instructional experiences serve as the teacher's guideline:

1. The child has an active role in planning the activity.
2. The experiences selected call for activity rather than passivity.
3. The activities foster the development of cooperation through sharing of materials and ideas.
4. The child is an individual.
5. The experiences enhance self-esteem.
6. The activities provide for exploration of real-life, practical problems.
7. Concrete materials and real situations are the chief media for exploration.
8. The curriculum grows out of the personal interests of the child.
9. Experiences are planned.
10. Experiences have sequence and continuity.
11. The emphasis is on the process rather than the product.
12. The teacher assumes a mediating, guiding role rather than a didactic role.
13. Child talk is valued.
14. Play is an important vehicle for learning.
15. Time is valuable.
16. Various levels of success are possible.
17. More than one solution is possible and there are alternate routes to a solution.
18. The child engages in decision-making and understands the consequences of his actions.
19. The activities preserve and enhance understanding of cultural group mores.
20. The activities are enjoyable.

SUGGESTED ACTIVITIES

Observe in several early childhood programs in your community. The following suggested activities are based upon your observations.

1. Identify the educational objectives of each of the programs you visit. Select five of the objectives you identified, and determine what areas of development —affective, social, psychomotor, and cognitive—are promoted in the attainment of each objective.

2. Determine how each program conducts diagnostic, formative, and summative evaluation.

3. Select some activity you observed in your visits to the early childhood programs. Perhaps the activity is a field trip (a trip to a supermarket, a farm, an apple orchard, a class picnic), or it may involve some learning center (water table, doctor's office, celebration of a holiday). Apply the principle of task analysis and build a sequence of educational objectives in each of the developmental domains, cognitive, affective, social, and psychomotor. Use the objectives outlined in this chapter as guides. Be sure to include the introductory and the follow-up portions of the activity or event in your planning. Determine at what points along the continuum of learning the objectives from each of these domains can be intertwined during the instructional process.

4. Select some learning centers you observed in the early childhood programs. Describe how the learning centers were used for instruction. Describe how the learning centers were used to obtain evaluative information.

5. Determine the method of program evaluation for each early childhood program you visited. What aspects of the program are evaluated? Who conducts the program evaluation and how often is it conducted? How are the results of evaluation utilized for program improvement?

6. Select several instructional experiences you observed. Apply the criteria for instructional experiences to the activity. Discuss your conclusions.

7. Prepare a case study of a 3-, 4-, 5-, or 6-year-old child.

8. Use the developmental checklist found in Appendix A as a guide in observing a young child. On the basis of your findings, describe what the next steps in the developmental-instructional sequence might be for this child. Design the program activities for this child. Give reasons for your choices.

9. Prepare several inventories or surveys. Use them with 3-, 4-, 5-, or 6-year-old children. Analyze and explain your findings.

10. Look at copies of standardized tests described in this chapter. Read the directions. Note how the tests within each area of development are similar and how they are different.

REFERENCES

Bloom, B. S., J. T. Hastings, and G. F. Madaus. 1971. *Handbook on Formative and Summative Evaluation of Student Learning.* New York: McGraw-Hill.

Brenner, A. 1967. "What Is the Nature of Reading Readiness?" in J. L. Frost, *Issues and Innovations in the Teaching of Reading.* Glenview, Ill.: Scott, Foresman.

Doll, W. E., Jr. 1971. "A Methodology of Experience: An Alternative to Behavioral Objectives," paper presented at the American Educational Research Association Conference, Section B-22, February.

Downing, J., and D. V. Thrackray. 1971. *Reading Readiness.* London: University of London Press.

Gagné, R. M. 1968. "Learning Hierarchies," presidential address, Division 15, American Psychological Association, August 31.

Gagné, R. M. 1962. "The Acquisition of Knowledge," *Psychological Review,* 69:355–365.

Gagné, R. M., and L. T. Brown. 1961. "Some Factors in the Programming of Conceptual Learning," *Journal of Expermental Psychology,* 62:313–321.

Holpfner, R., et al. 1971. *CSE-ECRC Preschool/Kindergarten Test Evaluations.* Los Angeles: UCLA Graduate School of Education, Center for the Study of Evaluation and the Early Childhood Research Center.

FURTHER READING

Association for Childhood Education International. *Testing and Evaluation: New Views.* Washington, D.C.: The Association, 1975.

Eisner, E. W. "Educational Objectives: Help or Hindrance?" *School Review,* 1967, 75(3).

Frost, J. L. "Analyzing Early Childhood Education Programs: The Nature of Educational Objectives," *Educational Leadership,* 1971, 28(8):796–801.

McAshan, J. H. *Writing Behavioral Objectives.* New York: Harper & Row, 1970.

Popham, W. J., and F. L. Baker. *Establishing Instructional Goals.* Englewood Cliffs, N.J.: Prentice-Hall, 1970.

Raths, J. D. "Teaching without Specific Objectives," *Educational Leadership,* 1971, 28(7):714–720.

Ford Foundation, William Simmons

CREATING THE CLASSROOM ENVIRONMENT

Once the broad objectives of an early childhood program have been determined, a classroom environment must be prepared within which these goals can be achieved. This environment must allow activities and events to occur which meet the criteria for instructional experiences listed in Chapter 8. The creation of such a learning environment must consider the selection and development of the physical facility, the arrangement of the classroom, and the choice of materials and equipment. It is to these areas of the learning environment that this chapter is addressed. Examples of the kinds of activities and experiences that can occur within this environment are discussed in this chapter and in the remainder of this book.

SELECTION AND DEVELOPMENT OF THE PHYSICAL FACILITY

Early childhood programs provide some type of care for children outside of their homes for some portion of the day. The kind of care provided—whether the emphasis is educational, developmental, remedial, custodial, or a combination of these—varies according to the purpose of the individual program and the particular needs of its clientele. An early childhood program may be a nursery, nursery school, preschool, child development center, day care home, day care center, play school, day camp, and so on. It may be public, such as the Head Start program or a public school kindergarten, or private, such as a church- or organization-sponsored program. In the selection and development of the physical facility, an early childhood program must meet the minimal standards prescribed by the particular state and local agency under which it operates and is licensed. There are also federal standards established to serve as program guidelines. Although standards vary from state to state for day care services, for example, agencies that receive federal funds for child care services are subject to the Federal Interagency Day Care Standards (U.S. Department of Health, Education and Welfare 1968). Moreover, local and state standards cannot be implemented at a level lower than the federal standards. State and federal standards govern such areas as building safety, amount of play space per child indoors and outdoors, food service, fire regulations, bathroom facilities, and adult-child ratio. These guidelines serve to protect the child with regard to physical safety, personal comfort, and security while in group care.

CREATING THE INDOOR ENVIRONMENT

The indoor environment of the early childhood program is heavily influenced by the philosophy of the staff and the curriculum objectives. It is also influenced by the location of fixed features in the physical plant such as doors, windows, sources of running water, and permanent storage areas. Within this framework, a general blueprint of arrangement as defined by the nature of early childhood activities can be organized. Art work, for example, needs to be conducted near the running water and sink, while books should be located in a quiet area conducive to reading and browsing. At the same time, such variable features as tables, chairs, cabinets, equipment, and supplies are arranged to suit the individual tastes and needs of teachers and children.

The General Blueprint for Classroom Arrangement

One appropriate arrangement of the classroom for young children is illustrated in Figure 9-1.[1] The plan calls for four basic divisions of space—quiet–dry, active–dry, quiet–wet, and active–wet. Wet activities are located as far as is feasible from the dry activities or areas, and active areas are located away from quiet areas. The *quiet–dry* quadrant (I) is for book and listening activities, story time, writing, sharing, and planning, games, and small-group lessons. The *active–dry* quadrant (II) is for large motor activities, block construction, woodworking, housekeeping, rhythms, and toy play. The *wet–quiet*

[1] This plan was shared with Joe L. Frost by Sue Dalziel at the annual conference of the Florida Association for Children Under Six in November 1972. The idea is credited originally to Nancy Rambusch.

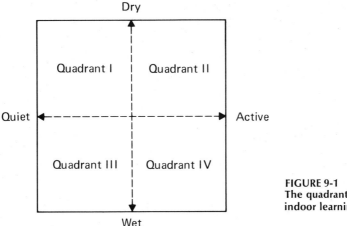

FIGURE 9-1
The quadrant plan for the
indoor learning environment.

quadrant (III) is for cooking, eating, pasting, papier mâché, and clay. The *active–wet* quadrant (IV) is for outdoor wraps, sand and water play, toilet and wash area, painting, and wet science experiments.

The wet area quadrants (III and IV) should be covered with a washable surface because of the spills that occur frequently. Quadrants I and II are dry areas and should be covered with a carpet to keep down noise and provide comfort for sitting on the floor. Over time, children learn behaviors appropriate to the various quadrants and modify their actions as they move from area to area. Thus, quadrants are zoned for type of activity and behavior rather than subject-matter emphasis. Subject matter is integrated with the activity and materials of the area, or center, as illustrated in Table 8-2. The teacher arranges large equipment that can be moved, such as tables and dividers, to accentuate the particular centers and make their purposes known.

The Center Plan for Classroom Organization

The physical space in early childhood programs is generally organized into learning areas, or centers (see Table 8-2). The areas themselves are more permanent than the materials and activities that occur there and that reflect the unique objectives of individual programs. In general, learning centers in early childhood programs are defined by the type of activity conducted in them, such as housekeeping or block play. The mere existence of centers of activity indicates that the curriculum is flexible and is characterized by movement, activity, exploration, and integration of content. The keynote is balance —between formality and informality, structure and flexibility, teacher direction and child responsibility.

THE HOUSEKEEPING CENTER.   The housekeeping center is located away from the main line of traffic and the quiet area. It is a miniature home, containing role-playing devices that allow children to imitate the behavior of grownups. This is an essential activity for healthy growth. The child must learn firsthand the appropriate societal roles. Sex roles, for example, are not inherent. They are learned through practice and observation. The housekeeping center provides dress-up clothes and materials that can be used to play out occupational, economic, and social roles. By no means are children restricted to playing out stereotyped roles designated by their own sex. Boys frequently choose to dress in girls' clothing and to play with dolls, while girls frequently elect to work in the carpentry area or be the "daddy" in their play. These chosen roles help the child to learn the real meaning of maleness and femaleness in society. The teacher does not insist or direct children to assume one role or another. Rather, the housekeeping center is available for the children to *explore*. The teacher merely provides the setting and materials and guides children toward taking advantage of the wide variety of resources available. The housekeeping center is also a rich arena for intellectual, motor, and social development. As children cook, dress up, and role play, they use language, enlarge their vocabularies, and grow in understanding of concepts. The potential for such language usage is everywhere: pint, quart, cup, dozen, spatula, laddle, electrician, repairman, wrench, screwdriver, and so on. Children improve motor ability as they pour, measure, button, zip, tie, fold, pin, put on, take off, iron, set the table, wash dishes, dress the baby, and cook supper. All this goes on in the midst of social interchange. As children interact with materials and with each other, they engage in language and materials exploration essential to concept development. Teachers assist by moving through the arena to listen, to engage in informal conversation, to add new props or materials, to question, and, on occasion, to explain.

Children share in making rules and setting limits for playing in the area. When children share in the responsibility, it is possible for activities such as water play and real food experiences to be part of the play in the housekeeping area. A small dishpan of water for "cooking," washing dishes, or washing doll clothes adds another dimension to the learning there. Children and teacher share in making a simple picture-word cookbook and then following the directions for occasionally "cooking" peanut butter and jelly crackers, Kool Aid, and stuffed celery.

Materials and furniture to stock the housekeeping area may be commercially purchased, or they may be recycled junk. Parents, relatives, garage sales, rummage sales, junk stores, and thrift shops are all sources of useful items for housekeeping play. Materials in this area include the following, in appropriate sizes for children:

Table and chair set

Rocking chair

Stove, refrigerator, sink, cupboard (wooden crates or boxes can be

Miscellaneous "real" appliances (broken toaster, iron, alarm clock, telephone, etc., with sharp and dangerous parts removed)

converted into appliances and cab-
inets)
Mirror (full size and hand mirror)
Ironing board
Brooms, mops, dustpan
Doll furniture
Dolls and doll clothes of different
ethnic groups in the classroom and
community
Dress-up clothes (men's and women's,
including hats, shoes, boots, coats,
dresses, gowns, suits, purses, jew-
elry, scarves, wigs, gloves, etc.)
Props for various roles (doctor, nurse,
businessman, beautician, plumber,
secretary, camper, etc.)
Various pots, pans, baking utensils
Bed or cot

Silverware, kitchen utensils (real ones
such as measuring spoons, spatulas,
funnels, egg beaters, strainers, etc.)
Dishes, cups, saucers, plastic glass-
ware
Aprons, tablecloths, napkins
Pillows, quilts, blankets
Empty, cleaned food containers of all
varieties
Modeling material for making "food"

Activities and materials in the housekeeping center or adjacent to it are arranged and rearranged with the changing interests and needs of the children. The area may become a restaurant with the following added: paper and pencil to print menus and take orders, pretend food made of papier mâché or clay, a cash register and money, waiters and waitresses. Illness in one child's family may prompt the housekeeping area to turn into a doctor's office or a hospital complete with bandages, stretcher, stethoscope, and doctors and nurses in "uniform." Or a visit to the school by a dentist may expand it into a dentist's office. The possibilities for learning through the housekeeping area are as limitless as are the children's interests and activities.

THE BLOCK-BUILDING CENTER.   Blocks are a universal medium for expression by preschool children. Almost every element of the early childhood program can be addressed in the block-building center. Sociodramatic play in the block area often rivals in intensity that of the housekeeping center. Children build clubhouses, forts, airplanes, cars, boats, fire stations, jails, and stores, and with the addition of a few dress-up clothes and props, they become pilots, drivers, sailors, storekeepers, and so on. Number, size, shape, and positional concepts are natural by-products of children's play. "How many do you need?" "Should this one go on top or bottom?" "This one is square." "Let's put the little one on top of the big one." Children's language grows as their concepts grow. They also learn to work with others, to articulate their ideas, to plan projects, and to assume responsibility for cleanup— all in an enjoyable manner.

The block area is located in the active–dry area of the room, perhaps next to the housekeeping area, since both are relatively noisy areas. Animal cages are not kept adjacent to the block-building area, since children may injure pets in their active play. Furthermore, some animals are frightened by noisy activity. The block area is carpeted to reduce noise, and it must be kept dry because blocks will warp and deteriorate if wet for extended periods of time. The area is sufficiently large to allow three to six children to engage in active construction play. Some block constructions are kept intact over a period of time, allowing children to return to their creations for modification and further play. Signs and stories are frequently dictated and attached to the structures. The building area may be bounded by low shelf dividers for storing the blocks. Large blocks are stored on the lower shelves and smaller blocks on the higher ones to facilitate removal. The shapes of different-sized blocks are traced on paper and taped as labels to appropriate shelves. These pictures are then used for classifying the blocks during cleanup. One end of the block area should be kept open so large construction activity can expand into a broader area.

Several types of blocks are available for the center. The most common are the solid wooden ones. They are durable and appealing and can be refinished periodically for even longer service. Hollow blocks provide size and less weight, allowing children to construct large structures to climb on and walk through. Hollow blocks are available with hand grips and rope handles. Many of these are too large for 2- and 3-year-olds but appropriate for children of 4 and 5. A variety of interlocking blocks or bricks are available in brightly colored plastic. The very large ones can be interlocked to form structures large enough for children to crawl through. They are adaptable to a wide variety of building tasks. Smaller interlocking bricks are often placed in the manipulative skills area for small muscle activity. Cardboard blocks are also available for purchase. Their light weight makes them especially appropriate for 2- and 3-year-olds. They can be handled easily and do not injure toes and fingers when accidently dropped.

Certain supplementary materials add to the functions of the block-building area. Props representing people, traffic signs, animals, and vehicles are used creatively by children. A variety of smooth building boards are also available from supply catalogs. These are indispensable to large construction and activities involving toy vehicles. Wooden cars and trucks complement the use of boards and blocks as ramps, bridges, and highways are constructed. Because of space limitations, the more extensive activity with wheeled vehicles is carried on outdoors. Cardboard packing boxes large enough for children to get inside are also added to the block area from time to time. They quickly become trains, houses, cages, and so on.

THE CONSTRUCTION OR WOODWORKING CENTER.   The major items required in the construction area are a sturdy workbench or table with attached vise, hammers, saws, nails, wood, and assorted tools and materials. A large, sturdy crate or wooden packing box may suffice as a workbench. Materials for the construction area are chosen with care. Most of the cheap, miniature sets of carpentry tools found in department stores are inappropriate for real hammering and sawing. Children need real tools with which to work, tools large enough to provide the weight needed for genuine activity and of sufficient quality to ensure that they will function well. Faces of hammers should be smooth and symmetrical. Nails should have large heads—common nails as opposed to finishing nails. Saws should be kept sharp enough to cut the soft woods such as pine, fir, cedar, and balsam. An assortment of scrap wood pieces can be secured from most lumber yards at no cost. Hard woods such as oak, elm, or ash are not appropriate in the construction area because children have great difficulty sawing or pounding nails into them.

The construction activity is carefully supervised to avoid cuts from sawing and bruises from hammering. The use of tools is demonstrated by the teacher, who gives direct assistance to children in learning safe techniques. Because of the noise level and the possibility of injury, no more than three or four children work in this area at one time. The children are not required to make something, yet the activity of nailing and sawing will ultimately lead to the desire of some children to make a tangible product. The teacher offers suggestions, assistance, and additional materials toward this end. Adding junk materials periodically to the construction area stimulates new ideas and new challenges for the children working there. Such materials include bottle caps, jar lids, popsicle sticks, wooden ice cream spoons, spools, old hinges and latches, nuts and bolts, and small pieces of scrap wood in assorted shapes. Sometimes the construction area becomes part of the creative arts area when sturdy glue and paint are substituted for the tools. Many creative wood sculptures result from combining the wood scraps and junk material with glue. In mild climates and in warm weather, the construction area may be moved outdoors. In early childhood centers where space is a problem, the workbench may be opened to the children only every other day and alternate with some other area.

Materials in the construction area include:

Workbench	Nuts and bolts
Vise	Screws
Hammers	Containers for nuts and screws
Screwdrivers	Scrap lumber
Coping saw	Rulers
Pliers	Yardstick
Saws	Sandpaper
T square	Junk materials (latches, hinges, bottle caps, wood chips, spools, tile samples, popsicle sticks, ice cream spoons, etc.)
Adjustable wrench	
Nails	Paint and glue

WATER PLAY CENTER.   An indoor water play area is a rich storehouse of concepts for children—sinking, floating, weight, volume, color, solubility, and density. Language development is a natural by-product. Water play can be conveniently located outdoors when the climate is mild and when the outdoor activities become a natural extension of the indoor program. The essential elements are a suitable large container, assorted utensils, and proximity to a faucet and drain. The most appropriate arrangement for indoor water play is a specially designed table with built-in faucet and drain. However, a variety of containers can be used instead, such as a plastic swimming pool, a plastic basin, or a large tub. Children can help in filling and emptying the water.

The teacher makes materials available according to the level of development of the children. At first, only a few containers are on hand, allowing children to dip and spill, splash, and test. Soapsuds and food coloring added at different times enhance interest and add interesting dimensions of form and color. Later, a variety of floating and sinking objects, water wheels, tubing, funnels, measuring cups, strainers, squeeze bottles, and so on are made available. The activity itself creates the only definition of area that is necessary. Children are clustered around the water. Materials are stored nearby in such a manner that children can remove and replace them without teacher assistance. Waterproof aprons are essential for water play. Simple plastic materials are appropriate. Materials in the water play area include:

Large central container	Buckets
Cans	Tubing (assorted)
Corks	Funnels
Water wheels	Straws
Soap	Food coloring
Sponges	Boats
Assorted floating and sinking objects	Hand mixers
Strainers	Egg beaters
	Squeeze bottles

When space is limited, the teacher may alternate the water play area with an indoor sand play area and appropriate equipment for measuring, weighing, pouring, digging, and sifting. The water in the water play container itself may also be substituted occasionally with other mediums for exploration and discovery through the senses such as autumn leaves, snow, mud, a cornstarch and water mixture, small styrofoam shapes used for packing, or pure sawdust.

THE LIBRARY-LANGUAGE CENTER.   The library area is a place where children can relax in comfort over a favorite picture book. It includes picture books such as the Caldecott Award books, Mother Goose rhymes, poetry books, ABC books, novelty books containing textures or smell, magazines, and books and stories the children themselves have dictated to the teacher for sharing. The area may be bounded by low bookshelves, open-face magazine racks, plants, and mobiles. There is a child-size table for browsing or reading, comfortable seating such as an old sofa or stuffed chair, a carpet or rug for bellywhopping, favorite pictures hung low enough for children to see, changing displays of book activities, puppets, flannel board stories, and children's art. The library area may include a listening station, filmstrip projector, filmstrips, felt boards, magnetic or felt letters, picture-word cards, sound-symbol games, and file cards and magic markers for dictating important words to the teacher for saving.

When locating the library area, lighting is a major consideration. Natural light is desirable, and proximity to a window allows children to see the outdoors. Glare should be avoided and artificial light of good quality should be provided as needed. Library activities are located in the quietest portion of the room, away from such areas as block building and housekeeping.

Materials for the library-language center include:

Flannel board
Story characters
Posters
Pictures
Photographs
Writing materials
Felt, magnetic, and sandpaper letters
   of the alphabet
Magnetic board
Sound-symbol games
Picture-word cards

Favorite story books
Picture books
ABC books
Mother Goose books
Children's magazines
Hand puppets
Typewriter
Listening station
Slides, filmstrips, and projectors

THE CREATIVE ARTS AREAS. Art, music, and rhythm areas may be established as separate or combined areas. The art area is relatively active; the music and rhythms area is active and noisy. The need for ready access to water and sink sets the art center apart to some degree. In the art area, the activity is valued over the product. Art is an outlet for emotions, a means for expression of creative abilities, a source of enjoyment, *and* an avenue for developing motor skills and concepts of form, texture, color, and spatial organization. The wide variety of activities in the art area include painting, fingerpainting, spatter painting, drawing, cutting, pasting, coloring, vegetable printing, rubber stamp printing, making collages, murals, and mobiles, and modeling with papier mâché and clay. The art center is extended to the outdoors in pleasant weather. The easels are taken outside and set in a picturesque spot away from the area of active play. At other times, very large paint brushes and buckets of water are brought outside for the children to "paint" on the sidewalk. The classroom art center is extended in other ways. A local artist or sculptor, perhaps a parent, is invited to school to share his or her talent with the children and thus stimulate thought. The class may take a trip to the public library and borrow a reproduction to hang in their classroom and talk about. Art may also be combined with other creative arts through such activities as fingerpainting to different types of music.

Music too is an activity to explore and enjoy. At the same time, the secondary learnings that occur through music cover a wide range of intellectual skills, particularly when music is combined with rhythm and dance activities. Language, mathematics, and social skills are also natural outcomes of the carefully planned music program. One popular record[2] illustrates the range of skills deliberately taught through music:

Side I	Side II
Parade of Colors	Triangle, Circle or Square
Paper Clocks	Something That Begins Like
Let's Dance	Words on the Board
One Shape, Three Shapes	Let's Hide the Tambourine
Lucky Numbers	Partners

Many of the materials in art, music, and rhythms are handmade. Children can assist in their construction and, at the same time, learn basic principles of recycling and ecology. Musical instruments such as drums can be made by covering the ends of coffee cans with inner tubing. Orange juice cans filled with seeds or pebbles make interesting shakers. Parents, children, and teacher all contribute to stocking a "junk box" for the art area. It is filled with such castoffs as hair curlers, plastic tomato cartons, plastic hoops from soda six-packs, margarine lids and containers, round tissue and waxed paper rolls, cardboard tubes, round bouillon containers, bottle caps, springs, wheels, wire coils, spools, beads, meat trays, styrofoam packing materials, and so on. Some of the basic materials in the art area include:

Easels	Scissors
Aprons, old shirts for smocks	Butcher paper
Juice cans, margarine tubs, baby food jars	Fingerpaint paper
Drying racks or rope and clothespins	Drawing paper
Plastic garbage can for clay	Brown paper
Chalkboard	Newsprint
Tissue paper	Tagboard
Wax paper	Stamp pads, stamp pad ink
Construction paper	Cotton
Tinfoil	Crayons
Metallic paper	Magic markers
Wallpaper books	Pencils
Clay	Erasers
	Staplers

[2] H. Palmer, "Learning Basic Skills Through Music" (Freeport, N.Y.: Educational Activities, Inc., 1972).

Clay boards	Pipe cleaners
Flour and salt	Popsicle sticks
Cornstarch, laundry starch	Tongue depressors
Toothbrushes for spatter painting and spatter paint boxes	Yarn and string
	Sponges
Armature wire	Macaroni and assorted seeds
Colored toothpicks	Cardboard meat and fruit trays, tinfoil dishes and trays
Colored chalk	
Masking tape, clear tape, thumbtacks	Junk box materials

The music-rhythms area contains the following materials:

Piano	Rhythm sticks
Record player	Cymbals
Records	Gongs
Tape recorder	Guitar
Autoharp	Kazoos
Assorted bells	Rattles
Assorted drums	Tambourine
Triangles	Xylophone
Tone blocks	Maracas
Handmade instruments	Shakers

THE MANIPULATIVE SKILLS AREA.　In this area, children engage in a great deal of independent exploratory activity. The area is stocked with a variety of materials designed to foster the development of small muscle control, number concepts, shape and size concepts, language, and group cooperation. The materials are placed on low shelves readily accessible to the children. Work spaces, tables, and carpeted area are provided within the area. To facilitate selecting and replacing the materials, the shelves are not cluttered, and the materials themselves are shelved by color, picture, or function. Small items are kept in color-coded and picture-coded containers which may be adapted from throw-away cartons. Contact paper is useful for covering such storage items as ice cream cartons, cereal boxes, and coffee cans. The materials are carefully selected to match the age group in attendance. Two- and 3-year-olds, for example, work with very simple puzzles and games. Some 4- and 5-year-olds are quite sophisticated and able to use relatively complex materials. Puzzles, for example, should become gradually more complex as children grow in ability. Only a portion of the available materials are displayed at one time; new materials are brought into the area periodically. The teacher demonstrates their use and children then explore them on their own.

The activity in the area ranges from quiet and reflective to active and noisy. The area may be subdivided by zoning different work spaces and storage areas according to the type of activity required. Puzzles and other table games can be placed in one area and blocks, construction sets, and pegboards in another. Materials in the manipulative skills area include:

Design blocks	Erector sets
Lotto games	Stringing materials (beads, seeds, macaroni, etc.)
Commercial and homemade games involving number, size, shapes, matching, discriminating, classifying	Table blocks, tiles, logs
Pegboards and pegs	Interlocking blocks
Puzzles (assorted)	Abacus
Shape sorters	Stack puzzles
Pounding benches	Nesting toys
Large and small dominoes	Lock box
Lacing and tying boot	Weaving frame
Geometric forms	
Tinkertoys	

THE SCIENCE CENTER.   Although science concepts are taught in several areas such as in the construction and water play areas, science is also given a special area in the preschool. Live pets are often a part of the science area or adjacent to it. An assortment of materials and equipment with which children can manipulate, explore, and make discoveries are also included. Prisms, magnets, a microscope, magnifying glasses, compasses, scales, a balance, and assorted objects to weigh and balance are important items to include for the young child's exploration. Natural objects which the child brings to school such as leaves, acorns, toadstools, seed pods, ants, worms, pollywogs, pine cones, seashells, and a bird's nest are also displayed in the science area. Learning from these impromptu interests is always extended as far as possible by incorporating books, reference materials, a magnifying glass, discussions, or even resource people and related field trips when possible. Such displays are not given simple lip service but are always exciting, stimulating, and useful sources of learning. They grow and change with the growing and changing discoveries of the children. Old machines and gadgets which the children can take apart and manipulate are also available in the science area. A bin of "things to measure with" (string, paper handprint, tube, block, ruler, tape measure, timer, and so on) is readily available at all times. Other resources which are added with interest and with need include separate containers of "things to sort" (bottle caps, buttons, beans, macaroni, toys, and so on), "things to weigh," "things to order," and "things to classify and group." Discovery boxes including objects with which to experiment, such as bulbs and batteries, assorted magnets with objects to test, weather instruments, seeds with planting and germinating materials, and mystery smell containers, are periodically added. These, too, are accompanied with pictures, photographs, books, dictated stories, magnifying glasses, microscope, and so on to encourage interest, stimulate curiosity, and extend learning.

OTHER CENTERS.   Additional centers of interest and learning emerge with need and the various interests of the children. Sometimes these learning centers become part of an existing center. For example, the housekeeping area may be turned into a restaurant or doctor's office, as described earlier. At other times, a separate new center may be arranged in an appropriate place in the room. For example, if an early childhood center has an accessible stove, the cooking center may be permanently located in that area. If the only equipment is an electric frying pan or portable burner unit, however, the cooking center may be established only on days when a cooking activity has been planned. The learning and development that are possible from cooking activities are numerous, thus making the cooking center a valuable part of the early childhood program. A center need not have a stove to benefit from cooking experiences. Many noncooking recipes are available as well as recipes that call for the use of a simple piece of equipment such as an electric frying pan, corn popper, or toaster. Examples include preparing raw vegetables, tasting new fruits, stuffing celery, making popcorn, ice cream, gelatin, toast, juices, peanut butter, oatmeal, French toast, vegetable salads, applesauce, and sandwiches. The prepared food is shared with the entire group for snack time. Recipes are printed in picture-word form on large chart paper for every cooking experience. Some of the tools, such as measuring cups and spoons, are actually traced alongside their referents on the recipe chart. "Reading" recipes during the cooking activity allows children to follow directions, practice left-to-right reading progression, classify, discriminate letters, learn sound-symbol relationships, enlarge vocabularies, increase understanding, talk, socialize, and share fun. In addition, the cooking experience itself promotes muscle development as children chop, cut, mold, stir, mix, beat, and grate. They also engage in measurement and number activities and grow in understanding of science concepts. (See Chapter 10 for additional examples of learning in the cooking center.)

IMPLEMENTING THE LEARNING CENTERS

In implementing the learning centers at the beginning of the year, the teacher introduces the children to each of the activity areas. She demonstrates the proper use of equipment and continues to do so whenever new equipment and materials are added. Together, teacher and children set limits and make appropriate rules for working in each area. Rules are changed throughout the year as teacher and children sense the need to do so. The teacher models pride in a tidy, orderly room. There are appropriate storage places for the materials, and they are accessible and clearly evident. Children are given ample warning and time to complete their activities so that cleanup time becomes an accepted part of daily routine and not an intrusion and source of frustration.

Communication among children and between teacher and children is a vital part of working together in the learning centers. Children share in the choosing, planning, and scheduling of activities. They are aware of such things as acceptable behavior, safety points and rules, and the number of children who can work in each area at any one time. When particular learning centers are not available at times, a traffic sign ("STOP") is placed at the entry or a sign printed: "Closed"; or "No water today." Children quickly learn to read these important notices. As children work in the activity areas, they share their interests, discoveries, and learnings. Communicating and sharing are everywhere evident in the form of charts, graphs, records, displays, labels, stories, and signs dictated to the teacher: "The temperature today is 77°"; "How to feed Parakeet Pete"; "This is a castle. I made it from blocks. A princess lives here"; "How much do you weigh?"; "Jimmy's seeds"; "Timmy found some acorns on the way to school today."

All the physical objects—the blocks, puzzles, vehicles, picture books, dress-up clothes, art materials—are limited in the absence of humans and their unique abilities of language and emotion. Physical things are the working stuff for development, but human language and emotion are the mediators between objects and intellect and between adult and child. As children move about in the activity areas, the teacher assumes a helping, facilitating role. *She observes carefully,* diagnosing individual problem areas and noting the need for follow-up activities. *She listens,* assessing concepts, depth of understanding, interests, and attitudes. *She encourages,* offering a smile, a pat, a suggestion, or a helping hand. *She guides,* bringing in a piece of equipment or some resource material, diverting frustration or a difficult moment. *She facilitates learning,* asking, "Why?" "How can you tell?" "What if ——?" "Could you——?" "What else?" *She enjoys,* marveling in a new discovery, laughing with the children, and having a cup of tea in the housekeeping area. The teacher's role is illustrated in the "Ten Commandments to Creative Teaching" (Brunswick 1971):

1. Thou shalt not acknowledge ANY blindly accepted answers by students but shall become a wondering, questioning echo saying, "Is it? . . . Are you sure? . . . How can you tell? . . . Did it? . . .
2. Thou shalt bite thy tongue every time thou wants to settle a disagreement between two children quickly by telling them the right answer.
3. Thou shalt turn thy ears up to HIGHEST to be sure thou doesn't miss any child's comment which might lead to a self-initiated learning opportunity.
4. Thou shalt not remove the string from thy finger to always remind thee to let the learning come from the children's interests, the children's motivations, the children's wonderings.

5. Thou shalt write on the chalkboard 100 times, "I must not let an alarm clock run my classroom activities."
6. Thou shalt honor thy own "crazy" ideas, curiosity and divergent thinking to cultivate a taste for those of others.
7. Thou shalt hold thy breath until the feeling passes if thou ever feels like saying, "We don't have time to waste or fool around with this idea."
8. Thou shalt remember to make every day the day to offer that encouraging word, that pat of security, that smile of comfort.
9. Thou shalt not commit thyself to rigidity in content, method or materials.
10. Thou shalt recite these every day so that thou will come to practice what thou preaches.

SUMMARY AND CONCLUSIONS

The classroom environment must allow activities and events to occur within which the program objectives can be achieved and that meet the criteria for instructional experiences (Chapter 8). The creation of such a learning environment must consider the selection and development of the physical facility, the arrangement of the classroom, and the choice of materials and equipment.

In the selection and development of the physical facility, an early childhood program must meet the minimal standards prescribed by the particular state and local agency under which it operates and is licensed. Federal guidelines concerning the development of the physical facility are also available.

The indoor environment of an early childhood center is influenced by the philosophy of the staff, the curriculum objectives, fixed features in the physical plant, and by the nature of early childhood activities. One appropriate arrangement involves four basic divisions of space: quiet–dry, active–dry, quiet–wet, and active–wet. Wet activities are located as far away from the dry activities as is feasible. Active areas are located far away from quiet areas.

The space in early childhood centers is generally organized into learning areas, or centers. In general, learning centers are defined by the type of activity conducted there. Learning centers for early childhood programs include housekeeping, block-building, construction or woodworking, water play, library-language, creative arts, manipulative skills, science, and cooking. Classroom organization around learning centers advocates a flexible curriculum characterized by movement, activity, exploration, and integration of content.

Communication is a vital part of implementing the early childhood learning centers. The teacher introduces the children to each activity area and demonstrates the proper use of equipment. Teacher and children set limits and make appropriate rules for working in each area together. Rules are changed throughout the year as teacher and children sense the need to do so. Children share in choosing, planning, and scheduling activities. As children work in the activity areas, they share their interests, discoveries, and learnings. The teacher assumes a helping role—she observes, listens, encourages, guides, facilitates, and enjoys.

SUGGESTED ACTIVITIES

1. Note the variety of buildings used for early childhood programs in your community. How has each of these facilities been prepared to protect the physical safety of the children? Determine the state and local agency under which each operates and is licensed.
2. Note the variety of classroom arrangements in the early childhood centers in your community. Determine how the classroom arrangement and organization fosters movement, activity, exploration, and discovery.
3. Note the variety of learning areas, or centers, in the early childhood programs in your community. Note the materials, equipment, and activities in each area. Determine the kinds of learning that occur in these centers.
4. Observe the activity in one particular learning center. Determine the kinds of rules established for behavior and activity in the area. Determine if they are rules made by the teacher or by the children.

REFERENCES

Brunswick, J. 1971. "My Ten Commandments to Creative Teaching," *Journal of Creative Behavior,* 5 (3) : 199–200.

U.S. Department of Health, Education and Welfare. 1968. *Federal Interagency Day Care Requirements.* Washington, D.C.: Federal Panel on Early Childhood.

FURTHER READING

Association for Childhood Education International. *Learning Centers: Children on Their Own.* Washington, D.C.: The Association, 1970.

Association for Childhood Education International. *Equipment and Supplies: Tested and Approved for Preschool/School/Home.* Washington, D.C.: The Association, 1968.

Association for Childhood Education International. *Housing for Early Childhood Education.* Washington, D.C.: The Association, 1968.

Association for Childhood Education International. *Bits and Pieces: Imaginative Uses for Children's Learning.* Washington, D.C.: The Association, 1967.

Association for Childhood Education International. *Toward Better Kindergartens.* Washington, D.C.: The Association, 1966.

Educational Products Information Exchange Institute. *Early Childhood Education: How to Select and Evaluate Materials.* New York: EPIE Institute, Educational Product Report #42, 1972. (386 Park Avenue South, New York, N.Y. 10016.)

Elardo, R., and B. Pagan (eds.). *Perspectives on Infant Day Care.* Orangesburg, N.C.: Southern Association on Children Under Six, 1972.

Evans, A. M. "How To Equip and Supply Your Prekindergarten Classroom," in J. L. Frost (ed.), *Early Childhood Education Rediscovered.* New York: Holt, Rinehart and Winston, 1968.

Evans, E. B., B. Shub, and M. Weinstein. *Day Care: How To Plan, Develop, and Operate a Day Care Center.* Boston: Beacon Press, 1971.

Frost, J. L., M. L. Richardson, and R. M. Rawson. *Early Childhood Education,* Curriculum Bulletin No. WOC-ECE-001. Orange, Tex.: West Orange-Cove Consolidated School District, 1969.

National Association for the Education of Young Children. *Ideas That Work with Young Children.* Washington, D.C.: The Association, 1972.

National Association for the Education of Young Children. *The Good Life for Infants and Toddlers.* Washington, D.C.: The Association, 1970.

National Association for the Education of Young Children. *Planning Environments for Young Children: Physical Space.* Washington, D.C.: The Association, 1969.

Project Head Start. *Equipment and Supplies: Guidelines for Administrators and Teachers in Child Development Centers.* Washington, D.C.: Office of Economic Opportunity, n.d.

Schmidt, V. E. *Early Childhood Education: Learning Experiences for the 3-, 4-, and 5-year-old Child.* Lincoln, Neb.: State Department of Education, Division of Instructional Services, 1971.

Southwest Educational Development Laboratory. *Setting up the Classroom* (tape, filmstrip, guidebook). Austin, Tex.: The Laboratory, 1971, 1972.

Wortham, S. *Bilingual Education in the Open Classroom.* San Marcos, Tex.: Bonham Early Childhood Center, 1973.

V

The Child and the Educative Process

William Tyler Page Elementary School, Montgomery County, Maryland

10

ENHANCING LANGUAGE
AND THINKING
IN YOUNG CHILDREN

In Chapter 6, we followed the emergence of the young child's inherent language ability and explored the external influences of the environment upon language development. Chapter 7 described Piaget's theory of intellectual development. The present chapter concerns the role of the teacher in enhancing both language and thinking in young children. The close relationship between language and thinking suggests that conditions which facilitate growth in one of these areas of development will foster growth in the other.

EXPERIENCE, SOCIAL TRANSMISSION, MATURATION, EQUILIBRATION, AND EDUCATIONAL TRANSMISSION

Piaget, it will be recalled, postulated that intellectual development is dependent upon the factors of experience, social transmission, maturation, equilibration, and educational transmission. The teacher's role in arranging the environment, planning activities, and extending the child's actions and interests are discussed here in terms of each of these major factors.

Important Early Experiences

EARLY EXPERIENCES AT HOME.   Before the child arrives at school, he has usually spent several years exploring the home environment. Healthy growth in the home is a result of planning. Soon after birth adults begin to interact with the infant. The child's first language teacher, his mother, uses a variety of techniques for promoting his language. She attends to his needs, soothes him, talks to him, and makes simple toys available. Adults "play" with the child. As the child grows over time, his physical boundaries are extended from the crib to the floor where increased mobility and space bring many new objects into reach. The wise adult does not unnecessarily hamper the child's movement and inquisitiveness; rather, potentially dangerous objects or valuable and breakable objects are removed from the child's reach. If the child enjoys a particular drawer, he may find that drawer available to him, complete with a favorite toy inside. The child also gains access to the outdoors early in life, crawling about on a blanket and on the grass, lapping up all the delights of new sensations. Through such simple activities, the child exercises his sensorimotor apparatus, growing daily toward more complex and differentiated behavior. He acquires his first words by matching environmental labels to his own concepts, which he has derived from his interactions with objects, people, and events.

With increased mobility and greater facility of language, the child requires a greater variety of objects to explore. Very simple toys give way to new challenges, even though favorites may be kept and enjoyed for a long time. The adult recognizes that the complexity of materials must keep pace with growing complexity of mental schema and physical development and arranges for the gradual introduction of novelty in the child's environment. The provision of a rich physical environment must not be taken lightly, for operations on objects is the basic process for the development of intelligent behavior. Piaget's fundamental factor of *experience* is at stake here.

THE IMPORTANT SCHOOL EXPERIENCES.   The task of providing for richness of experience, initially assumed by parents, is later taken over by the teacher. When the child arrives at school—or day care center, nursery school, kindergarten—his new environment must reflect the same care and knowledge so essential to his continuous, uninterrupted development. The new environment does not represent a radical break with the home environment. Rugs and pillows to curl up on, cots, a cozy chair, snacks, many familiar toys and objects, a consistent caretaker or teacher, all give school a comfortable, homelike atmosphere. The atmosphere is not only stimulating but it is responsive as well. There are materials, toys, equipment, people, and animals with which the child may interact actively. Nelson (1973:1–2) found that the earliest words spoken by the young child are those primarily related to his actions. He learns the names of things he directly acts upon (toys, keys, bottles, and so on). He does not learn the names of things that are present in his environment but that are not the object or source of action (table, plate, grass, and so on).

A second critical feature of the first learned words is that they do something (bark, roll, growl). Similarly, teaching materials for the young child do something; they don't just "sit there." The classroom is filled with objects the child can actively manipulate, using all of his senses. Even bulletin boards, displays, and mounted pieces of work are functional. They are planned and arranged with the child's help and are constantly changed to reflect ongoing, changing activity in the classroom. They are placed on the child's eye level so that he can refer to them and use them. Even inanimate objects such as pictures gain instructional power when an adult asks relevant questions to spur action: "If you were this tiger in the jungle, how would you move and sound?" An aquarium moved from its obscure position high on a counter down to a low bench where children can scrutinize its contents from numerous angles stimulates new, exciting interest and observation.

CLASSROOM PETS AND EXPERIENCE.   Classroom pets have the potential to become more than just a task on the weekly helpers chart. Firsthand experience with a parakeet set free daily within one kindergarten enabled the children to generalize and symbolize as follows:

BIRDS ARE
Feathery.....soft.....scared.....tiny.....Parakeet Pete.....light.....blinky and winky black eyes.....nice.....to go to my house over vacation.....pretty .....fun..... my friend.....

The bird became "blinky and winky black eyes" to one fascinated child able to scrutinize the tiny form perched upon his finger. It became a "friend" with whom to share private thoughts as it sat on top of the art easel watching another child paint. A third kindergartener, who loved to care for the parakeet, interacted on still a different level with the pet. She labored over two signs she had asked the teacher to spell for her and then hung one on either side of the bird's cage. One sign read simply "Parakeet Pete" and the other gave these directions:

Take out the dirty paper. Fill the seeds. Put in good water.

EXPERIENCE AND TIME.   To be able to experience, children need a great deal of time. Schedules, though necessary, must be flexible enough to allow children to pursue and complete their self-selected adventures. At the same time, teachers must gauge wisely when to let children experience on their own and when to offer encouragement, new direction, or merely help with spelling or dictation. Generally, children need an initial period of free manipulation and exploration with objects and ideas. This requires concrete objects and materials with which all of their senses can become involved: things to look over, observe, listen to, take apart, put back together, taste, smell, shake, pinch, push, pull, squeeze, and so on. Subsequently, free exploration can lead to involvement and commitment on increasing levels of complexity under a teacher's thoughtful guidance.

Objects and materials must be strategically located—a stopwatch to time Parakeet Pete's flight across the classroom, a scale near the bird seed to weigh his food, paper and pencil to keep records or dictate a story for later sharing, and a teacher nearby to take dictation and to encourage with "What if . . .?" "How about . . .?" "Why not . . .?" A trip to a pet store so the children can purchase bird seed and pet supplies or to a zoo affords numerous opportunities for related firsthand experience in the areas of science, social studies, mathematics, and language arts. Resources brought into the classroom must not be overlooked. A visit by a veterinarian or a local bird-watching enthusiast can invite children along new avenues of thought and investigation. Real objects and events take precedence, but these should be supplemented and extended with models, photographs, pictures, poems, and stories, both commercially as well as creatively inspired.

COMMUNICATING WITH PARENTS.   Broadening experience for children requires extending the classroom into the neighborhood and community, tapping public, private, and parental resources. An inquiring newsletter should be sent home early in the year inviting parents to list the talents, hobbies, and interests they would be willing to share with the children during the year. It may turn up a handy father willing to help make birdfeeders, to demonstrate bird calls, or to share his interest in taxidermy. An artistic mother may be willing to help the children experience making ceramic birds or share her knowledge of wildlife or of training animals. Newsletters should be a constant source of communication between parents and classroom happenings throughout the year. Besides drawing home and school closer together, they often lead to news of untapped and exciting resources, supplies, or trip possibilities.

Social Transmission

SOCIAL TRANSMISSION AND LANGUAGE.   Simultaneous emphasis upon the affective element which gives cognitive activity its source of energy reflects the fundamental factor in development that Piaget has identified as *social transmission*. The introduction to school is slow and gradual. Hopefully, the child has had an opportunity to meet one or more of the adults in charge before entering the program and already knows that there is a warm, responsive person there who can be trusted. Whenever possible, the children's entrance to the school or center could be staggered throughout the first few weeks so that they attend in small groups. This enables the teacher to give more time and attention to fewer children in the very beginning when routines, expectations, and relationships are first being established.

When the child first arrives in the morning, he is personally greeted by an adult who is thereby conveying to him the importance of his presence there. Arrival time, this private one-to-one encounter between teacher and child, is an opportune moment for informally promoting language development. In one way, the teacher asks questions based upon her intimate knowledge of the child and his world. The personal and relevant nature of her questions encourages the child to talk ("I've been waiting for you to come, John. What happened at your birthday party yesterday afternoon?"), helps him recognize the importance of language as one form of communication ("How did you win this puppet at your party?"), and encourages critical thinking ("You won the prize for pinning the donkey's tail? How did that make you feel?"). In another way, the teacher models language and expands the child's utterances.

Child: It's red and yellow.
Teacher: Yes, the puppet you won has a yellow head and a bright red body.

Nelson (1973) identified a number of environmental factors associated with rate of language acquisition by the very young child. On the positive side were the number of outings and the number of adults to which the child was exposed. Outings introduce the child to novel situations and objects, thereby stimulating language production. Knowledgeable adults with positive attitudes are sensitive to the child's needs and interests, encourage him, and influence his thinking. On the negative side were excessive time in watching television, excessive time spent with other children, and the high use of commands by mothers in their interactions with their children. The child who watches television passively is taking time out from action with objects and people, a factor shown to be closely associated with language growth. Nelson's conclusion that time spent with other children can have a negative effect on language development is probably influenced by the egocentricism of very young children and the fact that their early play is parallel rather than social. By age 3–4, social-dramatic play begins to emerge and peer interaction gains a more potent influence upon language.

Nelson's studies of children at age 30 months confirmed earlier findings of maternal influence on child speech. The mother who is not "tuned in" to the child's concepts and speech imposes her expectations upon him by controlling and directing his language and behavior. She rejects his language system by ignoring it, a negative effect upon verbal behavior. On the other hand, the supportive adult responds to the child's behavior, listens, observes, interprets it, and feeds back relevant data to the child. (See also Chapter 8 for a discussion of observation and interpretation of behavior in evaluation.) If language development is to be optimal in programs for young children, there must be a great deal of naturalistic conversation and play situations planned to stimulate linguistic interaction. If one is to learn to talk, one must talk. There must be a reasonably low child-adult ratio that allows a great deal of dialogue between adults and children. However, a low pupil-adult ratio is effective only under organizational conditions that allow effective language intercourse. Such conditions include freedom to move and explore both indoors and outdoors, opportunities for child-to-child interaction, stimulating learning centers, a flexible schedule and grouping patterns, pupil-teacher planning and evaluating, resource people, and field trips.

The teacher demonstrates that she values child talk by incorporating the children's ideas and suggestions in her own verbalizations: "Cindy thinks some children are staying on the tricycles too long in the first part of play time and other children don't have a long enough turn near the end of play time. Today, I'm going to bring the clock outdoors, and each person riding a tricycle will have a 10-minute turn." The teacher asks questions to encourage the child to talk: "What did you like best about the trip, Joey?" "What do you think you will need to make your spaceship, Danny?" "Why do you think the little rabbit in our story felt so sad?" "Both of you want to play with that truck. How do you think we can solve this problem?" "What shall we do to celebrate your birthday in school, Jan?" "What would happen if we had no books to read for story time?" The teacher gives the children numerous opportunities to use language: "Jane, you explain to the children how we play that game." "Certainly we can sing that song, Jimmy. Will you sing it for us once so we can remember the words?" "Tell us about the invention you made at the workbench today, Stevie." "Shawn, please explain to Jamie how the new crane works." "Kathy, please tell the children in the music center that our snack is ready."

ORGANIZATION OF THE CLASSROOM.　The arrangement and organization of a classroom can help children move toward self-responsibility and independence. (See also the discussion of classroom arrangement in Chapter 9.) Having a "cubbie," even if it is merely a shoe box above each coat hook, encourages care of property and respect for ownership. When the shoe box is labeled with each child's name and even his picture, the right to individual privacy is established and valued. Later, perhaps even an address may be added for the maturing child.

Time taken at the beginning of the school year and whenever something new is introduced to show children how to work and care for the equipment and materials invites children to function independently in obtaining and returning materials. Arranging basic activities and supplies in rather permanent areas and interest centers makes it easy for children to function independently. Teacher and children share in rearranging the interest centers as the need arises and in making rules for a harmonious classroom. Young children need the security of having limits, such as being expected to use the equipment properly, to know how many children can work comfortably in a learning center at any one time, and to clean up an area when finished there. In such ways, children are experiencing how to be responsible for their own behavior, how to share, and how to cooperate.

INVOLVING CHILDREN IN PLANNING.   The program includes regular times for children to engage in activities in which they will experience the desired learnings. In a brief group session at the beginning of each day, children experience planning, organizing, making decisions, and evaluating their outcomes. They experience short-range planning (scheduling the day's activities and events) and long-range planning (making plans for a forthcoming holiday). They are developing receptive language skills in listening to one another's ideas as well as expressive language skills in the sharing of ideas. Verbalizing what the problem is, listing all of the alternatives, and choosing the best course of action makes children aware of the steps in the decision-making process.

It is not enough merely to give children choices. They must be conscious of the fact that they are making them and have numerous opportunities to practice the steps in making decisions if they are to become thoughtful planners of their time and managers of their behavior. One group of 4-year-olds, for example, faced the question of how to celebrate Thanksgiving in their classroom and were invited to plan all of the things they possibly wanted to do. Their alternatives included (1) hanging assorted decorations, (2) making homemade bread, and (3) having a Thanksgiving feast which included a turkey and sauerkraut. The wise teacher accepted sauerkraut because it was her role to encourage the children to offer and weigh their alternatives and not to impose her own conventional ideas and values upon them. The feasibility of each alternative was discussed and voted upon when necessary. The calendar was brought out to schedule the activities. Pictures and labels were attached to the calendar so that the children could refer to and interpret their plans independently. Volunteers chose jobs they preferred. These were meaningful choices to make, realistic and important decisions, because they stemmed from the children's interests and ideas.

Teachers can increase children's awareness of the steps in the decision-making process on a one-to-one basis throughout the day as well. The choices may be as broad as deciding in which interest center to work that day. The teacher asks relevant questions and makes tactful suggestions to ensure that children make choices that are reasonably consistent with their needs and abilities. As the teacher guides the learning in moving from center to center and from child to child, she facilitates more specific planning, organizing, and decision-making.

Teacher: We don't have a puppet stage for the puppet you won. Is there something else you could use?

Child: I could make one.

Teacher: Yes, you could make a puppet stage. What things would you need? How would you make it?

The final critical skill in learning to make decisions wisely is evaluating the chosen alternative. The teacher expects the children to evaluate their work with her at one interest center before moving on to a new project. She encourages critical thinking on the part of the child with such questions as: "How do you feel about the puppet stage you built? Where do you suppose you first got the idea to make your puppet stage like this? Was it easy or hard to decide how to build it? If you could do it again, how would you do it differently? What if we didn't have a cardboard box? What else could you have used?" Discussing and evaluating with children is a rich time for language development. Children talk, identify, enlarge their vocabularies, extend concepts, and evaluate ideas. The teacher asks high-level thinking questions which call for the children to explain, classify, compare, infer, create, and evaluate as opposed to low-level questions which call for merely yes-no answers, simple descriptions or meanings, and sheer recall or memorization. The teacher introduces new vocabulary and she models and expands language.

Child: It's big.

Teacher: Yes, your puppet stage is big. You made the shape of the stage long and narrow.

Just before dismissal, perhaps after a story at the end of the day, children evaluate their day together as a group. It is an appropriate time to review the day's accomplishments, to evaluate successes and failures, and to look forward to tomorrow.

Maturation

Children learn because they have an inborn predisposition to do so. They are busily engaged in seeking and exploring, questioning and constructing, exchanging ideas and looking for alternatives. Innate exploratory powers of the child represent maturation, a third fundamental factor in accounting for development. The child is an active learner who will seek out and literally devour intellectual activities that are matched to his present developmental status.

Equilibration

The teacher can exercise only indirect control over the fourth fundamental factor in development, equilibration. Assimilation and accommodation, which work together in the equilibration process, are the result of the child's operations on objects. The teacher assists by creating a climate in which equilibration may occur; that is, she plans activities that sufficiently match the child's developmental status to enable him to assimilate their content (see Chapter 8 on evaluation and planning). He is somewhat familiar with the nature of the activity to be able to absorb it or to act upon it. At the same time, the activity introduces just enough complexity and novelty into the child's current scheme of things to enable him to accommodate. He must adjust his old way of thinking and acting to include this bit of newness. Thus, it is of critical importance that the teacher prepare an environment for activity suited to the needs and developmental level of the particular child.

Educational Transmission

The fifth fundamental factor in development, *educational transmission* (teaching), is planned on the basis of some particular view or views of learning and development. It is safe to say that no one has demonstrated that any one view is better than all others. However, a carefully thought-out view is better than a haphazard, random approach. The teacher must first of all understand that development is a whole process and cannot be fragmented. Although various aspects of development are separated for clarity of communication, the curriculum is not separated into airtight compartments. It is an integrated one in which the daily schedule encompasses large blocks of time for a wide range of planned activities designed to enhance the total development of the child.

Much of the activity is initiated, planned, carried out, and evaluated by the children under careful guidance of the teacher. The content focus on language arts, music, reading, science, mathematics, and so on, stems from these interests of the children (as well as diagnostic data collected by the teacher) and is appropriately integrated by the knowing teacher. Her role is to facilitate and extend the child's learning as far as his developmental level dictates is possible. The child's self-confidence and his curiosity is fostered by having many success experiences. Teachers do not have to continually tell children they are wrong; the activity itself should feed back information about right and wrong. The critical difference is that activity and material feedback are more likely to relate to the child's standards rather than the teacher's. The teacher should help the child examine his standards and values (see Chapter 11), but she should use care in judging his products. The case of Timmy below illustrates the factors of maturation, social transmission, and educational transmission intertwined in the educative process. In the example, the teacher attempted to extend the learnings as far as possible, based upon her knowledge of the child's individual needs and interests. The child responded to the teacher as far as his individual needs, interests, and level of maturation permitted.

TIMMY

Timmy loved to build with the large blocks. Usually he constructed forts and houses, one or two rows of blocks high. One day, he worked for a particularly longer period of time, arranging and rearranging the large blocks about four feet high. He was very proud of his unusual construction. "Look, Teacher, my BIG fort, my BIG fort!" "Yes, Timmy. You built a tall fort today, didn't you?" said the teacher. "I wonder just how tall your fort is. Can you think of a way we could find out how tall it is?" Timmy first shook his head no and then, flashing a broad smile, thoughtfully added, "It's as tall as Steven!" Steven was another boy in the classroom and Timmy's best friend. The teacher encouraged with, "Let's see if it is as tall as Steven." Together they invited Steven to stand next to the fort and ascertained that Steven and the fort were approximately the same height. Periodically, the teacher attempted different ways to further extend Timmy's learning: "Do you think your fort is as tall as anything else in the room? Can you think of a different way to measure your fort?" Timmy's interest in measurement had been satisfied, however. He repeatedly shook his head no and went on to readjust a few of the blocks. The teacher attempted to encourage Timmy's interest and language development in another way. "Would you like to make a sign about your tall fort, Timmy?" she asked. "Yeah," replied Timmy as he faced her with renewed interest. "Okay. Choose the materials you think you will need and we'll make your sign." When he returned, teacher and child got down on the floor together and Timmy dictated:

COME SEE OUR TALL FORT
TIMMY AND STEVEN

The teacher offered to print the words on scrap paper and have Timmy copy them himself, but he wanted her to print the sign. As she printed, she commented that words "tall" and "Timmy" began with the same sound and invited Timmy to print the "t" in "tall" himself, which he eagerly agreed to do. Later, she invited him to print his own name under the message as well as Steven's name, which he also eagerly did. After Timmy had hung his sign on the fort, he and the teacher read it again together. The expression on Timmy's face reflected his pride indeed. The teacher attempted to help Timmy examine his values and evaluate his work that morning. "I can tell by the expression on your face that you're very happy, Timmy. Are you proud of your tall fort? What made you decide to build a tall fort today? Was it easy or hard for you to build your tall fort? Would you make the same kind of fort again on another day or try a different kind?"

Later that morning, as he played in his fort with Steven, Timmy brought in the toy telephone. After playing with it for awhile, he approached the teacher with a small piece of paper and a magic marker and asked her to write down his and Steven's telephone numbers. Since neither boy knew his own phone number, the teacher said, "Well, let's go get a telephone book and look them up." Both boys were excited about finding their own listings. They listened with surprised interest as the teacher helped them look under their last names instead of under *Timmy* and *Steven* as they had suggested. They declined the teacher's offer, however, to copy down their phone numbers themselves or to add any other important numbers to their list. For many days thereafter, they were seen referring to the scrap of paper and proudly dialing their phone numbers.

Emerging Functions

As the child moves from one stage of development to another, he acquires different abilities and ways of interacting with his environment. Each newly acquired ability or mode of interaction does not emerge in isolation but is built upon previously acquired abilities and actions. All of the major factors discussed above—experience, social transmission, maturation, equilibration, and educational transmission—together influence the emergence of each new ability or mode of interaction. Here, various abilities are discussed individually for the sake of communicating the teacher's role in enhancing their development.

The Semiotic Function: Levels of Representation

According to Piaget, the child moves from the sensorimotor stage into the preconceptual phase of development at about 1½ to 2 years of age. This phase of development is marked by the appearance of the symbolic function, the ability to represent an object, event, or scheme (significate) by means of language, mental image, or symbolic gesture (signifier). Because linguists distinguish between the symbols and the signs that may be used to represent things, the term *semiotic function* has been coined for all activities having to do with signifiers. Children pass naturally through three levels of representation, the *index* level, the *symbol* level, and the *sign* level. The early childhood center striving to enhance thinking and language in the young child designs activities to improve his thinking processes as they develop on each level. The early childhood curriculum, then, develops representation by exposing the child to an appropriate sequence of activities that move from the specific and concrete to the abstract.

Initially, instruction emphasizes concrete activities and experiences with real objects. In order for a child to grow in abstraction ability, he must have many firsthand, concrete experiences with the things around him. If the child has seen only his own dog, the word "dog" will evoke a mental image of only that particular dog. But as he has opportunity to observe other dogs, the word "dog" will take on generalizing power, perhaps *over*generalizing power in the beginning. The child may call all animals "dog" that even remotely resemble his pet. Even at this primitive level the development of language is dependent on experiences that allow for the growth of symbolization or mental imagery.

The teacher schedules field trips to provide real-life experiences that cannot be provided in the school content: you can't bring elephants into the classroom. A visit to the zoo is rich in opportunities for symbolism. The child sees many different animals; hears their names; sees their distinctive characteristics—horns, ears, tail, and so on; hears them described; tries the words for himself; grows in imagery and language. Rather than constantly bombarding the child with just words, the teacher is selective in her scheme to promote language growth. As a language model for her students, she uses complete sentences in her own speech. She answers, "That *animal* is a giraffe" instead of "A giraffe"; "That *man* is the zoo keeper. He is throwing some fish to the seals" instead of "some fish"; That *color* is gray" instead of just "gray." She is careful to include the category or classification in the sentence as well (*animal, man, color*). She uses specific words in communicating rather than nonspecific, vague referents: "The monkey house is that big, green building over there next to the seals" instead of "They're over there"; "Your lunch bag is with all the other lunches at the front of the bus next to Mrs. Jones" instead of "There it is." She helps the child build an adequate image by giving information precisely and clearly: "The elephant's skin looks wrinkled" instead of "It's wrinkled;" "The lamb's fur feels soft" instead of "It's soft." Such concrete activity provides the tools of language and thought for symbolic play in which new meanings are attached to concrete objects.

THE INDEX LEVEL.   The index level of representation emphasizes operations on some *portion* of a real object, the *sound* of that object, or some distinguishing *feature* it has. For example, Kelly can identify her doll when only its head sticks out of her toy box. Scott recognizes his coat when only the sleeve is shown or recognizes his shoes after naptime when only the tips stick out from under the shelf. Wendy laughs and says "bow-wow" when she hears the tags on her dog's collar jingle as he moves around in another room. During a small-group activity, the children reach inside a "feel box" and name what the objects are simply from the way each object feels. In another small-group activity, children are blindfolded and name foods by the way they smell or the way they taste. Circle games are played in which the children close their eyes and identify a classmate from the sound of his voice. Sounds of objects (telephone, piano, drum, keys, animal sounds, vehicle sounds, and so on) are made for identification using either real objects or a record or tape recording.

Tape recorders offer rich opportunities for language development. One is taken along during the trip to the zoo and various noises recorded during the day: animals moving, vocalizing, eating; people walking, talking, buying and selling refreshments; the sound of the wind, water, trees. Later, in small groups or individually, children listen to the tape, guessing what each of the sounds could be and discussing why they think so. Parts of objects such as a bird's wing, bicycle handle bars, a cat's tail, and wheels from a car are shown to the child from which he identifies the whole object. Parts of tangible items may be shown or pictures of the object may be illustrated on cards. Marks of objects and silhouettes are made in the sandbox indoors or in mud or snow outdoors for identification. Examples of such marks include handprints, footprints, workbench tools such as a hammer, a spoon or a fork, a leaf, an animal outline.

THE SYMBOL LEVEL.   At the symbol level, the child uses his imagination to represent objects that are no longer present. In the art area, he creates animals from clay or he paints pictures with tempera. He creatively positions his body on large paper on the floor in the shape of an animal when the teacher asks him, "If you were a zoo animal today, what animal would you feel like being?" After a classmate or teacher traces his animal body shape, he paints in the features according to his mental image, cuts the animal out, and dictates a story about it. He spatter paints with the silhouettes of zoo animals and fingerpaints alongside a record of zoo animal noises, which stimulates both color and design. Zoo animals are painted on rocks whose shape or texture resembles a particular animal to the child. A title, sentence, or story is dictated to accompany the child's art work. In the music and rhythms area, the child recreates the sounds of the animals and reenacts their movements. A listening station is available for him to listen to a record of zoo animal sounds, to hear a story of a particular animal while following the story in a book, or to listen to songs about zoo animals.

Commercial or hand-made puppets of people and animals are provided for reenactment of the field trip, for creative dramatics, and for spontaneous linguistic interaction. The teacher uses puppets in a variety of ways to announce cleanup or outdoor play time, to get the group's attention, or to move the children from one activity to another. The children make their own zoo animal puppets from socks, potatoes, paper bags, styrofoam, popsicle sticks, cardboard tubes, and scrap materials. Cutouts are used on the flannel board to tell stories about the trip and the animals, name different animals, discuss their appearance, and describe their features. The teacher enhances language by being precise in referring to size, weight, height, and other dimensions or characteristics. For example, two or more animals are compared visually to help children grow in their comprehension (*big, bigger, biggest; tall, taller, tallest*), or the teacher verbalizes as to *how* things are alike or different ("Yes, both the elephant and the hippopotamus are the same color, gray," rather than "Yes, they're the same").

Outdoors, the child engages in simple games with rules as he plays "being zoo animals" with a group of other children: "You be a lion and these are your rocks so you can't come over here on my monkey's tree." Outdoor play equipment is turned upside down or combined with other pieces of equipment to symbolize cages. Through all of these symbol-level activities, the child learns that his world is not restricted to the immediate presence of an object.

THE SIGN LEVEL.   At the sign level, the child represents objects through words. The activities designed to enhance development at the symbol level underlie development at the sign level. The child is encouraged to talk in the presence of real objects and in his symbolic play or pretending activities. (Attending and language as program objectives are also discussed in Chapter 8.) During the field trip, talk helps to enlarge vocabularies and build comprehension through the naming and identifying of animals, objects, and events. The teacher is alert to identify immature syntactical structures in the children's language. She models mature syntactical forms herself: "That's the *seal's* fish to eat"; "There are three monkeys in this cage"; "The zoo keeper threw the fish *into* the water"; "The elephant's trunk is moving around the concrete *because* he is searching for more peanuts to eat"; "*If* you don't hang on to the string of your balloon, *it* will float away." Animals are compared and classified (reptiles, amphibians, two-legged, four-legged, those with fur, those with hide). Concepts are clarified and new ones formed (tortoise–turtle, rabbit–hare, calf–bull, goat–kid). Thought is stimulated (laugh like a hyena, roar like a lion, tall as a giraffe, strong as an elephant, graceful as a gazelle).

Back in the classroom, language and thinking are continued. Familiar words and newly acquired ones are used in discussing the trip, telling stories about it, and reenacting it. The children dictate stories, which may be typed on a primary typewriter, mimeographed, and collected in booklet form for each child to add to his own personal library. Story books such as *May I Bring a Friend?* and *Where the Wild Things Are* are read, dramatized, and reflected upon. Games involving anywhere from two people to a large group are structured to promote language, thought, and perception: (1) The child, blindfolded, reaches in a bag of objects and identifies each by touch. (2) A child identifies various zoo animals from another child's verbal description: "I am thinking of an animal. It is very large. It has wide ears, a short tail, a long trunk and is gray." (3) A child acts out an animal's movements behind a shadow screen while the others identify the kind of animal being represented. (4) Children play zoo animal lotto games. (5) Pictures are used as a basis from which to tell stories, locate information, follow directions, or predict outcomes. Out of these language experiences emerge sight vocabulary, work with auditory discrimination of consonant sounds (*l*ion, *l*eopard, *l*izard; baboo*n*, lio*n*), directionality and left-to-right ocular motility, form perception (matching capital and lower case letters, alike words, word parts), and early identification of adjustment problems (fatigue, poor vision, hearing loss).

Building from a base of concrete experiences with real objects and events requires that the teacher build a systematic plan for the child's development. She begins with his interests, capitalizes upon his natural curiosity and desire to know, and integrates her knowledge of child growth and development. A detailed case study of a project centering on policemen, as well as other representative activities, follow.

POLICEMAN, POLICEMAN[1]

A group of the 5-year-olds played policeman at school for several days. Outdoors, the tricycles became police cars and the concrete tunnel became a police station. Indoors, they built a jail from blocks and locked up whatever "prisoner" they could talk into assuming the role. Noting their continuing interest in policemen, the teacher introduced several new policeman puzzles and added some toy police cars and a wooden policeman to the block area. She also arranged for a field trip to a local police station and invited a policeman to bring his patrol car to school and speak to the children. In these index level activities, all the senses were involved in firsthand, concrete encounters with real policemen. The children were able to see and touch the various parts of the policeman's uniform and patrol car, as well as hear the names or labels for the objects. They were fingerprinted and shown how money was invisibly marked. They watched a demonstration of the safe use of flares and were permitted to explore and manipulate the cruiser lights, siren, and communication system. So many new and exciting things to absorb—and it was all reflected in their rapt attention and intense concentration. The trip to the police station proved to be just as engaging as a result of the firsthand experiences of being inside a jail cell, being locked in handcuffs, and standing so close to a tall figure in blue as to fully feel the impact of his presence. Such concrete, firsthand exposure to the real person and objects enabled the children to absorb a vivid mental image of many facets of a "policeman."

The teacher then went on to provide opportunities for numerous symbol level activities to enable the children to use that mental image. She brought in several old navy blue caps and shirts which were readily turned into police "uniforms." She taught them a song and finger play about the police. A large variety of fiction and nonfiction books about police were set out and were read aloud as well as taken into corners or to a block police station to be looked over again and again. One day a quarrel erupted over who would get to wear a tin police badge one boy had brought to school. The teacher encouraged the children to solve the problem for themselves: "There's only one police badge and five of you," she said. "How can we get more badges so there is one for each of you to wear?" When one child suggested that they could make badges, the teacher encouraged them to discuss the way they wanted the badge to look and, consequently, what material they would need. She printed the word "police" in large letters for them and hung it up for each child to copy himself on his own badge, giving assistance where needed. Dramatic play alternated between turning the blocks into a police station, a jail, and a police cruiser. On one occasion, several of the children were sitting upon a pile of blocks which had become a squad car. "I wish this police car really worked!" said one child wistfully. The teacher invited the group to sit down and discuss it with her and see if they could find a way to build one that did "really work." They made a list of exactly what they wanted: "We want to get inside it"; "It's got to have

---

[1] Reprinted, with revisions, from *Instructor.* Copyright © January 1976 by The Instructor Publications, Inc. Reprinted by permission of The Instructor Publications, Inc.

doors and a roof"; "It needs lights and a siren"; "Can we make it move?" and so on. Together they looked around the school grounds and found the perfect large packing crate. The teacher encouraged the children to go home that evening, talk about it with their families, and draw a picture of how each wanted his or her police car to look. The next morning, they eagerly showed and discussed their ideas. The teacher helped each of them label the important features he or she had put into their pictures. She brought in car magazines and they cut out and labeled additional necessary features. All of their plans and labels were mounted on a bulletin board display for reference.

Then they began to work. Their project took about six weeks, with the initial group of children maintaining their steady interest and the rest of the class periodically offering ideas and some manual labor. There were many problems to solve: how wide should the doors be, how high up should the roof go, how do you get it to stay there, how can we make the car move, how do you hook up lights and a siren. With each new problem the teacher encouraged the children to think of ideas, to discuss them together, and to reach their own solutions. Often they could visualize a problem more clearly if they drew a picture of it. Sometimes it was frustrating and the solutions took several days to reach. Sometimes the solutions came quite accidentally, such as when the children decided to mark the width of a child standing next to the crate to see how big to make the doors. Their measurement techniques were primitive, but they were acquiring new math and science concepts. They were making deductions, thinking and reasoning, and enlarging their vocabularies. The teacher made sure the appropriate props were available to facilitate their learning, such as a science book to look up a bulb and battery diagram for the police car lights. She encouraged their creativity and the symbolic potential they saw in material from the "junk box": shiny tunafish cans as headlights, padding from the halves of a long necklace box as brake and gas pedals, and two empty masking tape spools mounted on the car as support to keep the battery for the lights in place. Weekly class newsletters kept the parents informed about progress and needs. They also forewarned them of and enlisted their cooperation on such occasions as the day when everyone was to wear old clothes and paint the police car with "real" household paint. As a result, parents shared their children's enthusiasm about the project and frequently stopped by the classroom to look at its progress.

Throughout the period of interest in policemen, the teacher nurtured thought on the sign level as well, with representation through words. The children's pictures and plans of the police car parts were labeled, hung on a bulletin board display, and referred to frequently. Another display of the parts of a police uniform was labeled and arranged. Pictures of different kinds of policemen (detective, state trooper, harbor police, mounted police, FBI, secret service agent, traffic policeman, security guard, and so on) were discussed, captions attached, and hung in the room. The children were encouraged to constantly dictate sentences and stories to communicate their excitement and discoveries. These too were always read by teacher and child alone as well as shared later with the whole group. Periodically, the teacher typed the children's stories on a primary typewriter and made booklet copies of them for each child to add to his personal library. Each child in the classroom also had a box in which he kept his own special words during the year. These were words important to the particular child, such as the name of something new he received, a favorite toy or person, something he asked the teacher to print or spell for him, and so on. The word "police" printed on the handmade badges was added by many children to their word boxes, along with words like "prisoner," "bad guy," "sheriff," "'stop," "go," "arrests," and "ticket," and various words for types of police uniforms and automobile parts. The children frequently used their word boxes. Since these were personally important words, they were learned quickly as sight vocabulary. They were brought out to copy the spelling for a sign or simply just to play with and read for fun. The use of both the *spoken* word on the sign level as well as the *written* word was encouraged. Throughout the police car project, the children listened to each other, made plans, shared ideas, and evaluated them critically. They were constantly following directions, each others' or from a reference book on their own pictorial plans.

Classroom Experiences

COOKING.   Cooking experiences in the classroom provide numerous opportunities to extend language and thought from the concrete to the index, symbol, and sign levels of representation. On the concrete and index levels, children work with real food. Frequently the cooking experience stems from the children's interest in a particular item and serves to extend their thought and understanding of it. Acorns or walnuts found and brought to school by children in autumn can lead to a nutcracking party at snack time. Children experience breaking the shells with nutcrackers or hammers as well as the names, shapes, and tastes of such assorted varieties as hazel, brazil, pecan, almond, and walnut. Children may be introduced to other types of nuts such as boiled chestnuts and roasted peanuts. Children can shell roasted peanuts themselves and then use the nuts to make homemade peanut butter. Their understanding is further broadened when they are introduced to nutmeg, a metal nut, coconut, a nuthatch, and ballet of "The Nutcracker Suite." A fresh coconut is brought in to touch, examine, open, drain, and taste. It can be compared in taste to shredded coconut.

On the symbol level, pictures of foods and plastic models may be classified into food categories such as fruits, vegetables, meats, and dairy products. Plastic food models and the packages and containers in which foods come are placed in the housekeeping corner for dramatic play. Clay or an asbestos modeling mixture is placed in the art area for the children to make replicas of food. Once hardened, they may be painted. Real foods such as halves of apples, potatoes, carrots, and onions are used for stamping and printing experiences and for decorating wrapping paper, stationery, or greeting cards. Fruits and vegetables cut into varying designs such as a flower, arrow, or X and used with different-colored stamp pads inspire creativity in printing. Newsprint may be cut into large, distinctive shapes of different foods such as

El Paso Community College Child Development Center   Corpus Christi, Texas, Early Childhood Development Center

A-Bar-Z Ponderosa School, Austin, Texas   National Playing Fields Association, London

The young child's play is not dependent upon the existence of concrete and steel jungles. Simple, natural materials allow relatively safe, aesthetically pleasing, and enjoyable play.

John Arms

Play Schools Association

As children begin to learn games with rules, new terrain and new equipment are needed. The need for adults to provide outdoor materials appropriate to the child's development is just as crucial as the provision of developmentally relevant classroom materials.

255

National Playing Fields Association, London

National Playing Fields Association, London

National Playing Fields Association, London

National Playing Fields Association, London

The adventure playgrounds, popular in Europe, are stimulating the development of imaginative designs for children in the United States. Children can create and re-create with the materials of these playgrounds. Every form of play—exercise, construction, dramatic, social, games with rules—can be accommodated.

Corpus Christi, Texas, Independent School District

Corpus Christi, Texas, Independent School District

Corpus Christi, Texas,
Independent School District

Corpus Christi, Texas,
Independent School District

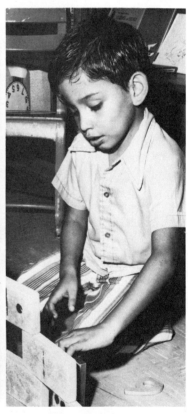

Corpus Christi, Texas,
Independent School District

It is often tempting for teachers to replace the active, concrete learning experiences of the young child with the neat, tidy world of academia. There are fundamental differences between the way many adults think and the way children develop.

258

James A. Dever School, Valley Stream, N.Y.

James A. Dever School, Valley Stream, N.Y.

James A. Dever School, Valley Stream, N.Y.

James A. Dever School, Valley Stream, N.Y.

In the high-quality early childhood program, parent participation, both in the form of conferences with the teacher and involvement in classroom projects, is the rule, for healthy development of the child is deeply rooted in positive family relationships. The school and the home are mutually reinforcing, but if second fiddle is played, it is played by the school.

259

apples, bananas, pears, or bread slices and used on the art easel for creative painting.

Both the written and spoken word are used on the sign level of representation. Children follow directions, both verbal and from a recipe, discuss and follow health and safety rules, plan menus, parties, and snacks, question food changes, predict the effects of heat and cold upon food, and generalize from one cooking experience to the next. (Program objectives of attending and language are also discussed in Chapter 8.) Vocabularies and concepts are broadened during the actual cooking experience, which lends itself to the use of words for *ingredients, food preparation* (scrape, beat, whip, refrigerate, brown, squeeze, chop, press, melt), *utensils* (mixing bowl, eggbeater, broiler, paring knife, measuring cup, grater, serrated-edge knife, spatula), *temperatures* (hot, warm, preheat, lukewarm, chill), *size and quantity* (miniature, teaspoon, medium, small, ounce, pound, cup, pint, dozen, pinch, half, bunch, dash), *texture* (stiff, stringy, lumpy, creamy, crunchy, firm, granular, crisp), and *flavor* (tart, salty, sweet, tangy, bitter, sour). During the art experiences, the names of foods as well as their color, texture, shape, and size are discussed and compared with the real object whenever possible or with pictures. The written word which represents the food is used. The children refer to recipes printed and illustrated on large chart paper, create their own recipes, or dictate stories about their cooking experiences. Poems, stories, and finger plays are additional ways to extend thought and language about food.

Cooking experiences are not limited to the classroom, nursery school, or day care center equipped with a stove and refrigerator. There are numerous recipes that require no cooking whatsoever or that may be partially prepared at home ahead of time. Cooking experiences are an appropriate time to enlist the aid of parents and their supply of such equipment as a popcorn popper, waffle maker, toaster, juicer, blender, food grinder, or ice cream maker. Many more recipes may be followed in the classroom using nothing more than a hot plate or an electric frying pan. Cooking experiences are an ideal way to make holidays more meaningful to children or to introduce them to other cultures. The seeds from a Halloween jack-o-lantern, for example, can be washed, dried, and saved. Later, they can be toasted in the oven with a little oil and salt for a delicious snack. The pumpkin itself can be peeled and the cooked pulp used in pumpkin bread or pumpkin pudding.

Parents should be invited to share their family holiday traditions. One mother shared the traditional gingerbread cookie house her family makes every year at Christmas with her son's classmates. She brought an extra batch of the cookie walls and roof to school and helped the children finish the gingerbread house to share themselves. There was something for everyone to do: glue the walls and the roof with icing, put in windows (Hershey bar squares), and snow in the yard and roof (vanilla frosting), shingles on the roof (ribbon candy), a sidewalk (peppermints), and trees (upside down ice cream cones covered with green frosting). Classrooms with children of different nationalities can take advantage of a unique way to introduce students to other cultures by inviting the parents to help the class prepare Indian or Mexican food, an Italian dish, or soul food. Children themselves often lead the way for exciting experiences with food. Literature becomes more meaningful when they have the opportunity themselves to make and taste "curds and whey" or "porridge." When one Oriental 5-year-old was asked by her teacher what she was preparing in the housekeeping area, she replied that she was very busy serving customers in her Chinese restaurant. Upon questioning her about her play, the teacher discovered that she was full of ideas for her restaurant, some realistic and others not. The teacher encouraged her dramatic play on all levels of thinking. She arranged a class trip to a real Chinese restaurant in a neighboring city where the children met the hostess, waiters, waitresses, and cook. They experienced placing the order, eating the new food, being billed, and paying.

Back in the classroom, they were encouraged to plan and rearrange the furniture in the housekeeping area into a Chinese restaurant of their own. On the symbol level, various roles were tried, discarded, and retried by the children at different times. Modeling material and paints were brought out for the children who wanted to make "food" for the restaurant. On the sign level, the children discussed the kinds of Chinese food to make and its appearance based on their trip to the real restaurant. They listened to each other's ideas, shared materials, and used new words. Afterwards, with the teacher's help, they printed menus, took and filled orders, and transacted with money in billing and paying. The multitude and range of activities encouraged here enabled each child to play and grow on his own level of development. The Chinese restaurant experience was subsequently extended by inviting the Chinese girl's mother and grandmother to school to actually prepare a Chinese meal with the children.

DRAMATIC PLAY.   Dramatic play becomes a rich opportunity for enhancing language and thinking on the symbol level of representation if the stage is properly set to broaden familiar roles and to introduce new ones. The teacher who changes the props in the dress-up center suggests new roles for the children to try on for size. These are real people with whom modern-day children come into contact in their daily lives. For example, a box containing hair rollers, comb, brush, bobby pins, wig, mirror, old hair dryer cap, and so on, inspires dramatic play as a beautician. Other old items can be collected, combined, and set out at different times for playing such roles as mechanic, business executive, astronaut, dentist, nurse, teacher, or farmer. Newsletters can invite parents to save castoff items from which dramatic play can be enlarged. Sometimes setting props in different parts of the classroom suggests new lines of thinking and playing, such as adding them to the block, housekeeping, or music area. Symbol level activities are accompanied by real experiences with roles on the index level and extending them to the sign level with written and spoken words in songs, poems, stories, and discussions.

One teacher felt the need to extend the 3- and 4-year olds' thinking and understanding about "daddies." Some daddies were invited to school to share their different occupations with the children. One father, who was an electrician, worked with the children in a classroom interest center set up about electricity. Another, a carpenter, helped the children make little wooden boats. The class took several trips to visit still other daddies at work, such as a construction worker and one who worked in a bakery. Along with these firsthand encounters with many different daddies, the teacher encouraged symbol and sign level activities. Various clothing and occupational props were set out at different times for role-playing. One corner of the classroom was periodically rearranged into an office, a barber shop, post office, fire station, and so on, to further inspire the children to role play what they were experiencing. Blocks were a good medium with which to role play being a bus driver and a trailer truck driver. The sandbox was an excellent medium for a farm, a busy construction site, and a highway department road repair project. Pictures of many fathers engaged in different work and play roles were displayed. The children painted portraits of their fathers and dictated stories about them. They heard library stories and poems about daddies as well as shared each others' stories. The teacher took photographs of each child and his daddy and the children made their own library book.

LOGICAL AND MATHEMATICAL OPERATIONS

Logico-mathematical operations include the major classes of classification, seriation, and number. These operations do not emerge all at once but are built from the accumulation of almost infinite physical operations or direct physical action upon objects. Thus from an early age the child is assisted in activities that enhance later development. The early school curriculum can help the young child's transition from physical actions to logico-mathematical operations by again providing activities that move from the concrete and specific to the more abstract.

Before the child develops logico-mathematical knowledge, or knowledge structured from activity of the mind, he must develop physical knowledge, or knowledge structured from bodily activities with objects. There are three levels in the transition from physical actions to logico-mathematical operations. The first is direct action upon reality. Physical knowledge is dependent upon the child's immediate perceptions and direct experience. As objects are explored, feedback allows the child to identify properties, to change, to compare, and to construct new objects. For example, the child picks up a rubber ball, squeezes it, bangs it against the floor, bites it, places it in a pan of water, holds it against his face. In so doing, he discovers that the ball is relatively soft, light in weight, smooth, and yielding and that it will float in water and bounce when struck against another object. During this stage the teacher supports the child's physical operations by providing materials and promoting inquisitiveness and by asking children to predict events. At this stage the child cannot be expected to provide causal explanations. He will learn that balls bounce, but he will not be able to explain why they bounce.

The second level in moving toward logico-mathematical operations is a transition from the child's centering on his own body and actions to a *decentered* state. In the decentered state, body and actions are distinguished from and form a meaningful relationship with other objects and events in the child's world. Decentering, a lengthy and difficult process at the physical operation stage, is even more complex at the representation, or logical thought, level.

It is at about four or five that a child is able to designate his right and left hands, though he may have been able to tell them apart since he reached the level of action. Yet, even though he knows how to use these notions as regards his own body, it will be two or three more years before he understands that a tree seen to the right of him when he is going one way will be on the left on the way back, or that the right hand of a person seated opposite him is on his own left; and it will take even longer to accept the fact that an object B located between A and C can be at the same time to the right of A and to the left of C. (Piaget and Inhelder 1969:94–95)

Finally, the development of the semiotic function and language places the child in an interactive role with others, requiring him to expand physical decentering to a third level of affective and social decentering. The teacher assists by planning experiences for both physical exploration and social interaction.

Classification

The child of 3 or 4 puts objects together because of certain likenesses or differences, such as their shape, color, or size. Or he may group the objects according to a particular figural collection or spatial relationship; that is, he may randomly arrange the objects in a straight line, a circle, or a square or even make a picture with them. At about 5 or 6, the child arranges objects purely by likenesses and differences, without any particular spatial form, and he is able to form subgroups with the objects. For example, he can identify a group of round objects from a larger collection of objects, and he can also identify red objects which are round (nonfigural collections). The emergence of genuine classification does not take place until the child is in the first period of concrete operations (7–9 years). In this stage the child extends his ability to differentiate by single characteristics. He can now respond correctly to the question, "Are there more round objects or more red objects?" He can classify by more than one property at a time; he recognizes that one object may belong to more than one group; he recognizes that all the members of a group may be red but that only some are round, some are square, and so on (all-some classification). Table 10-1 illustrates levels in the development of classifications.

Initially, the young child is provided with opportunities to classify in activities in which he has direct, physical encounters with concrete objects and on the index level of representation. For example, the teacher uses classification as a transition technique for moving children into learning centers or to and from a group planning session or story time: "All those children with brown shoes may . . . ; all those with blond hair . . . ; with blue eyes . . . ; all the boys . . . ; all the girls . . . ; all the children with pockets on their clothes . . . ; wearing a sweater . . . "; and so on. The teacher involves children in classification of real objects at snack time by having them sort all the chocolate chip cookies, all the red paper cups, all the spoons, all the big napkins, all the square cookies. A learning center may be set up to sort real objects in containers: buttons of different sizes or colors, autumn leaves or seeds of different varieties, things that are attracted to a magnet and those that are not. The list of ordinary concrete objects that may be collected for classification activities is limitless: seashells, cars, trucks, blocks, beads, animals, macaroni, nuts, bottle caps, mittens, fabric scraps, balls, cups. While on a field trip, children are told to look for all the objects they can find that are red or round or smooth. They arrange bulletin board and table displays of such objects brought back from a field trip or collected from home or

TABLE 10-1 Levels in the Development of Classification

Level I	*Level II*	*Level III*
First preoperational period (3–4 years)	Second preoperational period (5–6 years)	First concrete operations period (7–9 years)

| *Figural collections* Child groups by likenesses and differences and by spatial relationships. | *Nonfigural collections* Child forms groups and subgroups. | *Genuine classifications* Child classifies by more than one property; objects may belong to more than one group; all-some classification. Answers questions with understanding. |

around the classroom: things that are blue, sweet, sour, hard, shiny, soft, triangular.

Materials and equipment within the classroom may be classified along the symbol level of representation. Each type of block is traced on paper, cut out, and tacked to the appropriate shelf. Children classify the blocks by size and shape as they put them away at each cleanup time. Similar classification activities are arranged for the objects in the dramatic play area (shoes, purses, hats, bracelets, necklaces, rings, and so on). The shapes of cooking utensils are traced on a large pegboard where they are hooked for storage or in boxes on a closet shelf. Classroom supplies similarly lend themselves to classification activity: different sizes and colors of art and writing paper, pencils, crayons, chalk. Three-dimensional displays that the children have arranged on the index levels can be accompanied with a corresponding activity on the symbol level. A table display of real objects classified according to those that are round, square, oblong, and triangular, for example, is set under a bulletin board display of pictures of familiar objects containing those shapes (pillow, clock, door, window, pine tree, ice cream cone). Children's books are used for similar activities in which the children locate specific shapes within pictured objects. Graphs and charts such as those illustrated in Figure 10-1 are an ideal way to symbolize discoveries the children have made on an index level. The children consult mirrors and/or each other and classify physical appearance by hair color, eye color, height, and weight. Other charts and graphs may be made for the children's month of birth, likes, dislikes, number of brothers and sisters, pets, favorite TV show, and so on.

The above activities incorporate sign level activity as well. In grouping themselves into committees to assess hair color or height and weight, and to make the graphs or charts, children must engage in planning, listening, sharing, discussing, and evaluating. Appropriate labels need to be selected and printed. In discussing outcomes and drawing inferences from the charts, the class as a whole dictates sentences and stories about findings. On the sign level, classification is possible on a more abstract level. Displays are arranged

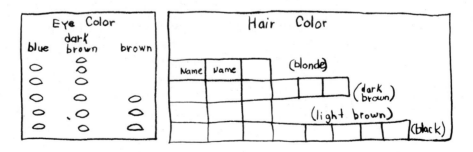

FIGURE 10–1   **Sample charts to aid classification activities.** (From Kissinger 1973:51.)

on abstract concepts and topics such as "The Sea" (sand, shells, water, seagulls, fishing net, sea animals) or "Shoes" (baby's, father's, sneakers, patent leather, loafers, horseshoes, old-fashioned, wooden, ceramic). These are accompanied by stories, poems, and songs.

Language and thinking are extended through exploration of multiple word meanings: *shell*—seashell, turtle shell, gun shell, Shell gasoline, eggshell, peanut shell; *tooth*—child's tooth, tooth of a comb, teeth on a saw blade; *board*—wooden board, checkerboard, ironing board. In simple handmade picture and word thinking games the child must classify the things that go together and explain his reasoning. (*Example*: On an oaktag strip containing pictures of a dog, girl, clown, and boy, the latter three are chosen as going together because they are all people.) Groups of pictures and matching word labels are handmade for classifying other objects as fruits, vegetables, farm animals, zoo animals, things that fly, things that make noise, things that are quiet, and so on. Word labels such as "hat," "spoons," and "shoes" are attached to their corresponding pictures and objects to be used in classifying the equipment at cleanup time. The children's names are used as a dismissal or transition technique. For example, the letter "b" is held up to classify all those children whose first names begin with that letter sound as the ones who may leave the circle. Names that rhyme with a word like "berry" (Mary, Larry, Jerry) are also used in the same type of activity.

Seriation

Simple seriation consists of ordering the elements of a group according to some property, for example, size, weight, or color intensity. Later, the child learns to seriate according to two or more properties at the same time, for example, size and weight. He not only identifies objects according to differences (classification) but he must expand his knowledge to order them according to relative variation. Seriation activity allows the child to learn greater-than and less-than relationships. When objects are ordered in ascending order, A is less than B is less than C, and so on ($A < B < C$). Conversely, in seriating in descending order, the reciprocal relationship is seen; C is greater than B is greater than A ($C > B > A$). With increased skill the child can engage in even more complex representational seriation. For example, he can plan (mentally) for a seriation operation and draw a diagram representing the operation in advance of actually performing it. Table 10-2 illustrates levels in the development of seriation.

Children are physically involved with seriation when they measure each other's height and weight and order themselves accordingly. They are occasionally called to line up by height or weight when going to and from the room as a group. The teacher uses the order of their heights and weights as a dismissal technique or for transition between activities. These index level activities are further strengthened with follow-up symbol level activities. Chil-

TABLE 10-2 Levels in the Development of Seriation

Level I	Level II	Level III
First preconceptual period (3–4 years)	Second preconceptual period (5–6 years)	First concrete operations period (7–9 years)
Preseriation	*Simple seriation*	*Operatory seriation and one-to-one serial correspondences*
Empirical grouping; child arranges and rearranges by trial and error.	Child seriates systematically; first the smallest, then the smallest left over, and so on.	Development of transitivity—If $A > B$ and $B > C$, then $A > C$; furthermore, $C < B < A$. Child can serially match two or more sets of objects simultaneously.

dren work in pairs to trace each other's body outlines on large paper. Each child then cuts out the figure and paints in his features and clothing details. These cutouts are hung on a wall in ascending or descending order. On the sign level, the children discuss the row of cutouts together. They make inferences and draw conclusions which are printed, read, and displayed for further reference. It is important for the teacher, through questioning, to help draw the children's attention to what it is they have done. Merely to do the activity is not enough. Through numerous opportunities to see likenesses and differences, to classify, compare, and seriate, children are sharpening their perceptions.

"I could tell that's Judy 'cause her braids stick out."
"That's Randy. He's the only one that gots glasses in here."

They are learning to observe details and then to stretch their minds and imaginations to utilize what they have observed.

"Susan has brown hair same as me."
"Joey's the biggest one, and he weighs the most, too."

As they grow in ability, these skills are generalized to solving problems in real-life situations. The mind has been disciplined to observe, analyze, evaluate, and draw logical conclusions.

"Go get Joey. He's the biggest one, and if he can get through the door everybody can fit in our block fort."

Children use their bodies to physically seriate: they curl up in balls of different sizes on the floor, separate their feet in varying distances, clap their hands increasingly louder or softer, lift their legs increasingly higher or swing their arms farther while marching. A learning center is set up for children to seriate groups of such objects as boxes, envelopes, cans, pencils, toy animals, cars, and blocks or natural materials the children bring to school such as rocks, leaves, and pine cones. The teacher asks them to order three different cookies on each napkin at snack time or to order the utensils or containers the ingredients come in before a cooking activity. The supplies or equipment in the room, such as paper, tables, or library books, are deliberately ordered by the children. Occasionally, the teacher asks them to order the play materials at cleanup time: "Put away the biggest item in each area first" (biggest block, biggest play food package, biggest dress-up hat). They make collages using different sizes of paper, fabric, buttons, or seeds or different shades and tints of a specific color.

The flannel board is used to have the children order cutouts (clothing, toys, animals, their families) while using words like "tallest," "biggest," "heaviest," "darkest," and so on. While playing in the sandbox and at the water table, the teacher questions them about the size and weight of different buckets, pails, or cans. For fun, pulleys are attached to carry different-sized containers across the sandbox. Children dig holes and make roads and tunnels of different depths and widths in the sand and use trucks of ordered sizes. In these activities, the teacher either directs the children to do a specific task or seizes upon the situations as they occur naturally in children's play to draw their attention to the seriation. She asks them high-level questions that call for explaining, inferring, judging, and problem-solving, not simple recall or memory questions.

Number

The development of whole numbers is connected to the development of seriation. Understanding number is not the same as parroting "one, two, three," and so on. Number is constructed from two types of one-to-one correspondences: (1) matched correspondences in which objects are related one to one by their resemblance to each other (car to car; circle to circle) and (2) random correspondences in which elements are assigned one-to-one correspondence without reference to relational qualities (apple to circle to horse). Number requires that the child distinguish elements and seriate them in space and time—one and then another one (two) and then another one (three).

The teacher focuses on opportunities to draw attention to number as it occurs naturally in daily activities. The child symbolizes the real object or event with a picture or model and then dictates a label, sign, or story about it on the sign level: Amy lost 1 tooth today; Joey is 5 years old today; Jimmy has 3 big brothers; Miss Beck brought 4 fish to school. Such learning experiences are relevent and personal for the child and, hence, are readily dictated and read. There are numerous opportunities during the day for children to make one-to-one correspondences: cookie to napkin and cup to chair at snack time; partner to partner going for a walk; boot to foot and mitten to hand preparing for outdoor play time; instrument to child for a rhythm band; record to cover and jacket to book at cleanup. One-to-one correspondence is carried out on a more abstract level through handmade games in which the child must match pictures such as basketball to basket, tennis ball to racket, astronaut to space-ship, dog to doghouse. It is important for teacher and child to discuss the matches he has made in such games because it is the reasoning and logic the child has used that determines what pictures can be paired. In some activities, a concrete object may be related one to one with an abstract idea: a red cube for each classmate who prefers apple juice for a snack and a green one for those who prefer cherry juice. Seeing and discussing tangible findings like these increase understanding of more than-less than concepts and numerals when the cubes are counted. Red and green construction paper cubes are pasted in chart or graph form later to visually symbolize the concepts. Cooking experiences are relevant opportunities to develop understanding of number: The recipe says 5 teaspoons, the cup of chopped nuts is more than the half cup, the cake pan was lighter before we put the batter in it, the turkey weighed less before we stuffed it.

INTEGRATING A SERIES OF OPERATIONS AROUND ONE THEME. Sometimes an entire unit of activities spontaneously develops in which children are able to increase their understanding of number in a multitude of realistic and meaningful ways, as the following case study illustrates.

A CIRCUS IS COMING

The week the posters and advertisements went up all over town that a circus was coming to a nearby college campus, the children in one 4- and 5-year-old room talked of little else. Only two of them had ever been to a circus before. One morning, as they were again discussing the circus in group time, the teacher said, "If we could arrange for all of us to go to the circus together, what kinds of things do you think we'd have to do to be able to go?" After the initial wave of excitement, the children offered such ideas as "We have to ask our mothers if we can go" and "My father said me and my brothers can't go cause it costs money to go in and he don't have any." "Yes Billy, it does cost money to go to the circus," replied the teacher. "Each person must buy an admission ticket to get inside the circus tent. It can cost more money once you're inside the tent also. People come around and sell popcorn, peanuts, soda, and other kinds of refreshments to eat. Can you children think of a way we could get money to go to the circus?" "We could ask our mothers for it" was the instant reply. "Well," said the teacher, "after mommies and daddies pay for their children's food and clothes and a place to live, they don't always have enough money left over for things like going to a circus, just as Billy's dad explained to him. Maybe if we think hard we can think of some other way to get the money, a way to earn the money." Someone else suggested, "We could make cookies and stuff and sell them"—and the circus project was underway!

There was much to be done. After clearing their ideas with the center director, children and teacher sat down in a group and figured out together exactly how much money they would have to raise for both admission and refreshments for everyone. They brought out the calendar and taped an elephant picture to mark the day they would go to the circus. They counted the working days they had in between. Next, using a cube to represent each child in the class, they matched cube to working day to figure out how many children had to work together in a cooking committee each day so everyone would have a turn making something and selling it. Each committee discussed with the teacher what they would like to cook and made a corresponding picture-word label to mark their day on the calendar. Using this picture-word method, the children in this program frequently referred to their calendar and were able to read and interpret any week's events independently. The group dictated a letter that was mimeographed and sent to the other rooms and to all the parents explaining their project and inviting everyone to come purchase a snack. Several parents, brothers and sisters, and older children in the center volunteered to help with the activities. The committees' choices of snacks to make and sell ranged from brownies, cupcakes, and cookies to lemonade and jello. One creative 5-year-old steered his committee into wanting to make "tunafish cookies." The teacher quickly accepted his vivid imagination and, with some talking and thinking, helped find a way to make them (a bread base cut into different shapes with cookie cutters and spread with tuna salad).

Each cooking session offered that particular group its own number experiences. There was limitless counting of ingredients and turns, dry and wet measuring with spoonfuls, cupfuls, and quartfuls, reading and rechecking of recipes, dividing of things like nuts for chopping, following directions, timing the baking, checking the clock, tasting, talking, and laughing. Two boys even picked up a stopwatch and had a race to see who could carefully empty a rack of cooled cookies faster, an idea that caught on with several others on subsequent days. Throughout, the teacher was guiding the children's interest, enlarging their vocabularies, encouraging their thinking with "What if" questioning, and expanding their language. Each committee discussed the monetary value of what they had made with the teacher, decided upon a sale price, and sold their products on the following day. Some of the children had had more experience with money than others and they shared their knowledge. Each was permitted to grow and learn on his own developmental level. Older children from other rooms who came to buy things seemed to enjoy helping the 4- and 5-year-olds make change and check to see that they had received the correct amount. Sometimes an explanation by an older child to a younger one of why two nickles are the same as a dime made the concept clearer to the child than any explanation his teacher could give. The children became "clock watchers" waiting for selling time to come and grew in their understanding of time.

A few days after the circus project began, Amy came bursting into the morning group planning time with an idea she had had the night before. "We could open up a boutique across the hall from our snack shop," she poured out excitedly. "Everybody who wants to can make things from clay and play dough, and we could paint pictures and glue wood sculptures and sell them in our boutique!" The children loved Amy's idea and willingly gave up treasured creations under her enthusiastic overseeing of The Boutique. Again the children were encouraged to discuss their ideas with the teacher and place their own sales price on what they had made. Kathy brought up her painting and insisted it be priced at $5. The teacher talked with her about the value of five dollars and the unlikelihood that school children would have that amount of money to spend on a picture. Kathy remained adamant and simply stated, "I know all that. My daddy told me $5 was lots of money, and that's what I want it to cost." The teacher accepted her value judgment, and Kathy's $5 painting went into The Boutique among the other items selling from 1 cent to 25 cents.

Every day the children counted their earnings and grew in excitement as the teacher helped them visualize how much nearer they had come to their goal. Many parents and relatives stopped by the shops to make a purchase or to share in their children's enthusiasm. "Eric announced at the supper table last night," said one mother laughingly, "that you have enough for the 'mission' tickets now and only have to get money for refreshments." Time to informally check vocabulary and understanding! In the end, the children had earned enough money to go to the circus matinee and even had some extra which they saved for a class treat later in the year. After several play sessions in school for practice and with whatever help was needed from a chaperoning parent, each child purchased his own admission ticket and bought his own refreshments. This particular group came to school only in the mornings, and one surprising outcome was the number of children who were fascinated with returning to school in the middle of the afternoon on circus day to attend the matinee. Sensing the change from their usual routines, they talked at great length about the clock and the time of day. The other unexpected outcome concerned Kathy's painting, which, as anticipated, did not sell. Later, when the painting was returned to her, she smiled knowingly as she took it and said, "I knew I'd get it back!"

INFRALOGICAL OPERATIONS

Infralogical operations (space, time, and speed) are so named because they have characteristics of both physical and logico-mathematical operations. They resemble physical operations by having exterior referents, being observable, but logical operations by the child are also involved. The teacher's role in enhancing the emergence of these operations again is to provide a range of activities and materials on the index, symbol, and sign levels.

Space

The development of spatial reasoning in the child begins with topology—the identification of spatial relationships and forms irrespective of size and shape. Initially, the young child is encouraged to explore space for himself. He is exposed to open space: large fields and playgrounds and efficiently organized classrooms within which to move his entire body freely. He is exposed to confined space: tunnels, tubes, and boxes to climb in, on, over, and under. He becomes aware of whether his body is standing still in space or moving through space. Directionality, later highly refined in the reading process, becomes evident to him. The young child learns to move his whole body or parts of it up and down, left and right, forward and backward. He also learns the direction of his body and its parts in relation to other objects. In games, he is asked to adjust his body or some specific part of it to an object: near, far away, farther away, between, next to, alongside of, on top of, underneath, behind. The correct vocabulary is supplied for him and he grows in language power as well as body awareness. He grows further in body awareness when asked to solve problems in space using large cardboard boxes, large blocks, old tires or tubes, and so on: "Hide inside the box so we don't see any part of you"; "Hide inside the box so only your finger tips show"; "Go through the tire feet first"; "Go through the tire a different way"; "Get inside the tube and move it to another space"; "Move between the blocks on your back without touching any of them"; and so on.

Free movement, with music as a stimulus and involving a group of children in a room, helps the child learn how to cope with changes in space, seek alternatives to problems, and gain skill and agility in moving safely around obstacles: "We're going for a walk in the woods now. Choose your own path. Walk as fast or as slow as the drumbeat. Be careful—don't bump into anyone else walking in the woods." Later, such spatial exploration on the totally physical level is refined to similar activities using two or more objects such as a dollhouse and furniture or farm animals: "Put the doll inside her dollhouse"; "Put the doll's chair next to her bed"; "Put the horses outside the gate." Similar activities on a more symbolic level can be purchased or made: "Find the picture of a book under a table" (from a series of four pictures of books in different positions in relation to a table); "Find the picture of a tree next to a house"; and so on. On a still more abstract level, children are divided into two groups, one group to draw a map of a trail around the room or school yard and the other to follow it. At another time, the group makes a large map of their neighborhood, locating and marking their homes and discussing their relationship to each other.

At 3–4 years the child can distinguish open figures from closed figures; he can copy a closed figure, but he cannot copy a distinctive shape such as a square or circle. At 5–6 years, he can copy a circle or a square but not a triangle. The curriculum provides opportunity for the young child to explore closed figures physically at first, with his whole body. In gamelike fashion, with and without music, children are asked to use their whole bodies or body parts to make different shapes: "Curl up into a ball on the floor, raise one arm and one leg until they touch, and make a triangle"; "Make a rectangle with your arms"; "Three of you join hands to make a circle"; "Now can you find a way for all three of you to use your whole bodies to make a circle"; and so on. They look at, touch, talk about, and label different shapes. On the symbolic level, children make different shapes from clay and play dough, paint and draw on large paper cut into different shapes, make collages out of one particular shaped paper or material scraps, and glue together abstract sculptures using particular shaped three-dimensional objects (oatmeal boxes, tissue tubes, salt boxes, boullion cube containers, tin cans, plastic hair rollers). They create pictures and stories, arranging and pasting a limited number of cutout shapes such as one rectangle, one triangle, and two circles. One creative 4-year-old made a picture of a garbage truck and labeled it (Figure 10-2).

Euclidean (figures, angles, and so on) and projective (problems of perspective) geometry are developed simultaneously. The child learns to copy and construct complex geometric forms (triangle, rectangle) beginning at about age 7. A child at the preoperational stage does not know how an object will appear when viewed from different perspectives. He cannot set his eating utensils in the same position as those of his friend across the table until the stage of concrete operations.

Spatial measurement develops independently but usually within six months after number. It consists of dividing continuous space into segments and using one of these segments as a standard to be applied successively to the whole without overlapping. Thus measurement requires certain classification, seriation, and number operations. The child accomplishes this task during the early concrete operations stage. Over time, he selects or invents units, or standards of measure, and applies them.

In measurement activities, the understanding of basic concepts such as equal to, as much as, more than, less than, greater than, bigger than, heavier than, wider than, and so on, are more important than the unit of measure itself. Pan scale, hourglass, timer, stopwatch, and rulers are visual aids to deepen understanding. Buttons, marbles, nuts, stones, macaroni, beads, seeds, sand, water, or string become standards of measure.

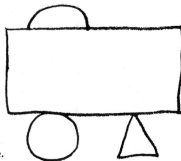

FIGURE 10-2   A garbage truck with a flat tire.

Snuffy weighs 40 marbles. Coco weighs 45 marbles. Coco is a heavier guinea pig than Snuffy.

It takes 2 small cans of seeds to balance this pail of sand.

To facilitate learning and independence, materials are organized in large containers of "things to measure with" and "things to sort" and are readily accessible.

The teacher is always alert to utilize the child's self-initiated activity to encourage spatial measurement: "I wonder whose hole in the sandbox is deeper, yours or Andy's? How could we find out?" "You climbed higher on the bars today, Pamela, than you ever have before. Let's measure and see how much higher." "What if you didn't have that board to put over the puddle. What else could you use to get across it?" "What makes you think your toy car is faster than John's?" "What do you think would happen if you put more bottle caps on this side of the pan scale?" At the same time, picture and/or word task cards (Figure 10-3) may be appropriately placed alongside such equipment as a balance beam, pan scale, water table, or sandbox to suggest an avenue of thought for the child to explore. (See also Chapter 8 and the use of task cards in learning centers for instruction and evaluation.)

The ability to conserve is perhaps the clearest single indication that the child has attained concrete operations of thought (age 7–11). The absence of this ability, therefore, places the child's thought in the preoperational stage. The child discovers conservation of substance at 7–8 years. He learns, for example, that the amount of clay in a ball does not change simply by modifying the shape of the clay ball into a clay sausage. Further, he knows that the process can be reversed. At 9 or 10, he discovers conservation of weight. Only later, at 11 or 12, does he discover conservation of volume. At this level, the child understands that the amount of liquid remains the same despite the size or shape of the container into which it is poured. Table 10-3 illustrates levels in the development of conservation.

Time

The concept of time develops little by little beginning in infancy. The 4- or 5-year-old confuses age and height. The tallest person is the oldest person. Later, he understands that one person is older than another but expects that younger people will "catch up" to older people. At age 7–8, he separates age from size, he understands that adults have a past, and he is able to extrapolate to the future. His older brother will always be older and he will always be younger.

The early childhood curriculum helps the child grow in his ability to *live* time wisely. He is given opportunity and support to plan out how he

FIGURE 10-3   Sample task cards.

TABLE 10-3   Levels in the Development of Conservation

Level I	Level II	Level III
First concrete operations period (7–9 years)	Second concrete operations period (9–11 years)	Late concrete operations period (11–12 years)
Conservation of substance Amount of substance remains unchanged despite change in appearance.	*Conservation of weight* Weight of substance remains unchanged despite change in appearance.	*Conservation of volume* Volume remains unchanged despite change in appearance.

will use his time each day, in which learning centers he will work, and what he plans to do at each. Equally important is giving the child the chance to evaluate for himself at the end of the day if he did in fact live his time to its fullest. (See also "Self-Evaluation" in Chapter 8.) The teacher teaches the child *how* to evaluate, but the child sets his own standards. The children actively participate together in setting up the daily schedule for the group during morning planning time. They verbalize about the sequence of the day's events and why some activities must occur at particular times (lunch, dismissal) or in a particular order. With repeated, meaningful practice in planning and evaluating, children become increasingly adept at living time to its fullest and richest extent.

The early childhood curriculum also helps the young child increase his awareness of the *passage* of time. In so doing, he becomes increasingly able to relate to quantities of time and, thus, utilize time more wisely. The child's attention is periodically drawn to time: "In five more minutes, it will be cleanup time"; later, "Five minutes have gone by, and it's time to clean up our room now." Changes in routine are an ideal opportunity to draw the child's attention to time and to help him learn to cope with change. The fascination of the group of children who had returned to school the same afternoon to go to the circus, described in the case study earlier in the chapter, is an excellent example of children's sensitivity to change and their need to learn how to handle it. As another example, "We usually go out to play now, but we're going to the puppet show instead." The passage of time is pointed out during stories: "What happened at the beginning (middle, end) of our story?" "The little kitten was lost all night long"; "The man ate his supper very, very slowly." The child is helped to associate the passage of time with relevant events in his life: "It will take us about as long to get to the orchard as it usually does to have our snack"; "Jimmy told us the drive to his grandfather's house will take 6 hours. About how long do you think 6 hours is?"

Cooking activities focus on time: stir 1 minute, bake 1 hour, refrigerate overnight, let rise for 2 hours, instant pudding mix sets in just 5 minutes. At the end of the day, the sequence of the day's events are reviewed. The calendar and the clock are constantly used to order events. Pictures and words are chosen and attached to the calendar by teacher and children together to help them realistically grasp an understanding of yesterday, tomorrow, next week, last week, the holiday weekend, and so on. Simple clock sketches are hung in the room to indicate when significant events or activities will occur. These are referred to often and are continuously updated as the children's activities dictate. Children easily become "clock watchers" and learn to tell time with understanding when exposed to time in realistic and meaningful ways.

Activities that focus upon the passage of time as it brings changes in the young child himself are important and appealing, since he is, by nature, self-centered at this age. A display of baby pictures of the children as compared to current ones leads to thoughtful discussions of the many changes 3, 4, 5, or 6 years have brought. Using sand or water, weight at birth as compared to the child's present weight is visually represented. Marks on paper tacked to the wall to contrast height, a comparison of footprints, and pictures of people in different stages of life also visually present the passage of time in the child's life. Reading and discussing popular children's stories offer the same food for thought on the sign level. Children are encouraged to verbalize their thoughts, feelings, concepts, and misconceptions by dictating their own stories, individually or as a group: "Being 3 years old means . . . ," "Old is . . . ," "Young is. . . ." To the children in one kindergarten, being 5 years old meant:

BEING 5 YEARS OLD MEANS . . .
. . . you play games; you play more rougher; ride a bigger bike; play football and kickball; ride a two wheeler—you can balance on it now; you get a training wheel bike; you can whistle; you lose a tooth; help make pizza; your clothes don't fit—

they stretch out and break and you'll be naked; you can't be a teenager; you can't drive a car; you can't mow the lawn. (Kissinger 1973:23)

Feeling the passage of brief periods of time is enhanced with games that measure it. New cars brought to school can be raced down inclined slopes, the race timed and talked about. In creative thinking games, a timer is set for 5 minutes while the children call out as many different uses for an item as they can think of. The teacher records their ideas. Three-year-old David seemed to be more fascinated with the paper shoe bag in which he carried his new shoes home than with the new shoes themselves. He brought the shoebag to school with him the following day and never put it down. Before dismissal his teacher set their cooking timer for 5 minutes and asked the group to think of as many different uses for David's shoe bag as they could. Their list included a laundry bag, put books in it, put puppies in it, carry lunch in it, collect rocks, bring groceries home, and make a superman costume with it.

The 4- to 5-year-olds' introspective estimates of time are linked to speed of activity and results of activity. The faster one works and the more he produces, the more time is spent. The 7- to 8-year-old understands that time is not a direct function of speed or results.

The concept of speed is relatively complex. It is not until the later concrete operations stage (9–10 years) that the child understands the relationships between distance (space) and time. The concept of speed does not emerge full-blown until the early formal operations period.

SUMMARY AND CONCLUSIONS

The teacher can enhance language and thinking in young children through her actions and her language, through her selection of materials and equipment in the classroom, and through the nature of the activities she plans and utilizes. The following checklist summarizes the teacher's role in enhancing language and thinking in young children.

Enhancing Thought

NATURE OF THE ACTIVITIES
1. The experience stems from or incorporates the children's ideas and interests.
2. The interests expressed by the children are followed up with appropriate related activities wherever possible.
3. The activity provides the children with a meaningful firsthand experience.
4. The children are allowed enough time to fully experience the activity.
5. They have time to freely manipulate and explore on their own at first.
6. They are able to actively investigate on the concrete level, with real objects and materials.

7. The experience incorporates activity on the index level of representation, the symbol level, and the sign level.
8. The activity is extended as far as possible to involve poetry, books, trips, resource people, cooking activities, audiovisual aids, and artifacts.
9. The activity is integrated with other areas such as mathematics, science, language arts, social studies, music, art, and dramatics.
10. The children are encouraged to be creative and original.

EQUIPMENT AND MATERIALS (OBJECTS, TOYS, PETS, DISPLAYS)

1. The equipment and materials (objects, toys, pets, displays) are stimulating.
2. The equipment is useful. It "does something."
3. The children can act upon the equipment. It engages their senses.
4. The equipment is functional. It serves a purpose. It is used by the children.
5. The equipment provides feedback to the children so that they can act independently.
6. Equipment and materials are in strategic locations in the classroom.
7. The related bulletin boards and displays in the classroom are the work of the children. They reflect the children's current interests and activities.
8. The related bulletin boards and displays are functional. The children refer to them. They are located on the children's eye level and are accessible to them.

INVOLVING CHILDREN IN PLANNING AND DECISION-MAKING

1. The children share in the planning of the classroom experiences.
2. There is opportunity for the children to weigh alternatives.
3. Time is taken after each activity for the children to critically evaluate the outcome of their decisions.
4. Throughout the activities, the children are encouraged to think for themselves through the types of material provided and through the behavior of the teacher.
5. The children are encouraged to solve problems for themselves.
6. They are guided to know where to seek help in solving problems (reference book, resource person, trial and error, and so on).

Enhancing Language

LANGUAGE USAGE

1. There are numerous opportunities provided for the children to use language instead of the teacher (by giving directions, explaining, telling a game or song, and so on).
2. Throughout the activities, there is time for the children to talk.
3. The teacher capitalizes on engaging the children in naturalistic conversation within the play situation.
4. The teacher asks questions that encourage the children to talk.
5. The teacher's questions are of a high-level nature. They call upon the children

to explain, classify, group, compare, make inferences, pretend and think creatively, evaluate and judge, and solve problems.

6. The teacher demonstrates that she values child talk by incorporating the children's ideas in her own speech and in the classroom activities.
7. There is personalized talk (greeting, recognition of achievement, recognition of personal events).
8. The children are encouraged to communicate their interests, ideas, and feeling by dictating labels, sentences, and stories.
9. The dictated ideas are shared with the other children.
10. The children are encouraged to verbalize what their own feelings, values, and standards are.

LANGUAGE SKILLS
1. The teacher listens carefully to the children's talk to identify such things as misconceptions, immature syntactical structures, and level of comprehension.
2. There is opportunity to enlarge vocabularies and to extend multiple word meanings.
3. Real objects and visual aids are used to increase comprehension and to clarify concepts.
4. There is opportunity for the children to classify and to compare.
5. The activities engage receptive language skills (listening).
6. The language experiences utilize reading readiness activities (building sight vocabulary, auditory discrimination, ocular motility, comprehension, and so on).
7. The teacher serves as a language model for the children. She uses full sentences. Her sentences include the category or classification. Her words are specific, precise, and accurate descriptives. She models mature syntactical structures (possessives, plurals, tense, condition, and so on).
8. The teacher expands the children's utterances wherever possible.
9. The teacher's verbalizations help to clarify for the children (*how* things compare, *what* the feelings are, and so on).

SUGGESTED ACTIVITIES

1. Observe a unit of activity in an early childhood center. Use the checklist found in the chapter summary as a guide and determine all of the ways in which the teacher enhanced language and thought during the unit.
2. Select several themes or units of study for 3-, 4-, 5-, or 6-year-olds. Build a file of ideas of ways to enhance language and thought if you were to implement these units of study in a classroom. Use the summary checklist as a guide.
3. Select several themes or units of study for 3-, 4-, 5-, or 6-year-olds. Analyze the language potential in each theme or unit as follows. List as many opportunities as you can think of for the children to use language during this unit instead of the teacher. List examples of questions the teacher could use that would encourage the children to talk throughout the unit. Give examples of

questions of a high-level nature that the teacher could ask. Determine ways that the children could communicate and share their activities, ideas, and feelings during the unit of study.

4. Talk to a 3-, 4-, 5-, or 6-year-old child. Show him some unfamiliar objects and talk with him about them or teach him how to do something. Tape record your conversation. Play back the tape recording and analyze your language. Give specific examples from the tape recording. Consider the following in your analysis:

   a. As the language model, did you use full sentences?
   b. What did your sentences include? what categories or classification?
   c. Were your words specific, precise, and accurate descriptives?
   d. How did you expand the child's utterances?
   e. How did you model mature syntactical structures?
   f. How did your verbalizations serve to clarify for the child?
   g. What were the opportunities to enlarge vocabularies and to extend word meanings?

REFERENCES

Kissinger, J. 1973. *A Process Curriculum for Five-year-olds*. Occasional Paper 7. College Park, Md.: Center for Young Children, College of Education, University of Maryland.

Kissinger, J., and J. Yabu. 1976. "The Police Car," *Instructor*, February.

Nelson, K. 1973. "Structure and Strategy in Learning to Talk," *Monographs of the Society for Research in Child Development*, 38(1–2).

Piaget, J., and B. Inhelder. 1969. *The Psychology of the Child*. New York: Basic Books.

FURTHER READING

Aebli, H. "Piaget and Beyond," in J. L. Frost (ed.), *Revisiting Early Childhood Education*. New York: Holt, Rinehart and Winston, 1973.

Almy, M., E. Chittenden, and P. Miller. *Young Children's Thinking: Studies of Some Aspects of Piaget's Theory*. New York: Teachers College Press, 1966.

Biber, B., E. Shapiro, D. Wickens, and E. Gilkeson. *Promoting Cognitive Growth: A Developmental-Interaction Point of View*. Washington, D.C.: National Association for the Education of Young Children, 1971.

Coody, B. *Using Literature with Young Children*. Dubuque, Iowa: William C. Brown, 1973.

Kamii, C. "One Intelligence Indivisible," *Young Children*, 1975, 30(4): 228–238.

Kohlberg, L., and R. Mayer. "Development as the Aim of Education," *Harvard Educational Review*, 1972, 42: 449–498.

Lavatelli, C. S. *Piaget's Theory Applied to an Early Childhood Curriculum*. Boston: American Science and Engineering, Inc., 1970.

Piaget, J. *To Understand Is To Invent: The Future of Education.* New York: Grossman Publishers, 1973.

Piaget, J. *The Language and Thought of the Child.* Cleveland, O.: World Publishing, 1955.

Special Study Institute. *The Application of Piagetian Learning Theories to Curriculum Development for Exceptional Children.* Austin, Tex.: The Texas Education Agency, 1973.

Ford Foundation, Roy Stevens

11

Enhancing Affective Development: Motivating and Managing Behavior

Teachers of young children are concerned with the promotion of every dimension of the child's development. Unfortunately, many devote a great deal of attention to cognitive development and academic achievement and neglect to plan for affective development, or growth in attitudes, interests, appreciations, values, and emotional sets. It is relatively easy to identify learning objectives for cognitive development and to devise activities for their attainment. But the dimensions of affective development are not so readily observable or understood in classroom action. The teacher may see, for example, that Billy is able to read a given selection with understanding, but she is much less secure about why he is not motivated to engage in out-of-class reading or what attitudes he holds about reading. Essentially, teaching for affect is not so much a process of defining "content to be taught" as it is a process of creating a stimulating, positive, emotionally secure climate for the child's living. The teacher is the key element, for she, more than any other variable, is responsible for creation of a rich environment that enhances affective development. The teacher

1. Accepts the child's feelings.
2. Assists the child in understanding his feelings.
3. Provides safe outlets for the child's emotions.

4. Focuses attention upon the positive side of the child's development and behavior.
5. Accepts the child's attitudes.
6. Plans activities to increase the child's awareness and understanding of other people, their attitudes, and feelings.
7. Helps the child examine and evaluate his personal values for himself.
8. Personally exemplifies an attitude of care, respect, warmth, consideration, openness, and acceptance in her interactions with the children.
9. Listens to the children with undivided attention.
10. Respects and utilizes the child's ideas.
11. Ignores some behaviors and uses positive reinforcement of other behaviors.
12. Builds the curriculum around the interests of the children.

The present chapter examines each of the dimensions of affective development and the teacher's plan for enhancing them.

ATTITUDE

The child's attitude about himself is a basic dimension of affective development, for it affects his motivation, his learning capacity, and his relationship with peers and adults. John does not think he's good at physical activities such as sports. Pam finds it difficult to print her name and shies away from all printing, coloring, and other small muscle activity. Jennie's mother believes that playing in school is a waste of time and insists that Jennie stay out of the housekeeping area. Tim is a poor reader, and his mother thinks he is lazy and doesn't read enough at home. How does the teacher effectively deal with these attitudes? Initially, she analyzes the situation to identify the underlying attitude, acknowledges its existence, and accepts her responsibility to deal with it.

Dramatic play with puppets, stories that accompany paintings, observation of the child, a private outing or talk with the child, all are ways in which the teacher gains insight into a child's attitudes. For John and Pam, the teacher first focuses on the strong areas of their development. John may not be able to kick a ball, but perhaps he blends colors beautifully in his art work or creates thoughtful poems or has a wonderful sense of humor. The teacher consistently comments to him, both privately and in front of his peers: "The dark blue and gray you used in this part of your picture really does make it feel as though a storm is coming, John"; "All the orange and yellow you used in your picture makes it bright and warm"; "I noticed you tried something new at the easel today, John. You made a design using only circles and triangles." The teacher's comments are specific rather than such vague generalizations as "Look at John's picture!" or "What an interesting painting, John!" At the same time, she verbalizes what it is John has done, but does not interject value judgments such as "That's a pretty painting" or "How nice" or "What a good job," since the words "pretty," "nice," and "good" may not hold the same value for John as they do for the teacher. Similarly, specific and objective statements are made for creative writing: "You used seven words that all begin with the sound of 'b.' They give your poem a special sound." "The words 'jump,' 'bounce,' and 'hop, hop, hop' you used in your poem tell me exactly how that rabbit went home." "All these nonsense words you made up give your story a very funny sound. Let's share it with the other children at story time and make them laugh too." Before long, everyone becomes more aware of John's strong qualities—the teacher, his peers, and John himself.

At the same time, the teacher initiates plans to change John's attitude about his weaker developmental area, his motor skill. Her careful observation indicates John needs to improve in eye-hand coordination and gross motor movement. To strengthen the skill, she schedules a series of small-group and individual activities involving rolling, catching, tossing, kicking, reaching for objects, and placing objects in designated places. The activities are carefully sequenced so that they begin on John's present developmental level and increase in difficulty and complexity. (See "Task Analysis" in Chapter 8.) She does not force him into any activity for which he does not feel ready, but sets the stage indoors and outdoors by the equipment she arranges to encourage him to engage in large muscle activities in his play: to use ladders, to walk and crawl the boards, to use the beanbags and balls, and so on. Initially, she reinforces his mere willingness to try these activities, however brief the attempt. (See "Managing Behavior Externally Through Reinforcement" later in this chapter.) "You tried the beanbag game today!" (as John makes two experimental tosses); "You played catch with Mary Ann today!" (as he throws back the ball which accidentally rolled to him and then plays briefly with the other child). As his skill begins to improve, the teacher is alert for opportunities to offer encouragement and praise: "You threw the ball farther today than you did yesterday, John!" "Wow, that kick put the ball as far as the sandbox!"

Working with Parents

In the cases of Jennie and Tim, the teacher must deal with the parents' attitudes as well as with the children's. Again, the teacher accepts the reality of their feelings and then tries to help. Discussing the mother's concerns during a parent conference and illustrating through an observational record of Jennie's daily activities over a period of time may reassure her mother that Jennie is receiving a balanced curriculum. (See "The Case Study" in Chapter 8.)

The teacher also gets Jennie's mother involved in some volunteer work with the children or merely some visitation and observation of their play within the classroom. She takes time to point out the learnings and discoveries occurring there to increase the mother's awareness of how math, science, language arts, social studies, reading, and writing are integrated in the child's play. She prepares a series of newsletters for all parents, each focusing on a different area of the classroom such as blocks, the easel, the housekeeping area and giving examples of the vocabulary development, math and science concepts, social skills, and so on, that are learned in each center. Sharing pamphlets and professional literature on the value of play is very helpful to parents in understanding their children. Open house, PTA meetings, and special parents' nights may focus on the same topic by using films, specialists, or a slide presentation the teacher herself has put together from pictures of the children at work in the classroom.

The Teacher's Role in Promoting Positive Attitudes

In providing for affective development, the teacher plans for growth with respect to attitude toward others. She examines her own attitudes toward various ethnic groups, the handicapped, the advantaged and the disadvantaged, and more specifically, toward each of the individual children within her classroom. Serious personality clashes, prejudices, or feelings of ineptness in dealing with specific problems all have a demoralizing effect. Such attitudinal problems are realistically faced and quickly corrected by transferring the child to another classroom, seeking the aid of specialists, and systematically working to change the attitude with or without counseling.

The teacher strives to increase awareness and understanding of other people in her students as well as in herself. She focuses upon the various backgrounds found within her classroom and other cultural and religious groups to which the children are exposed in the school and community. By helping the students become more informed about the individuality of each other, their understanding and acceptance of each other is strengthened. Cooking experiences in the classroom provide an opportunity to taste the traditional foods of other countries and cultures. Various parts of our own country are not to be overlooked. A new child moving in from New England or the South may afford an experience with making maple syrup or sampling hush puppies. Children help plan for and participate in the celebration of various cultural and religious holidays such as Easter, Chanukah, and Hina Matsuri (Doll's Day in Japan). Stories, legends, folktales, and poems are used to further increase awareness and information about people from other countries and from different parts of the United States, people with handicaps and special problems, and people of other races and religions. Native costumes, songs, festivities, dances, and special customs give new meaning to the peers and adults children encounter in their daily lives. These are all opportune moments to invite a parent, grandparent, neighbor, or friend to demonstrate his or her special heritage, whether it is a craft, a song, a dance, a food, or some artifacts. Emphasizing our own country's special days in the curriculum, such as United Nations Day, Election Day, Flag Day, and the birth of the "Star Spangled Banner" help children grow in knowledge and appreciation of their own heritage. More common holidays such as Halloween are used to develop additional attitudes focusing on safety and on UNICEF. Christmas is a time to lay the foundation for attitudes about ecology and wildlife preservation, for making parents aware of safety standards when buying toys, and for sharing directions with parents on how to make creative and inexpensive toys with their children from things around the house.

In teaching for affective development, the teacher is a constant example of the attitudes she is emphasizing. She illustrates an attitude of care and respect when she greets each child every morning and remembers important personal events in his life. She gets down to the child's eye level to talk to him and does so with warmth and politeness rather than coldness and negativism. The teacher refers back to his suggestions, accepts his ideas, and integrates them in the curriculum. She handles his work carefully and proudly and takes the time to arrange it neatly and aesthetically for sharing. She mounts displays on the child's eye level and arranges equipment and materials within his easy reach, because she believes the classroom is the children's place to live and work and not solely her domain. She has time to stop and listen to the child with undivided attention. She believes her students are capable, interesting, responsible, and unique individuals. She reflects this attitude by inviting them to plan and make daily decisions with her, encouraging and praising them, and sequencing and individualizing activities for them.

The teacher believes that learning is fun, worthwhile, and a lifelong activity, and she demonstrates this attitude by being enthusiastic, creative, and eager to learn herself. She plans meaningful activities, not busy work, and activities that call for the children to be active rather than passive and that lead them to make discoveries for themselves. She shares her own discoveries with the children and provides time for the children to share theirs with her and with each other. She acknowledges their personal work styles and tastes and provides a balance of noisy and quiet areas and a mixture of large space for some activities and small, cozy areas for others. She allows children to work alone, in small groups, and in large groups as the need arises. She varies the time schedule, the choice of learning centers, and the methods for working at each so that children are not forced to all be doing the same thing at the same time and in the same manner. She uses the classroom environment to set the stage for healthy attitudes to emerge—playing soft music on the record player to invite children to slip quietly into an assembly or a story time circle; using one color all around the room to set a particular mood, such as sunny yellow during a dark, stormy winter week; spreading quiet around the room to gain the students' attention by whispering in ear after ear rather than shouting. It doesn't take many whispers before everyone's attention is captured. Sometimes she gives simple directions in stick figure form on the chalk-board, thus giving children a chance to think on their own instead of always being bombarded with teacher talk.

INTERESTS

The teacher builds the curriculum around those things in which the individual child is most interested. (See Chapter 8 for ways to diagnose the child's interests.) If the curriculum is established by the teacher in advance of meeting the child and the child is expected to "fit" the curriculum, the critical interest variable is not taken into account, and likelihood of the child's working at a high motivational level is diminished. What the teacher can and should direct her attention to in *advance* of meeting her children is the logic of subject matter, sequences, and choices of media. She uses the child's interests as the basis from which to teach, whether the focus is math and science concepts, writing, reading, increasing vocabulary, socialization, or problem-solving.

A child may find learning to read much more appealing if he can read about dinosaurs or outer space or whatever the topic is in which he's most involved at the time. The teacher encourages his interest and attempts to extend it to the depths of new learning. She brings in books, objects, pictures, displays, and resource people on the subject. Lack of easy-to-read books on the topic is no obstacle because teacher and child write their own language experience stories. These then become the focal point for sight vocabulary development, phonic lessons, thinking and reasoning skills, and for sheer pleasure in listening. Related trips, learning centers, and activities are arranged. Music and art are incorporated, all to stimulate new thinking and discoveries for the child. The *Tyrannosaurus rex* in the created stories goes on to become the focal point for work with measurement, numbers, size, weight, comparisons, proportions, animal habitats and food, and so on. The children may even work together in planning and building a model of a dinosaur, creatively solving all the problems that arise from such a project.

Relating to Out-of-School Interests

The teacher is always listening and watching for the child to express his interests in the things he says in his play and in the things he brings to school. The child who eagerly wants to tell the teacher some unrelated item when the class is involved in other things should not be dismissed lightly as interruption. He may not be tuned in to what the rest of the class is doing, but his mind is definitely on important matters elsewhere: "You know what, teacher? My Grandma is coming from Massachusetts tomorrow." The teacher acknowledges his thinking: "We're listening to this story right now, Peter, but when we're finished, we'd like to hear about your grandmother's visit." And following the story and its discussion: "Peter wants to tell us something now." What an opportune moment to develop the interest in Grandma! Locating Massachusetts on a map may lead other children to locate where their grandparents live. A better concept of time and distance may emerge from a discussion of how long it will take Peter's grandmother to travel and relating it to the child's world—will it take as long as snack time or outdoor play time or all day in school? From this beginning, perhaps a unit of study on transportation will emerge. Stories and drawings of grandmothers may yield a picture different from the typical stereotype and awaken new interest in the way of life and dress when Grandma was a little girl. Best of all, perhaps Peter's grandmother can come to school for a visit.

In extending children's interests, the teacher makes sure the content of the activities she plans are appropriate to the particular age and level of the group with which she is working. She plans carefully so that the activities are properly sequenced and individual children may progress through them at their own developmental rate. She communicates frequently with parents by phone, notes, newsletters, and conferences to share knowledge about the child's background and interests. She maintains the teacher-parents communication while projects are ongoing and as they change so that parents also may participate in the educative process as observers, helpers, and advisers.

Extending Interests

While planning the curriculum, the teacher strives to *broaden* the child's interests by introducing him to new ones. The child who continually chooses only the block area, for example, occasionally finds a sign there when he arrives in the morning. Children in a classroom where messages are transmitted pictorially and graphically as well as verbally quickly learn to read a sign's simple message: "No blocks today" or "Closed today." The wise teacher is there, however, to guide the child with a thoughtful suggestion. "Since the block area is closed today, Stephen, maybe you'd like to try the clay modeling this morning"; or "I brought in a special game to play with you this morning, Stephen."

Experimenting with new foods in the classroom may spark a child's interest in a special area, such as a different culture, shapes and textures, the effects of heat and cold, or things that dissolve and those that don't. The perceptive teacher notes the initial interest and follows up with relevant activities for further investigation and discovery. The teacher continually changes the displays in and around the room to awaken new interests. She brings in interesting and unusual objects which tempt curiosity—an old clock, radio, cash register, typewriter, or other old machines can be looked at, touched, manipulated, taken apart and put back together again. Similar gadgets from which thinking, discovery, and a new adventure may stem can be handmade, such as a board of assorted latches and hooks, nuts, and bolts to assemble, a pulley system rigged to hoist a flag or send messages, a bulb and battery connection, and a box of various magnets and objects to test. New avenues of interest and thought are opened up by stories about nature and wildlife, important historical and contemporary figures, legendary characters and folk heroes, faraway lands and people, our own country's history, pioneer life, and space travel.

The teacher creates opportunities for the children to be sources of new interests for each other. She arranges time and space for them to share each others' work in all its forms—written, spoken, and three-dimensional. She also provides opportunities for children to work and play together in ever-changing groups, teams, and committees.)

APPRECIATION

In attempting to develop children's appreciation, the teacher strives to strengthen their awareness of each other, of personal style and taste, of property, and of the nature and beauty that surrounds them. She utilizes opportunities for children to learn to appreciate *each other*. She encourages and guides them to listen to each others' ideas: "It's Mary's turn to tell us her idea now, Susan. You can have a turn next"; "As we take turns telling our suggestions for the project, I'll write them down here so we won't forget any of them"; "Yesterday, Jimmy told me an idea he had for changing our snack time. Jimmy, will you tell all the boys and girls your idea now so we can try it today?" "Maureen had the same problem working that truck the other day, Vincent. Let's go ask her how she solved it."

The teacher fosters situations where children work together in changing numbers and groups so that they become aware of the need to share both ideas and assistance: "We're going to make Matthew's birthday cake this morning. All the children who want to choose that activity should go wash their hands now"; "Mark needs some help making his garage in the sandbox. Who can help him?"; "Maybe I can help you choose something to do today, Amy. Let's go see if Brenda and Joe need any help in their doctor's office"; "Here's the list we made of each thing we have to do to get ready for our Thanksgiving feast. You listen as I read the list again so you can tell me which committee you want to work on." The teacher acknowledges the diversity and uniqueness of the children's work. She shares their stories and poems by reading them aloud at story times and by hanging them up. Periodically, she types them and mimeographs a copy for each child to add to his personal library at home. She lists the children's suggestions and plans for class problems and projects, hangs them, and refers back to them frequently. She carefully mounts and displays the children's work, hanging it at the child's eye level so it can be seen and used. Children's work, not the teacher's, is everywhere, and it is changed as soon as its functions have been served. Because children are individuals, there is an obvious diversity in the nature of their work around the classroom and in the methods in which it is accomplished.

Appreciation of Property

The teacher creates a climate for appreciation of *property*. Each time a new piece of equipment is brought into the classroom, she spends time showing the children the proper way to use it. She sees that everything in the room has a clearly marked place for storage and that each child is familiar with the layout. Cleanup time is treated in a matter of fact manner in the daily life of the classroom from the first day of school. The teacher realizes that children become deeply involved in the things they are doing. Out of consideration for their feelings, she signals them as cleanup time draws near so that they have a chance to prepare for continuation the following day. Each child is expected to put away what he has used before going on to something else and to share in the general room cleanup. The teacher provides a separate place for each child to keep his personal belongings. Even a simple shoe box with the child's name on it placed above his coat hook will suffice.

Aesthetic Appreciation

A foundation for aesthetic appreciation is laid. The children are introduced to a variety of tastes in music. They sing folk songs to a guitar, learn to square dance, and slip quietly into group times to the accompaniment of Beethoven. They hum patriotic and pop tunes, learn holiday songs and finger plays, and form their own rhythm bands. The teacher plans for the children to grow in awareness of art styles. They go to the local library to borrow copies of art masterpieces to hang in the classroom. They invite a local artist to come to school and demonstrate his or her talent for them. They experiment with a variety of materials and mediums—tempera, fingerpaint, crayon, watercolor, magic marker, charcoal, chalk, clay, papier mâché, silk screen, printing, spatter painting, tie dyeing, découpage, pasting, cutting, and sewing.

Appreciation of Nature

An appreciation of nature and beauty is cultivated. Appreciation of wildlife begins with the classroom pet—an aquarium placed low to the floor so that children can closely observe the life there, a dozen chick eggs to care for until they hatch, a guinea pig to hold and stroke, a classmate's box turtle to see and talk about when it is brought to school for a visit one day. As winter draws near, the children turn milk cartons into bird feeders. They hear a story about animal tracks in the snow, go on a trip around the school to identify some themselves, and are enticed to continue the new discovery on their own outside of school. Lifetime impressions are created when children learn about such things as endangered species and the dangers of forest fires.

In one school, the principal walked into a kindergarten classroom unannounced one autumn day to observe the beginning teacher in that room. At the same moment he opened the door, he was dismayed to see all the children clamoring toward the windows, when moments before, from the hall, he had observed a quiet room with everyone intently involved in work. His surprised expression, however, was equally matched by the look of surprise and uneasiness on the teacher's face. After a brief hesitation, she continued toward the windows after the children. The window of this particular classroom faced a heavily wooded area adjacent to the school. Apparently, while teaching a language lesson to a small group of children, the teacher had observed a flock of birds leaving the woods and had told her students to quickly go to the windows to watch. Hundreds and hundreds of birds could be seen pouring out of the woods to head South for the winter. Children, teacher, and principal watched from the windows, spellbound by the sight they were witnessing.

The conscientious young teacher later went to the principal's office to apologize for not doing what her plan book indicated she should have been doing in that time period, but explained that she did not want her students to miss that moment of beauty. The principal replied, "If your students have thought about the wonder of those hundreds of birds as many times as I have today, education for the day in your room was achieved early this morning!" That same enthusiastic young teacher took her students to the top of a nearby hill to feel the wind pulling and shoving their little bodies on a gusty day; had them listen to the sound of the rain on the tin roof of the playground storage shed; made a class pet out of a spider that spun its web in the sunlight of the classroom to observe and record its movements; found a toadstool on her way to school one day and used it for teaching science, language arts, and health. This class gathered and created natural flower arrangements with the changing seasons to brighten each table in the lunchroom. They periodically planned and arranged an interesting display for the school entrance way—a bouquet of fall foliage, a library book about autumn, and some poems they created; acorns in and out of the shell with a sign that read, "Allan found these acorns on his way to school," a picture of an oak tree and its leaves, and some pictures of things made out of oak wood.

VALUES

The teacher does not impose her own values upon the students but strives to help each child identify his own personal values. Neither does the teacher judge or criticize a child's values, however different they may be from her own. Her primary objective is to help the child increase his awareness of what he values and to encourage him to evaluate his values for himself. The teacher's most effective tool in dealing with this dimension of affective development is her questioning technique. The following examples illustrate the range of daily opportunities the teacher has to focus and refocus the child's attention on his personal values.

Steven, a 5-year-old, has just taught himself how to ride a two-wheeled bike. The teacher uses the occasion to help Steven examine his values. She helps him to think about what he has done by asking the following: "Was learning to ride the two-wheeler very important to you, Steven?" "Can you tell me why it was important to you?" "How did that make you feel inside when you finally were able to ride it?" "Are you proud of having learned to ride the two-wheeler all by yourself?" "Will that be important to anyone else do you think?"

Ben complained to his teacher that it was too noisy in the classroom. When the class was all together for group time, the teacher guided the discussion as follows: "How do you like our room when you're trying to work?" "What good is it to have our room like that?" "Should it be like that all of the time?" "Should everyone like it like that too?"

Ann wanted to play in the sandbox and was throwing sand at Jeffrey to keep him out. The teacher sat down at the edge of the sandbox beside her and asked: "What do you think might happen if you throw sand at Jeffrey, Ann?" "What else might happen?" "What can we do about it?" "Do you think you would want to throw sand at someone again?"

A few days later, the teacher noticed Jeffrey and Ann playing together in the sandbox. The teacher joined in their conversation and then asked Ann: "How do you feel about playing together with Jeffrey in the sand, Ann?" "Do you like to play alone or with someone else?"

One morning, during a group daily planning time, the teacher asked: "When you come to school in the morning, do you know exactly what learning center you want to choose to work in or do you have to look for things to do?" "What do you like to do best? Why?" "What do you like to do least? Why?" "Do you like to work alone or with other children? all of the time?" The teacher recorded the children's answers to use at later dates for reexamining their values to see if they had changed in any way and why they might have changed.

Johnny handed in his work papers. They were messy, torn, and very carelessly done. The teacher asked: "How do you feel about the work you did today, Johnny?" "Would you want to change it in any way?"

In the daily life within the classroom, the teacher perpetuates some of the broader values of the community and society as a whole. For example, the social value of a democratic way of life is implemented in a daily group planning time by encouraging children to share, take turns, and cooperate and by teaching them how to make decisions wisely.

EMOTIONS

Before they can learn to handle their emotions, children must first be able to identify what it is they are feeling and the cause of that feeling. The teacher collects a file of pictures depicting a range of situations from happy ones to occasions of problems and conflicts. The subjects in the pictures are varied, including children, adults, and animals. The pictures are taken from magazines, books, newspapers, and photographs taken in and out of the classroom. The teacher uses them as a basis for involving children in group discussions about what they think is happening in each of the pictures, how each of the characters may feel, and how the children can tell what the character's feelings are.

After discussing the emotions they have identified in a picture, the group dictates a story about it. The teacher cuts out an assortment of facial parts from felt which the children arrange on the flannel board to depict various emotions. They are used in free play by the children and a story is dictated to describe the emotion each has created, or they are used in conjunction with the "problem" pictures in a "matching feelings" game. In addition, the teacher may work with small groups, describing a situation and asking the children to arrange the flannel board pieces to show how the character may have felt. The children make murals of such emotions as happiness, sadness, worry, and fear, using pictures cut from magazines or drawing their own.

By verbalizing their emotions, the teacher helps the children learn how to express their feelings. Marie arrives at school and shows the teacher her new shoes. "The smile on your face tells me your new shoes make you feel happy." Billy hits Robert because he wants to play with his truck. Robert begins to cry. "Look at Robert's face, Billy. The tears and his unhappy mouth tell us he feels very sad because you hit him." Virginia and Betty argue over a dress-up hat. "Your loud voices and your faces tell me you are both very angry." The children also learn that teachers, too, can express emotion! The children use mirrors to depict various emotions on their own faces. Later, they work in pairs, using each other's face as a mirror to depict various emotions. The teacher sets the stage by telling a short background story and naming the emotion for the children to show on their faces. She draws attention to their eyes, brows, mouths, and so on.

The children depict various emotions with their whole bodies during creative dramatics. They act out both animals and people feeling particular ways. Sometimes the teacher has the whole group freely act out the emotions. At other times the children take turns acting out a feeling without words while the others guess what emotion the actor is portraying. As the children become more skilled at identifying and expressing emotions, the teacher moves them into more difficult activities. The children dictate, draw, paint, or discuss answers to such questions as "If you could be an animal today, what animal would you feel like and why?" "If you were a color today, what color would you feel like and why?" Such activities are repeated on different days, since the children's thoughts will change with their changing moods. The children are also engaged in group or individual creative writing experiences on such topics as "Sadness is . . ."; Happiness is . . ."; "Love is . . ."; "Anger is . . ."; and so on.

INTERNALLY AND EXTERNALLY MOTIVATED BEHAVIOR

When a person does something solely for the pleasure of the activity or because of an inner desire to do so, we say he is internally motivated. Engaging in the activity is the reward. In contrast, when an individual does something for an outside reward such as praise, money, or a toy, he is externally motivated. The section that follows introduces several emerging approaches to motivating behavior through internal means. These approaches are discussed briefly merely to introduce the reader to alternative methods that are available for changing and motivating behavior. Interest in and utilization of these methods is growing rapidly, and as a result, a number of books and articles are available that describe the methods in depth. In a later section, the technique for motivating behavior through external means, using behavioristic principles, is discussed. The teacher's choice of particular internal and external techniques for motivating behavior within her own classroom is a matter of personal choice based upon the individual situation and need.

Motivating Affective Behavior Internally

External reinforcement is employed by teachers as a *control* technique. They decide in advance which behaviors are "right," "good," or "desirable" and then reinforce those behaviors. The child may or may not have a voice in the process of discriminating between "desirable" and "undesirable" behaviors. If he is excluded from making decisions about his own behavior, he can hardly be expected to know the difference between right and wrong, for the distinction is solely in the mind of the teacher. Socially acceptable or teacher-acceptable behavior must be learned by the child. Consistent reinforcement will condition the child toward that end, but it will not necessarily cause him to *understand* the consequences of his behavior on others. Nor will it help him to gain insight into the meaning of his behavior for self-analysis and self-growth. Behavior controlled by others is blind, uninformed, uninspired behavior. Intrinsic motivation, which stems from inner urges to grow, is maintained by external reinforcement, particularly in early stages. But as the urge to grow gains force, the sources of motivation and self-esteem are information, awareness of one's own behavior, the possibilities for that behavior, and the motives, consequences, and implications for behavior.

A new breed of professionals (Horney 1950; Rogers and Coulson 1969;

Sullivan 1950; Berne 1964, 1972; Glasser 1965; Harris 1967) has broken from traditional methods of psychotherapy to develop practical methods of changing the behavior of people. The emerging views hold that people are *responsible* for their own behavior. Unlike operant conditioning, an external motivation system, the new therapy approaches emphasize that freedom is knowing *what* we are doing. Something happens when a child thinks that is not bound exclusively to final results. Thinking is also a true and creative *cause* for behavior.

KNOWLEDGE, MASTERY, SOCIAL INTERACTION.   Horney (1950) builds from the basic view that everyone has strong inner drives for competence and approval. She proposes that *knowledge*—or awareness of one's thoughts, feelings, and actions—coupled with *mastery*—or capacity to use one's abilities—and *social interaction*—or getting to know and understand other people—are the major areas of experience that assure healthy emotional growth. These general dimensions are important because they are significantly related to teaching for affective development. As we saw earlier in this chapter, the teacher strives to increase the child's awareness of feelings, attitudes, interests, and values in himself and in those around him. She attempts to use and extend his interests and attitudes. She helps him learn to express and control his feelings and to examine his personal values. Horney's basic principles, however, are in need of more detailed study and organization before they can be practically employed by the classroom teacher in changing affective behavior.

HUMAN DEVELOPMENT PROGRAM.   The Human Development Program (HDP) (Bessell and Palomares 1973) focuses upon the same three areas of experience—awareness (knowing one's thoughts, feelings, or actions), mastery (knowing one's abilities), and social interaction (knowing other people). The HDP scheme is designed to *prevent* emotional problems by focusing upon the very young school child.

A circle arrangement ("magic circle") is used to promote communication. In the beginning, seven to twelve children are seated with the teacher in the circle. They are encouraged to share their feelings and personal thoughts about themselves and others in a physical arrangement that allows every child to see every other child. Thus nonverbal as well as verbal language is communicated. The teacher gently directs the discussion in such a way that children learn from the interaction. As children gain skill, the circle is expanded and modified until the entire class joins in two concentric circles.

The role of the teacher is not to teach directly but to *relate* to people, listening and helping others to focus on feelings, verbal and nonverbal, rather than content. She begins the session by describing the task. "Everyone has both good feelings and bad feelings. Today we are going to talk about the good feelings we have about school." In the beginning, the children may not react to the invitation to be first and the teacher may give an example of her own. As children respond, the teacher accepts and points out feelings: "Painting at the easel gives you a good feeling, Nancy. We are pleased to know that this makes you feel good. We are interested in your feelings." Listening is stressed by modeling good listening habits, referring back to previous statements, and giving approval to those who listen carefully. Every child is given an opportunity to speak each day, usually several times. Speaking is to be passed around, but no one is forced to speak unless he wishes to. The circle is constructive and criticism is not allowed. A touch may resolve inappropriate behavior; the child may be asked to change his seat; or the teacher may ask the child to explain the feelings underlying his behavior. Toward the end of the session, the discussion is summarized, setting the stage for future sessions. As the group gains skill, leadership is transferred from the teacher to a child. Through coping with feelings in a helping climate, the child grows in ability to articulate and understand feelings and thus gains self-confidence, leadership ability, and fuller acceptance of responsibility.

TRANSACTIONAL ANALYSIS (TA). Berne (1972) and Harris (1967) identified and emphasized social interaction as a basic unit in their development of Transactional Analysis.

The unit of intercourse is called a transaction. If two or more people encounter each other . . . sooner or later they will speak, or give some other indication of acknowledging the presence of the others. This is called the *transactional stimulus*. Another person will then say or do something which is in some way related to the stimulus, and that is called the *transactional response*. (Berne 1964:29)

In TA as a therapeutic method for changing behavior, a person-to-person transaction is examined to determine which part of the person is communicating. The multiple-natured person has three parts, Parent, Child, and Adult. The Parent in a person is developed during the early years. The Parent is recorded by the young child with high fidelity because he is unequipped to make interpretations; pain, horror, do's, dont's, delights, sorrows are recorded as truth, coming as they do from infallible adult-parent sources. It matters little that Daddy was drunk when he beat up Mommy. Only the obvious, observable behaviors were recorded by the child. In the absence of parents, Parent data are recorded from other adults or from television. These earliest experiences will be replayed by the child as he lives out his life. We do not have to explore deeply to determine what has been recorded. Although the affective position is established and will continue to influence the child's behavior, it can be changed. The behavioral clues to Parent responses, which are relatively immature, are physical—finger pointing, wringing hands, looking horrified, pursing lips, sighing, and so on—and verbal—"How many times have I told you?" "I can't for the life of me . . . ," "If I were you . . . ."

Parent expressions are archaic, automatic, unthinking, verbal responses often associated with body gestures.

The second type of recording is that body of data called the Child. These data are the internal responses of the young child to what he hears and sees. The Child emerges again and again as the individual relives or feels again the emotions that an experience originally produced in him. During the early years, the person has little language, so most of his reactions are feelings. He is subject to the endless demands of parents, who may convey to him that he is forever at fault or "not OK." The child who is supported in his innate urges to explore and create, feel and experience, records a series of "I'm OK" experiences. Later, as a grown-up facing frustration, he may be transferred into the Child state. If he becomes a captive of his feelings, the Child takes over. When anger and frustration dominate logic and reason, it is the Child who is in command. Clues to Child responses are physical—tears, tantrums, whining, nailbiting, laughter, giggling, and so on—and verbal—baby talk, "I want," "I guess," "I don't care," many superlatives, such as "mine is best," and so on. By the time the child enters school at age 5, he has been exposed to almost every attitude and admonition of his parents. Further communication with them serves to reinforce previously recorded data. He is now ready to "use his Parent" on others in the classroom.

The third source of data a child may accumulate is the Adult. Until about 10 months of age, the child remains a captive of his immobility and subject only to the recording of Parent and Child data. With the onset of walking and increased locomotion, however, he is gradually freed to explore, manipulate, and test his Parent and Child by gathering information for himself. He moves about the room, experimenting with new tasks, throwing and picking up objects, and going from sitting to creeping and eventually to walking. The child now begins to accumulate Adult data which are recorded from his own information gathering and processing. Harris (1967:30) has pointed out: "Through the Adult the little person can begin to tell the difference between life as it was taught and demonstrated to him (Parent), life as he felt or fantasied it (Child), and life as he figures it out by himself (Adult)." The physical and verbal clues to Adult responses indicate active data processing. The listening Adult is in constant movement, with frequent eye blinking. The face is straightforward, reflecting the mental activity of the listening person. The basic vocabulary of the Adult is inquisitive—"Why," "What," "When," "Where," "Who," and "How." Adult data processing is indicated by words and phrases such as "I think," "possibly," "it is my opinion." The maturing person learns to recognize the four different life positions in himself and in others: (1) I'm not OK—You're OK position (immature, anxious dependency); (2) I'm not OK—You're not OK (give up or despair); (3) I'm OK—You're not OK position (criminal); and (4) I'm OK—You're OK position (the mature adult, at peace with self and others). He is sensitive to the life positions of others and is sympathetic about others' needs for support. He listens carefully and avoids hasty responses that could result in uncomplimentary transactions.

Types of transactions. Communication between two people is characterized by a stimulus by one person and a response by another which generates a new stimulus for the original person to respond to. Transactions can be parallel, complementary, or crossed. Parallel transactions are Parent-Parent, Child-Child, or Adult-Adult:

$$P \longleftrightarrow P$$
$$C \longleftrightarrow C$$
$$A \longleftrightarrow A$$

Such transactions are generally harmonious despite the fact that Parent-Parent and Child-Child are relatively immature. Consider the following exchanges in a typical teacher's lounge:

$$P \longleftrightarrow P$$

Miss Jones: (Drinks coffee. Wrinkles her nose and makes choking sound.) It tastes awful.
Mrs. Smith: (Tastes her coffee. Makes gagging noise.) Well, at least its consistent—always bad.
Miss Jones: They just don't make coffee the way they used to.
Mrs. Smith: They don't make *anything* the way they used to.
Miss Jones: We should have known. But you have to pay more for it, anyway.

$$C \longleftrightarrow C$$

Miss Martin: That Billy Jones will be the death of me. If his IQ weren't so low, I'd think he was lazy.
Miss Doll: Do you think he is retarded?
Miss Martin: Undoubtedly, but the psychologist doesn't agree with me.
Miss Doll: Well, what do psychologists know? I can tell a retarded child when I see one.

$$A \longleftrightarrow A$$

Mrs. Rice: Tommy came to school late again this morning. He said his mother was still asleep when he left.
Mrs. Reed: Have you talked to the social worker? Perhaps she can go by and talk with Tommy's mother again.
Mrs. Rice: No, but that's a good idea. I think I'll go with her. Mrs. White has never been to a parent-teacher conference.

Complementary transactions also take place whenever each party enjoys his or her role or receives support and satisfaction in the role, whether or not both participants are communicating from the same life position. The husband who is having trouble on his job may come on Child to get stroking (Parent) from his wife (C↔P) or to get factual reassurances (Adult) from her (C↔A).

Uncomplementary, or crossed, transactions take place when the individual does not receive the type of communication that his stimulus called for. Sylvia Ashton Warner (1972:8–9) in *Spearpoint* illustrates a classic example:

"What about picking up your blocks, Henry?" (Adult response called for)
"I dowanna." (Child response)
"You used them. Come on, I'll help you." Kneel and start. (Adult)
"I said I dowanna and I don have to." (Child)

TA seems to be more comprehensive and more clearly defined than some methods of psychotherapy for use with older children and with adults. TA can be taught directly in both pre- and in-service programs of teacher education. Harris calls for the application of TA in education:

Education is heralded as the greatest medication for the ills of the world. Those ills, however, are deeply imbedded in behavior. Therefore, *education about behavior* through an easy-to-understand system like P-A-C- (Parent-Adult-Child) could well be the most important thing we can do to solve the problems which beset us and threaten to destroy us. (1967:161)

Through TA therapy, the individual is freed from predominating Parent and Child recordings by strengthening and emancipating the Adult. The method is geared to both teaching and learning. Consequently, through use of TA the teacher can *learn* to analyze her own and others' transactions toward the end of emancipated behavior. As preventive teaching she can apply principles of TA in her work with preschool children. As children become more mature the principles of TA can be taught directly as remedial teaching.

The initial TA session takes place in a group setting with the leader describing the major principles of the method. This is a straightforward lecture-demonstration approach followed by discussion and clarification. In the following sessions the participants are guided through a series of exercises, including role-playing of ego states and life positions, games, and group interactions about feelings. The leader helps individuals identify their Parent, Child, and Adult by asking direct questions. "What are you feeling now?" "Who is talking—Parent, Child, or Adult?" "What are you aware of in yourself right now?" A mutually restraining and supporting relation is maintained among the members of the group. They are beginning to "arrive" when they can state individually and in understandable language what is happening in the transactions. The major goal is to free the Adult from the negative influences of the Parent and Child. TA is a teaching-learning device, not a confessional. Group members are partners in the process of learning. A text (James and Jongeward 1971) and related workbook (Jongeward and James 1973) are available as resources for exercises in TA.

For younger children, who are still forming life positions, TA can be considered preventive rather than remedial or therapeutic. The principal assumption is that young children are more likely to grow into healthy, Adult-oriented people if the adults around them practice an Adult life-style in their relationships with children. The teacher also reinforces the emerging Adult in the child and uses the four life positions that Harris has proposed to identify the behavior of particular children. Equipped with this kind of knowledge, the teacher is better prepared to reinforce the Adult behavior in the child as well as help other adults who deal with the child—his parents and other teachers—to do so.

REALITY THERAPY. Another method of therapy, Reality Therapy (Glasser 1965), breaks with Freudian psychoanalytic procedures that delve into the patient's past in a reconstructive effort aimed at interpretation rather than evaluation of behavior. In Reality Therapy, the initial job of the therapist is to become involved with the person and help him face reality. The therapist rejects the unrealistic behavior but remains involved with the person. Finally, he teaches the person better ways to meet his needs in a reality context. Reality Therapy can take place with a group on an individual basis. The therapist (teacher) must be willing to become emotionally involved with the patient (student) and must show the student that she (the teacher) can act responsibly and that the student must be responsible for his own behavior. The emphasis is on behavior rather than attitudes; on the present rather than the past.

Reality Therapy is in some ways similar to TA. Like TA, it is a reaction against conventional methods of psychotherapy. Observable behavior rather than attitudes or morality is the focus of both approaches, and both emphasize that the individual must become responsible for his own behavior. One difference in the two approaches is in the language. Unlike TA, Reality Therapy lacks a specific language to describe the therapist-patient or teacher-child relationship.

The patient in the beginning comes on Child and views the therapist as Parent. In the initial hour, Parent, Adult, and Child are defined, and these words are then used to define the contract, or mutual expectations from treatment. The therapist is there to teach and the patient is there to learn. The contract is Adult-Adult. If the patient is asked, "What happened?" he can tell what happened. He has learned to identify his own Parent, Adult, and Child. He has learned to analyze his transactions. He has acquired a *tool* to free up and strengthen his Adult, and only this adult can be responsible. (Harris 1967:243)

A second difference is that while TA deals with the individual's past, which is continually expressed in the Parent and Child of the person, Reality Therapy deals with the individual's present. Excuses are not accepted, and others are not blamed for one's behavior. The child has little control over others and cannot change them. He must learn to live with them *or* without them (adults sometimes intervene to deal with the behavior of others who are affecting a particular child). The child will search for reasons for his behavior, but until he is helped to become more responsible, he will not behave differently. Knowing reasons for his behavior is of secondary importance to knowing what he is doing, assuming responsibility, and increasing control over his behavior.

Certain steps (inferred from Glasser 1965) are taken in applying the principles of Reality Therapy to teaching for affective development:

Step 1: What are you *now* doing? (The child must reflect on his present behavior rather than give reasons or excuses.)

Step 2: Is that the right thing to do? (The child must make a value judgment— he may need adult help in doing this.)

Step 3. What will happen if you do that? (The child must examine the possible consequences of his behavior.)

Step 4: Is that what you want to happen? (The child must relate his value judgment to probable consequences.)

Step 5: What are you going to do? Or what is your plan? (The child must learn to assume responsibility for his own behavior.)

The teacher utilizes cooperative planning-evaluating group sessions. Such daily sessions are characterized by (1) discussion of previous activity, including behavior and progress on tasks; (2) sharing and discussion of new ideas and materials; (3) planning for the day. The plan of action is written on the board in complete sentences and recorded on experience charts for future reference. As children gain skill in sharing, discussing, evaluating, and planning, the teacher gradually relinquishes her leadership of the group. One child at a time leads portions of the discussion until all have eventually practiced the group leader role. Thus, children learn how to act responsibly and how to accept responsibility for their own behavior. Glasser (1965) believes that "the public schools [are] by far the most logical place to do any real preventive psychiatry."

Managing Behavior Externally through Reinforcement

How to motivate children to behave in particular ways in the classroom has long been a concern of teachers. Until recently, there were few systematic attempts to prepare teachers to employ objective, external techniques toward this end. Most efforts were intuitive in nature, with the individual teacher using whatever technique she felt would do the job. Too often the teacher's method to motivate the child, to change his behavior in some way or "get him to do what the teacher wanted," was negative and coercive in nature. The results were less than satisfactory.

Now a body of research and experimental evidence is accumulating to show that systematic reinforcement techniques, skillfully employed, can serve as another useful tool for the classroom teacher in changing child behavior. Changing behavior goes well beyond the sphere of modifying disruptive or inattentive (negative) behaviors. In the broad sense, altering the behavior of children encompasses the entire teaching framework. When the teacher plans and executes an oral language lesson for a group of children, she is expecting that each child will learn something—new language patterns, new vocabulary, and so on. Concurrently, she is concerned about the affective climate of the lesson, for she expects that positive feelings and attitudes will be fostered. The teacher is concerned that many aspects of behavior will change. Evidence is accumulating at the present time to support the use of the behavioristic principles of B. F. Skinner (1938, 1953, 1972) for *selective application* in classroom management, particularly with handicapped (mentally and emotionally) children. Moreover, the literature on application of behavioristic principles to instruction is growing at a rapid rate (Meacham and Wiesen 1969; Krumboltz and Krumboltz 1972; Russell 1971; Brown 1971; Spaulding 1970; Blackham and Silberman 1971; Hunter 1967).

BASIC CONCEPTS OF REINFORCEMENT.   A reinforcement is an event that increases the *probability* of some behavior occurring again or that strengthens the response it follows. There are two types of reinforcers, *positive* and *negative.* A positive reinforcer is a rewarding event or stimulus that fulfills some desire or need of the student and strengthens the response it follows. Praising a child for cleaning up his work area is an example of positive reinforcement. Saying, "That's great, you did a fine job" *immediately* after the cleanup activity increases the likelihood that Jimmy will perform such cleanup roles in the future. The reinforcer must be given *immediately* after the child's positive behavior in order to be effective.

Negative reinforcement is the removal of something that is potentially punishing. For example, the teacher may threaten to keep a child from his outdoor play period if he plays during his work period. When the student discontinues playing during the work period, the teacher removes the threat. Thus the student's attention to work is presumably reinforced. It is important that the teacher use great care in determining whether the *specific* behavior she wishes to reinforce is clearly relevant for the particular student. The assignment in the above case, for example, may be too difficult for the student in question, or the student may be bored with the activity. Negative reinforcement, commonly employing threats, is a tenuous practice, for it is obvious that students are likely to dislike persons who resort to threat and coercion to accomplish their ends. Unless caution and skill are employed, such techniques can result in a demoralized student group. The wise teacher will employ negative reinforcement selectively and rely more extensively upon positive reinforcement in dealing with problem situations.

On occasion the teacher finds that threats must be carried out, and *punishment* comes into play. Jimmy is aware that he will lose his outdoor play time if he allows talking to his friends to keep him from completing his work, but he ignores the threat and the teacher imposes the punishment. Punishment is an event—staying in during outdoor play or getting demerits, for example—that presumably weakens, or decreases, the rate of behavior it follows. The unfortunate side effects of punishment are so common and so likely to be unpredictable that teachers should give special attention to replacement of the technique. Instead of punishment, desirable behavior is identified to replace the undesirable behavior, and the teacher sets about to provide systematic positive reinforcement.

Yet another technique can be employed to assist in making undesirable responses disappear. The principle of extinction holds that a response may be extinguished by withholding reinforcement. Considering the drives of individuals for attention, it is common sense to assume that Mary's crying to get attention will stop if she receives no attention from adults or peers during the crying behavior. Threatening, scolding, or ridiculing are not likely to be as effective in stopping the behavior as simply removing all reinforcement of the response. It should be remembered that *desirable* behavior can also be extinguished by the teacher's ignoring behavior. Extinction is a very difficult technique for teachers to use, since its effectiveness depends upon *complete* ignoring of inappropriate behavior, a task that few teachers perform consistently.

Reinforcers may also be categorized as *primary* and *secondary*. Primary reinforcers are useful because they serve physiological needs—food, oxygen, water, and sex. According to Skinner (1953), secondary reinforcers are those simuli that gain reinforcing power by being associated with primary reinforcers. The range of secondary reinforcers is potentially enormous, since any stimulus that is associated with and precedes a primary reinforcer may acquire reinforcing power. A word, sound, or touch may function in this way, depending upon the particular experiences of the individual. Some stimuli become *generalized reinforcers* when paired with a number of primary reinforcers over time. The attention of an adult may become a generalized reinforcer to an infant because of its association with the fulfillment of several basic needs. In the classroom setting, children learn to *generalize* behavior learned in one context to behavior occurring under similar stimulus conditions. For example, children who learn to behave in one way in their own classroom with their regular teacher tend to behave in the same manner when under the direction of a specialist teacher, an aide, or a substitute. Problems are encountered when the child attempts to generalize from a teacher whose discipline style is weak and inconsistent to one whose style is firm and consistent.

Using Reinforcement Techniques To Change Child Behavior

Skinner's experiments led to the definition of two major classes of behavior, respondent and operant. Respondent behavior is nonvoluntary, or reflexive, resulting unconditionally from a known or observable stimulus. Examples are salivation at the smell of food and the knee jerk response to a blow beneath the kneecap. The individual does not exercise *voluntary* control over such responses. On the other hand, the individual's operant behaviors are voluntary, and they need not be correlated with any specific unconditional stimulus. Most of man's behavior falls within this category, the major exceptions being the basic life processes (food, water, oxygen, elimination of waste). Operant behavior is emitted voluntarily for the purpose of affecting or changing one's environment. The techniques discussed here will fall within the framework of operant conditioning, since involuntary behaviors such as muscle reactions and glandular activity are not normally of concern to teachers. The following steps illustrate the procedures followed in applying reinforcement techniques.

DEFINE THE PROBLEM IN BEHAVIORAL TERMS. The problem should be specifically stated: "The child will not talk to the teacher"; "Billy cries every morning upon entering the classroom"; "Sue chews on her fingers during small-group lessons"; "John cannot locate his name above his coat hook"; "Janey will not attempt to put on her coat and hat for herself"; "Emily cannot differentiate colors." The careful analysis of a case study or an anecdotal record (see Chapter 8) is an excellent way to gain preliminary information about a particular behavior. The anecdotes in the record must, of course, be written in objective terms if behavioral data are to be extracted. Generalizations should be avoided in the case study *and* in the definition of the behavior to be changed. The following anecdote taken from a teacher's written evaluation illustrates the point:

Mary doesn't seem to be interested in her work. She is a perfect wiggle-tail during music. Sometimes I think she is just lazy.

As the case study is analyzed, recurring patterns of behavior may be examined to determine whether modification procedures are in order. As the teacher gains skill in child study, she will devise reinforcement plans on the basis of ongoing observation of her students.

Although systematic changing of behavior is most often associated in the minds and practices of educators with behavior *problems*, behavior or discipline problems do not have to be present in order for reinforcement plans to be utilized. Indeed, there are many highly successful teachers who reject the concept of "problem children" and generally attempt to accentuate the positive. This view probably contributes to their success, for it inherently enhances teacher expectations of children. Reinforcement techniques apply equally well to ongoing classroom teaching toward "academic" behaviors. The teacher develops or selects a series of specific objectives for individuals and groups based on careful study and diagnosis. For example, the objective for Emily might be: "At the end of this series of activities, Emily will be able to differentiate between the colors red, yellow, orange, blue, green, and violet." The objectives are matched to the child's developmental level and teaching proceeds. Reinforcement strategies are then employed to assist in achieving those objectives.

OBTAIN AN OBJECTIVE MEASURE OF THE STRENGTH AND/OR FREQUENCY OF THE BEHAVIOR (BASELINE DATA). A common procedure is to observe the child in question during present time intervals, noting in writing the frequency or duration of the current behavior. If the behavior occurs only during a particular portion of the day, the observer may be able to cover the entire time period. If the behavior is not specific to a particular activity or time period, the observer may, for example, select 20-minute time intervals for her study. The behavior is then translated into a graph depicting the frequency or duration of the behavior in question. If, for example, the observer is dealing with "inattentive behavior" covering a range of activities from walking around the room during formal class period to playing with a toy car, the *duration* of such inattentive behavior would be the more appropriate measure. If, on the other hand, the behavior is more specific—James talks out during small-group lesson activity—the *frequency* is the more appropriate measure. Figure 11-1 illustrates baseline data for Billy, a 5-year-old kindergarten student.

ANALYZE TEACHING, AND SEEK POSSIBLE CAUSES FOR INAPPRO-PRIATE BEHAVIOR. Critics of the S→R model for changing child behavior point out that the model tends to deemphasize searching for *causes*

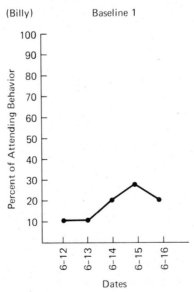

FIGURE 11-1 Baseline data for attending behavior during 20-minute, small-group teaching sessions.

of children's present behavior. The senior author's personal work in precision behavior modification—highly structured and planned reinforcement techniques for altering disruptive behavior—has shown repeatedly that the source of most so-called disruptive behavior of children can be traced to inappropriate teaching practices. Thus, modifying the behavior of the child may become a task, initially, of modifying the behavior of the teacher. The strict behaviorist tends to delete this step in dealing with child behavior, yet the successful application of behavior modification principles is dependent upon *changing the behavior of the teacher*. Further, in many problem cases, particularly in poverty area schools, physiological or even emotional problems that may readily be traced to concrete causes stimulate the inappropriate behavior.

A brief teacher behavior checklist is proposed for recording some of the teacher behaviors that are often linked to inappropriate or disruptive child behaviors. The teacher behavior checklist reprinted here was initially designed by a colleague of Joe L. Frost, Darryl Townsend, was field tested and modified in institutes for public school teachers, and is proposed for use after a specific inappropriate behavior of a child has been identified and measured (steps one and two above). The items on the checklist refer to the teacher's behavior in respect to the child in question rather than to the entire class. The results are to be employed in developing a behavior-changing plan for the child. It is expected and desired that such practice will have generalizing effects to the teacher's future interaction with other individuals and with groups of children.

The teacher behavior checklist can be used by one teacher or student teacher to record the behaviors of another teacher, or it can be used for self-analysis through videotape replay. In either event, the teacher will have objective data for subsequent modification of her reinforcing behavior. Actual application of the checklist has revealed a wide variety of teaching errors, notably the failure of teachers to observe certain relevant negative *and* positive behaviors of children. In brief, many teachers are not only poor *listeners* but they also fail to *see*. Other common errors are inconsistency in reinforcement, reinforcement of inappropriate child behaviors, and overreliance upon threats and punishment. Teaching effectiveness seems to be directly proportional to the ability and willingness of the teacher to *plan* carefully, giving attention to physical setting, appropriateness of content, and sequences of instruction. Employment of the whole range of reinforcement techniques is of no avail unless the academic program is one in which the child can succeed in learning.

The teacher also rules out other possible causes for inappropriate behavior before launching into a structured plan of behavior modification. James, 60 to 70 percent inattentive over a three-day period during small-group lesson activities, became the subject of a teacher trainee who proceeded to viodeotape the fourth lesson and bring the tape to class for analysis. As the lesson proceeded, James placed his fingers in his mouth, swiveled in his chair,

Teacher Behavior Checklist

Positive Control Methodology	Frequency (Check Marks)		Further Description of Teacher Behavior
Positive student behavior noticed			
Accepts student response (okay, yes, etc.)			
Approves student response (very good, etc.)			
Praises student response			
Builds on student response			
Refers to student's previous response			
Student answer repeated in reinforcing tone			
Special privileges awarded (feed the fish, etc.)			
Praises other children to affect child in question			
Employs positive physical contact (pats, hugs, etc.)			
Concrete reward given (toy, trinket, etc.)			
Employs humor as reinforcer			
Other positive reinforcement			
Negative Control Methodology			
Fails to detect disruptive behavior			
Notices disruptive behavior but tolerates it			
Employs nonverbal control (frown, silence, etc.)			
Signals for control (claps, hisses—shh, etc.)			
Calls student by name only			
Issues a brief command (stop that, etc.)			
Issues a threat or warning			
Issues elaborate reprimand			
Issues punishment			
Physical contact employed			
Student sent or taken from context			
Other behavior control			
	Yes	*No*	*Comments*
Instructional Variables			
Carefully prepared plan for teaching			
Instruction matched to child's ability:			
too hard			
too easy			
Instruction is interesting to the child			
Physical setting is appropriate			
Materials are appropriate			

banged his head with his hands, left his chair to walk around the room, and engaged in other "inattentive" behaviors. About midway through the lesson, he stated in an almost inaudible voice, "My teeth hurt." Neither the teacher nor the observers had detected this statement during the actual lesson. Upon examination, James was found to have gross cavities, a possible infection, and a temperature. The diagnosis and prompt treatment of such needs is prerequisite to the teaching-learning process.

A second case involved a student who engaged in crying, fighting, and other aggressive behavior on Wednesdays of each week. An alert teacher who happened to be keeping a case study on the child detected the Wednesday pattern and called the mother for a conference. She learned that the child's parents were separated and that the father came to visit the mother on Wednesdays. On occasion they picked up the child at school and took him along. At other times they left him to walk home alone to remain in a rat-infested apartment for most of the night. The child was horrified of the latter possibility, and this was expressed in crying and aggressive behavior. It was the cause that had to be removed. No amount of reinforcement applied at school was likely to have solved this problem.

IDENTIFY APPROPRIATE REINFORCERS.   Reinforcers are defined in terms of how they affect the learner, not on the basis of how the teacher feels about them. Reinforcers for one child are not necessarily reinforcers for another child. In addition, different reinforcers have varied degrees of reinforcing power for a particular child. The ultimate test of a reinforcer's power is through direct application to determine if the rate of desired response is increased. The teacher, however, must make advance decisions about which reinforcer or reinforcers to apply. The use of systematic techniques can take much of the guesswork out of this process. First, the teacher observes the child in various school-related activities to determine what he naturally selects from his surroundings, specific toys, activities, and friends. She also observes his reactions to her oral and physical communication. The child's responses, overt and covert, physical and oral, will give the teacher important clues to what he values. The teacher can then apply those valued objects and/or behaviors as systematic reinforcers. Mrs. Smith noted the expressions of pleasure (smiling, moving close to teacher, looking to see the signs of approval by other children, and so on) exhibited by Jose when she referred to him with pet names such as top cat. She built this language and accompanying physical expressions of pleasure into her reinforcement schedule for Jose.

A more formal procedure for determining the values and, consequently, the reinforcers for individual children is the use of a questionnaire. Experience has shown that a given questionnaire is not always appropriate to a given group or individual, but the alert teacher can make modifications as she proceeds. The questionnaire should not be administered in a formal fashion to young children. Rather, the teacher should familiarize herself with the content of the instrument, develop rapport with the child, and engage in an informal discussion or gamelike activity during which she seeks the type of information desired. The following are some questions that may be of value in identifying potential reinforcers. (See also Chapter 8 for the use of questionaires in evaluation.)

1. Who in the classroom do you like to play with the most?
2. What are your favorite toys (games, etc.) in the school?
3. If you could buy anything you wanted in a store, what would you buy?
4. What do you like to do the most in school?
5. What does the teacher do that makes you happy?

APPLY REINFORCEMENT.   Following the steps previously discussed, the teacher is now prepared to develop a plan for *behavior shaping*—the process of producing new behavior while extinguishing old or undesirable behavior. Undesirable behavior, if present, is punished or ignored. The terminal behavior to be reinforced is clearly identified: the sharing of materials during guided play activity; for John to be able to locate his name above his coat hook; for Emily to differentiate the colors red, yellow, orange, blue, green, and purple. Successive approximations toward this terminal behavior are identified, for children arrive at complex behaviors through successful efforts at simpler or lower-order levels. To illustrate, initially, the child might be reinforced for refraining from fighting over materials or for going toward all the coat hooks with his coat or for just talking about what color an object might be. Then, the child might be reinforced for allowing one additional child to share on occasion or for hanging his coat on a hook with a name that begins with the same initial consonant as his or for naming any color correctly. Finally, he is reinforced for making overt sharing gestures toward other children, for hanging his coat on the correct hook, or for correctly identifying the specified color. As the child develops complex sharing behavior, he is no longer reinforced for lower-order sharing behavior. The same principles would apply to the academics as well. Reinforcement must not be withheld until the child has mastered a series of complex developmental stages to arrive at a given terminal objective.

Having identified an operant behavior that occurs with reasonably high frequency, the teacher decides what the reward (reinforcement) is to be, under what conditions it will be administered, and who will administer it. In the case of Billy (Figure 11-1), the teacher worked with a consultant and an in-service training team and began a program of giving Billy verbal social approval after *every* correct response during a 20-minute, small-group lesson. Any undesirable behavior was to be ignored. After several sessions of this high-frequency reinforcement schedule, baseline data were again calculated for teaching behavior minus systematic reinforcement. At this point it is to be expected that the teacher's behavior has been "shaped," and her baseline 2 behavior toward the subject child will be different from her baseline 1 behavior. The data collected during baseline 2 is used to determine whether the teacher should now move to a variable-interval reinforcement schedule,

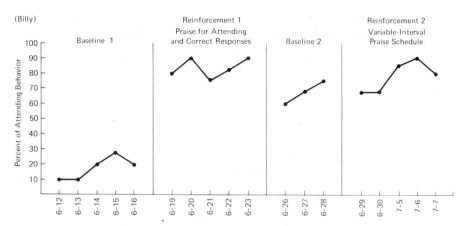

FIGURE 11-2   Record of attending behavior during 20-minute language lessons.

for example, reinforcing for every other correct response or overt sign of attention. Figure 11-2 illustrates the results of these procedures for Billy.

SUMMARIZING AND REPORTING THE CASE.   For teacher education purposes it is useful to develop a brief objective summary of the case of behavior change. This serves as a permanent record, and it may be used to communicate to other students, teachers, or professors in training sessions. Whenever possible, at least one videotape recording of each major segment such as baseline 1, baseline 2, and reinforcement 2 should be analyzed with other professionals to gain new perspectives. An example of a useful form for a case summary is given in Figure 11-3.

SUMMARY AND CONCLUSIONS

The dimensions of affective development include attitudes, interests, appreciations, values, and emotions. The teacher has an important role in enhancing affective development in the early childhood program. The teacher:

1. Accepts the child's attitudes.
2. Focuses attention on the child's strong areas of development while planning ways to improve his weaker developmental areas.
3. Increases the child's awareness and understanding of other people.
4. Exemplifies herself the attitudes she is trying to build in her students.
5. Increases her knowledge about the child and about the things in which he is interested.
6. Builds the curriculum around the interests and the diagnosed needs and strengths of each of the children.

RECORDER: Gail Smith and Bill Jones (independent observer).

CHILD: Billy Miller.

SCHOOL: Peabody Elementary.

SETTING: Billy is a five-year-old boy enrolled in a Peabody kindergarten class. Preliminary observations suggested that he was the most disruptive child in the class, and he was generally disruptive and inattentive during group activities. Specific behaviors included walking aimlessly around the room, poking other children, breaking crayons, banging his head with his hands, playing with his shoes, interrupting others with talkouts, etc.

BASELINE BEHAVIOR: The teacher used time sampling to record percentage of attending and nonattending behavior. The observation periods were approximately twenty minutes, or the length of the daily small-group (five children) language lesson. Every sixty seconds (one minute) the recorder observed Billy to see if he was attending, making a plus (+) for attending behavior and a minus (−) for unattending behavior. Attending behavior was defined as physical orientation (face, eyes, body) toward teacher and/or involvement in the lesson (desk work, oral language, etc.). All other behavior was recorded as unattending behavior. At the end of the initial observation period the recorder multiplied the number of pluses by five to get the percentage of attending behavior. The record was compared item by item with the record of the independent observer. Reliability was computed by dividing the number of agreements by twenty and multiplying by one hundred. Agreement percentage was 90.

EXPERIMENTAL PROCEDURES AND RESULTS: During baseline 1, Billy's mean attending behavior was 17 percent. During reinforcement 1, Billy was praised for every overt attending behavior and correct response. Attending behavior rose to 84 percent. When praise was withdrawn in baseline 2, attending behavior dropped to 68 percent (the teacher failed to withdraw all reinforcement and her planning for teaching the lessons had improved noticeably over baseline 1). During reinforcement 2, the teacher was instructed to provide verbal reinforcement on an intermittent schedule, every other correct response or overt attending behavior. Attending behavior rose to 78 percent.

DISCUSSION: In this case the teacher's planning and teaching appeared to be quite haphazard during baseline 1. Following the discussions of plans for experimental application of reinforcement, the teacher began to plan more carefully for the lessons, and she appeared to gain increased enthusiasm for her teaching. She did not withdraw all reinforcement during baseline 2; consequently, the effects of praise and other teaching variables are to some degree confounded. In any event, Billy's attending behavior increased dramatically, *and* the teacher appeared to improve her instructional procedures.

FIGURE 11-3 Sample summary form for experimental change of behavior.

7. Broadens the child's interests by introducing him to new ones.
8. Creates opportunities for the children to be sources of new interest for each other.
9. Utilizes opportunities for the child to learn to appreciate other children.
10. Creates a climate for appreciation of property.
11. Lays the foundation for aesthetic appreciation.
12. Cultivates an appreciation of nature and beauty.
13. Helps each child identify his personal values.
14. Teaches the child how to evaluate his personal values for himself.
15. Enables the child to identify his feelings and the causes of those feelings.
16. Helps the child learn how to express his feelings.

Behavior is motivated both internally and externally. When a person does something solely for the pleasure of the activity, or because of an inner desire to do so, he is internally motivated. In contrast, when a person behaves in a particular way for an outside reward such as praise, money, or a toy, he is externally motivated. There are several alternative methods available for the teacher to use in motivating and managing behavior. Some of the emerging approaches to managing behavior internally are the Human Development Program, Transactional Analysis (TA), and Reality Therapy. The Human Development Program focuses upon the very young child in an effort to prevent emotional problems. This method emphasizes awareness (knowing one's thoughts, feelings, or actions), mastery (knowing one's abilities), and social interaction (knowing other people). In TA, communication between two people is examined to determine which part of the person is communicating, the Child, Parent, or Adult. Through TA, the individual is freed from the negative influences of Parent and Child by strengthening his Adult. In Reality Therapy, the individual is helped to know what he is doing, to assume responsibility for his behavior, and to increase control over his own behavior.

The principles of reinforcement may be applied as a technique for motivating behavior externally. A reinforcement is an event that increases the probability of some behavior occurring again; that is, an event that strengthens the response it follows. Reinforcement may be either positive or negative. Positive reinforcement should be used more extensively than negative reinforcement. Desirable behavior is identified to replace the undesirable behavior, and the teacher begins a schedule of systematic, positive reinforcement. The procedure followed in applying the technique of reinforcement includes:

1. Define the problem in behavioral terms.
2. Obtain an objective measure of the strength and/or frequency of the behavior.
3. Analyze teaching, and seek possible causes for inappropriate behavior.
4. Identify appropriate reinforcers for the particular child.
5. Apply reinforcement.
6. Summarize and analyze.

SUGGESTED ACTIVITIES

Observe in several early childhood programs in your community. The following suggested activities are based upon your observations.

1. Select a 3-, 4-, 5-, or 6-year-old and observe him carefully over a period of time. Identify the positive attitudes that the child has about himself. Identify the child's negative attitudes. Determine some ways to help change the child's negative attitudes about himself to more positive ones if you were the teacher.

2. Determine the cultural and ethnic backgrounds of the children in the early childhood program in which you observe. Determine the cultural and ethnic backgrounds of other people in the school and in the immediate neighborhood of the early childhood program. Identify a number of ways in which you could increase the children's awareness and understanding of these varied backgrounds. Consider such things as cooking experiences, celebrations, songs, dances, guest speakers, crafts, demonstrations, displays, stories, folk tales, legends, learning centers, and field trips.

3. Observe several teachers of young children as they interact with the children in the classroom. Give specific examples of ways in which these teachers exemplified attitudes of care, respect, and learning as a worthwhile activity.

4. Observe the learning environments of the different early childhood programs. What attitudes do the room arrangement and the classroom environment invite in each?

5. Observe a young child in his classroom. Identify three interests of the child you observe. In what ways could you extend the child's interests in the curriculum? How could you incorporate other areas such as mathematics, science, language arts, social studies, music, art, and dramatics as you extend the child's interests? In what ways could you enable that child to share his interests with the other children in the classroom?

6. Give specific examples of the ways in which the teachers you observed help the children in their classrooms develop appreciation of each other. In what ways is appreciation of nature and beauty developed?

7. Listen carefully as you observe in different early childhood classrooms. Note examples of questions the teachers ask that encourage the children to identify their personal values. Note examples of questions the teachers ask to encourage the children to evaluate their personal values. Note the kinds of questions that cause the children to consider the consequences of their behavior.

8. Further investigate one of the emerging approaches to behavior management such as Transactional Analysis, Reality Therapy, or the principle of reinforcement. Read in greater depth about the approach you have selected. Observe a group or program in which the approach is used.

REFERENCES

Becker, W. C., et al. 1969. *Reducing Behavior Problems: An Operant Conditioning Guide for Teachers.* Urbana, Ill.: Educational Resources Information Center Clearinghouse on Early Childhood Education (ED 034 570).

Berlyne, D. E. 1965. *Structure and Direction in Thinking.* New York: Wiley.

Berlyne, D. E. 1962. "Uncertainty and Epistemic Curiosity," *British Journal of Psychology,* 53:27–34.

Berlyne, D. E. 1954. "An Experimental Study of Human Curiosity," *British Journal of Psychology,* 45:256–265.

Berne, E. 1972. *What Do You Say After You Say Hello?* New York: Grove Press.

Berne, E. 1964. *Games People Play.* New York: Ballantine Books.

Bessell, H., and U. Palomares. 1973. *Methods in Human Development: Theory Manual,* rev. ed. El Cajon, Calif.: Human Development Training Institute.

Blackham, G. J., and A. Silberman. 1971. *Modification of Child Behavior.* Belmont, Calif.: Wadsworth Publishing Company.

Brown, D. 1971. *Changing Student Behavior: A New Approach to Discipline.* Dubuque, Iowa: William C. Brown.

Frost, J. L., and G. T. Rowland. 1969. *Curricula for the Seventies.* Boston: Houghton Mifflin.

Glasser, W. 1965. *Reality Therapy: A New Approach to Psychiatry.* New York: Harper & Row.

Greenfield, P. 1969. *Goals as Environmental Variables in the Development of Intelligence.* Urbana: University of Illinois, Conference on Contributions to Intelligence, November.

Harris, T. A. 1967. *I'm OK—You're OK: A Practical Guide to Transactional Analysis.* New York: Harper & Row.

Helseth, I. O. 1939. *Living in the Classroom.* Ann Arbor, Mich.: Edwards Brothers.

Horney, K. 1950. *Neurosis and Mental Growth.* New York: Norton.

Hunt, J. McV. 1964. "The Psychological Basis for Using Pre-School Enrichment as an Antidote for Cultural Deprivation," *Merrill-Palmer Quarterly,* 10(3).

Hunt, J. McV. 1961. *Intelligence and Experience.* New York: Ronald.

Hunt, J. McV. 1960. "Experience and the Development of Motivation: Some Reinterpretations," *Child Development,* 31:489–504.

Hunter, M. 1967. *Reinforcement Theory for Teacher.* El Segundo, Calif.: Theory into Practice Publications.

James, M., and D. Jongeward. 1971. *Born To Win.* Menlo Park, Calif.: Addison-Wesley.

Jongeward, D., and M. James. 1973. *Winning with People: Group Exercises in Transactional Analysis.* Menlo Park, Calif.: Addison-Wesley.

Krumboltz, J. D., and H. B. Krumboltz. 1972. *Changing Children's Behavior.* Englewood Cliffs, N.J.: Prentice-Hall.

Lane, H., and M. Beauchamp. 1955. *Human Relations in Teaching.* Englewood Cliffs, N.J., Prentice-Hall.

Meacham, M. L., and A. E. Wiesen. 1969. *Changing Classroom Behavior: A Manual for Precision Teaching.* Scranton, Pa.: International Textbook Company.

Piaget, J., and B. Inhelder. 1969. *The Psychology of the Child.* New York: Basic Books.

Rogers, C. R., and W. R. Coulson. 1969. *Freedom To Learn.* Columbus, O.: Charles E. Merrill.

Rowland, G. T., and J. L. Frost. 1970. "Motivation: A Structure-Process Interpretation," *Psychology in the Schools,* 7(4):375–383.

Russell, I. L. 1971. *Motivation*. Dubuque, Iowa: William C. Brown.

Skinner, B. F. 1972. *Beyond Freedom and Dignity*. New York: Knopf.

Skinner, B. F. 1953. *Science and Human Behavior*. New York: Macmillan.

Skinner, B. F. 1938. *The Behavior of Organisms*. New York: Appleton-Century-Crofts.

Spaulding, R. L. (ed.), 1970. *Educational Intervention in Early Childhood*. Abstracts of the Durham Education Improvement Program: A project of the Ford Foundation, Duke University, Durham, N.C.

Sullivan, H. S. 1950. *The Interpersonal Theory of Psychiatry*. New York: Norton.

Warner, S. A. 1972. *Spearpoint*. New York: Knopf.

FURTHER READING

Ackerman, N. W., et al. *Summerhill: For and Against*. New York: Hart Publishing Company, 1970.

Biehler, R. F. *Psychology Applied to Teaching*, 2d ed. Boston: Houghton Mifflin, 1974.

Blackman, D. *Operant Conditioning*. New York: Harper & Row, 1974.

Coop, R. H., and K. White. *Psychological Concepts in the Classroom*. New York: Harper & Row, 1974.

Ginott, H. *Teacher and Child*. New York: Macmillan, 1972.

Glasser, W. *Schools without Failure*. New York: Harper & Row, 1969.

Greenberg, H. M. *Teaching with Feeling*. New York: Bobbs-Merrill, 1969.

King, E. *Educating Young Children: Sociological Interpretations*. Dubuque, Iowa: William C. Brown, 1973.

Matson, F. W. (ed.). *Without/Within: Behaviorism and Humanism*. Monterey, Calif.: Brooks-Cole Publishing Company, 1973.

Moustakas, C., and C. Perry. *Learning To Be Free*. Englewood Cliffs, N.J.: Prentice-Hall, 1973.

Rosenthal, R., and L. Jacobson. *Pygmalion in the Classroom*. New York: Holt, Rinehart and Winston, 1968.

Sears, P. S., and V. S. Sherman. *In Pursuit of Self-Esteem*. Belmont, Calif.: Wadsworth Publishing Company, 1964.

Skinner, B. F. *Beyond Freedom and Dignity*. New York: Knopf, 1972.

Williams, R. J. *You Are Extraordinary*. New York: Random House, 1967.

Henry Monroe

Enhancing Development
Through Play

Play is as old as recorded history. Toys have been located in the ruins and remains of ancient China, Egypt, Babylonia, and the Aztec civilization. History is rich with opinions about why children play, but until recently there was little systematic exploration of the nature and values of play. Over the centuries many people have viewed play as sinful and wasteful of time and energy. A popular nineteenth-century educational view placed little value in play aside from its function of expending excess energy. This "surplus energy" theory, originally proposed by Herbert Spencer, still prevails in many quarters today. Children are directed to "go let off steam" at recess, and play periods are scheduled to follow periods of sitting so that stored-up energy can be released. There is obviously some value to creating a balanced series of events, but some schools—and some parents—consider the release of excess energy to be the major or sole purpose of play. Such a view leaves nothing to imagination and planning. One form of play is as good as another so long as the child is active. Fortunately, such narrow views of play are rapidly being replaced by more dynamic views supported by a rapidly growing body of theory.

PLAY TIME IS LEARNING TIME

The early Greeks saw play as a vehicle for learning. They believed that play was important because it allowed the child to practice those functions that would be necessary for his safety and economic security as an adult. This view appears to have resulted from observations of animals playing out roles of escaping from danger and searching for food. In his play, the young child tries out the real world around him on a smaller, safer scale. He rehearses the social, emotional, and economic roles expected of him without fear of punishment or ridicule for his mistakes and clumsiness—after all, it is only play. (See also the discussion of dramatic play in Chapter 10.)

Four-year-old Rosalie was playing outdoors with two other girls. "Let's cook this," she says to the others as she puts a stone in the hole they have just dug. "It's almost ready to cook now." She picks up the rock and pats it many times, saying "tortilla, tortilla. That's a tortilla."

Five-year-old Christopher smooths out a paper towel on the edge of the sandbox. He pours sand in the middle of the towel and wraps it up. "Handywrap," he mumbles to himself. "Handywrap locks in the freshness." He looks up at some children playing next to him and with a smile says, "There. I'm going to lunch."

Following the Dark Ages, great thinkers continued to extol the virtues of play. Martin Luther censured monks and schoolmasters who prohibited children from playing at the proper times, thus making them "mere logs and sticks." John Locke believed that all activities of children should be "sport and play," that play sustained and improved children's health and strength. As he plays, the young child tests his limits to find out for himself what he can and cannot do.

Jose walks toward the swings where several other children are swinging. He watches their play as he sits on an empty swing. One of the children calls to the others, "Push me! Push me!" Jose says quietly, almost as if to himself, "I can push me myself," and does so. Another child calls, "Look at me!" as she stretches one foot way out in front of her and then way behind her as she swings. Jose says, much more loudly this time, "Look me. I can spin!" and makes his swing twirl around. A boy on the next swing watches, then makes his swing shake as he swings back and forth. Jose watches him, smiles, but continues to swing back and forth as before. Then Jose says in a very loud voice, "Look me how high I can go!" and swings very high.

Froebel, aptly called the apostle of play, gave play a central role in the educative process. He believed that spontaneous play is the most important avenue for children's learning. Unfortunately, many of Froebel's disciples overemphasized the importance of the "Gifts and Occupations" in his curriculum and failed to take into account the importance of play in using the objects as sources of learning. At a time when most teachers regarded play as an excuse for letting off excess energy or harmful impulses, Froebel maintained that play is valuable for its own sake.

Play is the highest phase of child development—of human development—at this period (early childhood) for *it is self-active representation of the inner—representation of the inner from inner necessity and impulse.* Play is the purest, most spiritual activity of man at this stage, and, at the same time, typical of human life as a whole—of the inner hidden natural life in man and all things. It gives, therefore, joy, freedom, contentment. Inner and outer rest, peace with the world. It holds the sources of all that is good. A child that plays thoroughly, with self-active determination, perseveringly until physical fatigue forbids, will surely be a thorough, determined man, capable of self-sacrifice for the promotion of the welfare of himself and others. . . . Play at this time is not trivial, it is highly serious and of deep significance. (1887:54–55)

John Dewey appears to have been influenced by Froebel, and his interpretations have seen widespread applications in schools around the world, notably in England and the United States. The curriculum of British primary schools reflects in practice Dewey's views on play and the role of play in children's learning. Consider the following comparison of Dewey's writing with the well-known Plowden Report on the British primary schools. On work and play, Dewey says:

What has been termed active occupation includes both play and work. In their intrinsic meaning, play and industry are by no means so antithetical to one another as is often assumed, any sharp contrast being due to undesirable social conditions. Both involve ends consciously entertained and the selection and adaptations of materials and processes designed to effect the desired ends. (1916:202)

Plowden writes:

Play is the central activity in all nursery schools and in many infant schools. This sometimes leads to accusations that children are wasting their time in school: they should be "working." But this distinction between work and play is false, possibly throughout life, certainly in the primary school. (1967:193)

Play totally absorbs the young child, mentally, physically, and emotionally. It thoroughly engages his attention, and in it he exercises persistence and problem-solving.

Danny watches a boy and a girl trying to drag a wagon out of a small ditch at the edge of the playground. Suddenly he runs over to them, gets down in the ditch, and straightens the front wheels of the wagon handle. "Now pull hard," he says to them. With a few big tugs, the wagon is freed. The three children look at each other and smile. Danny and the other boy climb into the wagon. The little girl picks up the handle and pulls them across the playground. After a while, they approach a small incline, and the girl struggles to pull the wagon's load up the incline. The two boys sit in the wagon momentarily, waiting for her to go again. Danny begins to rock his body back and forth with the motion of the wagon as the girl tugs on it. The second boy looks over the side at the back wheels. After a few moments, the second boy climbs out of the wagon, gets behind it, and pushes the wagon up the incline as the girl pulls. When they reach the top, he jumps back in and the three continue their play.

Children's interests merge as they play, bringing them into new social contacts and new social situations to learn to handle.

Josh sat down on the sandbox edge, letting the sand sift through his fingers as he watched and listened to two boys playing inside the sandbox. Each boy was pouring sand with his hand into a sock. Josh watched for a few minutes and then walked over to the far corner of the sandbox where another boy was playing with several cans. "Hey," said Josh as he picked up a can, "can I have one of these cans? We need it *so* bad. We need it *so* bad!" He takes the can over to the two boys filling the socks and says, "I'll pour for you." "We don't need a can," says one of the boys to Josh. "It'll go faster. It'll go *so* faster!" says Josh eagerly as he quickly fills one boy's sock to illustrate. All three smile, then continue their play together, with Josh pouring in the sand as each boy holds his sock.

Through his play, the child comes to understand concepts directly; he makes discoveries for himself. He finds out about inclined planes and the forces of gravity while racing toy cars down ramps, rolling down hills, and climbing elevated boards. He discovers that some things float and some things sink as he engages in water play. As he plays in sand, water, and mud, he learns that objects in his world have different textures, that they can be molded and manipulated, and that some things take the shape of their containers. His body feels the meaning of heavy while he carries a pail of sand or pulls a wagon load of blocks.

PLAY TIME IS DIAGNOSIS TIME

The child reveals himself—his social, intellectual, emotional, and physical development—in his play or failure to play. Some children select solitary play over group play. This may reflect insecurity in orienting themselves and getting along in social situations.

Patty is playing in the housekeeping area. She picks up a doll and sits it on her lap. She draws the doll close to her and hugs it. At the same time, she watches two other girls who are cooking at the toy stove a few feet from her. Patty cuddles the doll on her lap again. She looks into the doll's face for about a minute, then draws the doll closer to her again. She looks up at the other two girls again and watches them cook and laugh together for about three minutes. One girl feeds the other girl pretend food, and as the two girls laugh, a smile crosses Patty's face too. Patty gets up with her doll and goes to sit on a chair closer to the stove and the two girls, but she does not join their play.

Some children who engage in solitary play simply prefer independent activities that are more stimulating and challenging.

John watches two boys throwing a toy parachute in the air. He smiles and laughs with them as they enjoy watching it fall to the ground slowly and then toss it again. As it hits the ground, John runs after it with the boys, catches it first, and says, "Let me try it, okay?" They shake their heads yes and he tosses it high in the air, watches it fall to the ground, and all three boys laugh. One of the other boys picks up the parachute. John, still smiling, watches him toss it in the air, then turns and leaves. He goes to the side of the building where he left a hula hoop he brought to school. He picks up the hoop and spends the next 15 minutes struggling to get his body coordinated enough to turn the hula hoop around his waist for longer than three or four turns.

It is important to remember that most children need and seek solitude at times and this right should be preserved. In one classroom, the teacher and children discussed the need for privacy and together decided to turn a narrow refrigerator carton into a place of retreat. They cut a door in one of the long sides and opened the top for light and air. On one wall inside hung a supply of paper on which to write or draw out one's feelings. Sometimes a child would hang a special picture on another wall or bring a puppet, pillow, blanket, or stuffed animal inside. Gradually, the children added signs to the outside of the "quiet place," as it came to be known, which everyone quickly learned to read: "Private"; "Room for one"; "Keep out." At a later time, when one child first discovered an EXIT sign, he printed and hung the sign on the inside door. In another classroom, the teacher and children sectioned off a corner of the coat area with heavy cardboard and an old shower curtain for a quiet place in which to retreat.

As the child's inner, private world is revealed through play, the watchful teacher is alert to diagnose anxieties, fears, or hostilities. (See the section on using inventories and surveys in Chapter 8.) Sometimes it becomes apparent that a child is in need of professional counseling or therapy. At other times, merely playing out the feelings is all the therapy that is needed as a child strives to learn to cope with changes in his life.

Five-year-old Anna had been an only child in a warm and loving family until the arrival of a new sister. The teacher observed and recorded a sudden new pattern in the dramatic play of Anna and her best friend Maria: Maria lifts Anna and carries her to the doll crib. She lays Anna down in the crib and covers her. Anna closes her eyes and pretends to sleep. She begins to pretend crying in a baby, wailing tone. Maria comes to Anna and pretends to hand her something, saying, "Here's your bottle, baby." Anna puts her thumb in her mouth and sucks on it. Maria sits Anna up against the wall and covers her legs. She hands Anna a doll and leaves. Anna puts her arms around the doll, hugs it, and rocks it back and forth briefly. Then she stops and looks into the doll's face. She throws the doll on the floor and says, "I'm the baby."

Six-year-old Christopher was observed digging in the school yard with five boys and one girl: "I gotta dig it first. Then you all can see it when I take it out," he yells loudly. "Move back. Move back," meaning farther away from the hole they were digging. "It's gonna be a big one." "Teacher, we're gonna find a spider," says one of the other boys. "Oh, is there a spider over there in the ground?" asks the teacher. "No," says Christopher, "I'm digging for the devil." Then he looks up at the teacher, flashes a quick smile, and adds, "a toy devil."

Play time is an opportune time to diagnose level of motor development. (See the section on tests of psychomotor ability in Chapter 8.) The observant teacher notes the child who has difficulty coordinating his feet to pedal a tricycle or coordinating his eyes and hands to throw and catch. She detects signs of perceptual problems in children who constantly miss their targets. She notes the child who hesitatingly climbs boxes, stairs, and ladders one step at a time while hanging on tightly with both hands to any support. She watches for children whose coordination and balance make it difficult for them to hop, jump rope, crawl across boards, or walk along a marked line. The teacher watches the children as they move their bodies in their play as an indication of their body awareness and awareness of their position in space.

During play the teacher also has the opportunity to listen to the child's grasp of concepts and understandings as well as any misconceptions he may have.

A group of children were playing fireman outside. "There's a house on fire," someone yelled. "R-R-R-" sounded their voices, and tricycle firetrucks raced to the scene of the fire. Jamie ran and got the piece of hose from the toy shed. "I'll hook it up to the *faucet!*" he yelled to the other firemen.

A group of 3-year-olds were playing outside on the playground. Since it had rained the night before and early that morning, there were still a few puddles here and there on the play yard. The teacher observed Lori and Sandra squatting alongside a puddle and intently staring into it. She went over and joined them. "It rained all those worms," said Lori. "What makes you think it rains earthworms, Lori?" asked the teacher. " 'Cause there all over by my house when it rains," she replied.

PLAY TIME IS TEACHING TIME

Development does not take place in a vacuum, contrary to Froebel's notions of "free play" and Montessori's principle that one should demonstrate for the child and then leave him alone. Valentine (1942:174) pointed out: "Froebelian practice errs where it introduces make-believe play gratuitously, that is, where the child's spontaneity does not need its aid, and the Montessorians err in refusing that aid where it would serve to widen the child's range of serious interests and achievements." Since a great deal of the imaginative play of children is stimulated by the suggestions of other children, it would seem to produce no harm if suggestions were to originate in adults.

The central issue, then, appears to be the manner in which the adult offers suggestions and the nature of the opportunities that are provided.

Promoting Psychomotor Development

Children reveal deficiencies in their intellectual and/or motor functioning during play. These deficiencies may result from neurological handicaps stemming from birth defects, disease, injury, or lack of opportunity for self-expression in early play. The cause is usually less important for the teacher than early identification, which allows her to adjust her program for the child. Remediation may range from one-to-one direct instruction in psychomotor activities to adaptation of group play materials and techniques.

The teacher arranges special activities to enhance psychomotor development. She arranges and rearranges the outdoor apparatus—A-frames, ladders, boards, barrels, crates, tires, sawhorses, cardboard boxes, and so on—into obstacle courses designed to improve such motor-control activities as balancing, crawling, climbing, walking, throwing, hopping, and skipping. She is careful to include those children with poor motor performance in these games. They are fun-oriented times, accompanied by informal talk, laughter, singing, clapping, or a drum beat, so that children will see the activities as pleasurable and will choose to participate in them again. The teacher arranges the outdoor boards and blocks to create special and interesting tricycle and riding toy paths to encourage particular children to engage in pedaling and in activities that enhance foot coordination and spatial awareness. Sometimes the children bring out chalk to make a hop-scotch game or create their own hopping, walking, balancing, or combination course. The natural terrain is used to create bridges, tunnels, steps, and assorted obstacles. For developing eye-hand coordination, the teacher sets up beanbag and ring toss games. A large empty tin can is cut, smoothed, painted, and mounted low as a basketball hoop. The children make and blow bubbles. When the weather permits, large paint brushes and buckets of water are brought so the children can "paint" the brick and concrete walls. Sometimes a design or animal to paint is sketched on the wall first. Jumping rope, catching, kicking, and tossing activities with balls, beanbags, and yarn pompons are made available.

Promoting Emotional Development

For children who lack the necessary emotional control required in group play, the teacher provides special attention. She helps such children make choices of what to play with or where to play. In observing them closely to note signs of *impending* difficulty, the teacher is usually able to *prevent* difficulties in advance of "blow-ups." She may suggest a new setting for play or a secluded spot for a few moments of solitude. She may enlist the child's aid in arranging equipment or preparing a snack, or she may engage the child in a different game. The teacher redirects the troubled child so he can let off his anger or frustration by digging fast and hard in the sandbox, squeezing some mud, or punching away at a punching bag made from an old laundry sack securely suspended in an open area. At the same time, *outdoor play is not a time for every child to do his own thing all of the time.* Positive reinforcement such as praise or a gentle pat or hug helps to develop positive behavior. The helpful teacher looks ahead for potentially difficult moments and situations. The haphazard, threatening, dull activity can be enhanced by a few words of encouragement or suggestion by a friendly adult. Children like having such people around and look to them for glimpses of wisdom and signs of approval. The child who never completes a task is helped to examine the task and finds support for successful completion. A simple clue is often all that is needed to make the puzzle solvable. The teacher also keeps available objects or activities that help and soothe the troubled child. Knowing a particular child finds comfort or release of pent-up emotion in what are considered primarily indoor activities, the thoughtful teacher periodically makes those activities part of outdoor play as well: an easel set in a quiet place to paint out one's feelings, a soothing water table, some pans and a scrub board to wash doll clothes, a small table with clay to pound.

Promoting Social Development

Play time is the ideal time to help children grow in social development. The teacher encourages the children to cooperate, to help one another, to share, and to take turns. Where problems arise, teacher and children discuss the situation and reach an acceptable solution together.

Three new tricycles had been purchased for the playground. On the first day they were put out for the children to use, a great deal of quarreling erupted over who would ride the new tricycles. Tears flowed over who was forced to ride the old ones and who never got a turn on any at all. Before play time the following day, teacher and children discussed what to do to prevent a similar situation from occurring. "We can take turns on the new bikes," someone suggested. "But we had to come back inside before I got my turn yesterday," someone else retorted. After weighing many alternatives, the class decided that anyone who wanted to ride a new tricycle should print his name on a piece of paper. The paper was taken outdoors and taped to the spot where bikes were borrowed and returned. The children also brought out a large wooden clock. The teacher's job was to keep "real time" on her watch so that every child on the list had a five-minute turn on a new bike. The teacher fixed the starting and ending time on the large wooden clock, and each child was held responsible to watch for the beginning and end of his turn.

The good playground supervisor keeps records of each child's play choices, interests, and friends. Accordingly, she plans for modification of equipment and activities to extend and to enlarge both interests and contact. (See also Chapter 8 on interest inventories and Chapter 11 on extending interests.) Sometimes the children plan together before going to the playground, making choices of equipment and play areas. Teacher and children discuss safety rules, potential dangers, changes in routines, plans, and projects. The teaching possibilities in children's play are as many and as varied as are their interests. As young children rehearse the adult roles they see around them, they become policemen, firemen, astronauts, Superman, soldiers, cowboys, Indians, ambulance drivers, athletes, mothers, fathers, and teachers. Props including such assorted paraphernalia as clothes, tools, and equipment enhance their play. Signs and labels (STOP, GO, FIREHOUSE, HOOK AND LADDER TRUCK, AMBULANCE, ROCKET, SPACESHIP, TEPEE, TENT, BALLS, SAND TOYS, TRUCKS) are made and used in their play. Signs and labels are also an aid in putting toys and equipment away both indoors and outdoors. Children eagerly read and learn language skills from what is pertinent to them.

Weather and the changing seasons create opportunities for additional teaching at play time. Planning and building snow forts and snowmen foster cooperation and lead to a study of Eskimos and igloos. These creations can be measured, written, and sung about. When the sun comes out, they lead to experiments with melting, freezing, condensation, and evaporation. Recording and comparing the temperature throughout the school year eventually lead to discussions about the energy crisis. Play includes feeding the birds, identifying them, and investigating animal tracks in the snow. Play in the spring and summer leads to questions about rainbows, rain, and earthworms. Children dig in the dirt and are invited to learn how to prepare and plant a vegetable garden. They learn the names of seeds and tools and the value of sun and water. They record growth times and plant heights and discuss gardening as a means of fighting inflation. Children find bird nests and broken egg shells. They build bird houses at the work bench with all the planning, measuring, sawing, and hammering such a project entails. They experiment with their shadows and telling time by the sun. They run in the wind, build and fly kites, talk about tornadoes, hurricanes, and air pollution. They do wind experiments and let off helium-filled balloons with return-addressed postcards attached to see how far the wind carried them. As children play in autumn, they encounter people and animals preparing for winter. They plant flower bulbs for spring, discover frost, and discuss conserving heat and electricity. They rake leaves, jump and roll in them, throw them, and begin a compost heap for their spring garden.

In utilizing play as a time to diagnose, to learn, and to teach, the adult cannot assume a totally inactive role in the child's play. It is the teacher's responsibility to protect, guard, and cultivate. In the early stages, play is self-selected. As the child gains experience and seeks to extend his play, however, the teacher or parent must be there to assist.

PLAY TIME IS FUN TIME

Pleasure in the activity is a natural outcome of play. When enjoyment is absent, play passes over into drudgery and becomes self-defeating. Play is also serious business, but whoever maintained that one's play should be less than serious? Try taking it away! Play is at the same time enjoyable and demanding. The chief source of children's development during the early years is intellectually enriching, emotionally stabilizing, socially enlightening, and physically strengthening—yet it is fun. The teacher must be sure that it remains fun.

DEFINITIONS AND THEORIES OF PLAY

Since 1930, many writers have explored the topic of play. Valentine (1942:149) defined play as "any activity which is carried out entirely for its own sake." His definition is further clarified by noting that the play activity may be directed toward some end whch is a part of the interest element of the play. For example, in the building of a sand castle, the activity is more worthwhile because the castle results. Valentine explains that his definition does not rule out entirely certain previously developed theories of play, namely, Spencer's "surplus energy" theory, Karl Groos' (1898) theory that play has biological significance in preparing the child for problems of adulthood, and the theory that play represents biological repetition of man's history.

Defining Play by Motive

Ellis (1973) explored the historical evolution of definitions and theories of play. Play has been defined by *motive*. "Surplus energy" is one motive; "instinctive practice" of activities that will later be essential to life is another. Play has also been characterized as *intrinsically motivated* behavior: play is motivated by the inherent need to increase the amount of stimulation. Such a view contrasts sharply with the notion that play is motivated by extrinsic reward or by pleasure derived from the activity itself. Sapora and Mitchell cite definitons that view play as *voluntary activity* pursued for its own sake.

Lazarus—Play is activity which is itself free, aimless, amusing or diverting.
Dewey—Activities not consciously performed for the sake of any result beyond themselves.
Gulick—What we do because we want to do it.

Patrick—Those human activities which are free and spontaneous and which are pursued for their own sake. Interest in them is self-sustaining, and they are not continued under any internal or external compulsion.

Rainwater—Play is a mode of behavior, . . . involving pleasurable activity of any kind, not undertaken for the sake of reward beyond itself.

Pangburn—Activity carried on for its own sake. (1961:114)

Defining Play by Content

Play is also defined by *content*. If play can be differentiated from nonplay, some educators maintain, it should be possible to observe the attributes of the behavior and the setting that distinguish between them. Aggressive play, for example, is differentiated from real aggression by attention to a goal. In playful aggression the child is seeking interesting effects: the usual goals such as retaliation or rapid resolution are not pursued. Another view holds that attempts to define play are nonproductive, since play is not clearly distinct from nonplay or work. Teachers may choose to define play by *motive* or by *content*. If they choose the former, they must concern themselves with *why* children behave as they do. If they choose the latter, they may observe first-hand the overt behaviors of children at play and study these behaviors to understand the relevant features of the play activity. When both content and motives of play are taken into account and play is viewed in a unholistic sense, a "developmental interaction" point of view emerges. From this point of view heredity and environment are mutually reciprocating. Children inherit predispositions to engage in certain behaviors because they are intrinsically pleasurable. This intrinsic tendency interacts with external consequences of behavior to interest the child in a particular activity without detracting from his capacity to explore and change:

The formulations of play as caused by arousal-seeking and learning and the cognitive dynamics of development can be integrated in this way. The arousal-seeking model explains the mechanism driving the individual into engagement with the environment in ways surplus to the need of immediate survival. The consequences of such behavior comes, via learning, to condition the content of the behavior so motivated. The accumulative effect of such learning interacts with the arousal-seeking motive to produce an upward spiral in the complexity of the interactions. Similarities in that developmental path have led to the separation of the continuous process of growth into developmental stages where growing individuals are seen to move through similar phases at approximately the same time. (Ellis 1973:118)

An Integrated View of Play

Ellis believes that the most satisfactory explanation of play integrates three definitions: play as arousal seeking, play as learning, and the developmentalist view of the child. Play then becomes "that behavior that is motivated by the need to elevate the level of arousal towards the optimal"; and work is "the behavior emitted to reduce the level of stimulation" (Ellis 1973:110). This definition would suggest that pure play could exist only when all extrinsic consequences are eliminated. However, the need to produce effects, or get results, is in itself a kind of arousal-producing phenomenon. Play and work, then, lie on a continuum. The distinction between play and work is artificial. Pure play is only theoretically possible.

STAGES OF PLAY DEVELOPMENT

A review of the work of Piaget (1962, 1969), Valentine (1942), Smilanski (1968), Buhler (1937), Isaacs (1933), and Gesell (1946) gives the substance for a series of stages in the child's play development: functional play, sometimes called exercise play, beginning shortly after birth; constructive play, beginning around age 2; symbolic, or dramatic, play, emerging about 2½ years; and games with rules, emerging around age 6 or 7. The chronological ages are averages for middle-upper–class populations and are useful *only* as general guidelines. The *sequence* of specific play tasks that children engage in provides much more useful guidelines for program development than age-stage data.

Functional Play

The only kind of play that takes place during the sensorimotor stage of development is functional play. The child discovers the effects of his actions by chance and repeats them for the sheer pleasure of it. For example, he learns that he can strike at a suspended toy and cause it to move back and forth. At first, he strikes it for effect, which is not play. Play begins when the child engages in the activity for "functional pleasure" (Buhler 1937), that is, when the child begins to imitate himself. He repeats his actions and eventually tries new actions that are in some ways similar to previously learned ones. He also begins to develop foundations for language by making, repeating, and imitating utterances.

The first forms of play in the infant are hand movements and sound productions. He then moves to playing with parts of his body—fingers, toes, ears, nose—and with objects such as toys, clothing, or cups that come within his reach. He seems to gain special delight at his effects in splashing the bath water. Valentine (1942) observed the following age sequence in his work with infants. During the third month, there is movement such as shaking a rattle purely for the pleasure of it. During the fourth month, the infant practices "singing" or babbling for pleasure, "starting on a high note and running down a kind of scale." He also demonstrates extreme delight at playing with an adult's hair, illustrating both the influence of a parent and the early appearance of social play. At 5 months, the child is so fond of grasping things that he is difficult to dress or feed. He engages in real social play, responsively babbling and laughing in consort with a parent. At 6 months, the child practices for a week or more on newly acquired sounds; later, he engages in similar practice with newly acquired words. The child enjoys rough social play such as having a pillow or stuffed toy thrown at him. The infant eagerly tries to include anyone who is present in his play, thus engaging in increased social activity. Between 6 months and 1 year of age, Valentine's (1942) subjects demonstrated a rapidly growing sequence of development:

Six months: gyrated a spoon in a semicircular movement.
               drops a napkin ring for noise effect.
               bangs toys and drops them for effect.
Seven months: struck piano notes 100 times.
               bangs his cup with great gusto.
               makes new quacking noise repeatedly.
               is constantly active when awake.
Eight months: persistently plays with one object.
               persistently practices a new sound.
               begins with new play object by waving it about wildly.
               gnaws, seizes, moves, pushes, crawls over, lifts, kicks, bites, raises
                 play object in an active sequence.
Ten months: experiments with new more difficult tasks; games with mother,
                 stands up while holding ball in mouth, etc.
               throws object on floor, picks it up repeatedly.

Buhler (1935) gives an especially clear inventory of the child's play during the first year of life resulting from her Vienna study of 60 infants who were studied continuously for 24 hours. She differentiated four large behavior clusters: sleep and positive, negative, and spontaneous reactions. "Positive and negative reactions are movements toward or away from stimuli; spontaneous movements are those that occur independent of any ascertainable external stimuli." On the average the infant during the first week of life slept 21 hours each day. This time gradually decreased to an average of 13 hours a day for children at 12 months of age. Negative reactions such as fright and shock responses at 1 week and at 12 months, respectively, were 104 and 77 minutes, showing progressive reduction in negative reaction and suggesting increasing ability to cope with novelty. Positive reactions such as listening, looking, and grasping at 1 week and at 12 months averaged 47 and 112 minutes a day. Spontaneous reactions occuring independently of any determined stimuli increased from 14 minutes during the first week to 460 minutes at 12 months of age. Thus negative responses rapidly give way to positive ones, and the child engages in ever-increasing varieties of spontaneous movement. These appear to be reactions to *internal* rather than external stimuli and can be found in all living organisms. The purposeless movements, however, gradually become purposeful, leading to exploratory and creative play. By 1 year of age, spontaneous movements account for 30 percent of all activities and more than two-thirds of the child's activity while awake. This functional activity, along with exploration, underlie subsequent creative activity.

At about 12 months of age, play with imaginary objects, such as feeding a doll with a spoon, begins. The onset of walking adds new dimensions to exploratory activity, allowing the child to extend his range of movements and include objects previously out of sight and out of reach. The following illustrates the development of play from 12 to 24 months of age and its emergence into constructive and symbolic play.

12–18 MONTHS

Holds out hand for imaginary gift.
Turns pages of book.
Stares intently at pictures.
Rejects food for play.
Climbs stools and stairs.
Imitates bouncing of ball.

18–30 MONTHS

Resents other child touching his toys.
Shares toys upon mild reproval.
Imitates puzzle construction.
Plays for five minutes continuously at 19 months.
Make-believe-play emerges.
Pretends to drink from cup (20 months).
Looks for hidden objects.
Pretends sleep.
Feeds dolls with imaginery food.
Constructive play emerges.
Arranges bricks in row (22 months).
Builds with bricks.
Looks at pictures.
Compares notes on piano.
Draws with pencil (24 months).
Attempts imitation of drawn forms.
Shows interest in mechanical toys.
Plays with emotions (laughing, crying, etc.).
Pretense play increases (30 months).
Dramatic play emerges.
Offers imaginary food to dolls.
Mothers (nurses and pets) dolls.
Sometimes engages in nonsense play.

In applying these developmental principles to program development, the teacher observes firsthand to determine what her children can presently do or not do. She must rely upon past experience or normative tables to decide what should happen next. The teacher or caregiver of infants provides objects such as spoons, rattles, toy animals, and sound devices in an assortment of colors, shapes, and textures because these are the hardware for promoting functional play. They are placed in a variety of locations to foster looking, listening, reaching, and touching. As the infant moves into the more mobile toddler period, the range of materials is broadened to include picture books, stools, low steps, balls, dolls, containers, puzzles, stacking and nesting objects, and assorted sound-producing toys. The caregiver supplies the essential supplementary ingredients of safety and emotional security. She responds to the child and serves as a language model for him. She encourages him to use his own emerging language. She provides objects and situations that are intellectually stimulating and that invite him to explore, experiment, and manipulate.

Constructive Play

Genuine constructive play emerges around 22–24 months of age. The child in transition moves from the preliminary stage of functional play to play with a purpose. His activity now results in a creation. He can use play materials to fulfill a purpose. From sporadic manipulation the child now moves to purposeful building. His play is sustained over longer periods of time, and he views himself as a "builder" and a "creator." The products of constructive play may remain to challenge the child after initial activity has been put aside; that is, he can return to modify and refine his creations. Later, he begins to cooperate with his peers in constructive play. As building activities become more sophisticated, possibilities of combining this form of play with dramatic play emerge.

The materials of the 2- and 3-year-old are more complex, since the child is now engaging in constructive play and low-order symbolic play. He does not, of course, give up functional play but builds upon it, replacing random movements with purposeful movements, language, imitation, and dramatics. Later, he will include others in his activity, giving rise to sociodramatic play. The child feeds dolls and pretends other adult roles. He draws with a pencil and colors with crayons. The teacher must see that these materials are available. As the child grows into his third year, she also provides mud, clay, sand, building blocks, a tricycle, and a wagon, and she supports the child's play through informal talk, suggestions, praise, and questions. She is careful that the larger equipment for the 4- and 5-year-olds does not dominate the indoor and outdoor environment. In mixed age-group settings, a wider variety of materials and equipment is usually necessary.

Symbolic Play

Symbolic play begins during the second year. It is preceded by the stage Piaget has termed "deferred imitation" (see Chapter 4); that is, imitation that occurs after the model is no longer present. The child may see another child kick a toy repeatedly with his foot, for example. Later, he imitates this same activity with obvious pleasure. Symbolic play itself does not emerge until the child enters the preconceptual stage of development. It is the game of pretending. The child between the ages of 2 and 6 is unable to adapt himself to the unfamiliar world of objects and people around him sufficiently to satisfy his affective and intellectual needs. Since he cannot *accommodate* himself to reality, he must *assimilate* reality to himself. He constructs a system of symbols for self-expression, including both language and actions, from information transmitted to him by adults and peers. Through language and his actions on objects, the child resolves, through symbolic play, the conflicts that he observes or meets. He also explores and resolves role conflicts and unsatisfied needs, leading to liberation and extension of the self. The witnessing of an argument between mother and father will, in all likelihood, be played out and resolved in doll play. Play, then, represents an emphasis on assimilation over accommodation. Imitation, on the other hand, emphasizes accommodation over assimilation. The reader will recall from Chapters 7 and 10 that intelligence constitutes an equilibration between assimilation and accommodation. It is little wonder that play is viewed by many authorities as the chief instrument for intellectual development in children.

Children of 4 and 5 years engage in symbolic play in earnest. They are more social, and their materials needs are broader and more complex. Roller skates, jump ropes, scissors, puzzles, letters, and numbers are introduced. Interests that will later develop in school begin to be seen clearly for the first time. The children make more varied use of the playground, stacking, constructing, and climbing in ever-growing complexity. The bike paths become real highways with road signs, signaling the beginning of playing games with rules. The "scrap" or "creative" area becomes a focus of activity as children push their creative powers to the limit.

The most highly developed form of symbolic play is sociodramatic play. In dramatic play the child pretends or takes on the role of someone else, imitating actions and speech he has encountered in some situation. When the imitation is carried on with another role-player, the play becomes sociodramatic. The players interact with one another through imitation of adult talk, verbal substitution for objects, actions, and situations, and making plans to carry on the role-playing. Some major characteristics of sociodramatic play are imitative role-playing, make-believe in regard to objects, actions, and situations, persistence, interaction with others, and verbal communication (Smilanski 1968:9).

The values of sociodramatic play are far reaching, cutting across emotional, social, and intellectual domains of development. The child learns to integrate scattered experiences, to judge and select, to discern major features and main themes, to concentrate on a theme, to control his own behavior, to adjust to a social setting, and to act and react flexibly. The child also develops new concepts and the ability to generalize as he progresses toward the stage of abstract thought.

During the primary years, children expand constructive and socio-dramatic play into full-fledged games with rules. Individual differences are quite broad, and every primary school will need to continue supplying most of the materials and equipment of the preschool. Sizes are scaled upward, and new pieces are added. *Extra* space must now be available for organized games, including seasonal sports such as baseball and football and such games as jump rope and hopscotch. Most organized games can be enjoyed by both boys and girls (see Arnold 1972; Dauer 1972; Hammer 1970; McWhirter 1970).

Games with Rules

Full-scale playing of games with rules develops at about age 6. This form of play is generally regarded as the highest stage reached in play development. The child learns to adjust his behavior to the rules of the game. The major difference between playing games with rules and sociodramatic play is that the former is accompanied by relatively specific rules. The children agree, often arbitrarily, on what is allowed and what is not allowed. In socio-dramatic play, rules are also present, but they are imposed by standards of life. Dentists examine teeth; mechanics fix cars. Games with rules tend to emphasize one skill at a time; they are competitive rather than cooperative; and they demand a minimum of verbalization. Smilanski (1968) believes that games with rules are valuable in teaching specific skills or content, but that sociodramatic play is more relevant for overall social and intellectual development.

Sociodramatic play does not appear to be prerequisite to playing games with rules. Children who have had no experience in sociodramatic play are observed to enter into games with rules. By age 7, games with rules is the predominating form of play and continues so into adulthood. Although the majority of children begin to engage in socio-dramatic play at about age 3, certain elements are expressed much earlier. Valentine (1942) noted that "real play with an imaginary object" took place at about 1 year of age when a child pretended to feed a doll with a spoon.

RESEARCH PERSPECTIVE

Smilanski (1968) found that most disadvantaged children do not engage in dramatic play at all, and those who do play differently from other children. Certain environments do not support the development of increased skill in play, and children arriving at school from such environments may have skipped the stage of sociodramatic play altogether. Moreover, this lack has a negative effect on language and on social, emotional, and intellectual development. Smilanski's (1968) study of children in kindergarten and nursery school classes in Israel compared 18 low socioeconomic classes (disadvantaged D group) and 18 middle–high socioeconomic classes (advantaged A group). Fieldworkers recorded in detail their observations of the children on the basis of five categories: (1) play themes and roles; (2) use of toys and objects; (3) function and behavior of the leader; (4) verbalization during play; and (5) handling of problems, tension, and deviance.

Both groups of children tended to choose play themes and roles centered around the problems of adults close to them. There were significant differences favoring the A classes in the diversity and variety of roles, the range and depth of relationships portrayed, and the depth of understanding of main factors involved in a social situation. With respect to use of toys and objects, on a five-level scale of developmental stages that children pass through in playing with toys, most of the D children played at levels 1 and 2, with some at level 3. Most of the A children's toy usage was at level 3 and above. The toy and the activity constituted the play of the D children. With the A children, the toy was of secondary importance, being replaced by imagined objects and verbalization. Two possible reasons for these differences are the smaller number of toys that were available in the D children's homes and the different sources of satisfaction the D children derived from imitative activity. Since the A children tended to extend imitation by speech and make-believe, they were more independent of toys.

In the D group, there was a clearly designated, authoritarian leader, while the leader in the A group was difficult to pinpoint. Sometimes two or more children shared the role. Smilanski believes that parents of the A children tended to operate democratically, talking things over and refraining from giving orders and resorting to shouting and fighting. They also tended to teach a wider variety of behavior roles and to explain and give reasons for expected behavior. This and the converse pattern represented by the D children tend to be played out in school.

As one might expect, A children verbalized more than D children during play. The differences were in quantity, quality, and content. In a sentence, D children were "act- and object-minded," but A children were "concept- and word-minded." The A children exceeded the D children in amount of speech (698 to 415 words in 45 minutes), length of utterance (5.4 to 4.1 words per utterance), length of sentence (3.4 to 2.9 words), and range of vocabulary. The A children also used a higher percentage of nouns, adverbs, and words representing number and fewer adjectives, conjunctions, and pronouns.

In the matter of handling problems, the A children tended to criticize one another in an impersonal way, but D children criticized in a directly personal manner. Moreover, the A children were more likely to laugh with one another rather than at one another. During play the A children showed very little overt aggression, while those in the D group hit, cursed, threatened, and bullied each other. Possible explanations are that D children follow patterns set by parents. Toys for them are the main role support and objects of competition, since the concept of the game is not so fully developed as with the A children. They are bored with repetitive motor activity and are less able than A children to use argument and persuasion to solve their problems. These points should be kept in mind in interpreting the normative schedules of play. Those presented earlier for children from birth to 30 months and those that follow are based on middle- and middle-upper–class samples. It is important to note also that Smilanski's finding that many D children skip the stage of sociodramatic play is at variance with the common view of such experts as Piaget, Isaacs, and K. Buhler who hold that play is a natural process of stage development and that all children pass through all stages. The conflict appears to result from the nature of the children employed in the respective studies. Smilanski's A children followed the usual developmental pattern. The subjects of Piaget, Isaacs, and K. Buhler were from middle to high socioeconomic groups.

These conclusions strongly imply that the behavior of parents and the nature of the emotional and physical play environment is highly important in the development of play and associated language, intellectual, social, and emotional functions. The role of teachers and other adults who have considerable contact with the child would also seem to be critical. Adults who work with children from lower socioeconomic groups will need to emphasize the direct study of children over the selection of play sequences from existing schedules and curricula. Respective roles of parents and teachers would appear to be similar—to provide support for the child's play in ways consistent with his present level of understanding and activity. Ways the adult can enhance play for diagnosis, learning, and teaching have been discussed earlier in this chapter.

DEVELOPMENTAL SEQUENCE OF PLAY

The following is a summary of the development of play between the ages of 3 and 8.[1]

3 YEARS
Rides tricycle; pushes wagon.
Engages in domestic play (housekeeping, etc.).
Plays with imaginary playmates.
Plays house, store, etc., with other children.
Builds diverse structures with blocks.
Draws simple figures.
Colors with crayons and paints.

[1] Abridged and adapted from pp. 367–369 in *The Child from Five to Ten* by Arnold Gesell and Frances L. Ilg. Copyright 1946 by Arnold Gesell and Frances L. Ilg. By permission of Harper and Row, Publishers, Inc.

Plays in mud and sand.
Shows interest in Santa Claus.

4 YEARS

Combines real and imaginative in domestic play.
Prefers to play with other children.
Draws, paints, colors.
Rides tricycle.
Climbs and does tricks.
Makes detailed block and furniture constructions.
Admires own products.
Constructs with clay, paint, paper, blocks.

5 YEARS

Engages in more independent play.
Plays house frequently.
Runs, climbs, swings, skips, jumps, dances.
Tries roller skates, jump rope, and stilts.
Uses sand flexibly.
Paints, draws, colors, cuts, pastes, does puzzles.
Copies letters and numbers.
Matches pictures and forms (games).

6 YEARS

Elaborates and expands 5-year interests.
Engages in mud, sand, and water play.
Begins to play games with rules.
Plays tag, hide-and-seek.
Does stunts on trapeze, rope, tricycle.
Tosses, bounces, and throws ball.
Enjoys rough and tumble play.
Does simple carpentry.
Plays table games with cards, dominoes, and puzzles.
Collects odds and ends.
Paints, colors, draws; models with clay; cuts and pastes.
Prints letters to spell real words.
Plays oral spelling and number games.
Shows increased differentiation between boy-girl play.

7 YEARS

Develops intense interest in a few activities.
Has "mania" for certain activities: guns, funny books, etc.
Enjoys more solitary play.
Begins to ride bicycles, discards tricycle.
Plays with magic and tricks.
Collects and swaps items.
Shows strong interest in swimming.
Plays library, train, and post office with elaborate paraphernalia.
Plays simple ball games.

Writes letter to Santa Claus.
Plays with paper dolls and elaborate costumes.
Enjoys hopscotch, jump rope, roller skating, ball bouncing.
Plays cops and robbers; war play, tree houses, forts.
Begins to show interest in chemistry, etc.

8 YEARS

Prefers companionship (adult or child).
Differentiates work from play.
Plays elaborate table games.
Engages in dramatic play, giving shows.
Collects "gadgets."
Becomes interested in secret clubs.
Shows seasonal sports interest.
Begins to separate from opposite sex in play.
Shows beginning interest in group games such as baseball.
Enjoys unorganized group play.

ESTABLISHING AND MAINTAINING THE PLAYGROUND

Teachers must provide safe, challenging places for children to play. This space can be indoors or outdoors. Chapter 9 explored the creation of the indoor environment. In the present section, the outdoor setting will be discussed.

Children engage in spontaneous play wherever they are—on a vacant lot, in an abandoned house, in a street, on the roof of an apartment building, in an isolated wooded area. Many such places are potentially hazardous, particularly for young children, for they involve heights, broken bottles, moving cars, holes in the ground, and possibly deep water. The *ideal* playground environment has grass and hills, streams and rocks, sand and trees, birds and squirrels. All the mechanical paraphernalia designed by man pales in comparison to this terrain. But most children living in cities cannot have day-to-day access to such a playground paradise. Neither can they develop healthfully if the only alternatives are the hazardous conditions that exist in most high-density areas. Children need planned, supervised playgrounds. Man's ingenuity in building bad ones is exceeded only by his neglect to build any at all.

The first requirement is space, with a *minimum* of 100 to 150 square feet per potential child user. It is common practice to scrimp on this requirement by alloting space by the number of children actually using the area at a given time. Such playgrounds receive so much abuse that not a single blade of grass survives. The second decision typically made by those of the mentality required of the first decision is to cover the entire area with asphalt or concrete to make it smooth and "less dirty."

The playground should be adjacent to classrooms, with wide entries (sliding panels of glass) allowing natural extension of indoor activities to outdoor activities, and vice versa. If the building designers are wise and imaginative, they will locate the building with minimum alteration of the surrounding terrain so that rolling hills, trees, streams, and so on, can be preserved as functional areas of the playground.

The playground should be bounded by a fence at least 4 feet high to protect children from traffic and other hazards and to allow supervision by adults. Chain-link fence is sturdy and relatively inexpensive but not as aesthetically appealing as certain wood designs. However, nontoxic climbing plants can be planted to cover the entire expanse. The gates in playground fences need to be child-proof to prevent wandering away from the area.

A storage shed is provided for the wheeled vehicles and assorted other items that are moved on and off the playground as needed. Portable buildings are sometimes used for this purpose, but permanent ones, designed to fit into the overall building scheme, add to the attractiveness of the area. A drinking fountain on the playground allows children to drink without having to interrupt their play to return to the classroom. A water hydrant or some other source should be available to provide the water needed in water play.

Selecting Materials and Equipment

The typical playground is a jungle of steel and concrete. The major pieces of equipment are jungle gyms, swings, slides, and merry-go-rounds, all solidly fixed in concrete. Many architects add vertical concrete piers of varying sizes for children to climb on; oversize concrete tiles for climbing into, over, and through; and rock climbing pyramids for further climbing. The area, being limited in size, is sometimes covered with gravel to maintain a consistent surface and prevent erosion. Such undesirable playgrounds are aesthetically barren and extremely hazardous. To accentuate the problem, the equipment on many preschool playgrounds is too large for the children, having either been handed down by elementary schools or improperly selected. The one redeeming feature of these rock, concrete, and steel playgrounds is their durability and relative indestructibility. Willful destruction of equipment is a very real problem in many areas.

There is no single practical solution to the problems of creating a good playground for children. If vandalism is a continuing source of concern and sufficient supervision is not available, there are two alternatives. The first is to construct the "indestructible" playground already described. The second is to develop a "construction playground." All that is required is a fenced-in grass and sand area and several piles of construction material—scrap lumber, crates, old tires, barrels, and so on. The children construct and reconstruct their own playground. It has been said that children who "destroy" tailor-made playgrounds may in reality be expressing an urge to "rebuild" the area to suit their own tastes. On the construction playground, destruction is only a prelude to further construction. Tools can be made available during the regular school hours when adults are present to supervise.

NATURAL MATERIALS.   For most schools, the merits of free construction can be combined with the advantages of a carefully designed playground. On playgrounds truly designed with children in mind, a variety of natural and man-made materials are combined to be aesthetically pleasing but also relatively safe and challenging. A combination of grassy and sandy areas gives soft footing and prevents injuries so common on hard surfaces. Natural streams, trees, and slightly rolling hills provide climbing surfaces and additional textures to explore. These first priority natural materials should receive the most attention of the playground planner. If they are not initially available, they can be constructed. Fast-growing trees are planted; small hills are constructed; even a miniature stream can be built from concrete or plastic. If hydrant and drain are properly located, a stream can flow gradually across objects such as rocks and wood. The hydrant is turned off when not in use. An alternative method is to construct a circular stream using a small pump to recirculate the water, thus saving water that would ordinarily empty into a drain. Cleaning, however, is a problem with this system.

Certain large areas of the playground are kept in grass, the most desirable covering. Areas under and immediately surrounding large equipment are used too extensively for grass to survive and should be covered with concrete-type sand used in building construction. This task will require regular repetition, for small feet gradually beat away the sand to form mud holes and expose rocks and concrete.

SCRAP MATERIALS.   The second-priority materials that are provided include such objects as an old boat, an old car, a tree trunk, a large rock, and scrap materials for construction play. Many scrap materials can be used by adults to construct durable equipment. Cable spools, available from telephone companies, are painted and used for indoor or outdoor tables. They can be stacked to form climbing towers and forts and they can be used as bases for various climbing structures such as ramps and bridges. Old tires can be used for swings and can be bolted together to form tunnels and climbing towers. Large truck and tractor tires, laid flat and one-third buried, can be filled with sand for an ideal sand play area. Used railroad ties or sections of telephone poles partially buried also provide excellent boundaries for sand play. The ends can be cut from oil drums and smoothed to provide material for tunnels and various other usages. Scrap lumber and packing crates are the main stuff of children's construction. Houses are built as children engage in socio-dramatic play. New roles are taken on as they are completed and furnished for "housekeeping." Boys branch off to construct forts. With such materials children are not bound to present interests. They can continue to adapt and modify to keep abreast of their growing appetites for variety and complexity.

The following is a list of free or inexpensive materials that may be used in the construction of playgrounds for young children:

Scrap lumber
Wooden packing crates
Old furniture
Plastic wading pool
Old tires (truck, tractor, car)
Barrels (wood, metal)
Old doors
Wooden telephone-wire spools (all sizes)
Canvas
Carpet scraps
Heavy rope

Large nuts and bolts
Telephone poles
Railroad ties
Ladders
Old parachutes
Paint
Burlap
Metal poles and pipes
Short lengths of drain pipe
Shower curtains
Concrete sand

MANUFACTURED MATERIALS.   The third-priority materials are manufactured items. Interestingly enough, the planner who exhausts the available natural and seminatural (scrap) materials often finds that very few manufactured materials are needed. Even the steel climbing equipment and swings, if desired, can be constructed by a parent with access to pipe and a welder, usually at a fraction of the manufacturer's price. In either event, manufactured materials can be made safer by wrapping exposed legs on swings and climbing equipment with rubber padding. Swing seats are also padded to prevent injuries. These large pieces of equipment are located in open areas, away from fences and other apparatus so that they may be used safely.

A storage shed houses a variety of equipment. The tricycles are used on special hard-surfaced bike trails, preferably smooth concrete, bounded by grass. These wind around a section of the playground, up and down gentle slopes, to a return point. Road signs and markers are used to create real-life conditions for dramatic play. Wagons, wheelbarrows, and other wheeled vehicles are available to enhance play. Only heavy-duty vehicles designed to last many times longer than ordinary backyard toys should be selected, since equipment on school or community playgrounds is subjected to extremely heavy usage. In the long run, the best is the most economical.

Safety on the Playground

Earlier sections of this chapter described the teacher's role in ensuring that children learn and have fun on the playground. The teacher also has the responsibility to ensure that the playground is relatively free of hazards. This is best accomplished by planning with the children to observe needed rules and to assume responsibility for taking care of their own play area.

The performance of the safety function begins with the design of the playground and continues for as long as the playground is used. Many injuries result from poor equipment choices—items that are too large for children or not sufficiently sturdy—and from poor maintenance. One afternoon recently the authors visited three playgrounds in a single neighborhood. In the first, the entire area was paved with asphalt, which was in such a deteriorated state that large "potholes" and broken chunks of asphalt were scattered throughout the area. The playground was bounded by a tall, wire mesh fence. In one corner, a hole 3 feet wide led immediately to a vertical drop of 20 feet to a street below. The rock steps leading from the school were broken and falling apart, as were several of the wheeled vehicles stored in the hall. Play time for the Head Start children in attendance consisted of an organized game requiring the children to take turns running from one side of the playground to another. A second "playground" in the same school district was shared by kindergarten through elementary grade children. The equipment, a jungle gym and three concrete bridge tiles 4 feet in diameter, were all torn loose from their footings and could be rolled around the area, risking the life and limbs of the children. In the third playground, a private day care center, a wide variety of expensive equipment was secured in concrete throughout the small play area. The entire playground was covered by concrete and large gravel. Children from age 3 through 8 used the same equipment, which had been designed for primary ages. The lack of terracing, coupled with hard use and shifting gravel cover, had exposed the concrete moorings of the equipment and the jagged edges and foundations of the concrete covering. It is obvious that careful design and advance planning can prevent many safety problems.

The teacher inspects grounds and equipment regularly, removing broken equipment or declaring it off limits, and she takes the initiative to report needed repairs to the proper authority. The grounds are cleaned regularly to remove broken glass, rocks, and so on. The teacher also observes children at play, noting potentially hazardous activities and instructing children who may endanger themselves or others. Children are not allowed to abuse other children by hitting, using sticks, or in other ways bullying them. The offender is removed from the area for time out to reflect on the consequences of his behavior. Most of the minor behaviors can be handled simply by reminding children of the rules of conduct for outdoor play.

Proper supervision does not mean oversupervision. It is not possible to allow children to play and learn on a playground and at the same time reduce the possibility of injury to zero. Children must experience for themselves if they are to learn to avoid injury in everyday life. At the same time, however, they are relatively inexperienced and must be given controlled supervision by adults as they grow toward independence. Some common rules help to ensure safety:

1. Maintain open spaces around individual pieces of equipment.

2. Provide a soft surface such as sand around areas of hard impact—under swings and at the bottom of slides.
3. Pad metal legs of large equipment, the seats of swings, and other surfaces that may cause injury on impact.
4. Remove, replace, repair all broken or worn-out equipment.
5. Smooth all jagged and sharp edges.
6. Declare off limits all equipment designed for older children or equipment that is temporarily unsafe.
7. Clean the playground regularly to remove glass, loose rocks, and cans.
8. Develop buddy systems and provide *constant* supervision whenever pools or other deep water is being used.
9. Enclose slides in platforms or attach slides to broad platforms, such as on climbing towers, or to hills and mounds to prevent falls from the top.
10. Discuss essential safety rules with children so that they understand the limits of their play. Reasonable controlled conditions represent the desired middle ground between oversupervision and complete freedom in children's play.

INVOLVING PARENTS AND THE COMMUNITY IN PLAYGROUND DEVELOPMENT

The development of good playgrounds for young children has not kept pace with the rapid growth of enrollment in early childhood centers during recent years. Standards for playgrounds in day care centers are typically sterile. For example, the regulations pertaining to preschool playgrounds set by the state of Texas require that "the number of children *in the yard* shall not exceed the ratio of one child per 80 square feet of usable yard space." The playground must be fenced, and it must not contain "sharp objects, poisonous plants, highly inflammable materials, tanks, ponds, open wells, drainage ditches, sewage disposal equipment, dangerous machinery, garbage receptacles and garbage." The only required equipment specified is "large muscle equipment such as boxes, boards, sawhorses, tires, barrels, ladders, wagons and balls." The required materials and equipment for the indoor area covers several pages.[2]

The National Council of Jewish Women visited 431 day care centers throughout the country servicing about 24,000 children. They reported: "Almost all of the homes observed had some outdoor play area but one-fifth of the homes had no outdoor play equipment. Where equipment was provided it was regarded as good in fewer than one-half the licensed homes and in only one-fifth of the unlicensed homes" (Keyserling 1972:152).

Early childhood program personnel must take the initiative in stimulating action for better playgrounds. One of the authors, Joe Frost, collaborated with Barry Klein (Region XIII Education Service Center, Austin, Texas; now at Georgia State University) in an experiment designed to (1) build playgrounds at minimal cost; (2) involve parents and staff in playground

[2] As this material is being prepared for press, standards for playgrounds in Texas are being revised.

construction in ways that would enhance their interest and participation in school functions and their knowledge of the values of play; and (3) demonstrate the feasibility and characteristics of good playgrounds. The first step was to talk to a group of teachers involved in an in-service training program to identify a staff committed to quality education but with limited resources. Having identified a migrant preschool in a rural town and a church school in a metropolitan area, the team (professor, early childhood specialist, school supervisor, and teachers) formulated plans for securing administrative support. It was decided that the sponsoring school must make *some* commitment of resources as an indication of good faith and cooperation. In order to present a strong case to the school administration, a design for the proposed playground would be needed. At this point an architect with a special interest in playgrounds agreed to prepare working drawings for the team (Figure 12-1). A migrant preschool was selected as the first site. It was now time to approach the administrator of the school system.

Securing Administrative Support

During the conference with the school administrator, several salient points were made:

1. A professional team had laid the groundwork for the development of a playground.
2. All efforts had been and would continue to be on a voluntary, gratis basis.
3. The team could build a high-quality playground for children at minimal cost to the school system.
4. The team, however, felt that certain commitments must be made by the school: (a) construct a fence around the site and (b) agree to allow the team to provide training in the use of playgrounds for teachers and parents.

Each of these points represents a key concept in preparing a plan of action to be considered by administrators—a combination of careful planning, as evidenced by the professionally prepared design; good faith, as evidenced by the willingness of the team to contribute time and labor with no expectation of concrete reward; the requirement of training designed to ensure proper use of the product. Collectively, it would seem, the administrator is faced with "an offer he cannot refuse." Having received administrative approval, the team was ready for the next step.

Securing the Cooperation of Parents

At a regular meeting of the Parent-Teacher Association, the team presented slides depicting play equipment made from scrap materials. In the discussion that followed, the construction of a playground adjacent to the school was proposed. The parents were asked to pledge time and materials (Figure 12-2).

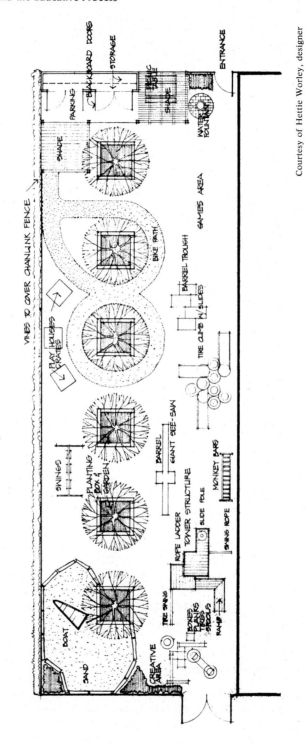

Courtesy of Hettie Worley, designer

FIGURE 12-1.

Name _____ Phone _____
Address _____
What materials do you think you will be able to supply?
1. _____
2. _____
3. _____
4. _____
5. _____
6. _____
Do you have any tools which you could lend for the construction of the playground?
1. _____
2. _____
3. _____
4. _____
5. _____
Would you like to help in the construction of the playground?
    Yes _____ No _____
What day of the week would be best for you? _____
What time? _____
What ideas, hints, comments, etc. do you have concerning the design or construction of the playground?

FIGURE 12-2. Parents' playground pledge form (developed by Barry Klein).

The social period that followed was charged with the excitement of parents and teachers planning together for children. A work day was scheduled. During the next week, trucks and cars of all descriptions dumped the following material at the playground site:

6 railroad ties	21 car tires
2 children's swing sets	Assorted plywood and masonite
2 clothesline poles	3 large crates
6 oil drums	1 door
9 tractor tires	1 book case
2 spools 66 inches in diameter	1 boat
3 spools 40 inches in diameter	Assorted carpet samples
3 spools 18 inches in diameter	29 gallons of auto paint
9 2-inch pipes	2 quarts of house paint
22 1-inch pipes	5 quarts of enamel
14 drain pipes	2 yards of sand

PARENT-TEACHER WORK DAY.   With these materials on hand, work could proceed. The original playground design was considered illustrative rather than definitive. As work proceeded, the equipment to be built was determined by the variable materials. For example, there were not enough telephone poles for the fort, so the two largest spools were stacked and rebuilt to serve the same purpose. The old door became the entry ramp for the second level. The sand pit, bounded by railroad ties, was located under one side of the oak tree and three types of swings were suspended from the massive branches. The sand play area was complemented by a nearby three-room playhouse constructed from packing crates. The planters were constructed in tires, since concrete tiles were not available. The remaining spools became tables for house play and support for construction and obstacle courses. As this is written, the second work day is being planned. Various tire structures will be built, the bike path will be constructed, the boat will be secured, and climbing structures will be built from the metal pipes. Water play containers may be supplied from a nearby faucet.

The work day was also a social day. Older children helped with digging and building. Adults painted the various structures and provided the tools and "technical" skills. Smaller children rushed to try out each piece of equipment as it was completed. (The team judged its success by the number of children engaged in a particular area. The sand pit was the winner.) At noon the entire group shared food brought by the parents and teachers.

This experiment illustrates that good functional playgrounds can be provided at little cost and that parents, teachers, and administrators can work together toward the solution of common concerns. Since the construction of the initial playground described here, a number of additional ones have been planned and work is in progress. Ideas generated are being disseminated through workshops and printed materials. Cooperation, careful planning, and initiative, coupled with sincere appreciation and respect for the talents of others, can build playgrounds.

ADVENTURE PLAYGROUNDS AROUND THE WORLD

Fortunately for children, there is now an awakening around the world to the need for playgrounds designed to encourage the spontaneous interests of children. Adventure playgrounds are a remarkable experiment for unleashing the creative energies of children through imaginative play with natural materials.

The adventure playground was the brain child of the Danish landscape architect and professor, C. Th. Sørenson (Bengtsson 1972:12). Sørenson's idea, proposed in the thirties, is now being adopted in many countries. The practical evolution began in 1943 in Emdrup, near Copenhagen, at the initiative of Sørenson and the Workers' Cooperative Housing Association. The materials were primarily bricks, boards, posts, and concrete pillars, with some tools for construction. The children, ages 4 to 17, constructed earth caves, buildings, chairs and tables, and assorted other functional pieces. As huts outlived their usefulness, they were demolished and rebuilt with greater sophistication. The children themselves gradually took over responsibility for operation of the area.

The adventure playground idea has been successfully implemented in Great Britain, Switzerland, Denmark, Japan, and the United States (Bengtsson 1972). In England, the playgrounds are so popular that nails and wood are rapidly used up, and spades are in great demand so that children can play in the only direction left—down into the earth. The reactions of neighborhood adults range from horror at the "eyesore with the weeds waist high" to "the most successful effort up to date." The most valued activities are digging, building, and cooking. Open fires are quite popular, ranking second only to earthen dens. Fires are subject to clearly established rules formulated and enforced primarily by children's committees. Cooking may evolve into the development of a canteen where food and treats purchased and prepared by the children are sold and shared. The canteen is also a popular socializing area. In one playground, sawing wood for old persons became a popular work-play activity. Older children often build dens, houses, boats, and other materials for younger children to use.

The adventure playground in Great Britain is a place where children are free to express themselves in ways not usually allowed. The playground may range in size from one third of an acre to two and a half acres. The children can "build houses, dens and climbing structures with waste materials, have bonfires, cook in the open, dig holes, garden, or just play with earth, sand, water and clay" (Bengtsson 1972:44). The usual age range is 5–15, but all age groups are welcome to participate. The playground usually has two full-time leaders who help children to plan and operate the area and to do the things they are attempting to do. Friendliness is stressed. Each playground has a playhut, a lavatory, and heating and cooking facilities. The site is fenced in, and the playground is covered by comprehensive insurance.

In other European countries, as in England, the rebuilding of entirely new neighborhoods following the devastation of World War II stimulated many people who work with children to think of new ways to create imaginative play environments. Experience in various countries has shown the most pressing problems to be (1) the provision of an endless supply of building materials (wood, tools, nails, and so on); (2) the provision of a qualified supervisor able to help children with the endless problems encountered in construction and who is warm, friendly, open, and supportive; (3) the provision of protection and defense for younger children who may be objects of aggression; (4) gaining the cooperation of adults who view the playgrounds as eyesores and the activities as means for teaching destructiveness.

The Danish playground plan calls for certain defined areas. The main building, which houses the supervisor's area, is where children borrow tools and materials, receive first aid, and go to the lavatory. The playground is also divided into a cave-digging and construction area; a building materials storage shed in an out-of-the-way spot; a communal area where children and adults can meet for special occasions; stables for a variety of domesticated animals; a fixed play equipment area with climbing materials, sand, and water; an asphalt area for skating and cycling; an open-air stage for plays; a bonfire site for burning rubbish, cooking, and warming; a garden for tending and learning; and an adjoining nature area that is left to grow wild.

The first adventure playground in the United States was sponsored by *McCall's* magazine in 1950. The vest-pocket parks in New York are similar in many ways to adventure playgrounds. Hopefully, American educators will spearhead a new effort to stimulate action by community groups to appraise the existing play facilities for children and take action to provide realistic contexts for creative expression.

SUMMARY AND CONCLUSIONS

Play time is learning time. The young child rehearses social, emotional, and occupational roles without fear of punishment or ridicule for his mistakes. In his play, he tests his limits to find out what he can and cannot do. The young child exercises persistence and probem-solving and makes discoveries for himself as he plays.

Play time is diagnosis time. In his play or failure to play, the young child reveals himself socially, emotionally, intellectually, and physically. The teacher may diagnose some anxieties, fears, or hostilities. She gains valuable insight into the child's concept development, language, and level of motor development.

Play time is teaching time. The teacher arranges special activities to foster psychomotor development. She helps children grow in cognitive, social, and emotional development. She provides encouragement and opportunity for children to cooperate, share, and help each other. She modifies equipment and activities to extend and to enlarge interests, contacts, concepts, and language. She provides safe outlets for emotions.

Play time is fun time. Play is the main avenue for children's development during the early years. As demanding and as serious as it is, play is also pleasurable activity. While the teacher uses play time to diagnose and to teach, she must make sure that play remains fun.

There are several stages in the development of play in the young child. Functional play begins shortly after birth. During this stage, the child exercises the actions he has acquired by repeating them and attempting variations of them. Constructive play emerges at about the age of 2 years. It is characterized by play with a purpose and generally results in some creation. Symbolic, or dramatic, play emerges at about 2½ years of age and is the child's game of pretending. A more advanced form of symbolic play is sociodramatic play in which the young child carries on pretense and imitation with another role-player. About the age of 6, children expand constructive and socio-dramatic play into games with rules.

Teachers must provide safe, challenging places for children to play. Playgrounds should be planned and supervised to ensure that children are safe, that learning occurs, and that play is enjoyable. The play yard should allow 100 to 150 square feet per child user and should be bounded by a fence at least four feet high. The playground should be adjacent to the classroom to allow the natural extension of indoor activities to outdoor activities, and vice versa. Natural terrain such as rolling hills, trees, and sandy and grassy areas should be functionally integrated into the playground design. Functional, creative playgrounds can be built at little cost through the use of such recycled materials as railroad ties, telephone poles, oil drums, car and tractor tires, packing crates, and spools. Parents can and should be involved in the construction of such creative playgrounds.

SUGGESTED ACTIVITIES

1. Visit the playgrounds of the early childhood centers in your community. Note the variety in the playgrounds with respect to size, type of equipment, kind of supervision, storage space, and use of natural terrain.
   a. Identify the ways in which each playground has been made safe for young children.
   b. Identify any dangers on the playgrounds. How could these dangerous aspects be improved?
   c. Identify the creative elements of the playgrounds you visited.
   d. Determine the amount of supervision on the playgrounds, the kind of supervision, and by whom.
   e. In what ways do you think each of the playgrounds you visited could be improved?
2. Observe a young child at play over a period of time. Prepare a case study (Chapter 8), including such information as what equipment the child plays with, the manner in which he plays, with whom he plays, what he says. Observe the child at play both indoors and outdoors. Discuss the child's social, emotional, motor, and intellectual development by analyzing your observations. Use the following questions as a guide. Share your case study with the child's teacher.

Social and Emotional Development
   a. What adult occupational and social roles does the child rehearse in his play? How does he handle these roles?
   b. In what ways has the teacher enhanced the child's understanding of the roles he rehearses? In what other ways could the child's learning be extended?
   c. How long does the child's attention focus on any one play activity (role, object, game, etc.)? Does his concentration and attention last longer on some activities than on others? which activities?

    d. Does the child play with other children? with whom? how often?

    e. Does the child share? cooperate? take turns? help? in what ways and to what extent?

    f. Does the child engage in positive behavior as he plays? What evidence is there of positive behavior?

    g. Does the child engage in negative behavior as he plays? What evidence is there of negative behavior? Does he exhibit negative behavior when he is playing with others? with someone in particular? when playing with certain equipment or materials?

Motor Development

    a. In what manner does the child pedal a tricycle? kick a ball? jump rope? run? walk up and down? climb?

    b. What control does the child have over his body and limbs when he crawls and walks the balance beam? when he hops and skips? when he follows an obstacle course?

    c. What control does the child have over his eye and hand coordination when he does things such as catch, throw, and aim at targets?

    d. Does the child seem to have any difficulty with his perception? with his hearing? in what way?

    e. What are the child's motor problems which the teacher has isolated to improve? How does she attempt to improve them through the vehicle of play?

    f. How has the teacher made enhancing motor development fun for the child?

Intellectual Development

    a. What understandings and concepts has the child revealed through his play?

    b. What equipment, toys, materials, resources, and so on, has the teacher employed to further strengthen those developing concepts?

    c. What new concepts and understandings have been introduced to the child through his play? How is the teacher further developing these?

    d. What misunderstandings has the child revealed in his play? How are these corrected through the vehicle of play?

    e. Does the child attempt to solve problems he encounters as he plays? what problems? How does he attempt to solve them?

    f. How does the teacher help the child become a better problem-solver?

REFERENCES

Arnold, A. 1972. *The World Book of Children's Games.* New York: World Publishing Company.

Bengtsson, A. (ed.). 1972. *Adventure Playgrounds.* New York: Praeger.

Buhler, C. 1935. *From Birth to Maturity.* London: Routledge and Kegan Paul.

Buhler, K. 1937. *The Mental Development of the Child.* London: Routledge and Kegan Paul.

Dauer, V. P. 1972. *Essential Movement Experiences for Preschool and Primary Children.* Minneapolis, Minn.: Burgess Publishing Company.

Dewey, J. 1916. *Democracy and Education.* New York: Free Press.

Ellis, M. J. 1973. *Why People Play.* Englewood Cliffs, N.J.: Prentice-Hall.

Froebel, F. 1887. *The Education of Man*. New York: D. Appleton.

Gesell, A. 1946. *The Child from Five to Ten*. New York: Harper & Brothers.

Groos, K. 1898. *The Play of Animals,* E. L. Baldwin, trans. New York: D. Appleton.

Hammer, B. M. 1970. *Children's Creative Dance Book*. Tucson, Ariz.: Mattler Studios.

Huizinga, J. 1949. *Homo Ludens: A Study of the Play Element in Culture*. London: Routledge and Kegan Paul.

Isaacs, S. 1933. *Social Development in Young Children: A Study of Beginnings*. New York: Harcourt, Brace.

Keyserling, M. D. 1972. *Windows on Day Care*. New York: National Council of Jewish Women.

McWhirter, M. E., L. Hawkinson, and J. Hawkinson. 1970. *Games Enjoyed by Children Around the World*. New York: International Recreation Association.

Piaget, J. 1969. *The Psychology of the Child*. New York: Basic Books.

Piaget, J. 1962. *Play, Dreams and Imitation in Childhood*. New York: Norton.

Plowden, B. 1967. *Children and Their Primary Schools*. London: Her Majesty's Stationery Office.

Sapora, A. V., and E. D. Mitchell. 1961. *The Theory of Play and Recreation*. New York: Ronald.

Smilanski, S. 1968. *The Effects of Socio-Dramatic Play on Disadvantaged Pre-School Children*. New York: Wiley.

Valentine, C. W. 1942. *The Psychology of Early Childhood*. Cleveland: The Sherwood Press.

FURTHER READING

Almy, M. "Spontaneous Play: An Avenue for Intellectual Development," *Bulletin of the Institute of Child Study,* 1966, 28(2). Reprinted in J. L. Frost (ed.), *Early Childhood Education Rediscovered*. New York: Holt, Rinehart and Winston, 1968.

Caplan, F., and T. Caplan. *The Power of Play*. New York: Doubleday, 1973.

Cass, J. F. *Helping Children Grow Through Play*. New York: Shocken Books, 1973.

Crowe, B. *The Playground Movement*. London: Allen and Unwin, 1973.

Ebbeck, F. N. "Learning from Play in Other Cultures," *Childhood Education,* 1971, 48.

Ellison, G. *Play Structures*. Pasadena, Calif.: Pacific Oaks College, 1974.

Erikson, E. *Childhood and Society*. New York: Norton, 1963.

Gordon, I. J., B. Guinagh, and R. F. Jester. *Child Learning Through Child Play*. New York: St. Martins Press, 1972.

Helick, M., and M. T. Watkins. *Elements of Preschool Play Yards*. Swissdale, Pa.: Regent Graphic Services, 1973.

Herron, R. E., and B. Sutton-Smith. *Child's Play*. New York: Wiley, 1971.

Lambert, J. *Adventure Playgrounds: A Personal Account of a Playleader's Work as Told to Jenny Pearson*. London: Cape, 1974.

Lowenfeld, M. (ed.). *Play in Childhood.* New York: Wiley, 1967.

Markun, P. M. (ed.). *Play: Children's Business.* Washington, D.C.: Association for Childhood Education International, 1974.

Omwake, E. "The Child's Estate," in A. J. Solnit and S. A. Provence (eds.), *Modern Perspectives in Child Development.* New York: International Universities Press, 1963.

Pickard, P. M. *The Activity of Children.* London: Longmans, Green, 1965.

Piers, M. W. (ed.). *Play and Development: A Symposium.* New York: Norton, 1972.

Southern Association on Children under Six. *Dimensions* (issue on play), 1975, 3(4).

Sponseller, D. (ed.). *Play as a Learning Medium.* Washington, D.C.: National Association for the Education of Young Children, 1974.

Stone, J. G. *Play and Playgrounds.* Washington, D.C.: National Association for the Education of Young Children, 1974.

APPENDIX A

Developmental Checklists for 3-, 4-, and 5-Year-Olds

A. ATTENDING

Level III						
1. Attends to a story 10–15 minutes						
2. Attends to an activity 15–20 minutes						
3. Repeats parts of stories						
Level IV						
1. Attends to stories and activities						
2. Listens to simple instructions and follows through						
3. Shares short stories with others						
4. Sustained attention span						
Level V						
1. Sustained attention span for a wide variety of activities						

B. SOCIALIZING (Inter- and intrapersonal relationships, play)

Level III

1. Engages in independent play					
2. Engages in parallel play					
3. Plays briefly with peers					
4. Recognizes needs of others					
5. Shows sympathy for others					

Level IV

1. Leaves mother readily					
2. Converses with other children					
3. Converses with adults					
4. Plays with peers					
5. Cooperates in classroom routines					
6. Takes turns and shares					
7. Replaces materials after use					
8. Takes care of personal belongings					
9. Respects property of others					

Level V

1. Cooperates in classroom routines					
2. Completes most self-initiated projects					
3. Replaces materials after use					
4. Takes turns and shares					
5. Takes care of his belongings					
6. Respects others' property					
7. Works and plays with limited supervision					
8. Engages in cooperative play					
9. Listens while peers speak					
10. Follows multiple and delayed directions					
11. Carries out special responsibilities (feed animal, etc.)					
12. Listens and follows suggestions of adult					
13. Carries out simple errands					
14. Sensitive to praise and criticism					
15. Enjoys talking with adults					

C. COORDINATING (Motor, fine and gross, hand-eye, self-help skills)

GROSS MOVEMENT
Level III

1. Catches ball with both hands against chest						
2. Walks a balance beam 6 feet						
3. Hops on both feet several times without assistance						
4. Throws a ball with accuracy						
5. Climbs up slide and comes down						
6. Climbs, alternating feet, holding onto hand rail						
7. Stands on one foot and balances						
8. Pushes a loaded wheelbarrow						
9. Runs freely with little stumbling or falling						

FINE MOVEMENT

10. Places small pegs in pegboards						
11. Holds paintbrush or pencil with whole hand						
12. Cuts with scissors						
13. Uses a knife and fork correctly						
14. Buttons large buttons on own clothes						
15. Puts on coat by self						
16. Strings beads with ease						
17. Hammers a pound toy with accuracy						

GROSS MOVEMENT
Level IV

1. Balances on one foot						
2. Walks on balance beam						
3. Climbs steps with alternate feet						
4. Climbs jungle gym						
5. Can skip haltingly						
6. Rides tricycle						
7. Throws, catches, and bounces large ball						
8. Stacks blocks vertically and horizontally						

9. Creates recognizable block structure						
10. Participates in outdoor play						

FINE MOVEMENT

11. Pounds and rolls clay						
12. Puts together fine-piece puzzle						
13. Forms a pegboard design						
14. Cuts and pastes						
15. Participates in finger plays						
16. Eats with spoon						
17. Holds cup with one hand						
18. Puts coat on hanger or hook						
19. Independent in toileting						
20. Is learning to button buttons, zip zippers, tie shoes						

GROSS MOVEMENT
Level V

1. Catches and throws small ball						
2. Bounces and catches small ball						
3. Can skip						
4. Skips rope						
5. Hops on one foot						
6. Creates tinker toy and block structures						
7. Climbs on jungle gym						
8. Rides tricycle with speed and skill						
9. Hammers and saws with some skill						
10. Can walk a straight line						
11. Descends stairs, alternating feet						

FINE MOVEMENT

12. Cuts and pastes creative designs						
13. Forms variety of pegboard designs						
14. Buttons buttons, zips zippers, ties shoes						
15. Plays jacks						

16. Creates recognizable objects with clay					
17. Independent in toileting					
18. Independent in eating					
19. Independent in dressing and undressing					
20. Learning to tie in out-of-sight locations (under the chin)					
21. Holds and manipulates pencils, crayons, and brushes of various sizes					
22. Combs and brushes hair					

D. RECOGNIZING AND DISCRIMINATING (Identifying—sensory activities)

Level III

1. Discriminates between two smells					
2. Knows and verbalizes smells are "different"					
3. May be able to label smell or smells (verbally)					
4. Discriminates between two sounds and verbalizes they are "different"					
5. May be able to label taste or tastes (verbally)					
6. Discriminates between two sounds and verbalizes they are "different"					
7. May be able to label sounds (verbally)					
8. Points to different food objects on request					
9. Points to basic shapes (circle, square, triangle) on request					

RECOGNIZING, DISCRIMINATING, CLASSIFYING

Level IV: Uses Multisensory Factors in Learning

1. Seeing, hearing, tasting, touching, smelling					
2. Discriminates differences in size and shape of concrete objects: big, little, long, short, square, round					
3. Classifies objects by weight: heavy, light					
4. Classifies objects by height: tall, short					
5. Identifies primary colors					
6. Discriminates likenesses and differences					
7. Concepts of relative loudness, distance, weight, time judgments					

Level V

1. Identifies and labels spatial relationships: far/near, in/out, front/back, top/bottom, first/last, over/under					
2. Identifies and discriminates value relationships: right/wrong, good/bad, pretty/ugly, sad/happy, like/dislike					
3. Identifies and discriminates value relationships: day/night, today/tomorrow, yesterday/today, before/after, now/then, earlier/later, never/soon					
5. Identifies primary colors (red, yellow, blue)					
6. Identifies secondary colors (green, orange, purple)					
7. Identifies pastel colors (pink, lavender)					
8. Classifies colors by intensity (dark, light, darker than, lighter than)					
9. Identifies the simple properties of an object					
10. Classifies foods: fruits, vegetables, meats					
11. Classifies tastes: sweet, sour, salty, bitter					
12. Classifies surfaces by texture: smooth, rough, slick, gritty, slimy					
13. Identifies and classifies common objects by shape: circle, square, rectangle, triangle					
14. Classifies objects by more than one property					
15. Seriates objects by size					
16. Seriates sounds by volume					
17. States functions of simple objects					
18. Reverses simple operations					

E. SYMBOLIZING AND IMITATING

Level III

1. Recognizes that pictures represent real objects					
2. Draws V or O from model					
3. Imitates grownups (play house, store, etc.)					
4. Imitates "correct behavior"					
5. Expresses frustrations in play					
6. Creates imaginary playmates					
7. Engages in housekeeping					

Level IV

1. Recognizes likenesses and differences in pictured objects					
2. Role plays wide variety of roles in housekeeping center and other centers					
3. Role plays a wide variety of adult occupations					
4. Participates in dramatization of familiar stories					
5. Uses puppets in self-initiated dialogues					
6. Differentiates between real and make-believe					
7. Draws pictures that symbolize events					
8. Tells experiences for an experience story					
10. Draws picture of arranged objects					
11. Draws picture before arranging objects					

Level V

1. Role plays in housekeeping and other centers					
2. Role plays on playground					
3. Role plays adult occupations					
4. Imitates reading behavior: turns pages front to back, talks about stories, mimics adult reader					

F. CREATIVE EXPRESSION (Exploring, Dramatics, Art, Play)

Level III

1. Creates new ideas from what he knows					
2. Paints and draws on large paper symbolic figures					
3. Builds simple structures with blocks					
4. Uses transportation toys, people, and animals to enrich block play					
5. Has imaginary companion					
6. Uses puppets to approach others					
7. Imagines any object into the object desired (symbolic function)					
8. Sings simple songs					

Level IV

1. Pretends dolls are real people					
2. Engages in rhythmic activities					
3. Sings alone					
4. Sings with group					
5. Experiments with rhythm instruments					
6. Creates art projects					
7. Constructs (paints, molds, etc.) recognizable figures					

Level V

1. Participates in a wide variety of creative activities: finger plays, rhythm band, working with clay, painting, outdoor play, housekeeping, singing, etc.					
2. Produces objects at the carpentry table; tells about them					
3. Produces art objects: tells about them					
4. Searches for better ways to construct					
5. Builds complex block structures					
6. "Plays" with new words					
7. Evaluates his work (compares, describes, suggests improvement)					

G. CONCEPT DEVELOPMENT (Cause-effect, conserving, sorting, grouping, space, weight, time)

QUANTITATIVE
Level III

1. Manipulates and experiments with simple machines					
2. Counts by rote 1–5					
3. Concept of "first" and "last"					
4. Concept of ordinal numbers through "third"					
5. Identifies pieces of money: penny, nickel, dime					
6. Developing value concept of money					
7. Concept of time: morning, noon, today, tomorrow					
8. Helps to create extended projects (block, sand table, etc.)					
9. Recognizes basic shapes					

10. Forms creative designs with materials					
11. Asks questions to gain problem-solving information					
12. Uses construction material for multiple purposes					

Level IV

1. Identifies pairs of familiar objects (shoes, socks, gloves, earrings)					
2. Uses ordinal concepts through fifth					
3. Demonstrates concept of number through 10					
4. Identifies penny, nickel, dime, quarter, dollar					
5. Compares distance (height, width) to an independent object (stick, etc.)					
6. Compares difference in dimension (taller, shorter, thinner, etc.)					
7. Compares volume in separate container Describes objects from different visual perspectives					

Level V

1. Compares methods of filling a space					
2. Groups objects into sets of equal number					
3. Compares elements of unequal sets (more than, fewer than, etc.)					
4. Demonstrates one-to-one correspondence					
5. Counts to one hundred					
6. Identifies numerals 1 to 100 (book pages)					
7. Orders numbers 1 to 10					
8. Identifies number in group (mark five cars)					
9. Combines (adds) total number and two small groups					

H. LANGUAGE

Level III

1. Most language is intelligible					
2. Knows the name of the school					
3. Responds correctly to simple instructions involving locations					
4. Uses pronouns correctly					

5. Uses sentences of 4–5 words					
6. Recognizes and labels (verbally) 100–200 common objects					
7. Knows parents' names					
8. 1000+ word vocabulary					

Level IV

1. Uses simple position words (over, under, etc.)					
2. Uses simple action words (run, walk, etc.)					
3. Uses complete sentences					
4. Uses personal pronouns					
5. Uses language for specific purposes: directions, information, etc.					
6. Repeats routine events					

Level V

1. Communicates ideas, feeling, and emotions in well-formed sentences					
2. Uses correct form of most verbs in informal conversation					
3. Uses correct prepositions to denote place and position					
4. Uses most personal pronouns correctly					
5. Repeats nursery rhymes					
6. Sings with group and alone					
7. Explains operation of simple machines (pencil sharpener, etc.)					
8. Uses language to get what he wants					
9. Vocabulary of about 2000–4000 words					

(SOCIAL KNOWLEDGE)

10. Can state full name					
11. Can state parents' full names					
12. Can state age					
13. Can state birthday					
14. Can state address					
15. Follows common directions					

I. READING READINESS

Level V: Auditory and Visual Discrimination

1. Discriminates between similar sounds made by different objects					
2. Discriminates between initial phonemes: bat/cat, fat/rat, plat/flat, sat/hat, fan/Dan					
3. Discriminates between medial phonemes: bet/bit, bat/but, bit/bat, bin/ban					
4. Discriminates between final phonemes: bat/bar, can/car, bet/bed					
5. Follows moving object with eyes, side to side at reading distance					
6. Draws circles with closed ends					
7. Connects dots with straight pencil lines					
8. Follows left-to-right progression of pointer as adult reads					
9. Identifies letters of the alphabet					
10. Matches upper and lower case letters					
11. Identifies his first name in print					
12. Picks out like words and symbols on a printed page					
13. Identifies reoccurring words on experience chart					

COMPREHENSION SKILLS

14. Listens to and follows verbal directions					
15. Locates elements in a picture (tallest, largest, etc.)					
16. Retells a story read to him in correct sequence					
17. Answers recall questions about story characters, actions, etc.)					
18. Draws analogies from story to his own experience					
19. Predicts and/or constructs story ending					
20. Suggests titles for experience stories					
21. Retells experiences in organized fashion					
22. Reorganizes pictures to show correct story sequence					
23. Makes value judgments about story events					

APPENDIX B

Addresses of Some Commonly Used Standardized Tests

INTELLIGENCE TESTS

Wechsler Preschool and Primary Scale of Intelligence
Psychological Corporation
304 East 45 Street
New York, New York 10017

Illinois Test of Psycholinguistic Abilities
University of Illinois Press
Urbana, Illinois 61801

Stanford-Binet Intelligence Scale
Houghton Mifflin Company
53 West 43 Street
New York, New York 10036

Pictorial Test of Intelligence
Houghton Mifflin Company
53 West 43 Street
New York, New York 10036

Torrance Tests of Creative Thinking
Personnel Press, Inc.
20 Nassau Street
Princeton, New Jersey 08540

READINESS TESTS

Metropolitan Reading Readiness Test
Harcourt Brace Jovanovich, Inc.
757 Third Avenue
New York, New York 10017

Harrison-Stroud Reading Readiness Profiles
Houghton Mifflin Company
53 West 43 Street
New York, New York 10036

ACHIEVEMENT TESTS

Preschool Inventory
Educational Testing Service
Rosedale Road
Princeton, New Jersey 08540

Basic Concept Inventory
Follett Educational Corporation
1010 West Washington Boulevard
P.O. Box 5705
Chicago, Illinois 60607

Preschool Attainment Record
American Guidance Service, Inc.
Publisher's Building
Circle Pines, Minnesota 55014

TESTS OF PSYCHOMOTOR DEVELOPMENT

Valett Developmental Survey of Basic Learning Abilities
Consulting Psychologists Press, Inc.
577 College Avenue
P.O. Box 11636
Palo Alto, California 94306

Developmental Test of Visual-Motor Integration
Follett Educational Corporation
1010 West Washington Boulevard
P.O. Box 5705
Chicago, Illinois 60607

Metropolitan Readiness Test (eye-hand coordination)
Harcourt Brace Jovanovich, Inc.

757 Third Avenue
New York, New York 10017

Southern California Perceptual-Motor Tests
Western Psychological Services
12031 Wilshire Boulevard
Los Angeles, California 90025

TESTS OF AFFECTIVE AND SOCIAL BEHAVIOR

California Test of Personality
CTB/McGraw-Hill
Del Monte Research Park
Monterey, California 93940

Coopersmith Behavior Rating Form
Coopersmith Self-Esteem Inventory (Form A and Form B)
Stanley Coopersmith
University of California
Davis, California 95616
Technical information available in S. Coppersmith, *The Antecedents
of Self-Esteem,* San Francisco: W. H. Freeman, 1967.

Measures of Self-Concept
Instructional Objectives Exchange
P.O. Box 24095
Los Angeles, California 90024

Cincinnati Autonomy Test Battery
Department of Psychology
Cincinnati University
Cincinnati, Ohio 45200

Glossary

Active involvement. Participation in the learning process with mental and physical action as opposed to being a passive bystander.

Concrete experiences. Activities and events in which the child participates directly and where he can observe firsthand and become actively involved with real situations, objects, and materials.

Controlled discontinuity. Facilitation of learning and growth by controlling the increments of challenge, novelty, and level of difficulty of educational events and activities.

Day care center. Group care for large numbers of preschool children generally at least 2 years of age. Day care centers often operate 10–12 hours a day and sometimes extend care to older children after school and during the summer.

Didactic teaching materials. Educational apparatus or materials designed to teach in themselves through the child's actions upon the material. Didactic materials generally fit together precisely or are used in particular ways, thereby giving the child immediate feedback as to whether his actions upon the material are correct or incorrect.

Family day care. Small-group care for no more than six children, including the day care mother's own children. Family day care is offered within the context of a family setting in a private home and is especially suited to the needs of infants and toddlers.

Group day care home. Before- and after-school care for up to 12 children within a home.

Individual differences. The uniqueness of each child with respect to areas such as interests, rate of development, and style of learning.

Infant stimulation program. A program designed to prevent that retardation in infants which stems from a barren, unstimulating environment. Such programs generally include human and material resources designed to influence such areas of development as sensory motor skill, language, and concept formation.

Instructional objectives. Particular skills or abilities that are identified as observable behaviors and that are the basis for planned lessons or teaching.

Kindergarten. An early childhood program for 5-year-olds that is either public or privately operated and full or part day.

Natural interests. Subjects, objects, and events upon which the child is naturally inclined to focus his attention.

Nonstandard dialect. In this book, any dialect that differs from the standard dialect of the predominating social class.

Normative stages of development. A standard pattern of the sequence and manner of development in some area(s).

Nursery school. Generally, a part-day program for 3- and 4-year-olds. Nursery schools vary greatly in sponsorship, type of facility, type of program, philosophy, and goals.

Parent-child center. A federally funded comprehensive program for children under 3 years of age and their families.

Parent cooperative nursery school. A school for young children organized by a group of parents who share the expenses as well as assist in the ongoing program. Typically, the parents are guided by a director qualified in early childhood education. Often there is an additional program component for the parents involving child-rearing, child growth and development, and related topics.

Predeterminism. A belief that the unfolding of human development has been determined beforehand through heredity.

Richness of experience. Activities and events that are abundant, meaningful, and educationally valuable to young children due to their nature and quality, and that are suited to both previous experiences and present needs.

Self-esteem. The child's feelings about himself, who he is, what he can and cannot do, and his importance to himself and to others. A child's self feelings are generally shaped by his personal experiences, his successes and failures, and the significant people in his life.

Sensory education. Learning through the senses; utilizing activities, materials, and events (sand, water play, music, texture board, size and shape boards, for example) that engage each of the senses and increase the discriminatory ability of each.

Standard dialect. In this book, the form of the English language that is used predominantly in speech and in print.

Structured program. An educational program that strongly emphasizes a particular aspect(s) of development and where all of the activities and materials are coordinated and integrated toward that end.

Wash-out. The loss noted by the second or third year of primary school of that gain in IQ achieved by some young children during their enrollment in early intervention programs.

Index

ABC books, 224, 225
Ability grouping, 105
Abstract thinking, 247, 334
Academic behaviors, 305
Academic Preschool, 87
Accommodation, 138–139, 166, 168, 244–245, 334
Achievement, longitudinal studies of, 79
Achievement tests, 57, 204–205, 368
Additive composition, 150–151
Adventure playgrounds, 348–350
Aesthetic appreciation, 291
Affective behavior, tests of, 206, 369
Affective development, appreciations, 290–292, 311
   attitudes, 284–288, 311
   emotions, 294–295, 311
   enhancing of, 283–295, 311
   interests, 288–290, 311
   values, 292–293, 311
Affective objectives, 183
Aggressive behavior, 65, 79, 309
Aggressive play, 329
Allport, G. W., 108, 109
American Council of Cooperative Preschools, 63
American Froebel Union, 58
American Institute for Research, 125
American Montessori Society, 45, 47
American Psychological Association, 53, 109
Anal period, 102, 104
Ancient Greece and Rome, early childhood education in, 14–15
Anderson, S. B., 85
Anecdotal record, example of, 189–193
Animal psychology, 54, 57, 69
Animals, deprivation studies on, 76
Anschauung, 19
Appreciations, affective development and, 290–292, 311
Aristotle, 15, 25, 42, 101
Arnold, A., 335
Assimilation, 138–139, 166, 168, 244–245, 334
   functional, 143, 149
   generalizing, 143

recognitory, 143
Association for Childhood Education International, 61
Association Montessori International, 45–47
Associative shifting, 54
Attending, developmental checklist for, 355
   educational objective of, 178–179, 212
Attitudes, affective development and, 284–288, 311
Austin (Texas) *Sportsman, The,* 16

"Back to basic skills" movement, 8
Baker, C. T., 78
Baldwin, B. T., 56, 78
Baldwin, J. M., 143
Bank Street program, 104
Baratz, J. C., 120, 123, 125, 126
Baseline data, 306, 310–311
Basic Concept Inventory, 205, 368
Bayley, N., 78
Behavior(s), academic, 305
   affective, tests of, 206, 369
   aggressive, 65, 79, 309
   inattentive, 306–308
   internalized organized, 137, 168
   learned, perception as, 76
   mechanistic, 57
   motivation and management of (*see* Motivation of behavior)
   nonobservable, 182
   observable, 182, 187
      stating objectives in terms of, 182
   operant, 305, 310
   organized, 137, 168
   respondent, 304–305
   social, tests of, 206, 369
   teacher, checklist for, 307, 308
Behavior modification, 3, 55, 106, 306–307
   See also Reality Therapy; Transactional Analysis
Behavior shaping, 310
Behavioral-environmental theory, 3, 106–107, 112

Longitudinal studies, 3, 78–79
Luther, M., 16, 26, 101, 320

McCall's magazine, adventure playground sponsored by, 350
McCarthy, D., 120, 123
MacFarlane, J. W., 78
Macmillan, M., 62, 63
Macmillan, R., 62, 63
McWhirter, M. E., 335
Madaus, G. F., 206
Make-believe play, 332, 334
Mallitskaya, M. K., 125
Manipulative arts center, 227–228
Maslow, A. H., 4, 107–110
Maturation, 140, 168, 237, 244
May, R., 108, 109
Meacham, M. L., 303
Measures of Self-Concept, 206, 369
Mechanistic behavior, 57
Meers, D. R., 6
Meizitis, S., 44, 46
Melzack, R., 76
Mental development, research into, 77–78
  See also Cognitive-developmental theory, Piagetian
Mental images, 148, 247
Mental retardation, poverty and, 3, 77
Mentally retarded children, educable, 2
  environmental deprivation and, 75
  Montessori method and, 35, 46
  sensory education as treatment for, 46
Merrill-Palmer School (Detroit), 56, 63
Methodology, Dewey's views on, 34
Metropolitan Readiness Test (eye-hand coordination), 206, 369
Metropolitan Reading Readiness Test, 205, 368
Mexican-American children, bilingual program for, 87
Middle Ages, early childhood education in, 15–16
Milton Bradley Company, 23
Mitchell, E. D., 328–329

Mitchell, L. S., 63
Montessori, M., 8, 17, 19, 24, 25, 30, 35–47, 62, 89, 101
  See also Montessori method
Montessori, Maria, 45
Montessori method, 35–47, 324
  contemporary research on, 42–45
  critical analysis of, 41–42
Montessori Method, The (Montessori), 42
Montessori Society, La, 36
Mother-Child Home Program, 90–92
Mother Goose books, 224, 225
Motivation of behavior, 295–313
  external, 295, 302–304, 313
Motivation of behavior (*continued*)
  internal, 295–302, 313
  intrinsic, 295
  See also Reinforcement
Motive, defining play by, 328–329
Motor training, 36–38, 44
Music, 226, 227, 272, 287
Mussen, P. H., 120
My Pedagogic Creed (Dewey), 30

National Association for Nursery Education, 60, 64
National Association for the Education of Young Children, 60–61
National Committee on Nursery Schools, 60
National Council of Jewish Women, 344
National Council of Primary Education, 61
National Council on Parent Education, 64
National Education Association, 53, 58, 60
National Research Council Committee on Child Development, 64
Nature, appreciation, 291–292
Nedler, S., 87
Negative reinforcement, 303, 313
Negro Head Start groups, 44
Nelson, K., 238–239, 241
Nelson, V. L., 78
New Schools Exchange, 110